IN THE
POST-COLD WAR ERA:

Does It Have a Future?

IN THE
POST-COLD WAR ERA:

Does It Have a Future?

EDITED BY

S. Victor Papacosma
and Mary Ann Heiss

ST. MARTIN'S PRESS
NEW YORK

355
N279

NATO IN THE POST–COLD WAR ERA: DOES IT HAVE A FUTURE?
Copyright © 1995 by S. Victor Papacosma and Mary Ann Heiss

ISBN 0-312-12130-X

⅃P

Library of Congress Cataloging-in-Publication number 95-35559.
A full CIP record is available from the Library of Congress.

First Edition: November 1995
10 9 8 7 6 5 4 3 2 1

Interior design by Digital Type & Design

To Ruth V. Young

CONTENTS

PREFACE
AND
ACKNOWLEDGMENTS

Over the past fifteen years, the Lyman L. Lemnitzer Center for NATO and European Community Studies at Kent State University has held many conferences on various dimensions of NATO's prominent role and challenges during the Cold War. These conferences yielded published volumes that detailed NATO's success in performing its assigned mission of securing peace for its member-states and averting military confrontation between the superpowers. The center's April 1989 meeting, to commemorate the fortieth anniversary of the signing of the North Atlantic Treaty, marked the end of an era. Within a relatively short period after this session, the Berlin Wall crumbled, the Soviet Union ceased to exist, and the Cold War came to an end.

The dramatic changes that followed generated a serious identity crisis for NATO. Whereas the East-West conflict that characterized the Cold War essentially defined who would be fighting whom in a future conflict, the uncertain post-1989 years have introduced new and potentially calamitous variables. The lines between enemies are no longer so clear-cut as they were during the Cold War, and communism no longer looms as the major threat to peace and stability in Europe. Despite the facts that hardly a voice has been heard calling for NATO's dissolution and that states from the former Warsaw Pact are seeking membership, the alliance's members face the demanding task of redefining NATO's strategic challenges and formulating appropriate policies and responses for present and future crises. To wrestle with these new, post–Cold War realities, the Lemnitzer Center on 8-9 April 1994 convened the conference "NATO after Forty-five Years: Does It Have a Future?" from which the essays in this volume were drawn.

The following articles combine to present a comprehensive investigation into NATO and its diverse problems, providing relevant historical background before analyzing recent conditions and projecting into the future. Two opening essays offer alternative assessments of NATO's accomplishments during the Cold War and are followed by others dealing with NATO's structural changes for the 1990s, NATO's shifting strategy, and NATO's developing connections with other international organizations, such as the United Nations, CSCE, and the European Union. The articles in the next two sections focus on NATO's association with the United States, the Anglo-American "special relationship," and the alliance's relationship with the former Warsaw Pact states, the Balkans, the Middle East, and

Scandinavia. The two final contributions offer the perspectives of officials from NATO and the U.S. government on recent NATO initiatives, particularly the Partnership for Peace.

The editors wish to express their special appreciation to the NATO Office of Information and Press for financially supporting the conference and to Karen Aguilar, U.S. liaison officer in that office, who with enthusiasm and creativity offered critical input for technical and other arrangements for the conference. Dr. Erika v.C. Bruce, then director of NATO's Office of Information and Press, and Dr. Joseph Kruzel, U.S. deputy assistant secretary of defense for NATO and European policy, took time out of their extremely busy schedules to present important papers during the conference. Panel chairs and discussants at the conference included Robert W. Clawson (Kent State University), James P. Cross (Heidelberg College), Leon Hurwitz (Cleveland State University), Chester T. Pach (Ohio University), Dennison Rusinow (University of Pittsburgh), and Frederick W. Schroath (Kent State University).

Dr. Mark R. Rubin, director of Kent's Center for International and Comparative Programs (CICP) once again displayed his marvelous expertise in dealing with logistical matters and other conference arrangements—as well as his talent as a translator/interpreter for one of the conference submissions. Phyllis Dreyer, CICP and Lemnitzer Center administrative secretary, had to deal with the totality of conference details and always responded with efficiency and a smile. Sandy Baker, CICP's administrative assistant, skillfully tackled budgetary problems. Student assistants providing important services during the conference were Tom Davis, Lynette Johnson, Denise Schneider, and William Smith.

A special debt of gratitude must be extended to two individuals. Dr. Lawrence S. Kaplan, director emeritus of the Lemnitzer Center, has maintained his dynamic involvement in the center's activities and contributed vitally from the first planning stages to the April 1994 conference's success. Now retired, Ruth V. Young, the Lemnitzer Center's administrative assistant for more than ten years, contributed so much to the activities of the center and to those associated with it —through her management artistry, spirited personality, creative ideas, and unflagging optimism—that we greatly miss her but also appreciate and draw on the rich legacy that she bequeathed us.

S. VICTOR PAPACOSMA
MARY ANN HEISS

ABBREVIATIONS

ABM	antiballistic missile (system)
ACCHAN	Allied Command Channel
ACE	Allied Command Europe
AF	Augmentation Force
AFCENT	Allied Forces Central Europe
AFNORTH	Allied Forces Northern Europe
AFNORTHWEST	Allied Forces North West Europe
AIOC	Anglo-Iranian Oil Company
APEC	Asia-Pacific Economic Cooperation
AWACS	Airborne Warning and Control System
BALTAP	Baltic Approaches Command
CEE	Central and Eastern Europe
CENTCOM	Central Command
CFE	Treaty on Conventional Armed Forces in Europe
CIS	Commonwealth of Independent States
CJTF	Combined Joint Task Forces
COMNAVSOUTH	Commander Allied Naval Forces Southern Europe
COS	chiefs of staff
CPC	Conflict Prevention Center
CSCE	Conference on Security and Cooperation in Europe
DPC	Defense Planning Committee
EC	European Community
EEC	European Economic Community
EFTA	European Free Trade Association
ESDI	European Security and Defense Identity
EU	European Union
Eurocorps	European Corps
FCMA	Treaty of Friendship, Cooperation, and Mutual Assistance
FOFA	follow-on-forces attack
FSC	Forum for Security Cooperation
FSU	Former Soviet Union
FYROM	Former Yugoslav Republic of Macedonia
GATT	General Agreement on Tariffs and Trade
GCHQ	Government Communications Headquarters
GDM	Group of Defense Ministers
GLCM	ground-launched cruise missile
HLG	High Level Group

ICBM	intercontinental ballistic missile (system)
IMS	International Military Staff
JNA	Yugoslav People's Army
LRTNF	long-range theater nuclear force
MC	Military Committee
MDF	main defense force
MILREP	Military Representative
MLF	multilateral force
MNC	Major NATO Commands
MSC	Major Subordinate Commands
NAC	North Atlantic Council
NACC	North Atlantic Cooperation Council
NPG	Nuclear Planning Group
NPT	Nonproliferation Treaty
OSCE	Organization for Security and Cooperation in Europe
PASOK	Panhellenic Socialist Movement
PERMREP	Permanent Representative
PFP	Partnership for Peace
PGM	precision guided munitions
PMSC	Political Military Steering Committee
PSC	Principal Subordinate Command
R & D	research and development
RF	reaction forces
SACEUR	Supreme Allied Commander Europe
SACLANT	Supreme Allied Commander Atlantic
SALT	Strategic Arms Limitation Talks
SDI	Strategic Defense Initiative
SHAPE	Supreme Headquarters Allied Powers in Europe
SIGINT	signal intelligence
SLBM	submarine-launched ballistic missile
SOFA	status of forces agreements
SSBN	nuclear-powered ballistic missile submarine
TNF	theater nuclear force
TSG	technical subgroup
UKAIR	United Kingdom Air Forces
UNPROFOR	United Nations Protection Force
WEU	Western European Union

Contending Counterfactuals: Negative and Positive Assessments of a Europe without NATO

■ ■ ■

1

NATO after Forty-Five Years: A Counterfactual History

Lawrence S. Kaplan

There are not many appropriate occasions for a historian to play with counterfactual history. To put it charitably, it is unreasonable for a scholar to venture into a realm where there are no records to provide guidance. For me to attempt to reconstruct a past for the Atlantic Alliance that might have been but never was invites ridicule, if not contempt, on the part of reputable scholars of the past. Despite the stigma attached to such an enterprise, I want to present a history of Europe and America with the North Atlantic Treaty Organization (NATO) after World War II and then to examine the difference that the alliance has made to its members over its forty-five-year history.

Before presenting this counterfeit history, I should like to note that the pundits who evoke a future rarely meet with the same suspicions that attach to the historian whose imagined past is no more preposterous than many an imagined future. "Futurology" even has a quasi-academic veneer of respectability; universities offer courses in the subject. And futurologists' projections are taken seriously in the press and podium, if not in the classroom, even if their counterfactual history proves to be mistaken or wrongheaded.

The triumph of the West in the Cold War opened the way for a host of predictions, most of which have not been realized; their authors have not been reproached for anticipating events that never happened. One of the most prominent visions, Francis Fukuyama's "end of history" in 1989, seemed absurd even as it was pronounced. Even granted that the afterglow of the destruction of the Berlin Wall could generate dreams of a new world order, it seems incredible four years later that Fukuyama's ideas were taken seriously. "What we are witnessing," he observed, "is not just the end of the Cold War, or the passing of a particular period of Cold War history, but the end of history as such: that is, the end point of man's ideological evolution and the universalization of Western liberal democracy as the final form of human government."[1] This statement gives a special pejorative meaning to "counterfactual."

Other predictions made as late as September 1989 became suddenly irrelevant after the dramatic events that followed later that year and in 1990. Such was the fate of the conference convened at NATO headquarters in Brussels to instruct the youth of NATO's member-nations about the problems facing the alliance as the decade of the 1980s ended. The key issue, according to NATO officials, was not how the West should match the deescalation of tensions initiated by Soviet General Secretary Mikhail Gorbachev, but how to win European, particularly German, approval for a modernized Lance missile. This was a short-range nuclear missile that would be employed in combat only on German soil. As a result, the Lance met with understandable resistance from its potential victims. The prospect of a unified Germany coming into being in the immediate future was raised only once, when one member of the conference, with mischievous intent, asked a German general dispatched to the conference from Casteau how much thought he was giving to the possibility of unification, and of its impact on NATO. With a broad smile the general responded that he and his colleagues were giving as little thought as possible to such an unlikely future. Less than two months later, the Berlin Wall fell; less than a year later, Germany was reunited; less than two years later, the Soviet empire dissolved. Meanwhile, the Lance missile itself became irrelevant.

But even when predictions go wildly astray their authors are readily forgiven. One distinguished authority, Ronald Steel, whose work is always worth reading, began predicting the demise of NATO as early as 1964. Its mission, the defense of Europe, was completed in Nikita Khrushchev's time, he claimed, as normal, if often hostile, relations prevailed between the Western and Eastern blocs. NATO had lost its function and should dissolve. Steel still anticipates its termination, although the date remains uncertain.[2]

Other commentators are more dogmatic about the necessity for immediate termination of the alliance. Political scientist Amos Perlmutter entitled a think piece in December 1993 "NATO Must Face the Fact It Is Obsolete" and judged that "the realities of contemporary international relations, with the United States on an inward retreat and Germany unwilling to become Europe's America, leave NATO with no reason to exist."[3] Newspaper editorials and columns played with variations of "obsolete" before and after the January summit meeting of the North Atlantic Council. The *New Statesman and Society* declared on 7 January 1994, that "NATO is Obsolete." *Newsday* (New York City) said the same thing more delicately by noting on 16 January that "A Treaty Becomes an Heirloom."

THE STATE OF WESTERN EUROPE, 1948–49

Responding to these pessimistic judgments, I shall venture to predict a past that might have come into being had NATO not been created. Knowing what we do about the state of Europe in 1948, some of my predictions may carry more weight than others. What can be said without hesitation is that Western Europe was on edge that year, fearful not of a Soviet invasion as such but of a Communist sweep into power through Soviet intimidation or through well-organized political parties. Despair over the economic future of a still-devastated Europe was a factor in the power of communism. Memories of Communists as the heroes of World War II resistance movements also gave an authority to the position of European Communists. Even though the Truman Doctrine had been pronounced and the Marshall Plan finally passed into law by the spring of 1948, the distance between the promise of those initiatives and their realization seemed vast. The former represented American unilateralism, a promise of aid for nations threatened by Soviet imperialism that could be unilaterally revoked. The latter was an economic program with great promise for the revival of Europe, but it would be wasted if political insecurity undermined the economic benefits among the beneficiaries. The American tradition of nonentanglement with European politics was still alive.

It required the combined efforts of American statesmen, such as Robert Lovett and Dean Acheson, and their European counterparts, Britain's Ernest Bevin and France's Georges Bidault, to break down American resistance to a binding alliance with Western Europe. In retrospect, the signing of the North Atlantic Treaty on 4 April 1949 was a logical evolution of American-European collaboration. This cooperation began with American support for the Brussels Pact in March 1948 and the Vandenberg Resolution in June of that year and continued with the Washington Exploratory Talks with the

Brussels Pact powers and the expansion of that alliance's scope in the winter of 1949. However, this was no easy transition. The path to the "pledge" of Article 5 had to overcome resistance from those in the American military fearing European raids on their own limited resources, from internationalists fearing the impact of a military alliance on the United Nations, and from traditional isolationists fearing infection from a close connection with the diseased Old World.

But what if the path toward the alliance had met with the insuperable obstacles that in the end would have doomed the North Atlantic Treaty? What would have been the fate of Europe—and the United States—if the Washington talks had collapsed in the summer of 1948, or if the Senate had succeeded in February 1949 in scrapping Article 5 of the treaty? The history of the West might have been very different from its actual experience in the first forty-five years of NATO's history.

THE NORDIC PAST

My speculations about what might have been begin with the "stepping-stone" countries on the periphery of the Western Union—Norway and Denmark—and then move to the Benelux countries and Italy before considering the major allies: Britain, France, and Germany. Scandinavia was an irritating afterthought for most of the European allies, considered in early 1949 only when the United States forced the allies to accept Norway and Denmark as stepping-stones valued for their position in the North Atlantic. Greenland and Iceland would provide bases for American aid to Europe. Norway, more than Denmark, was eager for the NATO connection as it worried about periodic pressure from the neighboring Soviet Union to enter into a bilateral nonaggression pact. For Norwegians these invitations were both an uncomfortable reminder of the Nazi invitation of 1939 and an incentive to come under the protection of the Western alliance. Denmark was more tempted to join a Nordic pact linking it and Norway with Sweden that would be independent of NATO and presumably less threatening to the Soviets. The Nordic pact never materialized, and Sweden remained outside the Atlantic Alliance. When Denmark joined Norway in accepting NATO membership, it nonetheless reflected its continuing concern over Soviet intimidation by not permitting NATO military bases on Danish territory.

Had NATO not come into being, what might have been the history of Scandinavia? First, the Nordic pact would have been signed. But how much security would it have given its members? Their combined military power was considerably less than even the skeleton military establishments of Western Europe. NATO had the potential to equal if not surpass the forces of the Soviet Union. Sweden's addition to Denmark and Norway would hardly be a deterrent to aggression. The future of Scandinavia without NATO would have been similar to that of another Scandinavian country, Finland. While there were worse fates than "Finlandization" under Soviet domination, the price to be paid for keeping the Soviet army at bay would have been high, both in a sense of freedom lost and very likely in prosperity unachieved. Of all the Scandinavian countries only Iceland might have managed well with or without a NATO relationship. It had no army and would have made a bilateral connection with the United States, whether or not it wanted it, similar to its position during World War II.

DISSOLUTION OF THE WESTERN UNION

The fate of the Benelux nations would have been somewhat different from Scandinavia's, but no less depressing. The Low Countries were physically separated from the Soviet Union, unlike Norway or Finland. They also had an existing alliance as an alternative, the Brussels Pact, out of which NATO developed. But the Western Union established under the pact was always a sham. It was essentially a device to lure the United States into a European entanglement. How long would have the fifty-year alliance survived with each of its "High Contracting Parties" affording, in response to treaty obligations, a "party so attacked all military and other aid and assistance in their power"? Given the rivalries among its leaders, the alliance would have broken up without even an external challenge to nudge it. The behavior of one of its major committees, the Commander-in-Chiefs Committee, suggested that it could not even decide on a military commander. But even if it had, the elaborate plans for economic and military coordination were all on paper and depended on an infusion of American funds that would come with American membership.

Without the rubric of the Atlantic Alliance, the strains within the Western Union would have become visible immediately. Even before the Brussels Pact was completed, American pressure was required to induce Britain and France to give Belgium and the Netherlands equality within the five-nation union. The Belgians and Dutch disapproved in particular of the larger members' intentions to have the lesser members sign a separate treaty with the two major powers. These fissures would have destroyed the pact had not NATO been present to subsume the core group under its aegis.

Among the casualties in a divided West would have been the Marshall Plan. If the Western Union had dissolved through impotence and mutual ill will, the self-help and mutual aid that Americans had asked as a price for their assistance would have been lacking. There would have been no European Economic Community developed to lift all of Western Europe into prosperity in the 1950s. In its place would have been a dispirited, disunited Europe, reminiscent of the 1930s, providing added opportunities for increasing the influence of domestic Communist parties. The Soviet Union could have then played the role of Nazi Germany a decade earlier; or even worse, a resurgent nationalist Germany could have taken its place.

For Belgium there was another price to be paid in the absence of an Atlantic alliance. While postwar Belgium was a leading advocate of European unity, it was also a nation divided by language, if not by culture and religion. Linguistic division was inextricably linked to class division. Since the nation had received its independence in 1830, French had been the language of government, of the military, and of industry. The beneficiary of the new industrial revolution had been Francophone Wallonia, not Flanders. French was also the language of the Flemish elite; the many dialects of Flemish reflected the parochialism of the peasant class. Flemish nationalism burgeoned in the twentieth century, aimed at the wealth and privilege of the Francophones. Nazi occupation during World War II had elevated Flemings above Walloons. In the postwar era, Flemings came into their own: Economic power shifted from the depressed coal regions of Wallonia to the north; the Flemish population rapidly outstripped its Francophone counterpart; and the government passed over to Flemish leadership.

A clash between the two Belgian populations had the potential to destroy the nation unless they were contained within a larger structure. With the failure of the Western Union, the demand for separation would have been irresistible, if only because Francophone Brussels was in the middle of the Flemish countryside. Consider that the distinguished bilingual University of Louvain split into two sectors, with the French-speaking wing moving across the linguistic line to build its Louvain-la-Neuve. The breakup of this ancient university occurred at a time when Belgium had a greater stake in unity than did any of its neighbors; Brussels, after all, was the capital of both NATO and the European Community. It hardly requires a great leap of imagination to envision the creation of two antagonistic nations emerging from a dissolved Belgium.

RED ITALY

Italy's history would have differed from that of Norway or of Belgium, if only because of the power of its native Communist party. The party commanded 25 percent of the voting population of the country, having won the reputation—fairly or not—of being the most effective opponent of Mussolini and his Nazi allies during World War II. Although the success of the Christian Democratic Union in the elections of April 1948 had eased American concerns about the Soviets seizing Italy through the polls, there still remained the possibility of Italy going Communist. It had taken a massive political campaign, orchestrated in the United States with the help of the new Central Intelligence Agency, to mobilize Italian-American influence in Italy. The prospect of failure in Italy had so shaken the composure of as cool a diplomat as George Kennan that he ruminated about American military intervention to prevent such a Communist victory. Without the benefit of the NATO ties, would the defeated Communist party have remained in the background? Defeated nationally, it still controlled a so-called Red Belt across the industrial center of Italy.

The Italian center parties succeeded in containing domestic Communist power, due to the split within Italian socialism between those who would accept the Western alliance and those who would follow Communist leadership. But it required NATO and the strong American connection to maintain a Western orientation. Italian communism never faded away. It assumed a putatively benign form in the 1970s under the name of Eurocommunism. Although its leader, Enrico Berlinguer, inspired considerable suspicion in Henry Kissinger's State Department, Eurocommunism won adherents in Europe because of its acceptance of NATO and its promotion of détente with the Soviet Union.

But what if NATO had not been in the background? Italy would have moved quickly into the Soviet camp, with serious consequences for the West. Where the Soviets were effectively removed from the Italian peace treaty in 1947, their continuing interest in a trusteeship over Tripolitania would have been intensified; and with the encouragement of a Communist government, they might have succeeded in establishing a Soviet presence both in Italy and in North Africa. Without NATO, the Mediterranean would have been as much a Soviet as a Western sea. The Adriatic would have been affected as well. The crisis over control of Trieste, which ended in Italy's regaining of the city, could have ended in war between a Communist Italy and a Yugoslavia that had escaped Soviet domination. Even if Italy rejected a Communist government, it would have had to attend to the warning that the leader of the party, Palmiro Togliatti, issued in 1949: namely, that if the Soviet army were to enter ·Italy, the Italian people would be obligated to come to the aid of the Soviet forces. In brief, it does not stretch credulity to envision a Communist Italy in the 1950s that would be as firmly in the Soviet orbit as Finland, and ideologically happier with this relationship than was Russia's western neighbor.

THE FOURTH BALKAN WAR

When one looks at the checkered history of Greece and Turkey inside NATO, a first reaction may be to wonder what difference the existence of NATO has made. The mutual antagonism between ancient enemies was not miraculously dissolved under the NATO umbrella. Fear of communism and hope of tapping American resources were the common factors that brought Greeks and Turks into uneasy harmony in 1952. Both nations were admitted into the organization in that year because the newly reorganized military command in Paris believed that Greek, and especially Turkish, manpower was necessary for defense of the southern flank against a possible Soviet attack. Turkey's twenty-five divisions would help fulfill the mandate of the Lisbon conference of the North Atlantic Council in February 1952 whereby NATO would have fifty divisions on hand to contain Soviet conventional forces.

The joint admission to NATO suggested a spirit of collaboration that did not exist between the two neighbors. When the short-lived Balkan Pact (including Yugoslavia) collapsed by the mid-1950s, the conflict between these two NATO members was resumed. Despite their participation in Supreme Headquarters Allied Powers in Europe (SHAPE) assignments, Greece and Turkey were at each other's throats for much of the next forty years over their respective positions in Cyprus and over air and sea rights in the Aegean. Greece left the organization's military wing in 1974, unhappy with American toleration of Turkey's invasion of Cyprus in that year. Turkey in turn denied use of vital bases to the United States and NATO when its military aid was cut off on the grounds that equipment intended for NATO purposes was channeled into an invasion that ended with 40 percent of Cyprus in Turkish possession.

Could an alternative history have been much worse? Very likely. Despite the tensions between them, neither Greece nor Turkey went to war, although not because of any particular act of reconciliation. Greece returned to the organization in 1980 for fear that Turkey would receive benefits by its continued participation that Greece would not enjoy. And Turkey's annoyance with the United States was balanced against continuing concern over the intentions of its Soviet neighbor. Greece and Turkey never went over the brink into open warfare.

Left outside NATO, the histories of Greece and Turkey would have been very different. Turkey would not have found the strength to resist Soviet pressure on its own. Not only would it have had to cede territory in the Caucasus but also its control over the Dardanelles would have been lost. Greece, for its part, might have had to fight over again the battle against communism, and this time it would have had no American partner or Yugoslav defector to help contain the pressure. And with both nations firmly in the Soviet grasp, there would have been no incentive for the Soviets to restrain their satellites from waging war over the Aegean or Cyprus.

FRANCE: 1939 REDIVIVUS

Gloomy as the prospects for Italy and Greece would have been, those of France and Germany, the major continental powers in Western Europe, would have been catastrophic by comparison. For France, the primary concern was always a revived and rearmed Germany, even when this concern seemed to have been subsumed under worry over a well-organized Communist party with 20 percent of the nation's vote behind it. The liberal Catholic party, Mouvement Républicain Populaire, anti-Communist Socialists, and conservative Radicals all saw Communist subversion as the more immediate threat. Even followers of Jean Monnet who looked to a long-term Franco-German reconciliation could not escape the memories of three wars with German reichs.

As noted in a different context, the Brussels Pact was no solution for France, although it did combine a program of containment of Communist power with a specific reference to "a renewal by Germany of an aggressive policy." Without American adherence, it lacked credibility to contain a Soviet invasion or, more relevant to the French, to restrain German economic recovery, German rearmament, and the revival of Germany's drive for dominance. France's perception of a German menace was obvious in its desperate attempts within the NATO fold to sabotage the European Defense Community, which would have opened the way for a German army in a European uniform.

In the absence of the Atlantic Alliance, France's paranoia would have been even more evident. What it had failed to do after World War I, namely, to use the Allied military victory to subject an essentially more powerful

Germany to France's leadership on the Continent, it achieved after World War II by retaining control of the Saarland and maintaining the division of Germany. France had failed ignominiously in the interwar period to achieve its objectives. Would it have done any better after World War II if Europe and America had failed to effect an alliance? Such a question is easily answered in the negative.

France would have found itself beset by enemies on all sides. From the West, the allies, America and Britain, if they acted at all, would have moved toward restoration of Germany as a bulwark against the Soviet Union. But even if the Anglo-Saxon powers had isolated themselves from the Continent, the only source of assistance in the containment of Germany would have been the Soviet empire. That the American connection was unreliable would have been obvious to the French, either because it would have substituted American for German or Russian domination, or because America would have eventually tired of its military role in Europe and brought its troops home. Such were the concerns that agitated France within the Atlantic Alliance. Witness the efforts of the hapless Fourth Republic to achieve a nuclear *force de frappe*. And, particularly, witness General Charles de Gaulle's none-too-subtle signals to the Soviets that the price for his removal of France from NATO's military organization and his frank acceptance of the Oder-Neisse line was a senior partnership with Germany in his projected *Europe des patries*. De Gaulle sought a revival of the old Franco-Russian entente without removing France from the protection of the North Atlantic Treaty's Article 5.

Without NATO there would have been no American lifeline. And had de Gaulle established his Fifth Republic, he would have been dealing with a Poland or a Czechoslovakia in a Soviet sphere. His only possible partner would have been the Soviet Union. In one sense, this Eastern connection could have been far more effective than France's alliance with the fragile new nations of the East in suppressing German militarism. In this circumstance, the price France would have had to pay for a neutral or a Communist Germany would have been a Communist France. De Gaulle's vision of Europe from the Atlantic to the Urals might have been realized, but not under French leadership.

THE FOURTH REICH

The nightmare of an irredentist Germany unrestrained by a Western alliance was not confined to France. It was never far from the thoughts of other former victims of German occupation. The Dutch and Norwegians had as many reasons as the French to prevent the reemergence of an armed Germany seeking restitution of lost territories. What was lost after World War II was considerably more than had been taken from the Second Reich in the Treaty of Versailles. This pervasive European worry may not have been shared by Americans, but it was recognized in Dean Acheson's repeated testimony before the Korean War that German rearmament was not possible even though German territory would be protected as long as occupation forces remained on German soil. When Germany finally entered NATO in 1955, it was only after its membership was cushioned inside the enlarged Western European Union. Britain's membership provided some reassurance to France, as did the special restrictions on Germany's ability to manufacture nuclear, biological, or chemical weaponry, or even to raise an army independent of NATO.

Without NATO there would have been no means of gradually bringing West Germany into the alliance. Our counterfactual history would have witnessed a Hobbesian Europe in which the powerful consumed the weak, in which there would be no chains to bind an aggressor. True, there were forces in Germany that recognized the ugliness of Germany's past and would make a heroic effort to prevent the reemergence of rabid German militarism. Such was the aspiration of the German Socialists, led at the beginning of the 1950s by Kurt Schumacher and later in the decade by Erich Ollenhauer. Their path was pacifism, which they hoped would appease the Soviets sufficiently to permit the unification of the divided Germanies. This policy's chance of success would have been stronger than that of the pro-Western Adenauer forces, which would have looked to incorporation with the West as a means of taming German expansionism.

But neither the Francophilic Adenauer nor the neutralist Ollenhauer would have been the dominant force in a Europe that resembled the 1930s. In their place, neo-Nazi parties would have had power thrust on them or would have seized control of West Germany. Such parties existed in the 1950s in the Federal Republic (for example, the Deutscher Reichspartei). They received sustenance from the huge influx of Germans expelled from the Sudetenland, Poland, and East Prussia. These displaced Germans played a role in the politics of the Adenauer era that was larger than the size of their political parties. Even with Germany firmly embedded inside NATO and committed to the goals of the Atlantic Alliance, one could find maps that identified East Germany as *Mitteldeutschland* and the lost territories as *Ostdeutschland*. While NATO may have claimed that unification would come from a position of strength vis-à-vis the Warsaw bloc, it did not include the retaking of parts of Czechoslovakia, Poland, or the Soviet Union. In a world without NATO, the irredentist parties would have overwhelmed the moderate democratic elements with promises of the recovery of territory and prosperity.

There would have been only one force that could inhibit the rise of a Fourth Reich, and that would have been the Soviet Union. Given the lively memories of World War II, the Communist empire would have done everything in its power to remove the threat of a neo-Nazi Germany. It would have followed a line attempted in the confrontation between the Atlantic and Warsaw blocs. Unification of East and West Germany would have been part of a package that would have left Germany at best a neutralist nation, without an army or major weaponry. In this scenario, a united Germany would be a Communist Germany, the German Democratic Republic extended to the Rhine.

Yet this is not the most likely history of German-Russian relations. German nationalists would not have been satisfied with a neutral state, even a united state; the lost territories would have been as much on the nation's mind as they were under Hitler. And a subservient role to the Soviet Union would have been even less acceptable. Germany unbound would have found a way to build a nuclear armory and then challenge the Soviet Union in a race far more dangerous than the NATO-Warsaw Pact contest was in its most volatile period. If the Russians had memories of German bestiality in two world wars, Germans remembered the dream of harnessing the resources of the Ukraine, as the Second Reich intended in the Treaty of Brest-Litovsk in 1918 and the Third Reich in its invasion of the Soviet Union in 1941. The image of a Europe under such German domination could be as unsettling as a Europe under Communist domination—and perhaps even more so.

ISOLATED BRITAIN

It has been over a century since Britain, with an empire on which the sun never set, could enjoy a "splendid isolation." The twentieth century witnessed the steady decline of the British Empire despite desperate attempts to maintain the influence it had enjoyed in the nineteenth century. Two world wars left it depleted in funds, resources, and morale. Such hope that the nation had in recovering its leadership rested on a "special relationship" with the United States. An astute British pundit, Alistair Buchan, expressed it in the form of the wise Greek slave manipulating the strong but inexperienced and naive Roman conqueror. America as the daughter of Britain would be instructed in the ways of the world by a wiser and older veteran.

This was the vision that moved Foreign Secretary Ernest Bevin to entice the United States into a European alliance in which Britain would share power with the United States. Britain's position as *primus inter pares* in a global commonwealth offered at least the illusion of substance to its claim as America's partner. When the Atlantic Alliance was forged, Britain appeared to have won its objective. It was soon disillusioned. Paris, not London, became the headquarters of NATO; American commanders, not British, were in charge of military operations. Even its hope for a naval command was denied. As NATO evolved, American concerns centered on France and Germany, forcing Britain to become part of a European rather than an Anglo-Saxon community. Dean Acheson brutally stated the truth of Britain's weakness in deriding its efforts to serve as broker between the Soviet Union and the United States, or as a special partner to the American superpower. In Acheson's words, expressed in 1962, "Great Britain has lost an empire and has not yet found a role."[4]

If Britain's fate within NATO was that it became a middle-ranked nation tied to a European community dominated by Germany, what would have been its future without NATO? Unquestionably, the decline of British power and influence would have been even steeper. In the collapse of an Atlantic alliance, Britain would have clung to the hope that some form of the informal wartime Anglo-American alliance would survive. Those hopes would have been dashed even more quickly than the Greek-Roman model that British leaders had anticipated under NATO. The military collaboration of World War II had little meaning for NATO when the United States helped to abort Britain's invasion of Egypt in 1956 and six years later abruptly canceled a nuclear weapon that Britain had counted on to sustain its position as a nuclear power. Without NATO and with a United States suspicious of all European connections, Britain would have turned to its Commonwealth without success. The rapid degeneration of its empire in the 1950s would have proceeded even more rapidly in these circumstances than it actually did.

After Britain had excluded itself from the Continent, any European policy it could devise would have been a reprise of traditional British alliances designed to keep in check any nation that could control the Continent. Whether that nation was Germany or Russia, a shrunken Britain, its economy in tatters, would have stood no chance of emulating the triumphs of the eighteenth or nineteenth centuries. Belated attempts to join once again with France would have failed in the face of a Communist France or a France under the German Bundesbank. Labor riots would have reduced the national state to anarchy.

If there was a ray of hope in this new world it would not have been in a revival of the American partnership but in a junior partnership with the Soviet Union in a new common front against German domination. Despite all the economic misery that Britain would have suffered, the British Communist party would have been unable to take over the country as its counterpart in Italy had done. Britain still had resources, and even far-flung friends in Canada and Australia as well as a hard core of Anglophile Americans. It would have survived as it did in World War II and joined the Soviet Union in an effort to keep German power in check. At best the future for Britain would have been an uneasy balance in which it would have played a significant but minor part. The alternative would not have been conquest by Communists or neo-Nazis but acceptance of a position as an offshore island living on the scale of a Third World country. The image of Britain in the Tudor years comes to mind. It was an offshore island of Europe before it became an island empire.

AUTARCHIC AMERICA

All of the foregoing scenarios are based on an assumption that the United States would have turned its back on Europe and reverted to traditional isolationism. This, of course, is not the only path the nation might have followed. One can conceptualize a powerful America with a military machine ready and able to take on any potential enemy and doing so alone. Given the disillusion with the Soviet wartime ally and the concurrent fear of Communist expansion, the United States might not have demobilized after the war. Instead, it might have used the atomic weapon as an instrument of blackmail to deter the Soviet Union from moving beyond its borders with either its armies or its ideology.

Whether or not such a posture would have succeeded is moot. The picture of an aggressive America puffed up by its success against the Germans and the Japanese to the extent that it would assume the burdens as well as the advantages of global supremacy is an unlikely one. Those Americans who had entertained such a notion were few in number and had little influence. Brigadier General Bonner Fellers, for example, hardly spoke for the air force, let alone for the military at large, when he urged America to threaten the Soviet Union with atomic destruction if it did not accede to American supremacy. This would have been an extravagant interpretation of the atomic diplomacy that critics have attributed to American policy toward the Soviets in 1945.

The form that American disillusion with Europe was more likely to have taken would have been to look either inward or to the Pacific. Isolationist tradition never applied to Asia; it had been directed since the end of the Franco-American alliance only to Europe. While bilateral agreements with specific European countries might have been possible after the war, particularly with Britain, the temptation to use such arrangements as buffers against communism would have been diluted by a sense of betrayal once again by an ungrateful Europe. The sentiment that led America to reject the Treaty of Versailles and the League of Nations in 1919 would have risen again, with even greater force than had been manifested a generation before. The massive demobilization of America's armed forces in 1946 was a portent of what would have happened if the United States had rejected an entanglement with Western Europe. Rather than rearming against Soviet communism, the nation would have turned its back on an Old World that would never reform; it would have let the former allies resume their feuds, and let the Soviets extend their reach to the Atlantic. The warnings of such old isolationists as former ambassador Joseph Kennedy and former president Herbert Hoover would have been accepted instead of being ignored as they were on the eve of the Great Debate in 1951 over dispatching U.S. troops to Europe. In December 1950, Kennedy had claimed that entanglement with Europe—and Asia as well—was suicidal. It would neither win friends nor assure America's security. It would only waste troops and resources in a useless effort. And if communism did succeed in Korea or Europe, what of it? It would be a short-lived triumph, as the West would break loose from the Soviets much as Tito's Yugoslavia did in 1948. Hoover invoked a "fortress America" in a public address, asserting that if Europe should be united under a hostile power, Fascist or Communist, it need not affect America. America, both he and Kennedy asserted, could be autarchic, independent of the rest of the world.

The national euphoria that would have accompanied this divorce from the Old World would have lingered for a decade. Not even the knowledge that the Soviet Union possessed an atomic device, and a few years later, a hydrogen bomb, would have jarred America from its complacency. Only when the limits of its own vast resources began to take a toll on the nation's prosperity and security would the price of autarchy have become increasingly unbearable. Raw materials for American industry, including nuclear weaponry, required imports from abroad while exports were needed to absorb American manufactures. Isolationism in the postwar world would have depressed America's standard of living as well as its spirits.

This new sense of insecurity would have coincided with changes in military technology to induce panic far more severe than *Sputnik* caused in 1957. Such would be the effect of the Soviets and the Germans possessing intercontinental ballistic missiles that these power shifts could have made America as vulnerable as Europeans felt themselves to be in the 1970s. German expansionist dreams expressed in Operation Barbarossa in 1941 would have become a reality as Russian resources were harnessed to the German economy. In a world made smaller by technology, the Atlantic Ocean was no longer a guarantor of American independence. Even belated attempts to mobilize China or Japan to counter the power of a united and hostile Europe stretching from the ocean to the Urals and beyond would have failed. When not fighting with each other, the Asian powers would have been intimidated by the Eurasian behemoth.

The consequence for the United States would have been a massive military buildup that would have drained the economy and damaged the fabric of democracy. In the 1940s, those who raised concern about America becoming a garrison state under military control recognized that Generals Marshall and Eisenhower were not men on horseback, no matter how high their civilian offices. And if General MacArthur aspired to that role, as some of his critics claimed, he quickly reconciled himself to exile in the Waldorf-Astoria when his autocratic style proved to be more attractive in Japan than it was in Washington. An America without an Atlantic alliance, however, might have turned to dictatorship in its struggle for survival.

Whether or not any of these visions of Armageddon—some of them contradictory—bear any resemblance to reality, it is reasonable to assume in any counterfactual historical study that both Europe and America would have faced a more difficult future than they did under the aegis of NATO. With all the stresses that the alliance produced, and almost all were clearly visible to any onlooker, the last half-century of European-American relations reflected no zero-sum relationship. Each of its members profited from the connection.

NATO AFTER FORTY-FIVE: A COUNTERFACTUAL HISTORY

What then of NATO's future? Most counterfactual pundits looking beyond the Cold War have decided that NATO will dissolve, or should dissolve. Judgments have been made, as noted, on the basis that a new world order would make the old alliance unnecessary, that successor organizations would replace NATO's function, or that the United Nations in the wake of the end of the Cold War would fulfill its original peacekeeping expectations. The most frequently mentioned replacement involves at least one or more of Europe's own organizations, ranging from a modest Franco-German brigade to a more satisfying Western European Union serving as the military arm of the European Union. In brief, there is no reason why a unified Europe, whether or not it should be the United States of Europe, should need an American presence on the Continent or in an integrated alliance.

The trouble with these projections has been the turbulent aftershocks of the termination of the Cold War. The breakup of the Soviet Union inspired not only ethnic conflict among the newly independent nations in the former Soviet empire but also new insecurity among the former Eastern European satellites of that empire. A Russia that has been disillusioned by the lure of a market economy and resentful of its loss of status could produce a new czar with imperial ambitions. Would the European Union be able to cope with these problems, offering the psychological as well as military security that NATO gave for two generations?

The answer to this question is clearly negative. Western Europe has not fulfilled the promises of economic, let alone political, union that the Maastricht meeting in 1992 was supposed to bring. Resentment against German domination, particularly the German Bundesbank, has divided the community. It has not been able to make up its mind about extending its membership or deepening its integration. Its vacillation over the Serbian challenge in Bosnia has weakened its credibility as a successor to NATO.

But does the new disarray in Europe, reminiscent as it is of the national relationships in the first half of the twentieth century, mean that only NATO can cope with the current crisis? The alliance's behavior since 1990 favors the views of those who would bury it as a useless relic of the past. The efforts at the North Atlantic Council meetings in London in 1990 and Rome in 1991 hardly inspire confidence. The new strategic concepts developed there, particularly rapid reaction forces for crisis management, seemed to fall apart in 1991 in the face of NATO's failure to deter Serbian aggression. And the offer of a "partnership" to East European nations at the Brussels summit meeting of January 1994 fell short of the security guarantees that those nations were demanding of NATO. Joint field exercises are no substitute for the pledge of Article 5, which the allies refused to grant in Brussels. Division among the allies over Bosnia continues into 1995 even as NATO acts as a UN surrogate.

Despite these negative signals, my counterfactual history of the next few years finds that NATO will not disintegrate. America's refusal to put its troops at risk in Bosnia until the warring parties had come to their own agreement does not necessarily mean that the United States has removed its commitment to defend the allies in the event of attack. The presence of even a handful of American soldiers in the Former Yugoslav Republic of Macedonia (FYROM) suggests otherwise. Article 4 of the North Atlantic Treaty, wherein the allies will consult whenever the security of any of the parties is threatened, applied both to Bosnia and to FYROM. Although NATO hesitated in Bosnia, it will have no choice in FYROM, where Greece and Turkey have interests at stake. NATO as a deterrent force will have more effect in deterring Serbia's Milosevic from intervening here than it did in Bosnia.

But NATO's survival will rest on more than a token presence in the Balkans. Insufficient as the Partnership for Peace may have been, it was a source of some comfort to the East Europeans. As Russia discovers that America's presence in Europe through NATO is a stabilizing force, it will become more accepting of the Western alliance. The unsatisfactory partnership with Eastern Europe will be replaced by membership, including the guarantees under Article 5. This does not mean that Polish or Hungarian armies will be rebuilt or their militaries integrated into a SHAPE command. What will make their membership acceptable is that Poland and Hungary's status would be much like Spain's or Iceland's—outside a military structure but inside a security system. NATO for Poland will resemble the alliance as it existed before the Korean War converted it into a military organization.

Beyond this arrangement, there will be the ineffable matter of the American presence in Europe. This is a symbol of stability that gives continuing significance to the alliance. America's commitment to Europe was also the glue that seemingly replaced the Soviet threat as NATO's centripetal force. The transatlantic bargain had always been the source of NATO's unity, even as it was obscured by the need to build a defense against an aggressive Warsaw bloc. With the demise of the Soviet Union, insecurity emanating from a potentially irredentist Russia and from a united Germany will require the continuation of the NATO umbrella.

Unlike the conditional tense I have used in my counterfactual history of NATO's first forty-five years, here I use an unqualified future tense as a measure of my conviction that NATO has a function for the immediate future: namely, to assure peace and order in Europe. The belief that membership in NATO is vital to their existence explains the desperate efforts of East European nations to come under the protection of the umbrella. It also explains why none of the charter members is asking for the withdrawal of American troops from its territory. Nor is any member, including France, so dissatisfied with the direction of America's current behavior that it intends to leave the alliance. Withdrawal would be a simple matter under Article 13 of the treaty. A country's membership could cease "one year after its notice of denunciation has been given to the Government of the United States of America, which will inform the Governments of the other parties of the deposit of each notice of denunciation."

The day may come when such a "denunciation" is made. Or, if NATO should become irrelevant through impotence, it may dissolve quickly in the manner of the Warsaw Pact in 1991, or gradually in the manner of SEATO in 1977. My counterfactual history of the 1990s may be as mistaken as Fukuyama's in 1990 or Steel's in 1964. But I suspect that my version may have more validity than theirs.

NOTES

1. Francis Fukuyama, "The End of History," *The National Interest* 16 (Summer 1989): 4.
2. Ronald Steel, *End of the Alliance: America and the Future of Europe* (New York: Viking, 1994).
3. Amos Perlmutter, "NATO Must Face the Fact It Is Obsolete," *Insight on the News* 9, no. 49 (6 December 1993): 31.
4. Acheson included this comment in his 5 December 1962 address, "Our Atlantic Alliance: The Political and Economic Strands," at the U.S. Military Academy. *Vital Speeches of the Day* 29, no. 6 (1 January 1963): 163.

2

NATO and the Soviet Bloc: The Limits of Victory

Walter L. Hixson

As the North Atlantic Treaty Organization (NATO) marked its forty-fifth anniversary in 1994, supporters of the alliance found much to celebrate. The enemy that NATO had been designed to contain, the Soviet Union, no longer existed. As General Colin Powell, then chairman of the U.S. Joint Chiefs of Staff, put it in 1991, "We have seen our implacable enemy of forty years vaporize before our eyes."[1] Russia still existed, to be sure, but it no longer remained an imperial power, having been shorn of authority over its onetime East European satellites, as well as the Baltic states, Ukraine, and to a lesser extent the Caucasian and Central Asian republics.

In their euphoria over the collapse of Eastern European and Soviet communism, national security elites viewed these developments as a stunning triumph for Western diplomacy, and by implication for NATO, the centerpiece of the postwar European security structure. In 1992, President George Bush declared that the Cold War had ended and that the United States and its NATO allies had "won" the conflict. Zbigniew Brzezinski, former national security adviser in the Carter administration, cited German reunification and absorption into NATO, dissolution of the Warsaw Pact, and efforts by Russia's former satellites to join the European Community and NATO as conclusive evidence that "the Cold War did end in the victory of one side and the defeat of the other. . . . The most likely conventional Western scenario of victory," Brzezinski declared, "has been exceeded to a degree that is truly staggering."[2]

Prominent historians Arthur Schlesinger, Jr., and John Lewis Gaddis are among those who embrace the "victory thesis" in explaining the dramatic changes in European politics since 1989. They perceive the Cold War as an ideological confrontation won by the West. As Schlesinger succinctly put it, "Democracy won the political argument between East and West. The market won the economic argument." Gaddis agrees, depicting the Cold War as a confrontation between freedom and dictatorship in which the West triumphed.[3]

By claiming victory, Powell, Bush, Brzezinski, Schlesinger, Gaddis, and myriad others echo the orthodox interpretation of Cold War history. All have been staunch defenders of postwar American foreign policy. They perceive the United States as having been justified in abandoning its traditional policy of European non-entanglement in 1949 in favor of a formal political and military alliance. Defenders of NATO believe that the alliance contained the USSR, thereby contributing to its ultimate demise, while keeping a "long peace" of almost half a century in Europe.[4]

The definitive tone of the triumphalist perspective notwithstanding, debate over the Cold War, far from being resolved by the disintegration of the Soviet empire, has been revived.[5] The debate is likely to continue for some time and, we can only hope, will be made richer by material unearthed from Soviet archives. Continuing historical debate over the origins, course, and consequences of the Cold War will necessarily include efforts to assess NATO's role in the East-West conflict. Was NATO part of the architecture of victory, or an impediment to liberal reform in Eastern Europe and the USSR?

Clearly, as Brzezinski pointed out, the collapse of Eastern European and Soviet communism more than fulfilled the most optimistic projections of American Cold War strategists. But the disintegration of European communism does not necessarily vindicate NATO, as the defenders of American strategy cited above would have it. An alternative interpretation exists, namely, that the Soviet Union collapsed from internal causes and may well have crumbled or reformed earlier in the absence of the external threat that NATO represented. If this is indeed the case, the historic Western alliance impeded rather than encouraged the progressive evolution of Soviet and Eastern European societies.

By confronting the Soviet Union and its allies with a hostile military alliance, NATO cemented East-West confrontation, deterring détente and political liberalization in the East. Would liberalization have come sooner to Eastern Europe and the Soviet Union if the West had pursued détente instead of a Europe divided into hostile military blocs? No one can embrace such a counterfactual argument with certainty, yet a strong case can be made that NATO was an unnecessary impediment to reduced tensions and liberalization of the East bloc.

NATO both reflected and furthered the course of the Great-Power rivalry between East and West that evolved in the wake of the Allied victory in World War II. The Grand Alliance deteriorated partly as a result of lingering wartime resentments, such as delays in the opening of a second front in Europe, but mainly because of a contest for spheres of influence. The Soviet Union, under the brutal dictatorship of Josef Stalin, reabsorbed the Baltic states (part of the traditional Russian empire) and used its position as liberator in Eastern Europe to impose Stalinist regimes in such border states as Hungary, Poland, and Romania. The 1948 coup in Czechoslovakia—in part a response to Marshall Plan appeals to Eastern European states—culminated a successful Soviet effort to establish a buffer zone on the Western frontiers through which it had been attacked twice in a single generation by Germany and its allies.

At the root of the hostile Western response to the Kremlin's actions was a determination to establish a liberal political order undergirded by U.S. economic power in postwar Europe.[6] This was the same goal that American diplomats and businessmen had pursued in the aftermath of World War I.[7] Western hostility to the establishment of a Soviet sphere of influence in Eastern Europe rested on solid ground insofar as Premier Josef Stalin had signed the Declaration of Liberated Europe at the Yalta Conference in February 1945. Although Stalin thus pledged to support self-determination in postwar Europe, he had also repeatedly emphasized to President Franklin D. Roosevelt and British Prime Minister Winston Churchill Moscow's intention to establish "friendly" regimes on the USSR's borders. The Western leaders understood that the Yalta declaration and Stalin's real intentions contradicted one another, but they saw little benefit in confrontation before securing the unconditional surrender of Germany and Japan.[8]

With the end of the war in both theaters, however, tension between Communist Russia and the capitalist West resurfaced. Exacerbating the situation after the end of the Pacific war was U.S. trumpeting of its sole possession of the atomic bomb, while Soviet scientists—and spies—worked feverishly to break the American monopoly.[9] The Western allies sharply condemned Soviet efforts to establish spheres of influence in Eastern Europe and the Near East. Western leaders denounced Marxist-Leninist ideology and attributed virtually all leftist uprisings to a Kremlin drive for world domination. As a result of these perceptions, the United States in 1947 sponsored the Truman Doctrine, buttressing a reactionary regime in Greece, and the Marshall Plan, promoting psychological and economic recovery to thwart the threat posed by Communist political parties in Western Europe.[10]

The Marshall Plan, or European Recovery Program, has rightly been judged "one of the most successful peacetime foreign policies launched by the United States in this century."[11] Under its auspices, American diplomacy contributed directly to Western European economic recovery, at the same time inspiring confidence and promoting close ties with Washington. By 1948, once-threatening Communist parties in France and Italy had been relegated to an "isolated opposition" that reflected the general weakening of the Western European left. By 1949, with the creation of the West German state, U.S. economic and political intervention had proven instrumental in reviving parliamentary democracy throughout Western Europe.[12]

Still reeling from the psychological, as well as material and physical, effects of World War II, however, Western Europeans felt vulnerable to Soviet power, especially in the wake of the Hitler-like coup in Czechoslovakia. By 1948 a virtual war—or Cold War—atmosphere prevailed, prompting the Soviet blockade of Berlin and the U.S.-sponsored airlift of supplies to the allied sectors of the former German capital. It was in the midst of these unsettling events that European and American officials launched the historic collaboration that would produce the NATO alliance.[13] The collective defense treaty, eventually encompassing sixteen member-nations, constituted a formal military alliance, one that clearly targeted the Soviet Union and its Eastern European satellites. An attack on one NATO member would be considered an attack on all. In the wake of the Czech coup, American and European officials emphasized the parallels between the Soviet Union and Nazi Germany in order to build popular support for the alliance.[14]

Despite the putative defensive motives underlying NATO, however, military considerations were secondary to political and economic goals, especially in Washington. Most U.S. officials concurred with a Central Intelligence Agency (CIA) assessment in the fall of 1948 that concluded, "We do not believe that the events of the past six months have made deliberate Soviet military action a probability during 1948-49."[15] Top Truman administration officials and advisers, including Dean G. Acheson, W. Averell Harriman, Louis Johnson, and General Omar Bradley, "did not expect and were not worried about Soviet aggression."[16] Neither Charles Bohlen nor George F. Kennan, the nation's preeminent Soviet experts, anticipated military action by the USSR.

While the emphasis on the chimerical Soviet military threat revived images of Nazi aggression in order to build public support for the "entangling alliance," the primary goal of American strategy was to promote Western integration. NATO furthered the cause of political, economic, and military integration begun by the Truman Doctrine and the European Recovery Program in 1947. NATO also provided a structure for assuaging French anxieties while reintegrating western Germany into the postwar liberal order. The formal military alliance thus fostered a heightened sense of security, although the foundation had already been laid for Western European economic recovery and the triumph of parliamentary democracy.

NATO quickly emerged as the centerpiece of Western Cold War strategy, one whose vitality rested on reinforcing the perception of an implacable Soviet enemy with whom negotiations were futile. As historian Melvyn P. Leffler has persuasively argued, the Western coalition, led by the United States, rejected negotiations with the USSR in deference to effecting "a preponderance of power" in the West. In the spring of 1948, Leffler notes, "virtually every American assessment of Soviet aims underscored the Kremlin's conciliatory demeanor and readiness to talk." Committed to integration and to gaining the upper hand in the East-West struggle, Washington rebuffed all diplomatic overtures. "With momentum in their favor," Leffler explained, American national security planners "would not diverge from their course of defeating communism in Western Europe, co-opting German power, and implementing the ERP [European Recovery Program]."[17]

Ironically, it was George Kennan, the nation's foremost Soviet expert and a man who had been credited with mobilizing both elite and popular support for the Cold War, who opposed the Western strategy of pursuing preponderance. In the summer of 1948, Kennan, head of the State Department's Policy Planning Staff, proposed a negotiated "disengagement" from Central Europe. Under the plan, both Soviet and allied forces would withdraw from Germany, which would then hold free elections intended to produce a neutral, nonaligned, and demilitarized state. Kennan envisioned "long and difficult negotiations" that could, however, ultimately achieve a settlement that would be "to the overall benefit of U.S. interests" while taking into account "legitimate Russian interests and requirements." If nothing else, he advised, the disengagement proposal could "offset charges that we do not really want any settlement with Russia."[18]

Kennan himself, as he later admitted, failed to realize at the time that the United States did not in fact want a settlement with the USSR. Not a single prominent figure in the Truman administration or in the British and

French governments embraced Kennan's call for disengagement. As Leffler notes, the West's "primary national security goal was not to unify Germany or ease tensions in Europe; it was to harness Germany's economic and military potential for the Atlantic community."[19] Truman administration officials rejected Kennan's proposal on the grounds that a neutral, reunified Germany might someday unite with Moscow, or reemerge as a threat in its own right. Either scenario would impede economic and political integration, leave France and other European nations insecure, and curb American efforts to ensure a preponderance of power.

Top Truman administration officials, including most notably the new secretary of state, Dean Acheson, shot down Soviet initiatives calling for a negotiated settlement in Europe. One such opportunity arose in late January 1949 when J. Kingsbury Smith, European general manager of the International News Service, sent a wire to Stalin noting that Truman's press secretary, Charles Ross, had stated that the president would confer with the Soviet premier should he be willing to travel to Washington. Stalin promptly responded that his doctors "strongly object to my undertaking any prolonged journey," but he offered to meet with Truman in any one of five Soviet sites or in Poland or Czechoslovakia. United Nations (UN) Secretary-General Trygve Lie endorsed the prospect of a Great Power summit that might reduce Cold War tensions and revive the prospects of a multilateral postwar order centered around the United Nations.

The Truman White House declined comment on Stalin's offer while making clear its hostility to a summit. "It is known that Mr. Truman does not look with favor upon a 'Big Two' conference to settle East-West differences," White House journalists reported.[20] The *New York Times* reported that "there is very little likelihood that the United States would now agree to postponing its plans for the political organization of western Germany."[21] American officials expressed concern that any meeting behind the Iron Curtain would be a propaganda boon for Moscow, but at the same time Truman declined an opportunity to suggest an alternative site. Had Washington proposed a summit in, say, jointly occupied Austria or neutral Switzerland, Soviet willingness to negotiate could have been tested. Instead, Acheson put the matter to rest in a news conference in which he blamed the Soviet Union exclusively for the Cold War and charged Stalin with staging an "international political maneuver" rather than offering a real chance for peace.[22]

As events moved toward NATO signing ceremonies in Washington in April 1949, the Kremlin again advanced proposals calling for a negotiated settlement. Not wishing to bear the onus for the division of Germany, and thus of Europe, Acheson agreed to a meeting of the Big Four foreign ministers. Acceding to Western demands, Stalin terminated the Berlin blockade in May 1949, reducing East-West tensions and allowing the allies to end the costly airlift of supplies into western sectors of the city. The United States, however, remained opposed to the prospect of disengagement and German neutralization. As Acheson explained to Truman and the National Security Council, the NATO allies would proceed with plans for effecting a separate west German government and would agree to unification only "on the basis of consolidating the Eastern zone into ours." Washington thus rejected negotiations with Moscow and would accept only a Soviet capitulation.[23]

Only Kennan, soon to resign as Policy Planning Staff director, continued to insist that Western policy, including NATO itself, was ill-conceived. The author of the famous "Long Telegram" and "X Article" had not suddenly gone soft on communism. Despite attempts, notably by Acheson, to dismiss Kennan as impractical, the Soviet expert had definite objectives in mind. A longtime Germanophile, Kennan did not want to see the former Reich partitioned between the United States and the Soviet Union, both of which he considered overextended. Moreover, and central to the focus of this chapter, Kennan argued that Western military integration would sacrifice indefinitely East-Central Europe to Soviet domination. Kennan's concept of containment had envisioned a gradual mellowing if not outright collapse of Soviet communism, but he now viewed the Western military alliance as an impediment to that goal.

To Kennan, the Atlantic Alliance represented the militarization of his containment strategy. By rejecting opportunities for a political settlement on the future of Germany, the West limited the prospects for the mellowing and retraction of Soviet power that he had predicted in his wartime and postwar essays. As a Soviet expert and longtime resident of Moscow, Kennan, despite his deep-seated anticommunism, showed a willingness to consider the Kremlin perspective on the creation of NATO and the incorporation of a rump German state into the Western alliance. The Russians, he observed in 1950, could not but have perceived NATO

> as, of course, an alliance against them. They must have realized that from then on, in giving up any influence anywhere in eastern or central Europe they ran the enormous prestige risk of abandoning territory to a military alliance in which their outstanding adversary in the eyes of the world played a dominant part. From then on it must have appeared to the Kremlin leaders that there were only two possibilities conceivable from the

standpoint of their interests: either the firm retention of their hold on eastern and central Europe, or a military conflict.[24]

While it is not clear just how seriously Stalin and his associates took the threat of Western aggression, Russian history offered little reassurance. Russia's influence in Europe had peaked in the mid-nineteenth century, leaving the country thereafter in a position of economic and technical inferiority to the West. That inferiority produced a high degree of insecurity, especially considering Western anti-Bolshevism, Allied intervention after World War I, and outright invasion by Germany in 1941. NATO could not fail but to fit into this pattern of Western hostility. The West, already materially and technologically superior, now sought to incorporate the greater part of the Soviet Union's wartime enemy, Germany, into a hostile military alliance encompassing more than half of Europe. Marxist-Leninist ideology, which viewed aggressive imperialist wars as a final stage of capitalism, exacerbated a sense of vulnerability still strongly felt in the wake of the deep Nazi penetration.

Not surprisingly, the USSR made NATO's alleged aggressive design the centerpiece of Soviet propaganda. Newspaper articles and radio broadcasts reflected an "enormous concentration on the single propaganda theme . . . that [NATO] is aggressive in purpose and is intended to bring about war."[25] By confronting the Soviets with a hostile military alliance, the West simplified the task of Communist propaganda in Eastern Europe and the Soviet Union. Many Eastern bloc residents, perhaps a majority, viewed NATO as a potential invasion force. Such perceptions undoubtedly fueled support for the Soviet regime and for the maintenance of hegemony over Eastern Europe.[26]

A hardening of positions on both sides characterized the period following the implementation of NATO. The Soviets harassed U.S. diplomatic missions, launched full-scale jamming of Western radio broadcasts, and conducted "an extensive, thoroughgoing effort to drive out Western cultural and charitable institutions" throughout Eastern Europe.[27] U.S. exports to Russia decreased by 90 percent in 1949 alone.[28] In the West, Truman in April 1950 approved NSC-68, a critical policy paper whose apocalyptic tone encouraged worst-case scenarios and buttressed a massive military buildup that institutionalized the Cold War and the military-industrial complex in American life.[29] The perceptions underlying NSC-68 accelerated the nuclear arms race and led logically to the conclusion, now known to be false,[30] that Stalin ordered Kim Il Sung's aggression in Korea in June 1950. The Korean War, coming on the heels of the Communist triumph in China, ensured the implementation of NSC-68 and the militarization of containment.

The strategy of incorporating West Germany gained momentum in December 1950 when Acheson won NATO approval for German rearmament. Economic integration proceeded apace. On 10 March 1952, Stalin issued a "peace note" in which he again offered to negotiate a settlement of the German question. The Soviet dictator proposed that all foreign troops be withdrawn from German soil within a year; that no military bases be permitted in Germany; that the former Reich be precluded from joining an alliance that included any of the World War II Allies; and that Germany be allowed limited armed forces but be free of any economic restraints. No less an authority on diplomacy than Henry A. Kissinger recently wrote that "the tone and precision of Stalin's note suggested that his purpose transcended mere propaganda." Perhaps anticipating a long Cold War that his country could not win, Stalin "might have been willing to pay a significant price for a relaxation of tensions."[31] The Truman administration dismissed Stalin's note as pure propaganda. If that was so, why not call the dictator's bluff, exposing Soviet insincerity and winning a propaganda victory for the West? Instead, the Truman administration "scorned the Soviet overture." As Leffler observed, Acheson aimed "to co-opt German power, not haggle over German unity."[32]

The death of Stalin on 5 March 1953, six weeks after the coming to power of the new administration of Dwight D. Eisenhower in Washington, offered another propitious opportunity to negotiate a settlement in East-Central Europe. Again, however, the United States and its allies dismissed the prospect. In the USSR, Stalin's apparent successor, Georgy Malenkov, called for peaceful coexistence with the West in a speech at Stalin's funeral. Subsequently, his publicly stated willingness to negotiate on all outstanding issues relating to European security had the support of other Soviet elites.[33]

In the West, Eisenhower enjoyed enormous prestige, and his Republican party, although strongly influenced by the right-wing zealots responsible for the hysteria known as McCarthyism, was far less vulnerable to charges of being soft on communism than Truman had been. But Eisenhower, architect of the Normandy invasion and NATO's first supreme commander, favored Western integration above all else, including a settlement with the USSR over East-Central Europe. Eisenhower embraced the advice of Secretary of State John Foster Dulles and West German Chancellor Konrad Adenauer over the more uncertain course now advocated by, among others, Winston Churchill. Serving once again as British prime minister, Churchill had undergone a change of heart and now urged his Western colleagues to drop all preconditions for a summit with the Soviets in order to achieve a Cold War settlement. Eisenhower refused, prompting Churchill to complain privately that the new American president was "weak and stupid" for declining an opportunity to pursue détente with Russia's post-Stalin leadership.[34]

"It is difficult to avoid the conclusion," historian Bennett Kovrig has observed, "that the West missed a rare opportunity in the spring and summer of 1953 to renegotiate the division of Europe."[35] Despite all the Republican rhetoric about the immorality of mere containment and the urgent need for liberation of the captive nations of Eastern Europe, the West refused to pursue avenues that carried any realistic prospect of an early achievement of that goal. A rearmed West Germany joined NATO on 6 May 1955. Days later, the USSR signed the Austrian State Treaty allowing for the neutralization of that country, but in the same month formalized its hegemony by incorporating the Eastern European regimes into the Warsaw Pact.[36]

Creation of a formal military alliance tied to the Kremlin severely limited the prospects for liberal reform in Eastern Europe. Moreover, West German rearmament offered an ideal issue to be exploited by Soviet propagandists in their appeals to the Warsaw Pact states. As C. D. Jackson, Eisenhower's staunchly anti-Communist psychological warfare adviser lamented, "The Russians can now say with a straight face, 'Now you can see what your fine Western friends think of you and your eventual liberation. They are rearming the Germans to prepare for another war. . . . We may not be perfect, but the best way for you to protect yourselves from those Nazi beasts is to stick with us.'"[37]

Under the direction of Jackson and others, Washington strove to counter Soviet propaganda through the Voice of America, Radio Free Europe, covert operations, and limited cultural exchange. These activities gradually contributed to a burgeoning desire for independence and liberalization in Eastern Europe, but the Warsaw Pact offered a convenient pretext for intervention when reformers renounced Soviet hegemony. The Kremlin's brutal repression of the 1956 Hungarian uprising showed that the Cold War, as Kennan had anticipated, was a zero-sum game in which the Soviets perceived that any defecting states, if allowed to proceed, would join a hostile Western European military alliance. Draconian measures, sanctioned by the Warsaw Pact, would be taken to prevent the erosion of Kremlin influence.

Thus, by the mid-1950s, the creation of NATO and the incorporation into the Western military alliance of a rearmed West Germany had prompted Soviet counterresponses that ended the prospects of neutralization or near-term reform in East-Central Europe. The diplomatic record clearly reveals that the USSR expressed more willingness to negotiate the fate of this region

than did Washington and its NATO allies. While no one can say that negotiations would have succeeded, the West abandoned all interest in them and
pursued the economic, political, and military integration of Western Europe
instead. Despite a rhetorical commitment to liberation, American policy left
Soviet leaders seeing little alternative to strengthening their hegemony over
Eastern Europe.

Liberalization, and ultimately the collapse of Communist regimes, came
to the region more than thirty years later. The disintegration of the Soviet
empire resulted in part from the persistent pressures—diplomatic, military,
and cultural—on the part of a Western coalition that was superior in material, technological, and, most would agree, moral terms. The reform policies
of perestroika and glasnost associated with Mikhail Gorbachev, although
designed to revivify socialism, served instead to reveal the glaring weaknesses and overextension of Soviet power. As the USSR wrestled with internal reform and steady decay, Eastern Europe broke free in 1989. The next
year, German reunification, opposed by the West in the early Cold War,
became a reality. Finally, in 1991, the Soviet Union itself collapsed.

The question now before historians is not really whether the West won
the Cold War—clearly the dramatic changes that have occurred since 1989
constitute a victory of sorts. The remaining questions, however, are those that
orthodox Cold War scholars prefer to ignore. Those questions focus essentially
on the costs of the Western victory and whether it could have been achieved,
in one form or another, at an earlier time, and thus at a lower cost. In other
words, future research must focus on which tactics of Western diplomacy
succeeded and which failed in the ultimate Western victory in the Cold War.

Although that debate remains nascent, a handful of American scholars
has already made the case that the United States and its allies overreacted
to the Soviet threat, invested too heavily in the Cold War and military
Keynesianism, and may well have retarded the process of liberalization in
Eastern Europe.[38] So-called revisionists (a term that serves more as an epi-
thet than a reflection of universally embraced concepts) have influenced discussion in the West for years, but what promises to invigorate the new
Cold War historiography is the entry into the debate of historians of the former Soviet Union, who are now free to make an honest evaluation of their
country's history.

Three historians from the former Soviet Union, none of whom carries
a brief for Stalin's diplomacy, nevertheless agree that Western policy—and
most especially NATO and the militarization of containment—retarded the
prospects of liberalization in Eastern Europe and the Soviet Union itself. One

of them, Georgi M. Kornienko, formerly of the Soviet Foreign Ministry, argues that "the far-reaching changes in the USSR would have started much earlier in a different, more favorable international climate." The arms race and intensification of Cold War tensions "could have been entirely avoided, I think, if only George Kennan's recommendation of 'containment' of the Soviet Union by means of principally political and economic methods had prevailed in Truman's second administration, instead of the policy of containment by primarily military means."[39]

Vladislav Zubok, who holds a doctorate from the Institute of USA and Canada Studies, agrees that the militarization of containment in the West created "an atmosphere of intense dangerous confrontation" that "strengthened reactionary elements in Communist ruling elites and weakened reform-minded elements." He argues that "new evidence demonstrates that Stalin in early 1950 showed anything but a high level of confidence" and offered only a "reluctant nod" to Kim Il Sung's notification of impending war in Korea. By adopting the extreme perceptions of NSC-68, Zubok suggests, U.S. national security planners "may have missed possibilities for exploiting 'seeds of decay' within the Communist world."[40]

Finally, Alexei Filitov, of the Moscow World History Institute, argues that "the Cold War could have been aborted and Soviet-American cooperation on the German problem could have begun on several occasions" in the late 1940s and early to mid-1950s. Filitov believes that the triumph of democratic and market forces across the former Soviet empire "would have come much sooner and would have cost much less . . . had the Cold War not militarized the historical dialectical argument between East and West."[41]

The possibility that NATO and the militarization of containment retarded Eastern European and Soviet liberalization and needlessly prolonged the Cold War should give pause to self-congratulatory proponents of the victory thesis. To the extent that the United States achieved victory, it came at great cost, both economic and moral (since the Cold War justified armed support of authoritarian regimes), and may well have left the nation in a state of premature "relative decline."[42] Even the scope of the Western victory—the complete collapse of political structure across a huge and vital region of the world—has left insecurity and violent unrest in its wake, forces that may well prove more destabilizing than the now-defunct Soviet regime.

NATO Secretary-General Manfred Wörner once observed that the alliance, more than just a security pact, "became the expression of a common purpose and a political vision, a community of values and destiny . . . to ensure the cohesion and solidarity of our liberal democracies."[43] Lawrence

S. Kaplan, the preeminent historian of NATO, agrees, terming NATO "the most successful as well as the most significant of the [United States's] initiatives after World War II." Kaplan rightfully credits the alliance with the seemingly impossible historic achievement of uniting France and Germany. For Western Europe, he argues, NATO achieved "the promise of a genuine community as outlined in the treaty's preamble."[44] As a result of dedicated efforts that cut across diverse languages and cultures, men and women scarred by the tragedy of a horribly destructive global war came together and rebuilt an integrated community in the heart of Europe. Like the Marshall Plan before it, NATO fostered Western European economic and political security in the wake of two devastating global conflicts.

In the interests of achieving Western unity, however, NATO planners foreclosed opportunities for an even more peaceful and integrated world, one that might have allowed Eastern Europe to have been less the victim and more the agent for shaping its own destiny. The Soviet Union, particularly under Stalin, did much to provoke the Cold War, but it also tried harder than the West, even under Stalin, to pursue détente. The Soviets did so because they sensed their own relative weakness. That weakness, compounded by the strains of more than forty years of the Cold War, culminated in 1991 in the disintegration of the Soviet Union.

A case has been made here for the plausibility of the argument that had the United States pursued negotiations in the wake of successful implementation of the Marshall Plan, liberalization may well have come sooner to Eastern Europe and the Soviet Union. Instead, American policymakers opted for the militarization of containment, as evidenced by the NATO alliance, NSC-68, intervention in Korea, and promotion of the nuclear arms race. U.S.-sponsored overreliance on military aspects of strategy in the first generation of the Cold War not only ruled out negotiations but limited economic and cultural penetration of the Iron Curtain. My own view, based on current research and extensive discussions and observations during a year's residence (1990-91) in the former Soviet Union, is that Western material success and the allure of advanced consumer society did far more to undermine Soviet authority than NATO and other conventional aspects of Western diplomacy.[45] Although much more work will have to be done on this neglected aspect of Cold War history before any definitive judgments can be made, it may well be that had the West tried harder to keep open lines of communication, thereby allowing for large-scale cultural infiltration, the Cold War might have ended sooner, cost less, and left a more stable world in its wake.

NOTES

1. Quoted in the *Washington Post*, 28 September 1991.

2. Zbigniew Brzezinski, "The Cold War and Its Aftermath," *Foreign Affairs* 71 (Fall 1992): 31-49.

3. Arthur Schlesinger, Jr., "Some Lessons from the Cold War," *Diplomatic History* 16 (Winter 1992): 47-53; John Lewis Gaddis, "The Cold War, the Long Peace, and the Future," ibid., 234-46; idem, "The Tragedy of Cold War History," ibid. 17 (Winter 1993): 1-16.

4. John Lewis Gaddis, *The Long Peace: Inquiries into the History of the Cold War* (New York: Oxford University Press, 1987).

5. On this point see Karen J. Winkler, "Scholars Refight the Cold War," *The Chronicle of Higher Education*, 2 March 1994; Gaddis, "The Tragedy of Cold War History"; Bruce Cumings, "'Revising Postrevisionism,' or, The Poverty of Theory in Diplomatic History," *Diplomatic History* 17 (Fall 1993): 539-69; and Michael J. Hogan, "The Vice Men of Foreign Policy," *Reviews in American History* 21 (June 1993): 320-28.

6. Few historians would dispute that economic motives played a powerful role in American policy in postwar Western Europe. Thomas J. McCormick, *America's Half Century: United States Foreign Policy in the Cold War* (Baltimore: Johns Hopkins University Press, 1991), employing a "world systems" model of capitalist development, offers a strong case for the primacy of U.S. economic motives. Historians employing the "corporatist" paradigm offer a more moderate analysis, but one still based extensively on economic determinism. See, for example, Michael J. Hogan, *The Marshall Plan: America, Britain, and the Reconstruction of Western Europe, 1947-1952* (New York: Cambridge University Press, 1987).

7. Warren I. Cohen, *Empire without Tears: America's Foreign Relations, 1921-1933* (New York: Alfred A. Knopf, 1987).

8. U.S. Department of State, *Foreign Relations of the United States: The Conferences at Malta and Yalta, 1945* (Washington, 1955).

9. David Holloway, *The Soviet Union and the Arms Race* (New Haven: Yale University Press, 1983); Gregg Herken, *The Winning Weapon: The Atomic Bomb in the Cold War, 1945-1950* (New York: Vintage Press, 1982).

10. The literature on the Truman Doctrine and Marshall Plan is enormous. On the former contrast Richard M. Freeland, *The Truman Doctrine and the Origins of McCarthyism: Foreign Policy, Domestic Politics, and Internal Security, 1946-1948* (New York: New York University Press, 1985), with Howard Jones, *"A New Kind of War": America's Global Strategy and the Truman Doctrine in Greece* (New York: Oxford University Press, 1989). On the Marshall Plan contrast Hogan, *The Marshall Plan*, with Alan S. Milward, *The Reconstruction of Western Europe, 1945-1951* (Berkeley: University of California Press, 1984). See also the essays in Charles S. Maier, ed., *The Cold War in Europe: Era of a Divided Continent* (Cambridge: Harvard University Press, 1991).

11. Hogan, *The Marshall Plan*, 445.
12. Derek W. Urwin, *Western Europe since 1945: A Political History*, 4th ed. (London: Longman, 1989), 47-56, quote on 53.
13. Lawrence S. Kaplan, *NATO and the United States: The Enduring Alliance* (Boston: Twayne Publishers, 1988), 16-30.
14. Thomas G. Paterson, "Red Fascism: The American Image of Aggressive Totalitarianism," in his *Meeting the Communist Threat: Truman to Reagan* (New York: Oxford University Press, 1988). See also Ernest R. May, *"Lessons" of the Past: The Use and Misuse of History in American Foreign Policy* (New York: Oxford University Press, 1973).
15. CIA Report, "Possibility of Direct Soviet Military Action During 1948-49," 16 September 1948, Harry S. Truman Papers, Intelligence File, 1948, box 255, Harry S. Truman Library, Independence, Missouri.
16. Melvyn P. Leffler, *A Preponderance of Power: National Security, the Truman Administration, and the Cold War* (Stanford: Stanford University Press, 1992), 282.
17. Ibid., 215.
18. Kennan, "Policy Questions Concerning a Possible German Settlement," PPS 37 and PPS 37/1, in *The State Department Policy Planning Staff Papers, 1947-1949*, ed. Anna K. Nelson, 3 vols. (New York: Garland Publishers, 1983), 2:325-71. See also the discussion in Walter L. Hixson, *George F. Kennan: Cold War Iconoclast* (New York: Columbia University Press, 1989), 80-84.
19. Leffler, *Preponderance of Power*, 283.
20. 2 February 1949 wire service reports, Papers of Charles G. Ross, Subject File, box 7, Truman Library.
21. *New York Times*, 1 February 1949.
22. 2 February 1949 wire service reports, Ross Papers, Subject File, box 7.
23. Leffler, *Preponderance of Power*, 283-85.
24. Hixson, *Kennan: Cold War Iconoclast*, 80.
25. "Foreign Radio Reactions to the Text of the North Atlantic Pact," 23 March 1949, Files of Clark Clifford, box 10, Truman Library.
26. Adam Ulam, *Expansion and Coexistence: Soviet Foreign Policy, 1917-1973*, 2d ed. (New York: Praeger, 1974), 439, 498-500, 505-6.
27. CIA report, "Soviet-Satellite Drive Against Western Influence in Eastern Europe," 2 June 1950, President's Secretary's Files: Intelligence Files, CIA Reports, 1949-1950, box 257, Truman Library.
28. Albert L. Weeks, *The Other Side of Coexistence: An Analysis of Russian Foreign Policy* (New York: Pitman, 1970), 131.
29. The best new study of this oft-discussed document is Ernest R. May, ed., *American Cold War Strategy: Interpreting NSC-68* (New York: Bedford Books, 1993).
30. Recent evidence from the Soviet Foreign Ministry Archive confirms what Nikita Khrushchev recalled in his memoirs, that North Korean leader Kim Il Sung initiated the offensive against South Korea. Stalin reluctantly approved Kim's

plans, largely out of concern that China's Mao Zedong would gain in prestige as a leader of world communism if he supported Kim in Korea while the USSR stood aside. See "New Findings on the Korean War," *Cold War International History Project Bulletin* (Fall 1993): 1. See also Strobe Talbott, *Khrushchev Remembers* (Boston: Little, Brown and Co., 1970). Some historians, including Bruce Cumings, emphasize South Korean provocations in the outbreak of the civil war. See his *The Origins of the Korean War*, Vol. 2, *The Roaring of the Cataract, 1947-1950* (Princeton: Princeton University Press, 1990).

31. Henry A. Kissinger, *Diplomacy* (New York: Simon & Schuster, 1994), 498.

32. Leffler, *Preponderance of Power*, 457-58.

33. Bennett Kovrig, *Of Walls and Bridges: The United States and Eastern Europe* (New York: New York University Press, 1991), 51-53.

34. Ibid., 53.

35. Ibid., 53.

36. Audrey K. Cronin, *Great Power Politics and the Struggle over Austria, 1945-1955* (Ithaca: Cornell University Press, 1986); Peter Zwick, *Soviet Foreign Relations: Process and Policy* (Englewood Cliffs: Prentice Hall, 1990), 191-96.

37. C. D. Jackson to Dillon Anderson, 19 April 1955, C. D. Jackson Papers, box 90, Dwight D. Eisenhower Library, Abilene, Kansas.

38. See, for example H. W. Brands, *The Devil We Knew: Americans and the Cold War* (New York: Oxford University Press, 1993), 187-228. See also the brief essays by Gar Alperovitz and Kai Bird, Richard J. Barnet, and Ronald Steel, in "The End of the Cold War: A Symposium II," *Diplomatic History* 16 (Spring 1992): 223-318.

39. "Kornienko's Commentary," in May, ed., *Interpreting NSC-68*, 124-29.

40. "Zubok's Commentary," in ibid., 189-93.

41. Alexei Filitov, "Victory in the Postwar Era: Despite the Cold War or Because of It?" *Diplomatic History* 16 (Winter 1992): 54-60.

42. Paul Kennedy, *The Rise and Fall of the Great Powers: Economic Change and Military Conflict from 1500 to 2000* (New York: Random House, 1987), 514-35.

43. "Fortieth Anniversary of NATO," speech by NATO Secretary-General Manfred Wörner, April 1989, Brussels, in *Change and Continuity in the North Atlantic Alliance* (Brussels: NATO Office of Information and Press, 1990), 43.

44. Kaplan, *NATO and the United States*, 183-84.

45. Walter L. Hixson, "Parting the Curtain: Propaganda, Culture, and the Cold War," book manuscript in progress; idem, *Witness to Disintegration: Provincial Life in the Last Year of the USSR* (Hanover, NH: University Press of New England, 1993).

PART 2

NATO's Structure and Strategy

3

NATO's Structural Changes for the 1990s

Robert S. Jordan

In the end, the past possesses us.[1]
—EDWARD W. SAID

The overarching theme of this chapter is that the basic confluence of the historical forces that have contributed to incessant European warfare is still very much with us. Even if we cannot agree entirely with Samuel Huntington's thesis concerning the clash of civilizations, we can certainly understand that the ethnic/religious hatreds of the past are being revisited in the present.[2] Additionally, we may be witnessing the gradual adaptation of the Cold War politics of Europe away from two (and then one) fixed coalitions, in the direction of shifting coalitions revolving loosely around various Great Power interests.

It follows, therefore, that in this turbulent post–Cold War international political world, writing about the circumstances and settings of the North Atlantic Treaty Organization's (NATO) post–Cold War military structure must be regarded as a highly contingent endeavor. Nonetheless, it seems clear that all of the states of the "new Europe" have similar defense goals. They want to protect their airspace; they want to protect their territories from incursions; and they want to defuse their domestic ethnic violence. To do this, they must rely for local defensive action on their standing military forces, coupled with reserve (or in some cases, militia) forces that can be swiftly mobilized. But they must also rely on outside historic "friends" or on coalition partners.[3]

This observation has been borne out, for example, as the disastrous warfare in the Balkans has unfolded. NATO member-states have, in effect, become partners with the United Nations and with the Western European Union (WEU) member-states in attempting to contain and resolve the warfare. These three international organizations have worked together to develop the means, at the very least, of diminishing bloodshed and the suffering of civilians while pressuring the combatants to cease their warring efforts.

It was clear as early as 1988 that the advent of the collapse of the Soviet Union would undoubtedly transform fundamentally the military structure of NATO but that the collapse could also enhance NATO's political responsibilities.[4] With the so-called interlocking relationships of NATO with the United Nations (UN) and the WEU and with other possible or actual coalition partners, such as the former Warsaw Pact states and those of the Commonwealth of Independent States (CIS), the political/diplomatic dimension of NATO has indeed taken on a new and unanticipated significance as NATO attempts to work out a renewed purpose and role.

In other words, more than a swift and, some would say, precipitous drawdown of NATO's standing military forces (or "forces-in-being"), especially those arrayed along the former Central Front, is taking place. A steady political realignment of those remaining military forces has also begun, in response to the altered circumstances that now exist in a Europe fundamentally changed as a consequence of the rapid reunification of Germany, the dissolution of the Soviet Union, and the demise of the Warsaw Pact.

With regard to NATO's relations with Central and Eastern Europe, four principles have been enunciated to provide a guidance framework:

1. The alliance's relations with the area will be carried out under the auspices and guidance of the North Atlantic Council (NAC).
2. They will include the range of military exchanges, assistance, and other activities conducted between NATO Headquarters, the Major NATO Commands (MNC), and their subordinate commands as approved and sponsored by the Military Committee (MC).
3. They should be reciprocal in nature.
4. They should not be seen to favor one cooperative state or group of states over any other.[5]

A prime example, discussed below, is the NATO policy of drawing the former Warsaw Pact states into a North Atlantic Cooperation Council (NACC).

More recently, a Partnership for Peace (PFP) arrangement for limited military cooperation was offered to these states—along with those states that gained (or regained) their political independence with the breakup of the Soviet Union.

CHANGES IN THE MILITARY GOVERNANCE OF NATO

> *Cooperation in international affairs and in NATO is not automatic. Even when interests converge . . . the effort that will go toward common goals, especially in terms of "blood and treasure," can never be predicted.*[6]

The Defense Planning Committee (DPC), a coordinate committee of the North Atlantic Council (NAC), provides the NATO Supreme Commanders, Supreme Allied Commander Europe (SACEUR) and Supreme Allied Commander Atlantic (SACLANT), with the direction they require in order to implement the military plans and policies approved by these two ministerial governing bodies.[7] The DPC is the highest military body in NATO, consisting of those member-states that participate in the integrated defense structure. It meets biannually in ministerial session with the defense ministers and otherwise at the level of the Permanent Representatives (PERMREP).[8]

The overall military governance of NATO takes place through the MC, composed of the chiefs of staff (COS) of all the member-states (except Spain, Iceland, and France) [see Appendix B].[9] The MC normally meets at least twice per year at the COS level and operates on a continuous basis through national military representatives (MILREP), who are appointed by each of the chiefs of staffs to act on their behalf.[10]

The Military Committee is responsible for providing military advice and guidance to the NAC and the DPC; as such, it is the body to which the two (formerly three) Major NATO Commands are responsible [see Appendix B]. The presidency of the MC rotates annually, but the day-to-day business of the committee is directed by the chairman, who is elected for a period of three years; by tradition the post is never held by an American. An International Military Staff (IMS), created in 1967, acts as the executive agent of the MC.

With the creation of the NACC, periodic meetings of the Military Committee "in cooperation session" (MC Co-op) were established. The MC Co-op meets twice yearly following the meeting of the MC. The first meeting at the ministerial level was held on 20 December 1991. The defense ministers then met on 1 April 1992, and the MC at COS level conducted its first meeting on 10 April 1992. In February 1993 the first meeting at the MILREP level was held.[11]

The second meeting of the MC "in cooperation" convened at the COS level in April 1993. The purpose of these meetings is to give the NATO chiefs the opportunity to share their views on matters of common concern with their cooperation partners and to provide a politically acceptable method by which they can jointly consider solutions to their common defense and security problems.

Military-related activities are conducted by the cooperation partners' military authorities with the two MNCs and their subordinate commands, subject to these guidelines:

- Cooperation activities at MNC level and below should normally focus on more practical areas, such as development of military doctrine, organization and structure of military forces, expert assistance, training and exercises, exchange programs, and logistic issues;
- MNCs are encouraged to notify the IMS of particular activities that may be of interest;
- MNCs should develop specific guidelines for subordinate NATO military staffs and agencies; and
- MNCs will submit forecasts on cooperation activities to the MC on a biannual basis.[12]

More specifically, a NACC Ad Hoc Group on Cooperation in Peacekeeping formed to develop plans and policies for the area embraced by the Conference on Security and Cooperation in Europe (CSCE). An open-ended expert working group, under the chair of the IMS, has been charged with developing studies concerning three areas: (1) the assets and capabilities required for the conduct of peacekeeping operations; (2) the possibility and utility of developing a database of available resources; and (3) the requirements for forces, procedures, and equipment to facilitate cooperation in peacekeeping operations.[13]

NATO's military cooperation program has six fundamental objectives:

1. to demonstrate the nonthreatening defensive posture of the alliance and its continuing dedication and contribution to peace;
2. to inform NATO nations about cooperation partners' strategies, concepts, and security concerns and their individual methods of operating in peace and crisis;
3. to provide concrete military assistance to individual cooperation partner states where possible, seeking help from NATO nations as appropriate;

4. to assist in the development of civilian-led, democratically controlled defense establishments, including development of civilian
expertise in defense and military affairs;
5. to influence and advise on the establishment of appropriate,
effective, and defensive armed forces that can contribute to stability and security in Europe within the context of the post-
Helsinki process;
6. to enhance transparency and mutual understanding in military
affairs as a vital component of confidence-building procedures.[14]

It is important to grasp the possibilities of the NACC. At the risk of being
exhaustive, the following are some of the "Defense Planning Issues and Military
Matters" that clearly provide opportunities for the NACC states, as set forth
in the NACC *Work Plan for Dialogue Partnership and Cooperation* for 1994.

1. principles and implications for security of strategy and military
doctrine;
2. issues of defense planning including organization and roles of
the Ministry of Defense and the general staff;
3. force and command structures, including reserve forces;
4. military contribution to conceptual approaches to arms control
and disarmament issues;
5. cooperation in the planning and development of military exercises, subject to political guidance and any related ministerial
decisions;
6. democratic control over the armed forces and promotion of
civil-military relations in a democratic society;
7. concepts and methods of training and education in the defense
and military fields;
8. consultations on concepts of modernization of command and
control systems, including communications and information
systems;
9. conceptual discussion on the potential role of the armed forces
in natural and technological disaster clean-up;
10. planning, organization, and management of national defense
procurement programs;
11. air defense related matters.[15]

Another area of NATO activity that can offer opportunities for cooperation should be noted. The DPC created a Group of Defense Ministers (GDM)
in December 1991 in order to provide a venue in which informal sessions of

the NATO defense ministers (without France, which declined to participate) can take place with the defense ministers of cooperation partners. It meets at least once yearly at the ministerial level, with additional meetings occurring as circumstances warrant. The purpose of the GDM is to make detailed arrangements for meeting the needs of the cooperation partners as they reform their defense establishments. As such, it has become the clearinghouse on defense-related cooperation activities with the NATO military commands.

The January 1994 NATO summit approved the Partnership for Peace program, providing even more opportunities within the framework of the NACC.[16] According to the U.S. deputy assistant secretary of defense for European and NATO policy, the PFP program follows these guidelines:

- NATO would invite NACC members and other nations of Europe to sign an agreement with NATO to join a Partnership for Peace. NATO would not impose conditions on membership, beyond the willingness and ability to participate.
- The partnership would be a NACC activity that would build upon existing NATO and SHAPE [Supreme Headquarters Allied Powers Europe] structures. Partners would assign officers on a full-time basis to a planning cell at SHAPE and would participate in the deliberations of appropriate NATO bodies and in Partnership exercises.
- Partners would submit implementation plans or work programs to the alliance as a means for assessing their progression toward the goals of joint planning, interoperability, transparency, and civilian oversight of their defense ministries.
- NATO allies and partners would agree to consult whenever the territorial integrity, political independence, or security of a partner state was threatened. This would not, however, involve extension of NATO's security guarantee under Article V of the North Atlantic Treaty.[17]

As was provided in the Framework Document:

> The other states subscribing to this document will cooperate with the North Atlantic Treaty Organization in pursuing the following objectives: . . . (d) the development of cooperative military relations with NATO, for the purpose of joint planning, training, and exercises in order to strengthen their ability to undertake missions in the fields of peacekeeping, search and rescue, humanitarian operations, and others as may subse-

quently be agreed; (e) the development, over the longer term, of forces that are better able to operate with those of the members of the North Atlantic Alliance.[18]

In this respect, there is the potential that PFP will, over time, draw a distinction between those states that can be considered as evolving toward some sort of formal NATO membership and those that probably never will be considered, such as those in Central Asia.[19] This can be regarded as clearly a limitation, at least for now, on how far NATO can go in coopting these states into a formal "Euro-Atlantic" alliance framework that would in effect rewrite the North Atlantic Treaty.[20]

Taking into account present European international political circumstances, the PFP states are provided opportunities to strengthen their security needs by gradually integrating their military establishments into NATO.[21] Moreover, the PFP program has the potential of moving the PFP states in an evolutionary way into a Western political and military posture without disrupting the evolving post–Cold War U.S.-Russian relationship. Thus, PFP status has the potential of drawing the states of Europe more closely toward (rather than away from) each other in their security relationships.[22]

THE EVOLVING COMMAND STRUCTURE OF NATO

NATO must continue the adaptation of its command and force structure in line with requirements for flexible and timely responses contained in the Alliance's Strategic Concept.[23]

If we accept the general principle that form follows function, then the evolution of NATO's command structure provides a perfect example of the application of this principle. The form was the appearance of a well-thought-out military command structure based on rational considerations of military effectiveness. But in reality the function has clearly been to satisfy the political imperatives that are so much a part of alliance relationships. There is ample literature discussing the motivations for the creation of NATO's command structure, stemming from the early years of the alliance (a few of which are cited in this chapter).

For our purposes, three authoritative statements that should suffice to support this observation are drawn from the literature. The first is a concise statement given by General Dwight D. Eisenhower, the first SACEUR to Averell Harriman, then serving as President Truman's special assistant on foreign affairs. At the time, Eisenhower was establishing SHAPE: "the task of 'devising an organization that satisfies the nationalist aspirations of twelve different countries or the personal ambitions of affected individuals is a very laborious and irksome business.'"[24] A later SACEUR put it even more bluntly: "I must say that it might be workable [referring to the Southern Region command structure]. My main criticism would be that making a greater monstrosity out of an already monstrous organization is something of an offense against common sense."[25] George Kennan put it more dispassionately:

> We shall have to insist on solutions which preserve the security and effectiveness of major strategic planning and which give recognition to the overwhelming relative importance of the contribution we shall be expected to make to the defense of the Atlantic area. Here, considerations of national pride and prestige are going to enter in, and we are going to have a hard time getting some of the others to accept realistic arrangements in which their own roles, and their own right to be informed on all aspects of strategic planning must necessarily be limited.[26]

Nonetheless, what emerged satisfied NATO's political needs for nearly forty years, which is no small achievement.[27] It is useful, therefore, to note briefly at this point how the command structure has evolved over the history of the alliance.

From the alliance's very beginning, immediately following the signing and ratification of the North Atlantic Treaty, its military side took the form of "regional planning groups," which permitted those states wishing to cooperate within a certain regional proximity to do so without involving every member-state in every command relationship. The regional planning groups reported directly to the MC. And in order to avoid the national rivalries for the command positions that would have been required, there was no overarching NATO military command structure. [An example of the United States's early conception as to how to organize NATO militarily is in Appendix A.] With the onset of the Korean conflict in 1950, however, the need for a more formalized command structure became obvious, and, as mentioned, thereafter General Eisenhower was persuaded to become the first SACEUR, charged with creating SHAPE.[28] [The structure that was worked out is in Appendix B.]

After the Cold War ended, NATO reappraised its military command structure, since the main arena of possible conflict had disappeared along with the Berlin Wall. At its December 1991 meeting, the DPC agreed to embark on a reorganization plan that would be completed on 1 January 1995. (Equally important, perhaps, was the fact that the alliance agreed to reduce the overall manning strength of its headquarters by 25 percent.) The new structure reduced the number of MNCs from three to two by eliminating the Allied Command Channel (ACCHAN). This made sense, since there was no longer a Central Front to reinforce and resupply. Instead, ACCHAN has been merged into Allied Forces North West Europe (AFNORTHWEST), a newly formed Major Subordinate Command (MSC) of Allied Command Europe (ACE), which also includes Allied Forces Northern Europe (AFNORTH), which formerly had been an MSC of ACE. The Baltic Approaches Command (BALTAP), which had been a Principal Subordinate Command (PSC) of AFNORTH, and the UK Air Forces (UKAIR), which had also previously been an MSC of ACE, were not included in the redefined AFNORTHWEST.[29] Instead, BALTAP is now under Allied Forces Central Europe (AFCENT).[30] [The post–Cold War military structure of NATO is in Appendix C.]

NATO forces were reformed into Main Defense, Reaction, and Augmentation Forces. Main Defense Forces (MDF) are still the backbone of NATO, composing for some member-states the primary basis for their national military establishments. They can comprise multinational and national formations and be left at a lower level of readiness, at peacetime manning levels, or at mobilization status. Most of the MDF are in the Central Region, comprising four multinational units: one German-Danish, one German-Dutch, and two German-U.S. There is also an agreement for the Franco-German European Corps (Eurocorps) to be made available to NATO under certain specified conditions.[31]

Reaction Forces (RF), comprising no more than about 10 percent of the total of NATO forces, include ground, air, and naval forces at relatively higher levels of readiness. They are "designed as mobile and flexible crisis management tools, offering a range of military options to NATO's political leadership in times of tensions."[32] The RF consist of Immediate Reaction Forces of brigade size and the ACE Rapid Reaction Corps, which can deploy up to four divisions with comparable air and maritime components.[33] Those forces required for a prolonged conflict would be drawn from lower-readiness MDF forces and from Augmentation Forces (AF) and would be provided as reinforcements for deterrence, crisis management, and defense purposes.[34]

We need to note at this point the introduction of a new term into the NATO lexicon: "multinationality." The term describes the formation of smaller forces whose composition can change and adapt as circumstances permit. These forces can enable the smaller member-states to participate more easily in possible situations where otherwise they might feel that the size, character, and structure of their forces would make them, relatively speaking, less useful. The UK/Netherlands Amphibious Force is one example; another is the NATO Airborne Early Warning Force. The ACE Rapid Reaction Corps, for which the United Kingdom takes the lead, is still another example.[35] Standards of battlefield interoperability can also, perhaps, be achieved.[36]

Thus, four types of multinationality can be identified: (1) the long-held NATO international headquarters concept; (2) the framework headquarters (ACE Rapid Reaction Corps); (3) the balanced headquarters (Multinational Airmobile Division Central [four member-states] and Multinational Division South [three member-states]); and (4) the limited framework (at both corps and divisional level, in which a discrete formation of one member-state is taken as a subordinate force into the operational structure of another).[37]

Further flexibility is provided by the creation of the concept of Combined Joint Task Forces (CJTF), which were endorsed at the January 1994 summit. The CJTF is described thus:

> Under this plan, NATO-trained and integrated military forces and assets can be assigned to European-only task forces and employed on European-only contingencies in those cases when the full NATO membership chooses not to participate. A task force could even include forces of countries outside NATO— perhaps our Peace Partners, once PFP is up and running.[38]

This is truly an innovation in that, while NATO member-states can retain the "privileges" of membership, they are not necessarily required to share equally—or even at all—in the "responsibilities" of membership. No better illustration can be provided of the major point of this chapter: that the political dimension of NATO remains in the forefront as the military dimension takes on entirely new aspects.[39] Put another way, "consensus" in NATO no longer necessarily requires unanimity.

Hopefully, these newly defined forces can be effectively employed in crisis monitoring and response, such as intelligence, early warning, surveillance, communications, and command and control. Certainly, surveillance of the "no-fly" zone over Bosnia, provided by NATO Airborne Warning and Control System (AWACS), has enabled NATO fighter aircraft to carry out their interdiction mission, which on 28 February 1994 resulted in U.S. F-16 jets shooting down four Serb Jastreb aircraft.[40] In addition, the maritime aspect of NATO and WEU has remained firmly in place in regard to "out-of-area" crises requiring the use of naval forces.[41]

One thing is also clear: France, which since the days of Charles de Gaulle has not been an active member of NATO's military organization, is now cooperating more fully with its NATO partners. In response, NATO has been discussing all peacemaking activities in the NAC, in which all sixteen members participate, rather than the MC, in which, as already pointed out, France has not been an active member.[42]

INTERLOCKING EUROPEAN "ARCHITECTURE"

It cannot be said that Europe is whole: there is still a tension between the factors of integration . . . and the forces of division ranging from regional particularism to ethnic differences, racism and intolerance.[43]

NATO Secretary-General Manfred Wörner stated in January 1992: "A collective security organization cannot be based solely on political commitments and legal procedures. It must be based on common values, the practice of very close cooperation, and, above all, on a demonstrable capacity to uphold the security of all its members, even in the most difficult circumstances, by this yardstick. The only collective security system in Europe both today and tomorrow is NATO."[44] As a practical matter, NATO will continue to be the predominant multilateral security organization in Europe for the good reason, as former SACEUR General John Galvin put it: "The US is committed to NATO with a fully deployed force. For that commitment, we get a seat at the table. We get an influence in the shaping of the security situation in Europe, and that's what we want."[45]

It may perhaps have been serendipitous that the demise of the Soviet Union, the other great European Cold War protagonist, coincided with the inaugural meeting of the newly formed NACC.[46] At that meeting, Ukraine refused to be represented by a Russian diplomat presenting himself as a Soviet official. As an American observer commented: "We got to see the Soviet Union disappear right before our eyes."[47] Events since then, including a more nationalist stance in Russian domestic politics, now preclude any serious contemplation of the possibility of Russian membership in NATO, although Russia, with reservations, did join the PFP.[48]

The new NATO Strategic Concept focuses on smaller forces, thus moving away from response to a massive attack by set armies in favor of crisis management that looks to political considerations as well as to considerations of balance of power. The concept contemplates "a strategy of an interlocking architecture of security structures," which would include NATO, the WEU, the UN, and the CSCE.[49] As one observer put it:

NATO can make available common assets to the UN for particular missions. In peacetime, forces under direct NATO command
are limited to the integrated staff at its headquarters, the airborne
early-warning and control force based at Geilenkirchen in
Germany, and a small number of multinational forces: the standing naval forces in the Atlantic and the Mediterranean, composed
of destroyer or frigate-class ships drawn from member countries;
and the Allied Command Europe (ACE) Mobile force which
maintains a small permanent staff near Heidelberg in Germany.[50]

In regard to the CSCE, in June 1992 the NATO foreign ministers signaled
NATO's willingness "to support, on a case by case basis in accordance with
their own procedures, peacekeeping activities under the responsibility of the
Conference on Security and Cooperation in Europe (CSCE)."[51] The CSCE was
declared a "regional arrangement" under Chapter VIII of the UN Charter,
which for the first time gave the CSCE peacekeeping and conflict-prevention
modalities. The CSCE is also mentioned in the Framework Document of the
PFP: "The other [non-NATO member] states . . . will cooperate . . . in pursuing the following objectives: . . . (c) maintenance of the capability and
readiness to contribute, subject to constitutional considerations, to operations under the authority of the UN and/or the responsibility of the CSCE."[52]

The purpose for this enhancement of the CSCE, which includes creating
more supporting institutional arrangements, is clear: to respond to the threat
of conflict in the CSCE area resulting from the end of the Cold War. The
CSCE has operations in Tajikistan, Moldova, Georgia, Latvia, Estonia, and
Macedonia, and it provides sanctions assistance missions in Macedonia,
Croatia, Albania, Bulgaria, Hungary, Romania, and Ukraine.[53]

In regard to the WEU, the Maastricht Treaty on European Union, which
went into force in January 1994, provides that the European Union's foreign
and security policy "shall include all questions related to the security of the
European Union (EU), including the eventual framing of a common defence
policy, which might in time lead to common defence."[54] The EU is authorized to "request" the WEU "to elaborate and implement decisions and
actions of the Union which have defence implications."[55]

The notion is to give the WEU, in its relationship to the EU, a greater
responsibility in European defense matters by working toward creating a
European Security and Defense Identity (ESDI). It was assumed that the
WEU's three main tasks would likely be humanitarian and rescue, peacekeeping, and crisis management. NATO has referred to the ESDI as "gradually emerging as the expression of a mature Europe."[56] In other words, the

WEU will be the bridge between NATO and the EU. At Maastricht, it was agreed that a forty-man planning cell would be established to deal with possible WEU duplication with NATO.

The Eurocorps is composed of French and German armored divisions and a Franco-German brigade, supported by Spanish and Belgian units.[57] Consideration is also being given to include the NATO-assigned, although on-call to the WEU, UK/Netherlands Amphibious Force and the Multinational Airmobile Division (Central).

The United States agreed to these arrangements, with the following provisions: (1) NATO is the avenue through which security consultations should be made; (2) NATO is the organization in which major issues are to be determined; (3) NATO is to have first refusal in confronting any security task; and (4) In order that NATO is not undermined, European formations should be "separable but not separate" from the alliance's force structure.[58] A joint session of the NAC and the WEU Council on 8 June 1993 approved a combined NATO/WEU concept of operations. The command and control arrangements for both NATO and WEU operations were placed under the authority of both councils, with operational control of the combined NATO/WEU Task Force delegated through the SACEUR to the Commander Allied Naval Forces Southern Europe (COMNAVSOUTH).[59]

The story is still unfolding as far as WEU naval operations are concerned.[60] In 1992, the WEU began coordinating those naval vessels that were participating with NATO forces in patrolling the Strait of Otranto and the Adriatic Sea. The purpose is to engage in surveillance/monitoring and in enforcement operations of the UN Security Council embargo on Serbia and Montenegro.[61] NATO AWACS and maritime patrol aircraft have been involved. Even though there are divided opinions as to how effective this arrangement has been, Sharp Vigilance is the first European operation for WEU.[62]

The tragedy that has unfolded in the former Yugoslavia simply underscores the general sense of unease that something similar may be repeated elsewhere in Europe. The smaller powers' search for patronage from among the Great Powers, whether through CSCE, NATO, or WEU, will continue unabated, as those smaller powers realize only too clearly that they cannot, by themselves or among themselves, guarantee each others' borders or even, perhaps, their domestic stability. This is clearly the motivation behind the desire of the so-called Visegrád states—Poland, Hungary, the Czech Republic, and Slovakia—to join NATO.[63] But they, along with other former Soviet bloc states together with Russia and the CIS states, must, at least for the time being, accept more limited affiliations in their search for security.

There are those who would prefer that a distinction be drawn between those states that comprise Central Europe (Poland, Hungary, and the Czech Republic) and those that comprise Eastern Europe (Russia, Ukraine, Belarus, and the Baltics).[64] The rationale is that the states of Central Europe are ethnically homogeneous and are moving steadily into the Western market-oriented international economy, which means that they would be able to participate effectively in Western international organizations—including the EU. It is unlikely that they could drag NATO into their internal civil conflicts. The Eastern European states do not yet, if they ever will, possess these features, and therefore are best kept in a looser relationship, such as that being formed through NACC and PFP.[65]

CONCLUSIONS: NATO'S CRISIS OF PURPOSE

We cannot do without force. . . . You cannot establish freedom . . . without force, and the only force you can substitute for an armed mankind is the concerted force of the combined action of mankind.[66]

The greatest immediate challenge to NATO in the post–Cold War period, of course, is peacekeeping responsibilities in what is now considered out-of-area. This area is not, however, out of post–Cold War Europe and therefore not out of NATO's area of immediate concern. During the Cold War, the major effort of NATO planning was collective self-defense: to deter a direct attack by the Soviet Union and its Warsaw Pact allies on the geographic area prescribed by the North Atlantic Treaty and to avoid being drawn into out-of-area disputes that one or more individual member-states might want NATO as a whole to become involved in. With the collapse of the Soviet Union and the demise of the Warsaw Pact, the issue has become one of collective enforcement on behalf of either the UN or the CSCE and of working in tandem with the WEU in such enforcement. How and under what circumstances NATO should become involved militarily outside of the treaty area—that is, in "the New Europe"—is far from resolved.

The major dilemma, however, as one NATO observer put it, is that "this new [post–Cold War] environment makes action much more difficult."[67] Even more skeptical is this appraisal:

There's no strategy for what the West wants to do in the Balkans, or anywhere else. The Western countries are afraid of the costs and risks to soldiers. They'll do anything to avoid involvement. They'll sit around waiting for some good news to turn up.

They'll wind up with another fresh disaster, and they'll have to bring in NATO like it's an ambulance.[68]

The problem, of course, is one of political will. Is there a sufficient degree of common interest remaining in NATO, now that the common threat of the Soviet Union has passed, to justify NATO's continuing as a credible military instrument in international politics? There is if we recall that throughout its history NATO has been responsive to a political purpose, supported by a highly adaptable military structure. The military structure will doubtless continue to change to reflect shifting Euro/Atlantic international political requirements, and NATO politically will continue to find itself responding to needs that are shared with other international organizations, such as the UN or other regional international organizations.

The most recent political innovation has been the enlargement of NATO to embrace in a qualified fashion the states of the former Soviet bloc and the successor states of the Soviet Union. This enables these states to engage with NATO in various consultative, planning, and joint exercise activities, which reassures them against any territorial incursions they might fear and perhaps also against domestic violence. But of course, a revived Russia—which is not likely to join NATO and thus restrict its own field of international political action in Europe—might well engage in interventionist attempts that would indeed test the will of the core NATO members as well as the other NACC and PFP states.

In regard to efforts at resolving the conflict in Bosnia-Herzegovina, the interest of Russia in the Serbians, the interest of the United States in the Bosnian Muslims, and the interest of Germany in the Croatians may or may not bode well for NATO in any future Balkan crisis. It is too soon to draw any conclusions. But Kosovo or Montenegro may be next, which could involve Albania, perhaps followed by Macedonia, which in turn could involve Greece, Turkey, and Bulgaria.[69] If NATO could demonstrate its political and military effectiveness in containing and coping with the violent disorder and chaos in the Balkans, then perhaps we can contemplate with some hope a stable post–Cold War Europe.

But as the former commander of NATO's naval forces in Southern Europe (and now U.S. chief of naval operations), Admiral Jeremy Boorda, put it: "Speed is real important. One of the tenets of all the planning we've done is to get there as quickly as we can. Because if you have the initial will to be peaceful, you don't want to let it degrade."[70]

APPENDIX A [71]

The Proposed Pre-Korean Military Structure of NATO

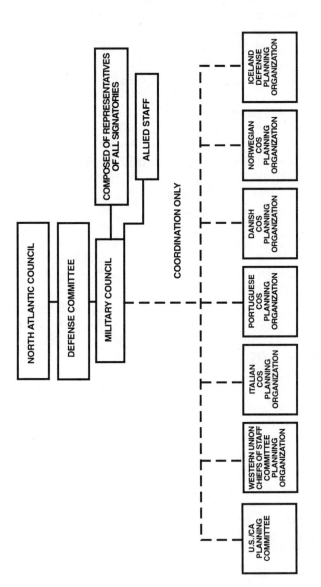

U.S. (JCS) Proposed Defense Organization: Plan D, July 1949

APPENDIX B [72]

The Cold War Military Structure of NATO

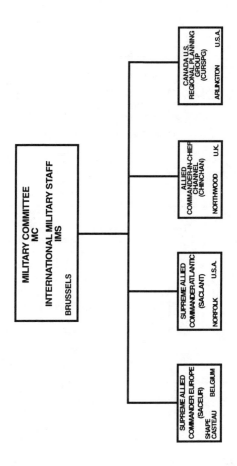

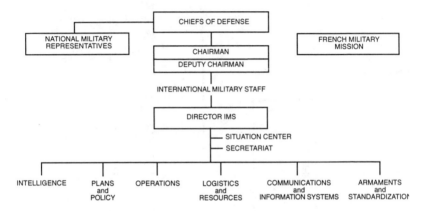

The Military Committee

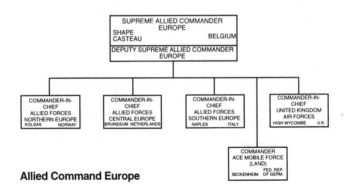

Allied Command Europe

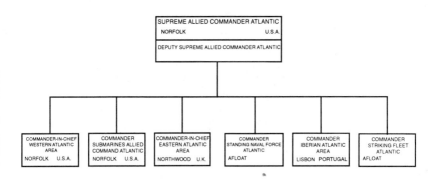

Allied Command Atlantic

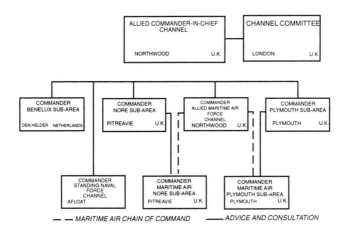

Allied Command Channel

APPENDIX C [73]

The Post–Cold War Military Structure of NATO

Old Structure

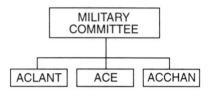

New Structure

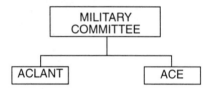

Major NATO Commands

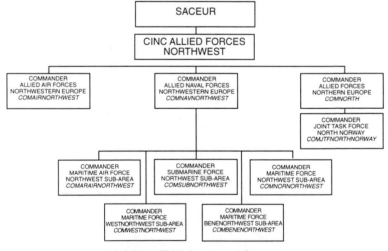

AFNORTHWEST Command Structure

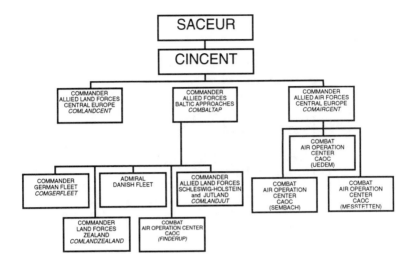

AFCENT Command Structure

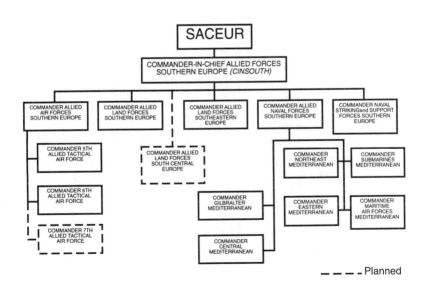

AFSOUTH Command Structure

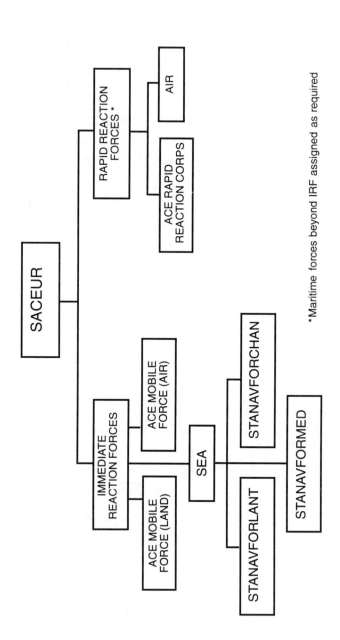

ACE Reaction Forces

*Maritime forces beyond IRF assigned as required

NOTES

1. Quoted in Diana Jean Schemo, "America's Scholarly Palestinian Raises Volume Against Arafat," *New York Times*, 4 March 1994. A thoughtful essay on this subject is J. E. Spence, "Entering the Future Backwards: Some Reflections on the Current International Scene," *Review of International Studies* 20 (January 1994): 3-13.

2. See Samuel P. Huntington, "The Clash of Civilizations?" *Foreign Affairs* 72 (Summer 1993): 22-49: and Josef Joffe, "The New Europe: Yesterday's Ghosts," ibid. (America and the World 1992/93): 29-43.

3. See *The United States, NATO and Security Relations with Central and Eastern Europe*, Policy Paper, The Atlantic Council of the United States, September 1993.

4. See Robert S. Jordan, "NATO: Has Anything Really Changed?—An American Perspective," *The World Today*, Royal Institute of International Affairs (London), October 1988, 180-82. An interesting assessment of the implications for world politics of the breakup of the Soviet Union is Donald M. Snow, *The Shape of the Future: The Post–Cold War World* (Armonk, NY: M. E. Sharpe, Inc., 1991). See especially his "Eight Propositions," as discussed in chap. 1.

5. Listed in *U.S. Defense and Military Relations with Central and Eastern Europe*, Headquarters, U.S. European Command (A White Paper by Lt. Col. Hammersen, The George C. Marshall European Center for Security Studies), 19 October 1993, 13.

6. Douglas Bland, *The Military Committee of the North Atlantic Alliance: A Study of Structure and Strategy* (New York: Praeger, 1991), 6.

7. There is a third, the Nuclear Planning Group (NPG), whose membership is limited.

8. Several committees report to the DPC, notably the Political Committee, the Economics Committee, the Defence Review Committee, the Conference of National Armaments Directors, the Science Committee, the NATO Air Defence Committee, and the Committee on the Challenges of Modern Society. See *NATO Handbook* (Brussels: NATO Office of Information and Press, 1992).

9. Spain and France, however, maintain military missions to the MC. The evolution of the NATO Chiefs of Staff structure can be traced from the early days of the British Committee of Imperial Defence. See, for example, Robert S. Jordan, "The Contribution of the British Civil Service and Cabinet Secretariat Tradition to International Prevention and Control of War," in *The Limitations of Military Power*, ed. John B. Hattendorf and Malcolm H. Murfett (London: Macmillan Publishers, 1990), 95-110. See also William Jackson and Lord Bramall, *The Chiefs: The Story of the United Kingdom Chiefs of Staff* (London: Brassey's, 1992).

10. Their role has been described thus: "The military representatives are the muscle and sinew of the Military Committee. Without their permanent presence little work of substance could be accomplished by the Committee, and 'discovering policy' would be impossible. In both formal and informal ways the

military representatives consult continuously with their peers, with NATO commanders, and with their 'political partners,' a routine that is at the heart of NATO's policy process." See Bland, *The Military Committee*, 182.

11. The initial NAC guidelines were approved in November 1990 and revised in November 1991 and June 1992.
12. Drawn from *U.S. Defense and Military Relations with Central and Eastern Europe*, 13.
13. Cited in the Documentation section of the *NATO Review* 41, no. 6 (December 1993): 28.
14. Ibid.
15. Ibid., 31.
16. The text of the summit is contained in *Declaration of the Heads of State and Government Participating in the Meeting of the North Atlantic Council Held at NATO Headquarters, Brussels on 10-11 January 1994*, NATO Press Communiqué M-1(94)3, 11 January 1994. The specific document is contained in *Partnership for Peace: Invitation*, NATO Press Communiqué M-1(94)2, 10 January 1994. This document has within it a so-called Framework Document, which sets out more specific terms and conditions for subscribing states.
17. Joseph Kruzel, "Peacekeeping and the Partnership for Peace," in *Peace Support Operations and the U.S. Military*, ed. Dennis J. Quinn (Washington: National Defense University Press, 1994), 97.
18. *Partnership for Peace: Invitation*, Annex, 1-2.
19. As the president of Azerbaijan said, perhaps excessively optimistically, at the signing of his nation's PFP program: "We hope that our participation in the NATO program . . . will make it possible to achieve . . . a peaceful and just settlement. NATO's authority can be a weighty factor for [ending] this murderous war." Several of the Central European states had not only pressed for, but had actually applied for, full NATO membership. Quoted in Reuter dispatch, reported in *Current News/Early Bird*, American Forces Information Services, 5 May 1994.
20. For a somewhat skeptical discussion of NATO's capacity to expand its membership see Ole Diehl, "Opening NATO to Eastern Europe?" *World Today*, The Royal Institute of International Affairs, December 1993, 222-23.
21. The PFP coordination cell at NATO Headquarters is located in the former Live Oak building, which had been the center, under the SACEUR, for NATO coordination on matters involving Berlin. As an example of how swiftly the PFP program has caught on, in May 1994 Danish, German, and Polish defense ministers announced their intention to hold joint military maneuvers under the auspices of the PFP.
22. All partners will formulate and execute their individual "Partnership Programmes," which are developed in agreement with NATO from "Presentation Documents identifying the steps they will take to achieve the political goals of the Partnership and the military and other assets that might be used for Partnership activities." (*Framework Document*, 2.) A liaison office for each such state has been set up at NATO Headquarters in Brussels so that they can participate "in

NACC/Partnership meetings and activities as well as certain others by invitation." (Ibid.)

23. *Declaration of the Heads of State and Government*, 3.

24. As quoted in Gregory Pedlow, "The Politics of NATO Command," in *U.S. Military Forces in Europe: The Early Years, 1945-1970*, ed. Simon W. Duke and Wolfgang Krieger (Boulder: Westview Press, 1993), 18.

25. Quoted in ibid., 35.

26. Quoted in Bland, *The Military Committee*, 137.

27. The origins of NATO can be found in Robert S. Jordan, *The NATO International Staff/Secretariat, 1942-57: A Study in International Administration* (London: Oxford University Press, 1967); idem, ed., *Generals in International Politics: NATO's Supreme Allied Commander, Europe* (Lexington: University Press of Kentucky, 1987); and idem, *Alliance Strategy and Navies: The Evolution and Scope of NATO's Maritime Dimension* (New York: St. Martin's Press, 1990).

28. For the story of the creation of the command military structure of NATO see Jordan, ed., *Generals*. For the story of the creation of the maritime command structure of NATO see idem, *Alliance Strategy*.

29. This is taken from William T. Johnsen and Thomas-Durell Young, *Preparing for the NATO Summit: What are the Pivotal Issues?* Strategic Studies Institute, U.S. Army War College, 8 October 1993, 18ff.

30. As Johnsen and Young put it: "Both political and military rationales drove this decision. Politically, Denmark wished to be considered an integral part of Central Europe and Germany wanted all of its territory located within one MSC. Militarily, the unification of Germany had greatly extended the AFCENT area of responsibility eastward and the defense of a unified Germany under one MSC made good sense." (Ibid., 21-22.)

31. *NATO's New Force Structures*, Basic Fact Sheet, NATO Office of Information and Press, September 1993, No. 5, p. 1.

32. General Vigleik Eide, "The Military Dimension in the Transformed Alliance," *NATO Review* 40, no. 4 (August 1992): 22.

33. *NATO's New Force Structures*, 1-2. The ACE Rapid Reaction Corps was created in October 1992, to be fully operational by 1995. The Air Reaction Forces Planning Staff was activated in April 1993. Already, elements of NATO's maritime reaction forces have been enforcing UN-mandated sanctions against the former Yugoslavia.

34. Ibid., 2.

35. The first field exercise, named *Arcade Guard* and involving nearly two thousand soldiers, took place in February 1994. The RRC is located in Bielefeld, Germany.

36. Interoperability has been described as "'equipment, procedures, doctrine, and training' and 'the ability of people, organizations, and equipment to operate together effectively.'" See Sterling D. Sessions and Carl R. Jones, *Interoperability: A Desert Storm Case Study*, McNair Paper 18, Institute for National Strategic Studies, National Defense University, July 1993, 1-2.

37. Gen. Sir Peter Inge, "NATO's Reaction Capability—The Cornerstone of Crisis Management," *NATO's Sixteen Nations*, No. 1/93, Special Issue, 60. For a discussion of NATO's concept of an international headquarters see Jordan, *Generals*, intro.

38. "New Europe, New NATO," *NATO Review* 42, no. 1 (February 1994): 13-14.

39. For example, in May 1994 NATO exercise Dynamic Impact 94, which included a joint evacuation operation as well as an amphibious assault for the first time, took place in the western Mediterranean. More than 11,000 amphibious and land troops, 70 surface and subsurface vessels, and 280 aircraft participated. Participating forces came from Belgium, France, Germany, Greece, Italy, the Netherlands, Portugal, Spain, Turkey, the United Kingdom, and the United States. (France and Spain participated although they are not part of NATO's military structure.) Reported by Sue Palumbo, "NATO Exercise Aims to Make Dynamic Impact on Cooperation," *European Stars and Stripes*, 15 May 1994.

40. The AWACS—modified Boeing 707 aircraft—operate in safe territory over Hungary or the Adriatic Sea and are manned by British, French, or multinational crews. They have a radar range of over two hundred miles and monitor humanitarian air activity—in fact, *all* air activity—over Bosnia. See Steve Vogel, "AWACS Planes Keep Close Watch on Bosnia," *Washington Post*, 5 March 1994.

41. NATO's CINCSOUTH has overall responsibility for NATO's participation in peacekeeping activities in the former Yugoslavia in accordance with relevant UN Security Council resolutions. NATO member-states, led by the United States, were directly involved in the war against Iraq. For this purpose, there was a realignment of NATO-earmarked forces. For example, mine seekers were diverted and, for the first time, German warships took up patrol in the Mediterranean to replace ships of other member-states that had been diverted to the Gulf area.

42. Quinn, *Peace Support*, 194. See also David Buchan, "France Goes on the Defence Offensive," *Financial Times* (London), 25 January 1994. The CJTF concept, linked to the European Defense Identity, which embraces a more formal role for the WEU, as pronounced at the January 1994 NATO summit, is very much to France's liking. See Michael Meimeth, "France Gets Closer to NATO," *World Today*, Royal Institute of International Affairs (London), May 1994, 84-85. However, France and the United States are not in agreement over how best to deal with the Bosnian crisis. See Thomas W. Lippman, "U.S., France Continue Jousting on Bosnia Policy," *Washington Post*, 12 May 1994.

43. Clive Archer, *Organizing Europe: The Institutions of Integration* (New York: Edward Arnold, 1994), 19.

44. NATO Press Release, 27 January 1992, NATO Press Service. The entire press release is a comprehensive review of the role of NATO in the post–Cold War period. See also "European Security Identity and Defence Role," *NATO Review* 36, no. 6 (December 1991): 19-20.

45. Quoted in Kurt Shillinger, "Commander Tells How NATO's Role Will Change," *Christian Science Monitor*, 2 December 1991.

46. It was held in Brussels on 20 December 1991. The initial Work Plan was issued on 10 March 1992.
47. Also, President Boris Yeltsin of the Russian Federation had written to the gathering expressing an interest in Russia's joining NATO "sometime in the future." See Thomas L. Friedman, "Yeltsin Says Russia Seeks to Join NATO," *New York Times*, 21 December 1991.
48. Russia was admitted to the NACC in December 1991, and the other CIS states were formally admitted on 10 March 1992. Georgia, at that time not a member of the CIS, chose also not to join the NACC. Turkmenistan became the eighteenth state to sign up for the PFP on 11 May 1994. Its objective, as is true for many of the CIS states, was as much to ensure its sovereignty vis-à-vis Russia as to support NATO and UN peacekeeping efforts. See "Turkmenistan signs as peace partner," *Washington Times*, 11 May 1994.
49. The *Declaration on Peace and Cooperation* agreed by the NATO heads of state and government at the Rome summit in November 1991 stated that: "The challenges we will face in this new Europe cannot be comprehensively addressed by one institution alone, but only in a framework of interlocking institutions tying together the countries of Europe and North America." See *NATO Review* 39, no. 6 (December 1991): 25-32, for full text of the *Declaration*.
50. Mats R. Berdal, *Whither UN Peacekeeping?* Adelphi Paper 281, IISS/Brassey's, October 1993, 71.
51. Quoted in *NATO's Role in Crisis Management and Peacekeeping*, Basic Fact Sheet, NATO Office of Information and Press, July 1993, No. 4, p. 1.
52. *Framework Document*, 1. "They also reaffirm their commitment to the Helsinki Final Act and all subsequent CSCE documents and to the fulfillment of the commitments and obligations they have undertaken in the field of disarmament and arms control."
53. The United States has provided funding for these CSCE activities because "low-intensity conflict prevention and peacekeeping activities, developed significantly by the CSCE since 1992, provide the U.S. and Europe unique opportunities to control and resolve conflicts before they rage out of control." U.S. Government Document, *Congressional Presentation for Promoting Peace*, FY 1995, Jointly Prepared by the Department of State and the Department of Defense, 34.
54. Treaty on European Union, 1992, Title I, Common Provisions, Article B.
55. Quoted in Robert Mauthner, "Common Policy Relies on WEU," *Financial Times* (London), 12 December 1991.
56. See NATO Press Communiqué M-1(4)3, 1. The declaration also reported on agreement "to adapt further the Alliance's political and military structures to reflect both the full spectrum of its roles and the development of the emerging European Security and Defence Identity."
57. See Thomas-Durell Young, *The Franco-German Relationship in the Transatlantic Security Framework*, Strategic Studies Institute, U.S. Army War College, 15 July 1991. It is to possess a "European vocation."

58. This section is adapted from Richard M. Connaughton, "European Organizations and Intervention," in Quinn, ed., *Peace Support Operations*, 194-95. The WEU also monitors river traffic on the Danube, and NATO's EUROGROUP is transferring some of its activities to WEU. Ibid.

59. See *NATO's Role in Crisis Management and Peacekeeping*, Basic Fact Sheet, NATO Office of Information and Press, July 1993, No. 4, p. 2.

60. The WEU first coordinated its naval presence in the Gulf during the latter stages of the Iran-Iraq War of 1980-1988. Technical coordination on the spot and at the admiralty level took place by five members with naval vessels in the area under the WEU's aegis. Then, after the Iraqi invasion of Kuwait in 1990, WEU foreign and defense ministers, meeting in Paris in August 1990, agreed to coordinate their response both at a political level and in the region by agreeing on areas of operation and on sharing tasks, logistical support, and intelligence. See Archer, *Organizing Europe*, 243ff.

61. This was in accordance with UN Security Council Resolutions 713, 757, and 820. Later, enforcement operations were extended into Albanian waters by agreement with Albania. In mid-1993, over 12,000 ships had been challenged, of which 803 were stopped; of these, 176 were diverted and subsequently inspected and 9 violators were detected. Six WEU members have contributed vessels and airplanes. See *NATO Review* 41, no. 3 (June 1993): 19. There has been no weakening of these activities.

62. WEU ground and air forces will not be involved in the former Yugoslavia in the absence of a lasting truce.

63. There are many more states in the band stretching from Finland downward than the four named. Furthermore, the successor states of the former Soviet Union that border on the Soviet bloc states are also very uneasy about irredentist claims. This would include Belarus, Ukraine, and Moldova.

64. For more on this see Robert S. Jordan, ed., *Europe and the Superpowers: Essays on European International Politics* (New York: St. Martin's Press, 1991), esp. part 3. See also Archer, *Organizing Europe*, chap. 2.

65. See, for example, Edward L. Rowny, "NATO and the difference between Eastern and Central Europe," *Washington Times*, 15 March 1994. Central and Eastern European states are being given associate membership in the WEU amid denials that this may be a backdoor way of giving them access to NATO. It has been described as "an attempt to find a new model for military and political cooperation on a limited space in Europe." See *Itar-Tass*, 12 May 1994, as reported in *Current News/Early Bird*, 17 May 1994.

66. President Woodrow Wilson, Speech at Sioux Falls, Iowa, 18 September 1919.

67. Quoted in Dick Polman, "Where Does NATO Go After Bosnia?" *Philadelphia Inquirer*, 6 March 1994. This does not mean, however, that there are no continuing military commitments. For example, more than half of the airmen in USAFE since 1991 have been involved in missions short of war, humanitarian or otherwise. See James Kitfield, "Between War and Peace," *Government Executive*, May 1994.

68. Quoted in Polman, "Where Does NATO Go After Bosnia?"
69. An example of the complexity of the problem is reflected in a report that, even as Greece enforces an embargo against Macedonia in contravention of its obligations as a member of the EU, Greece and Macedonia are cooperating in violating UN economic sanctions imposed on Yugoslavia for its support of the Bosnian Serbs. See Jonathan C. Randal, "Greece, Macedonia Said to Skirt Sanctions," *Washington Post*, 16 May 1994.
70. Quoted in ibid. For example, in March 1994, NATO developed a plan that called for the rapid deployment of fifty thousand troops to Bosnia if a peace agreement among the three warring factions was achieved. Code-named "Discipline Guard," the NATO forces would supplement the UN troops in Bosnia. Planning has been taking place in order that NATO can move quickly to implement whatever peace agreement eventually emerges.
71. Bland, *The Military Committee*, 122.
72. Ibid., 185, 170, 191, 189, 187.
73. Johnsen and Young, *Preparing for the NATO Summit*, 19, 20, 23, 27, 8.

4

NATO's Strategy: Past, Present, and Future

Steven L. Rearden

By the mid-1990s, the North Atlantic Treaty Organization (NATO) faced an uncertain future, its traditional strategy in disarray now that the Cold War was over. Some critics argued that, because of the disintegration of the Soviet Union, NATO strategy, like the alliance itself, had outlived its usefulness.[1] But as new dangers from ethnic and religious tensions along the periphery of the old Soviet empire erupted, the reasons for keeping NATO alive and well arguably remained strong. Even former members of the Warsaw Pact were clamoring to be part of NATO. The alliance was, in other words, a rallying point for peace and stability in a troubled world, and as such continued to serve a useful purpose. Accordingly, in preparing for the years ahead, NATO still needed an up-to-date strategic concept around which its members could organize themselves, plan for future contingencies, and allocate their national resources.

NATO's transition from an anti-Soviet alliance into one capable of dealing effectively with post–Cold War problems did not promise to be easy. Throughout its history, NATO had been basically a defensive coalition, organized for purposes of deterrence. War fighting, as such, had tended to receive mixed degrees of attention and would have represented, in any case, a failure of NATO's larger political mission. As NATO moved into the post–Cold War era, it continued to adopt a more or less defensive posture, but with greater emphasis in military and strategic planning on peacekeeping and humanitarian missions.

NATO'S STRATEGY: THE HISTORIC PATTERN

For most of its history, NATO operated with dual strategies—one political, the other military. The political strategy, always fairly constant and easy to identify, was that spelled out in the 1949 North Atlantic Treaty, which committed the member-states to a system of collective security. Although the treaty mentioned no specific threat, the first purpose of the alliance was always to provide mutual security in the face of a menacing Soviet Union. Whether the Soviet threat was exaggerated for political purposes, as some of NATO's critics have argued, remains a matter of conjecture. But at the time of the alliance's formation, with the consolidation of Soviet power in Eastern Europe a fait accompli, with West Berlin besieged by a Soviet blockade, and with Norway and Turkey under constant pressure to make territorial and political concessions to Moscow, it was little wonder that Western Europeans felt threatened.[2]

NATO was first and foremost a political alliance, fashioned to reassure Western Europeans that recovery from World War II would not be in vain and that they would continue to enjoy the peace and freedom being denied their neighbors behind the Iron Curtain in Eastern Europe. NATO's function was one of long-term deterrence of Soviet aggression. It was meant to build confidence and by so doing to strengthen the West morally and materially against the possible dangers of Soviet expansionism. Although it is entirely conceivable that the Europeans could have done this on their own, they looked to the United States for leadership and assistance. American involvement thus became crucial, not only to assure the immediate success of the enterprise that culminated in the signing of the North Atlantic Treaty in April 1949 but also to underwrite its future prospects.

Whether NATO's founders expected it to survive as long as it did is another matter. Internationalists, like the American diplomat Theodore Achilles, nourished the hope that the alliance would lead to ever closer transatlantic unity. But NATO was such a fundamental departure from the American tradition of avoiding entangling alliances that the preponderance of informed opinion on both sides of the Atlantic remained skeptical. Secretary of State George C. Marshall probably spoke for most when he privately predicted that sooner or later the United States would tire of foreign obligations and revert to some form of isolationism.[3] Both views, as it happened, missed the mark. The isolationist resurgence that Marshall and others expected failed to materialize, and NATO never became the catalyst for across-the-board Western integration that others hoped it would be. Yet its contributions to increasing the range and depth of political contacts among the Western bloc nations, adding in the process to the sense of common purpose that inspired the alliance in the first place, were rarely, if ever, equaled by other means.

NATO's military strategy, on the other hand, was never so clear-cut or constant. Until the outbreak of the Korean War, NATO's resources for combating a possible Soviet invasion of the West were negligible. Efforts to develop a medium-term defense plan in 1949-50 did more to expose NATO's weaknesses than to provide a strategy for repelling a possible Soviet attack. Although the Korean War brought an upsurge of concern for Europe's security, leading to increases in both American aid and the willingness of Europeans to make sacrifices in their own defense, requirements set by NATO planners consistently outpaced capabilities. What evolved instead, despite NATO's carefully laid-out plans on paper for a conventional defense, was a fallback strategy predicated on the only readily available source of military power: U.S. strategic air and nuclear weapons.

Broadly speaking, NATO's Cold War military strategy fell into three periods of development. The first was the period of massive retaliation, which coincided with the development by the United States of a nuclear-oriented defense posture.[4] Although the term "massive retaliation" did not come into use until U.S. Secretary of State John Foster Dulles suggested it in 1954, it was a fairly accurate summation of NATO strategy as early as December 1949, when the Defense Committee first acknowledged NATO's dependence on U.S. nuclear retaliatory power.[5] At the time, because the U.S. nuclear stockpile was still small, NATO's only choice was to continue to explore conventional means of repelling a Soviet attack. But as the stockpile grew and the enthusiasm for rearming inspired by the Korean War dissipated, hopes for a credible (and affordable) conventional alternative steadily faded. Finally, in 1954, after nearly five years of searching for other ways of shoring up Europe's defenses, the North Atlantic Council (NAC) approved a report (MC 48) sanctioning the inclusion of nuclear weapons in the planning and preparations routinely carried out by NATO military authorities.[6]

MC 48 became the first in a series of NATO planning papers setting forth requirements for the alliance's "integrated atomic capability," the bedrock of NATO military strategy until the adoption of flexible response in the mid-1960s. As a basic objective, MC 48 posited that NATO forces should be able to use atomic and thermonuclear weapons in their defense from the outset of a war with the Soviet Union. The assumption was that the Soviets would initiate any attack on the West by an atomic onslaught against which NATO would have to react in kind. For the NATO allies to be able to resist and defeat such aggression, they would have to have the ability to survive and gain superiority in the initial phase of the conflict. This meant controlling the battlefield at the outset and gaining the upper hand with tactical nuclear weapons.[7] With strategy thus conceived, NATO soon found itself on the way to a nuclear buildup that would profoundly influence alliance thinking and behavior for the next generation and a half.

Massive retaliation was a credible deterrent only while the United States possessed overwhelming nuclear superiority. By the late 1950s, growing Soviet capabilities in long- and intermediate-range ballistic missiles and air-craft posed an unmistakable threat to the United States and its NATO allies. Although intelligence estimates of the size of the Soviet strategic forces turned out to be exaggerated, the West generally perceived an approaching nuclear stalemate.[8] With the high costs of a nuclear arms race foremost in mind, Eisenhower, in his second term, decided to settle for strategic suffi-ciency rather than clear-cut superiority. But after *Sputnik* in 1957, pressure to regain and keep the lead in nuclear weapons increased dramatically.

FLEXIBLE RESPONSE

In 1961, with the advent of the Kennedy administration in Washington, mas-sive retaliation began to give way to a new strategic doctrine known as flex-ible response. The basic idea had been percolating for years among such notable strategists in the United States as Bernard Brodie, former army chief of staff General Maxwell Taylor, and William W. Kaufmann of the RAND Corporation; and Basil Liddell Hart, P. M. S. Blackett, and Sir Anthony Buzzard in the United Kingdom. In general, the aim of flexible response strategists was to shift the burden of defense from a general nuclear response to the graduated use of force, thereby lessening the threat of death and destruction while increasing the credibility of a Western response to a less than all-out Soviet challenge.[9] Kennedy was an easy convert. As a senator and presidential candidate, he had been highly critical of the Eisenhower defense program, faulting it for allowing the country to lag behind the Soviet Union in missile development and for failing to provide a viable limited-war capa-bility. "We have been driving ourselves into a corner," Kennedy complained, "where the only choice is all or nothing at all, world devastation or sub-mission—a choice that necessarily causes us to hesitate on the brink and leave the initiative in the hands of our enemies."[10]

The task of redeeming Kennedy's pledge to do something about this sit-uation fell to his secretary of defense, Robert S. McNamara. Although

McNamara accepted nuclear weapons as an integral part of the West's security structure, he agreed with Kennedy that there needed to be a broader range of options for the use of force. Nuclear weapons, McNamara believed, should be NATO's last resort, not its first, as planning guidelines had dictated in the 1950s. In practical terms this meant less reliance on the threat of immediate wholesale nuclear retaliation and more emphasis in U.S. and NATO planning on controlled nuclear responses and general purpose forces that could hold their own, at least for a while, against a conventional attack by Warsaw Pact forces.

While McNamara never advocated an exclusively conventional defense, his proposed revamping of NATO strategy struck many Europeans as risk-prone and costly. The rule of thumb advocated by U.S. planners was that NATO should be capable of mounting sustained conventional operations for up to ninety days.[11] Europeans worried that the more dependent NATO became on conventional forces, the more removed Europe would be from the umbrella of protection provided by the U.S. strategic nuclear deterrent. When halfway measures like the ill-fated multilateral force (MLF) failed to make any headway, McNamara turned to unilateral declarations of continued U.S. strategic nuclear support for NATO and closer cooperation within the alliance on how nuclear weapons would be used. Coordination for the use of tactical nuclear weapons fell to an interallied Nuclear Planning Group (NPG), created in 1966. Thus reassured, the following year NATO adopted a new directive (MC 14/3) incorporating flexible response principles.

Also in 1967, NATO endorsed the Harmel Report, named for the chairman of the drafting committee, Belgian Foreign Minister Pierre Harmel. Reflecting a European perspective, the Harmel Report postulated a dual policy of defense and détente. "Military security and a policy of detente," the report argued, "are not contradictory but complementary." Given the overall tenor of the report, it seems clear that, while the European allies were willing to accept flexible response in principle, they viewed it as a less than reassuring form of deterrence without a fundamental change in the East-West political climate. Flexible response appeared workable, in other words, only as long as it was accompanied by improvements in East-West relations.[12]

Whether flexible response would, as its proponents insisted, reduce the danger of nuclear war never ceased to be a hotly contested issue. With the United States preoccupied in Vietnam and with many European allies skeptical of the whole concept, the link between European security and nuclear weapons remained almost as strong and as close as ever. Tactical nuclear weapons continued to play a major role in NATO strategic plans and doubled in number, to more than seven thousand, by the end of the 1960s.[13] McNamara recognized that NATO's commitment to implement flexible response fell "short of providing for a capability to deal successfully with any kind of nonnuclear attack without using nuclear weapons ourselves." At most, he acknowledged, "NATO nonnuclear capabilities should help deter a deliberate nonnuclear attack by denying the Warsaw Pact any confidence of success except by using a force so large that it clearly threatens NATO's vital interests."[14]

In a 1975 report mandated by Congress, Secretary of Defense James R. Schlesinger described flexible response as resting on a "NATO Triad" of conventional forces to deter and defend against conventional attacks, theater nuclear forces, and strategic nuclear forces. Schlesinger insisted that these capabilities were mutually supportive—that the function of NATO's theater nuclear forces, for example, was not only to provide a capacity for credible retaliatory responses but also to deter conventional attacks by posing the threat of nuclear escalation "should the conventional situation warrant." Schlesinger did not elaborate publicly on what these conditions might be, but he did mention that theater nuclear forces could be used if NATO failed to mobilize quickly enough to meet a Warsaw Pact conventional attack, or if the Soviets drew divisions from the Sino-Soviet border. In any case, it was obvious that, despite a declared preference for confining any conflict to conventional weapons, nuclear forces remained an integral part of NATO's strategic concept. As Schlesinger observed: "Theater nuclear forces, in limited use, to complement conventional forces, could serve the political purposes of showing NATO's resolve and creating a situation conducive to negotiations, and could help avert major loss of NATO territory."[15]

THE FORWARD DEFENSE STRATEGY

The third and last phase of NATO Cold War military planning was that associated with the forward defense strategy formally adopted in 1984 and the accompanying maritime strategy. As explained by Supreme Allied Commander General Bernard W. Rogers, forward defense was not a revision per se of strategy, but an attempt to give greater credibility to flexible response. Conventional forces, made more effective by recent advances in electronics and computers, would have an even larger role than before. The principal new strategic feature was to add depth to the battlefield in Europe (thus shifting the fighting away from the densely populated areas of West Germany) by targeting and destroying Warsaw Pact rear echelon forces, probably the weakest link in the Soviet order of battle. This became the follow-on forces attack (FOFA) concept, which had been part of evolving U.S. Army "AirLand Battle" doctrine since the mid-1970s.[16] Although Rogers insisted that NATO and American army doctrine were the products of separate inquiries, the two so mirrored one another that the distinction appeared somewhat artificial. By concentrating on follow-on forces, forward strategy theorists expected to render attacking Warsaw Pact armies incapable of sustaining the offensive by making it impossible for them to bring up reinforcements and supplies. The proffered scenario of events was that, once the Warsaw Pact realized that it could not sustain an offensive, it would then be dissuaded from either committing additional forces or electing to escalate to nuclear weapons. Exactly how the Soviets and their allies were supposed to arrive at these conclusions, however, was never fully clear.[17]

The maritime strategy was likewise a more aggressive stance in the face of growing Soviet naval capabilities for offensive war in the North Atlantic and Arctic Ocean areas. Like the FOFA concept, the maritime strategy was largely the product of American initiative and received strong impetus under the Reagan military buildup of the early 1980s.[18] Its aim was to bring war into the Soviets' backyard with counterforce attacks on Soviet naval facilities and with massed amphibious landings by marines along the eastern Baltic and Black Sea coasts. Critics, including some U.S. army and air force officers, maintained that the maritime strategy was really nothing more than a ploy to justify building a six-hundred-ship navy in the 1980s and beyond, that it would drain resources from the more important task of defending Europe, and that the end result would be to weaken conventional deterrence.[19] Proponents argued that a naval defense in depth could wrest the initiative from the Soviets, clear the sea-lanes, and contain Warsaw Pact naval forces at their home bases.[20] According to analyst Robert S. Jordan, the overall effect was akin to the globalist naval strategy practiced by the United States in the aftermath of World War II.[21]

STRATEGY AND ARMS CONTROL

Behind NATO's shift to the forward strategy and a more nonnuclear stance during the 1980s lay the increasing acceptance among alliance members that the availability and use of nuclear weapons would be steadily curtailed, partly as a result of growing political opposition from groups such as the Greens, but more importantly because of the restraining influence of arms control agreements. The decision to forge ahead with nuclear arms control as part of NATO's standing agenda may be traced to the Harmel Report's call for "more stable" East-West relations, which in the early 1970s translated into the policy of détente. From that time on, even though détente eventually wore thin, arms control remained a constant factor in NATO's military planning, affecting practically everything from perceptions of strategic objectives to the procurement of new weapons.

At the center of the arms control process rested the Strategic Arms Limitation Talks (SALT) initiated between the United States and the Soviet Union in 1969, the object of which was to establish some measure of stability over a competition in strategic weapons that verged on being out of control. Soviet negotiators in SALT I (1969-1972) wanted the talks to include all offensive weapons capable of reaching the territory of the other side. This was a definition that the United States rejected because it would have included forward-based U.S. systems dedicated to NATO but not Soviet medium-range bombers and missiles targeted against Western Europe. The resolution of this impasse took the form of confining discussion to a rather narrow but significant spectrum of weapons—intercontinental ballistic missiles (ICBM), submarine-launched ballistic missiles (SLBM), and antiballistic missile (ABM) systems.[22]

SALT I produced two accords: the ABM Treaty, which imposed major constraints on the research, development, and deployment of strategic antiballistic missile systems; and the Interim Agreement on offensive weapons, mandating a five-year freeze on new construction and deployment of ICBM and SLBM launch systems. American negotiators generally agreed—and so testified before Congress—that the ABM Treaty was a significant first step toward curtailing the arms race and that it would generate momentum going into SALT II for the early conclusion of a permanent replacement agreement on offensive arms, expanded by the 1974 Vladivostok accord to include heavy bombers as well as long-range missiles. But as the negotiations dragged on, disillusionment set in. Not only did the East-West strategic buildup in offensive arms show few signs of abating, but also in its eagerness to reach a SALT II treaty the United States made concessions that critics deemed unnecessary and dangerous to crisis stability.[23]

Although not directly involved in SALT, the European members of NATO watched the proceedings with keen interest, mainly because of the impact the talks were likely to have on the continuing ability of the United States to provide effective extended deterrence. Viewed from this perspective, the results of SALT I were inconclusive. But by the time the outlines of a SALT II agreement began to appear in the mid-1970s, it was increasingly clear to many European leaders—the West Germans especially—that several of the concessions the United States was contemplating, notably in long-range cruise missiles and bombers, would adversely affect European security. Worse, the United States seemed inclined to accept a SALT II agreement that in appearance, if not in substance, would confer permanent strategic superiority on the Soviet Union: a 1.5 to 1 advantage in ICBM launchers and a significant edge in aggregate throw-weight and megatonnage. Only in the number of strategic warheads was the United States expected to maintain a meaningful lead.[24]

This looming shift in the strategic balance had two notable effects on NATO. One was that it heavily strained the alliance's continued commitment to détente, already burdened with growing East-West differences over Soviet activities in Africa and other issues. As Phil Williams argued, the European view of détente was always more cautious and skeptical than the American view. Although the Europeans were not about to pass up any benefits they might derive in the form of increased trade and cultural contacts with the East, few expected détente to lead to the resolution of fundamental differences. The most useful function it could serve was in narrowing areas of disagreement and potential conflict to the point where opposing ideological and political systems could safely coexist.[25] Even West German Chancellor Willy Brandt's ambitious Ostpolitik (eastern policy) of the early 1970s had rather limited objectives, focusing on improving relations with the East in order to strengthen the status quo. As détente faded, European political leaders thus found it easier to readjust their thinking and curtail their expectations than did their American counterparts.

Another salient consequence for NATO to come out of SALT was that it sent the European members scurrying for something that could augment U.S. strategic nuclear protection. The most obviously concerned were the West Germans who, unlike the British and the French, produced no nuclear weapons of their own and were therefore dependent on the United States to provide up-to-date nuclear deterrence. Failure to do so, as West German Chancellor Helmut Schmidt asserted in his celebrated speech of October 1977 to the International Institute for Strategic Studies (IISS), would inevitably weaken deterrence and détente at the same time by magnifying "disparities between East and West in nuclear tactical and conventional weapons."[26] Schmidt's major worry focused on the Soviet Union's decision (part of an ongoing weapons modernization program throughout the Warsaw Pact) to deploy a new generation of more powerful and usable theater nuclear missiles, the SS-20. Derived from the SS-16, an ICBM that apparently failed to live up to expectations, the SS-20 was a mobile missile carrying three independently targeted warheads, capable of reaching any target in NATO Europe. Nothing comparable to the SS-20 then existed in the NATO arsenal, although the United States did have five Poseidon missile submarines dedicated to NATO that posed a similar threat to the Soviet Union. However, these U.S. missile submarines were subject to the limitations being negotiated in SALT; the SS-20s were not. Alarmed by the danger the SS-20s posed, Schmidt tried first through diplomatic channels to draw American attention to the problem. When that failed, he went public with his speech to the IISS.[27]

The upshot of Schmidt's initiative was the "dual track" decision of December 1979. This committed NATO to the modernization of its long-range theater nuclear forces (LRTNF), while the United States, acting as the allies' agent, initiated new negotiations (separate from SALT) with the Soviet Union to head off any further LRTNF competition. At the same time, as a goodwill gesture, NATO announced that the United States would withdraw 1,000 tactical nuclear warheads from Europe. The new weapons that NATO planned to field, with deployment scheduled for 1983, were 464 ground-launched cruise missiles (GLCM) and 108 Pershing II ballistic missiles to replace an equal number of shorter-range Pershing IAs deployed in West Germany since the late 1960s. Militarily, a mix of both ballistic and cruise missiles recommended itself as a hedge against improvements in Soviet air and missile defenses. And since these weapons had the range to threaten targets well behind Warsaw Pact lines, they could be justified as contributing to NATO's military objectives by providing support, albeit nuclear, under the emerging doctrine of forward defense.

All the same, the dual track decision was, first and foremost, a political one, whose main purpose was to enhance NATO's bargaining power with the Soviets without seeming to engage in a costly new round of arms competition. Though important for credibility purposes, the military and strategic value of bolstering NATO's nuclear capability was a secondary consideration and was tacitly acknowledged as such by the allies at the time. Indeed, in its early deliberations, the High Level Group (HLG) to which NATO referred the problem summarily rejected the development of either an effective battlefield nuclear capability or the deployment of a theater nuclear force large enough to counter Soviet LRTNF without external support from the United States. The HLG urged instead that the allies concentrate on a third, less ambitious and less costly, option of improving NATO's intermediate-range nuclear forces on a moderate scale—what British and West German officials termed an "evolutionary upward adjustment" in NATO's nuclear capability.

In short, the deployment should appear credible but not overly threatening.[28] Subsequent technical analysis showed that, from a military standpoint, developing such a posture would depend on NATO's ability to demonstrate the survivability both of the weapons systems themselves and of support functions. Upgrading and hardening command and control facilities (the Achilles' heel of virtually all high-technology military systems) would have to be a top priority.[29] Once these requirements were met, according to one American participant in the planning process, the missiles would be "sufficiently survivable, even if not perfectly survivable."[30]

As discussion within NATO progressed, the nuclear modernization issue became, in effect, the most critical test of American leadership that the alliance had experienced since Charles de Gaulle's defection from NATO in the 1960s. Immediately following Schmidt's speech to the IISS, the inclination among American policymakers was to stall for time in the hope of reaching a comprehensive SALT agreement that would obviate the need for either the deployment of new weapons in Europe or separate arms control negotiations. But on 7 April 1978, President Jimmy Carter stunned the NATO allies by announcing that he was deferring production of the neutron bomb, an enhanced radiation weapon designed mainly for battlefield use against invading Warsaw Pact tank formations. Carter defended his decision on the rather narrow grounds that he could never get a satisfactory commitment from West German Chancellor Schmidt on deployment.[31] Yet it was clear that other factors were at work as well. As a practical matter, the neutron bomb's function was to kill people and leave buildings largely intact, a bonus perhaps for frontline countries like West Germany where wartime damage was liable to be severe, but a perversion of moral values as far as Carter was concerned. Zbigniew Brzezinski, Carter's national security adviser, readily acknowledged the president's moral qualms about putting things ahead of human lives and ruefully described the neutron bomb decision as "a major setback in U.S.-European relations." Indeed, it cost the United States dearly in terms of prestige and leverage with its allies and invited concessions that Washington might otherwise have been inclined to resist. From this point on, the upgrading of NATO's theater nuclear forces became a virtual certainty, although it remained a divisive issue in European—especially West German—politics.[32]

In sum, the dual track decision effectively committed NATO to a course of nuclear modernization that none of its members particularly wanted to see come to fruition. Despite NATO's declared policy of upgrading its INF capabilities, the preferred outcome all along was a gradual diminution of reliance on nuclear weapons. The ultimate objective was a negotiated settlement that would relax some of the pressure brought on by the Soviet nuclear buildup. Militarily, the weapons that NATO planned to deploy were likely to have a marginal impact on the strategic balance in Europe; politically, however, they filled a void that went far toward restoring NATO's sense of self-confidence. Even more important, they represented a calculated effort on the part of the European alliance members to regain some of the bargaining leverage they felt they had lost in the 1970s.

THE REAGAN BUILDUP

Then, in 1981, came the Reagan administration, with radically different priorities than its predecessor. Adopting an almost dismissive attitude toward arms control, the Reaganites launched the largest and most costly U.S. military expansion since the Korean War. Improvements in strategic systems received especially heavy emphasis. Included in what amounted to a wholesale refurbishing of the West's strategic nuclear arsenal were the MX missile, the Trident submarine, and the B-1 bomber, along with a host of futuristic follow-on weapons as well, such as the Stealth (B-2) bomber and, most innovative and ambitious of all, a space-based antimissile system known as the Strategic Defense Initiative (SDI).[33]

The Reagan buildup was not without political and strategic consequence for NATO Europe. Despite increased talk of conventional options, it seemed all too clear from the European perspective that U.S. policymakers were preoccupied with the U.S.-Soviet strategic relationship, rather than Europe, and that redressing imbalances in the nuclear arena was Washington's overriding priority. French Foreign Minister Claude Cheysson merely stated the obvious when he spoke of a "creeping divorce" between European and American security interests.[34] What worried many Europeans specifically was that the United States seemed bent on improving more than its posture of deterrence and would settle for nothing less than acquiring a war-fighting/ war-winning nuclear capability over the Soviet Union. Whether justified or not, such worries added immensely to growing antinuclear sentiment among European environmentalists and others and made it all the harder for NATO to coordinate and articulate a coherent strategic concept.

One of the most divisive issues was SDI, Reagan's hope for the future to render nuclear weapons "impotent and obsolete." Not only did SDI pose huge technical challenges, making it potentially the most costly defense program in history, but it also fed fears in the West of strategic instability leading to a new round of strategic arms competition with the Soviet Union. Furthermore, Europeans worried that, if the United States succeeded in insulating itself behind a strategic shield, it would lose interest in continuing to provide extended deterrence. Even close friends of the Reagan administration, such as British Prime Minister Margaret Thatcher, privately expressed misgivings about SDI and gave it only qualified support.[35]

A further consequence of the Reagan buildup was the apparent setback it dealt to arms control. While the Reagan administration went through the motions of endorsing and supporting arms control, its commitment to serious and productive negotiations appeared to some critics questionable. Skeptics viewed the administration's stubborn adherence to the "zero-zero" option—a NATO-approved concept calling for the total elimination of all intermediate-range missiles on both sides—not so much as a credible or realistic negotiating position, but as a thinly veiled excuse to thwart progress in the INF talks. Whether the Soviets were any more serious in reaching an agreement, however, is equally debatable. When in 1982 the U.S. chief negotiator for INF, Ambassador Paul H. Nitze, tried quietly to arrange a compromise—the celebrated but ill-fated "walk in the woods" episode—he encountered little enthusiasm either in Washington or in Moscow. The following year, to the surprise of no one, the Soviets broke off the INF talks when NATO, as scheduled, commenced deployment of its cruise and Pershing II missiles.[36]

The collapse of the INF talks in 1983 was not the political disaster it seemed at the time to some analysts, nor did it usher in a period of new and more dangerous East-West arms competition. On the contrary, it provided a cooling-off period that gave both sides a chance to step back and take a fresh look at their strategic and theater requirements. According to Ivo Daalder, senior defense officials in the Reagan administration viewed NATO's theater nuclear force (TNF) as an integral part of the West's strategic posture in case of a general nuclear response and now wanted to press on with modernization of NATO's shorter-range nuclear weapons.[37] But with the antinuclear movement gaining momentum in Britain and on the Continent, the European allies were reluctant to be seen unreservedly embracing such a policy. At its meeting in late October 1983 in Montebello, Canada, the Nuclear Planning Group announced a face-saving compromise under which SACEUR would continue to study improvements in the allies' shorter-range nuclear weapons while over the next five to six years NATO would unilaterally reduce its nuclear stockpile by an additional fourteen hundred weapons.[38] Observers credited the reduction, in part, to new methods developed by

NATO planners for calculating nuclear weapons requirements, and to the fact that many of the weapons designated for removal were of older vintage, due to be retired anyway. But with the strengthening of its conventional capabilities beginning to bear fruit, NATO's strategic posture was probably now less dependent on nuclear weapons than at any time in the past several decades.

Further nuclear cutbacks were just around the corner, the result to a considerable extent of unexpected flexibility on the Soviet side that led to the resumption of the INF negotiations in 1985 and to the signing, two years later, of the INF Treaty. Not only did the treaty incorporate the zero-zero option insisted upon by NATO; it also contained provision for the most extensive and intrusive on-site inspection verification measures yet seen.[39] By itself, the INF Treaty, as U.S. Ambassador Richard Burt observed at the time, did little more than to restore the status quo in Europe as it existed in the mid-1970s, prior to the SS-20 deployment.[40] But in view of subsequent developments—the disintegration of Communist power in Eastern Europe, renewed Soviet interest in negotiating deals on strategic and conventional arms, the dismantling of the Warsaw Pact, and, ultimately, the collapse of the Soviet Union itself—it might also be argued that the INF Treaty signaled the onset of a strategic realignment across Europe. By the early 1990s, the barriers that had divided East from West for nearly five decades had largely disappeared.

ENTERING THE POST–COLD WAR TRANSITION

With the ending of the Cold War, NATO military planning again entered an era of transition, this time facing an almost wholly unfamiliar set of challenges. Endeavoring to adjust, NATO leaders adopted a new strategic concept at their meeting in Rome in November 1991. This was NATO's first full-scale strategic reassessment since the breakup of the Soviet Union and as such represented barely more than a preliminary appraisal. Although flexible response remained the allies' basic military doctrine, it was modified to reflect as much as an 80 percent further reduction in NATO's nuclear forces and similarly large (but publicly unspecified) cutbacks in conventional capabilities. Instead of linear forward deployments facing eastward, NATO announced its intention to adopt a more mobile posture favoring rapid reaction to defuse crises and cope with less than all-out emergencies.[41]

Translating the new strategic concept into a working military policy was, as expected, not without difficulty. The reasons were several, starting with the tentativeness that necessarily surrounded the making of concrete plans in the absence of an identifiable threat such as the Soviet Union used to pose. The new strategic concept readily acknowledged that "Rather than facing the over-arching threat of a simultaneous full-scale attack on NATO territory, the alliance now confronts threats that are multifaceted and less predictable."[42] Viewed from this perspective, with the Warsaw Pact a fading memory, NATO's military strategy in the 1990s ceased to command the urgent attention it did during much of the Cold War. Instead, interest turned to the alliance's political strategy, emphasizing such issues as its role as a peacekeeper and its future relations with former members of the Warsaw Pact.

An added factor in the post–Cold War uncertainty over NATO's military posture was the ambivalence of the United States toward future obligations in Europe. Although President Bill Clinton insisted at the NATO summit in January 1994 that the United States remained committed to NATO, it was not a commitment with the same degree of interest or enthusiasm shown by previous U.S. administrations. Clinton promised to keep U.S. forces in Europe at "around 100,000" through the end of the century, a figure above what some analysts were projecting but well below what the Bush administration had said it would keep. According to Secretary of State Warren M. Christopher, Asia had replaced Europe as the focus of American foreign policy, mainly because of increased U.S. trade with Asia but also because of what Christopher and others in the Clinton administration considered the distorted Eurocentric approach of past policy.[43] Cooperative security through multilateral UN-brokered operations was the Clinton administration's preferred approach.[44]

Hardest of all to adjust to was the depletion of resources at NATO's disposal. Domestic needs took priority in post–Cold War Europe and the United States alike. Not only had the Soviet threat been a rallying point for alliance unity; it had also been a convenient device for sizing NATO's capabilities, for sustaining its requirements, and for driving new research and development (R&D). Future dangers were not likely to be as well defined, making it all the more difficult for NATO to decide what it needed and to be able to justify the diversion of resources for defense purposes. What once appeared vital additions to the NATO arsenal became unaffordable, if not questionable, luxuries. A case in point was the collapse of plans in 1993 for a joint Anglo-French air-launched nuclear missile. As Simon Lunn aptly summed up the situation, "Nobody seems to know what is sufficient for today's security environment in Europe."[45]

With the allies intent on downsizing their defense establishments, even maintaining a nucleus of ready forces posed serious complications for NATO planners and policymakers. Behind the public squabbling in 1993-94 among NATO members over how to deal with the Bosnian crisis loomed the hard fact that NATO could not count on having the manpower and other available resources to cope with a lengthy conflict in the Balkans. The Bosnian situation was perhaps a unique, extreme case, but it still pointed up the need for ready military forces to deal with security problems in Europe.

All the same, NATO continued to possess two valuable strategic assets that were hard to reproduce elsewhere. One was its command and control structure, which remained the most effective instrument of its kind in Europe for directing military, humanitarian, and peacekeeping operations. The other was a physical base for pre-positioning equipment and supplies in an emergency or for "out-of-area" ventures. Even though NATO's political leaders had generally been reluctant to sanction operations below the Tropic of Cancer, NATO naval planners had for some years recognized the numerous dangers to Europe's oil lines of communication with the Middle East and had planned accordingly.[46] The Persian Gulf War of 1990-91 and the crucial part that supplies and equipment pre-positioned in NATO Europe played in the success of that conflict testified to the continuing importance of NATO facilities in global strategic planning.

POINTING TOWARD THE FUTURE

As NATO looked ahead to the twenty-first century, further refinements in military strategy probably seemed likely to await the emergence of a new, or at least refurbished, political strategy. After four and a half decades, NATO was having to "reinvent" itself in order to deal with new problems in a world setting radically altered from that in which the alliance was founded. As this process of reinvention went forward, two questions dominated the agenda: Should NATO refocus its energies and assets on peacekeeping and related missions? And should it look eastward and draw new members into its ranks?

In addressing the first of these questions, NATO had to take into account not only the dwindling availability of military resources but also the willingness of the allies to concert their efforts in new directions. As the indecision and uncertainty that initially surrounded NATO's response to the Bosnian crisis suggested, the alliance's political leaders faced considerable difficulty reaching a consensus on how peacekeeping and humanitarian problems ought to be handled. Among alliance planners in Brussels, however, the governing assumption was that sooner or later NATO would find itself operating further and further afield and that it should prepare accordingly. The approval at the January 1994 summit of the reorganization of NATO's forces into "combined joint task forces" marked a major step in that direction.

As for the second question—should NATO look eastward and welcome new members into its ranks?—the January 1994 summit laid the ground-work for an answer here as well by endorsing President Clinton's proposal of a "Partnership for Peace" between NATO and its erstwhile enemies. Although the partnership program was open to all former Warsaw Pact countries, attention focused initially on the Visegrád states of Eastern Europe (Poland, Hungary, the Czech Republic, and Slovakia). The partnerships were to be an interim arrangement, part of an evolutionary process of integration, starting with various forms of military cooperation, that might or might not lead to full membership by these countries in NATO. The explanation offered by Secretary of State Christopher was that: "Participation in the partnership will build the qualifications necessary for membership [in NATO], but par-ticipation alone will not guarantee membership."[47] In other words, the aim for the time being was to pull these countries as firmly as possible into the Western orbit. Noting this, skeptics viewed the possibility of the partnership program evolving into a series of anti-Russian alliances supporting a Western policy of neo-containment.[48]

By leaving unclear the exact status the participants in the Partnership for Peace program were to enjoy, NATO avoided the more difficult problem of what kinds of security guarantees it would offer. Inevitably, questions arose as to whether these partnerships would be worth anything other than to pro-vide moral support. One obvious reason for not rushing into new commit-ments was that years hence NATO could discover that by extending its realm eastward it had accepted security obligations that its members could not or would not honor, much as France and Britain reacted when faced in 1938 with possibly having to honor their pledges to Czechoslovakia. Having suc-ceeded in ridding itself in the late 1970s and 1980s of overwhelming depen-dence on nuclear weapons, NATO was also divesting itself of a large measure of its conventional capabilities as well in the 1990s. While NATO's latent power remained substantial, the fact that its forces in being commanded less and less of each member's gross domestic product suggested a growing gap between the guarantees NATO could offer, on the one hand, and its capac-ity to act, on the other.

What NATO would use in the future to back up any new or enlarged obligations had yet to be ascertained. One possibility, as the size of NATO armies shrank, was greater reliance on advanced technologies such as Stealth fighter bombers and cruise missiles and precision guided munitions (PGM). All had proved exceptionally effective in the Persian Gulf War against certain targets like Iraqi command and control bunkers, communications systems, and military facilities with civilians nearby, where surprise and/or pinpoint accuracy were essential. But at the same time the high cost and other limitations of these weapons had greatly restricted their use. PGMs accounted for only 8 percent of the bombs and other ordnance dropped during the Gulf War and were of little use against large-area targets like supply depots or deployed forces. As appealing and promising as these new technologies appeared to be, the findings of the Gulf War Air Power Survey, initiated by the U.S. Air Force, cast doubt on whether they would soon, if ever, produce any radical or dramatic changes in tactics and strategy.[49]

Another possibility to come out of the Gulf War was increased emphasis on defensive systems like the Patriot antimissile missile. While not as militarily effective as first believed or as its manufacturer claimed, the Patriot still demonstrated that missile defense had an important mission.[50] Follow-on systems under development in the mid-1990s promised to be even better and more reliable. Despite having largely abandoned SDI, the Clinton administration continued to accord missile defense, now reoriented toward theater and battlefield applications, high priority as a precaution against the proliferation of various weapons of mass destruction (chemical, biological, and nuclear weapons). What was slow to emerge in the absence of a specific threat was a constituency within NATO and a willingness on the part of the European allies to share in the expense of future R&D.

Yet a third option, though not one that many people seemed ready to acknowledge, was a return to more reliance on battlefield tactical nuclear weapons. The danger of this course was that NATO could again find its military options severely constrained, its effectiveness hamstrung by dependence on weapons of questionable use politically. On the other hand, NATO military planners had to look ahead and adjust their thinking to an alliance with broadened responsibilities. Nuclear weapons, for all the political problems they posed, remained a viable military asset for this purpose, though it appeared unlikely that nuclear weapons would ever again have the central role in strategy that they had in times past.

The danger that NATO might overextend itself had to be balanced against the equally hazardous course of doing nothing at all and seeing the gains made for liberal democracy in Eastern Europe swept away by a tide of red fascism. Either way, NATO's continuing role in underwriting security and stability in Europe was likely to be considerable. NATO's emerging post–Cold

War political strategy, concentrating more on peacekeeping and humanitarian activities than on deterrence, suggested an alliance of the future with broader and more fluid interests than it had known in the past. It was also becoming a NATO with diminished American leadership and involvement, which placed more responsibility for strategic decisions on the European members of the alliance. NATO's future military strategy would undoubtedly reflect these new political realities.

NOTES

1. See, for example, Jonathan Clarke, "Replacing NATO," *Foreign Policy* 93 (Winter 1993-94): 22-40.
2. The best overview of NATO's origins and the ideas behind it is Lawrence S. Kaplan, *The United States and NATO: The Formative Years* (Lexington: University Press of Kentucky, 1984).
3. Such was Marshall's attitude as recounted in Paul H. Nitze, *From Hiroshima to Glasnost: At the Center of Decision—A Memoir* (New York: Grove, Weidenfeld, 1989), 59.
4. For a fuller discussion see Samuel R. Williamson, Jr., and Steven L. Rearden, *The Origins of U.S. Nuclear Strategy, 1945-1953* (New York: St. Martin's Press, 1993).
5. U.S. Department of State, *Foreign Relations of the United States, 1949* (Washington, 1975), 4:356-58; Christian Grenier, "Strategic Concepts for the Defence of Western Europe, 1948-1950," in *The Western Security Community*, ed. Norbert Wiggershaus and Roland G. Foerster (Oxford: Berg Publishers, 1993), 313-41.
6. Robert A. Wampler, "Conventional Goals and Nuclear Promises: The Truman Administration and the Roots of the NATO New Look," in *NATO: The Founding of the Atlantic Alliance and the Integration of Europe*, ed. Francis H. Heller and John R. Gillingham (New York: St. Martin's Press, 1992), 353-80. See also Ernest R. May, "The American Commitment to Germany, 1949-55," *Diplomatic History* 13 (Fall 1989): 431-60.
7. For the development of NATO strategy under MC 48 see Robert J. Watson, *The Joint Chiefs of Staff and National Policy, 1953-1954* (Washington: Historical Division, Joint Chiefs of Staff, 1986), 311-21.
8. For the controversy over Soviet strategic strength see John Prados, *The Soviet Estimate: U.S. Intelligence Analysis and Russian Military Strength* (New York: Dial Press, 1982), 67-126; and Lawrence Freedman, *U.S. Intelligence and the Soviet Strategic Threat*, 2d ed. (Princeton: Princeton University Press, 1986), 62-80.
9. The best analysis is Jane E. Stromseth, *The Origins of Flexible Response: NATO's Debate over Strategy in the 1960s* (New York: St. Martin's Press, 1988). See also Richard A. Aliano, *American Defense Policy from Eisenhower to Kennedy: The Politics of Changing Military Requirements, 1957-1961* (Athens: Ohio University

Press, 1975); and Lawrence Freedman, *The Evolution of Nuclear Strategy* (New York: St. Martin's Press, 1981), chap. 19.

10. Quoted in Alain C. Enthoven and K. Wayne Smith, *How Much is Enough?* (New York: Harper and Row, 1971), 122.

11. Ivo H. Daalder, *The Nature and Practice of Flexible Response: NATO Strategy and Theater Nuclear Forces since 1967* (New York: Columbia University Press, 1991), 74-76.

12. "The Future Tasks of the Alliance (Harmel Report)," December 1967, reprinted as Appendix D in Stanley R. Sloan, *NATO's Future: Toward a New Transatlantic Bargain* (Washington: National Defense University Press, 1985), 219-22.

13. See McNamara's statement accompanying his FY 1969 budget submission in U.S. Congress, Senate, Committee on Armed Services, *Hearings on Authorization for Military Procurement, Research and Development, Fiscal Year 1969, and Reserve Strength*, 90th Cong., 2d sess., 1968, 183.

14. Quoted in Daalder, *Flexible Response*, 69.

15. James R. Schlesinger, "The Theater Nuclear Force Posture in Europe: A Report to the U.S. Congress in Compliance with P.L. 93-365" (Washington: Department of Defense, 1975), 11-13.

16. For a summary of the evolution of army doctrine see John L. Romjue, *From Active Defense to AirLand Battle: The Development of Army Doctrine, 1973-1982* (Ft. Monroe, VA: Historical Office, U.S. Army Training and Doctrine Command, 1984).

17. Bernard W. Rogers, "Greater Flexibility for NATO's Flexible Response," *Strategic Review* 11 (Spring 1983): 11-19.

18. Testimony by Secretary of the Navy John Lehman and CNO Adm. James D. Watkins, 14 March 1984, in U.S. Congress, Senate, Committee on Armed Services, *Hearings on Department of Defense Authorization for Appropriations for Fiscal Year 1985*, 98th Cong., 2d sess., 1985, Pt. 8, 3852-94.

19. For a summary of criticism see John J. Mearsheimer, "A Strategic Misstep: The Maritime Strategy and Deterrence in Europe," *International Security* 11 (Fall 1986): 3-57.

20. The case for the maritime strategy was best made in a set of navy-sponsored articles published as *The Maritime Strategy, Supplement to the U.S. Naval Institute Proceedings* 112 (January 1986). See also Linton F. Brooks, "Naval Power and National Security: The Case for the Maritime Strategy," *International Security* 11 (Fall 1986): 58-88; and Francis J. West, Jr., "Maritime Strategy and NATO Deterrence," *Naval War College Review* 38 (September-October 1985): 5-19.

21. Robert S. Jordan, *Alliance Strategy and Navies: The Evolution and Scope of NATO's Maritime Dimension* (New York: St. Martin's Press, 1990), 139-41.

22. For an overview of the SALT negotiations see Thomas W. Wolfe, *The SALT Experience* (Cambridge, MA: Ballinger, 1979).

23. The most persistent critic of what became the SALT II Treaty was Paul H. Nitze, who had served as a member of the U.S. SALT I delegation. For a summary of his views on how SALT II threatened to damage U.S. and Western security see

Kenneth W. Thompson and Steven L. Rearden, eds., *Paul H. Nitze on National Security and Arms Control* (Lanham, MD: University Press of America, 1990), 149-240; and Nitze, *From Hiroshima to Glasnost*, chaps. 16-18.

24. Raymond L. Garthoff, *Détente and Confrontation: American-Soviet Relations from Nixon to Reagan* (Washington: Brookings Institution, 1985), 856-67; Daalder, *Flexible Response*, 166-68. See also Lawrence Freedman, "Negotiations on Nuclear Forces in Europe, 1969-83," in *The European Missile Crisis: Nuclear Weapons and Security Policy*, ed. Hans-Henrik Holm and Nikolaj Petersen (New York: St. Martin's Press, 1983), 123-28.

25. Phil Williams, "The United States and Détente: A European View," in *The Cold War Past and Present*, ed. Richard Crockatt and Steve Smith (London: Allen and Unwin, 1987), 110-27.

26. Helmut Schmidt, "The 1977 Alastair Buchan Memorial Lecture," *Survival* 20 (January-February 1978): 2-10.

27. Helmut Schmidt, "If the Missiles Go, Peace May Stay," *New York Times*, 29 April 1987.

28. Daalder, *Flexible Response*, 176-77.

29. J. Michael Legge, *Theater Nuclear Weapons and the NATO Strategy of Flexible Response*, RAND Rpt. No. R-2964 (Santa Monica, CA: RAND Corp., 1983), 74.

30. Lynn Davis (assistant deputy undersecretary of defense for policy planning, 1977-1981), cited in David S. Yost, "The History of NATO Theater Nuclear Force Policy: Key Findings from the Sandia Conference," *Journal of Strategic Studies* 15 (June 1992): 236.

31. Jimmy Carter, *Keeping Faith: Memoirs of a President* (New York: Bantam Books, 1982), 225-29

32. Zbigniew Brzezinski, *Power and Principle: Memoirs of the National Security Adviser, 1977-1981* (New York: Farrar Straus Giroux, 1983), 301-6. See also James A. Thomson, "The LRTNF Decision: Evolution of US Theatre Nuclear Policy, 1975-9," *International Affairs* 60 (Autumn 1984): 601-14; and Jeffrey Herf, *War by Other Means: Soviet Power, West German Resistance, and the Battle of the Euromissiles* (New York: Free Press, 1991).

33. Two good overviews of the Reagan buildup are William P. Snyder and James Brown, eds., *Defense Policy in the Reagan Administration* (Washington: National Defense University Press, 1988); and Daniel Wirls, *Buildup: The Politics of Defense in the Reagan Era* (Ithaca: Cornell University Press, 1992).

34. Quoted in Richard J. Barnet, *The Alliance—America, Europe, Japan: Makers of the Postwar World* (New York: Simon & Schuster, 1983), 434.

35. Margaret Thatcher, *The Downing Street Years* (New York: HarperCollins, 1993), 463-69.

36. Nitze, *From Hiroshima to Glasnost*, 366-98. See also Strobe Talbott, *The Master of the Game: Paul Nitze and the Nuclear Peace* (New York: Knopf, 1988).

37. Daalder, *Flexible Response*, 237-44.

38. Montebello meeting, Final Communiqué and Annex, 28 October 1983, Department of State *Bulletin* 83 (December 1983): 24-25.

39. See Joseph P. Harahan, *On-Site Inspections under the INF Treaty: A History of the On-Site Inspection Agency and INF Treaty Implementation, 1988-1991* (Washington: On-Site Inspection Agency, Department of Defense, 1993).

40. Richard Burt, "The Right Lessons of INF Treaty," *Wall Street Journal*, 7 January 1988.

41. "NATO's Evolving Role in Atlantic Security," U.S. Department of State *Dispatch*, 11 November 1991.

42. Ibid.

43. "Recriminations Intensify Strain in Atlantic Alliance," *Washington Post*, 25 October 1993.

44. See Ashton B. Carter, William J. Perry, and John D. Steinbruner, *A New Concept of Cooperative Security* (Washington: Brookings Institution, 1992).

45. Lunn quoted in "Britain Scraps Missile Project," *Washington Post*, 23 October 1993.

46. Joel J. Sokolsky, *Seapower in the Nuclear Age: The United States Navy and NATO, 1949-80* (Annapolis, MD: Naval Institute Press, 1991), 122.

47. Warren Christopher, "NATO Plus," *Washington Post*, 9 January 1994.

48. See, for example, Thomas W. Lippman, "NATO Peace Partnership's New Look: A Protective Shield Against Moscow," *Washington Post*, 8 February 1994.

49. Thomas A. Keaney and Eliot A. Cohen, *Gulf War Air Power Summary Report* (draft in galley proofs), chap. 9. See also Eliot A. Cohen, "The Mystique of U.S. Air Power," *Foreign Affairs* 73 (January-February 1974): 109-12; and *Gulf War Air Power Survey*, Vol. 2, *Operations and Effects and Effectiveness* (Washington: G.P.O., 1993).

50. The Patriot's controversial performance is discussed in Theodore A. Postol, "Lessons of the Gulf War Experience with Patriot," *International Security* 16 (Winter 1991/92): 119-71. The Patriot's manufacturer, Raytheon, published a separate rebuttal. See Robert M. Stein, "Patriot ATBM Experience in the Gulf War," ibid. 17 (Summer 1992): 199-240.

NATO and
Interlocking Institutions

■ ■ ■

5

NATO and the United Nations:
Toward a Nonallergic Relationship

Alan K. Henrikson

The United Nations (UN) traditionally has been allergic to the North
Atlantic Treaty Organization (NATO). I use this unusual word—from the
Greek *allos* and *ergon*, or *other* and *work*—because it suggests exactly that
odd reaction, a disagreeable sensitivity to or even actual antipathy toward
another, different kind of body, that has characterized so much of the UN
community's response over the years to NATO.

Perhaps revealingly, there is not a single reference to the North Atlantic
Alliance or NATO in the otherwise comprehensive annual *Report* (1993)
to the membership of the United Nations by Secretary-General Boutros
Boutros-Ghali.[1] However, this gold-covered document, of some 182 pages
(the longest to date), does mention the Organization of American States
(OAS), the Organization of African Unity (OAU), the Conference on Security
and Cooperation in Europe (CSCE), and even the Economic Community of
West African States (ECOWAS).

In fairness, of course, it should be noted that Secretary-General Boutros-
Ghali, both in this large document of September 1993 and in his *Agenda for
Peace* report of 1992 to the UN Security Council, has in a general way supported a larger role in the peace and security field for "regional understand-
ings." A brief chapter in that slim blue booklet treats "cooperation with
regional arrangements and organizations." But that earlier, shorter report
does not mention NATO either. The reference to Europe is noteworthy:

"Efforts undertaken by the European Community and its member States, with the support of States participating in the Conference on Security and Cooperation in Europe, have been of central importance in dealing with the crisis in the Balkans and neighbouring areas."[2]

A brief observation made late in 1992 by NATO Secretary-General Manfred Wörner speaks volumes about the difficult NATO-UN relationship. "Mr. Boutros-Ghali, in his 'Agenda for Peace' and letter to the CSCE, has welcomed the role of regional organizations in upholding UN decisions," the secretary-general wrote in the *NATO Review*. "At the same time, the habit of cooperation and looking to each other for guidance has yet to be established at the working level."[3]

This absence of a functional relationship between NATO and the United Nations is remarkable and profoundly ironic. The UN's reserved attitude toward NATO, like NATO's coolness toward the UN, contrasts strikingly with what has long been a historical reality: that the North Atlantic Alliance, the legal commitment along with the military forces and political infrastructure, constitutes the firmest foundation—organizationally, the best friend—that the UN system has had in the world. Arguably, NATO has done more in its forty-five-year history to contribute to international peace and security, and not merely stability in its own defensive treaty area, than has the United Nations organization itself, with its expressly worldwide mandate and purview. NATO has been a bedrock of international peace, globally as well as regionally.

This geographically extensive role, it should be more widely known, was part of the original intention of NATO. Article 4 of the 1949 Washington Treaty indicates clearly that the Atlantic allies expected to be able to rely on their working partnership as a basis for possible coordinated action even in other parts of the world. The article states that the signers of the treaty "will consult together whenever, in the opinion of any of them, the territorial integrity, political independence or security of any of the Parties is threatened." In a set of confidential "agreed minutes of interpretation," the signatories recorded their common understanding that "Article 4 is applicable in the event of a threat in any part of the world," including a threat to the "overseas territories" of any of the parties.[4] When President Harry S. Truman attended the signing of the North Atlantic Treaty in Washington on 4 April 1949, he stated that "to protect this area against war will be a long step toward permanent peace in the whole world."[5] In passing, I draw attention, for later reference, to the fact that President Truman said that the treaty would protect the North Atlantic area against "war"—a systemic goal—

rather than against any particular country, such as the formerly Nazi Germany or Soviet Russia—an alliance objective.

The relationship of the North Atlantic Alliance specifically to the United Nations, the organization having the formal responsibility of maintaining worldwide peace and security, is another matter. Some historians believe that the North Atlantic Treaty was essentially a way of circumventing, or bypassing, the United Nations, or, at best, "a method of shoring up a failing institution."[6] The fact that NATO's Washington Treaty contains numerous references to the United Nations and its charter—a "liberal sprinkling" of names, as Lawrence S. Kaplan describes it—is from this skeptical point of view of limited real significance. "A hasty reading of the treaty," Kaplan points out, "could leave the impression that the pact was actually a codicil of the charter itself, and this was precisely what was intended." Articles 1, 5, 7, and 12 refer specifically to the charter, and the preamble opens with the declaration "The Parties to this Treaty reaffirm their faith in the purposes and principles of the Charter of the United Nations." The executive branch and congressional proponents of the North Atlantic pact were playing a "semantic game," Kaplan argues. "There was an inherent conflict between the treaty and charter that could not be avoided."

Had the allies announced publicly that NATO "would be essentially a regional arrangement" like the 1947 Rio Pact, Kaplan rightly explains, their doing so would have required acceptance of the terms of Chapter VIII of the UN Charter governing "Regional Arrangements." That chapter requires deference to the Security Council "on which the Soviet Union would sit in judgment of their activities." Its Article 53 stipulates that no enforcement action could legitimately be taken under regional arrangements (except temporarily against former "enemy states") without Security Council "authorization." Article 54 requires that the Security Council "at all times be kept fully informed" of regional measures taken for the maintenance of international peace and security.

The "only rubric" of the charter then open to the North Atlantic Treaty signatories, Kaplan emphasizes, was Article 51, at the end of Chapter VII on "Action with Respect to Threats to the Peace." This article affirms the "inherent right of individual or collective self-defence" that UN members could exercise if attacked, "until the Security Council has taken measures to maintain international peace and security." The U.S. ambassador to the United Nations at the time, Warren R. Austin, expressed the view—probably the one prevailing within the Truman administration—that Article 51 does not grant a power. "It merely prohibits anything contained in the Charter cutting across existing power."[7]

My perspective on these same basic facts of adjustment of NATO to the UN Charter is somewhat different. Apart from taking the words in the North Atlantic Treaty and policy statements regarding it as constituting a real as well as formal commitment, and also apart from wondering why the United States and its allies should even be expected to declare their broadly influential, transoceanic alliance a "regional arrangement" in UN Charter terms, I would emphasize that the founders of NATO believed that they were doing what they could to strengthen the new UN organization and its purpose of collective security in the only way possible in the international circumstances of the Cold War that was settling in. Their action in forming the North Atlantic Alliance was not a washing of hands of the United Nations and its ideals, or even merely payment of lip service to it.[8] As Secretary of State Dean Acheson, certainly himself a realist, said of the treaty, "it is designed to fit precisely into the framework of the United Nations and to assure practical measures for maintaining peace and security in harmony with the Charter."[9] Highlighted here is the need "to assure practical measures" that, given the Soviet Union's use of the veto in the Security Council, could not be carried out in any other way. If there was hypocrisy in the administration's protestations of North Atlantic Treaty–UN Charter "harmony," it was a necessary hypocrisy—which sometimes is an ingredient of statesmanship.

The Canadian government, having a strong multilateralism that it wished to reconcile with its defense commitments, had perhaps the clearest view of the way the United Nations and an Atlantic pact could and should fit together. As Canada's minister of external affairs, Louis St. Laurent, suggested, speaking before the UN General Assembly, there could be formed "an association of democratic and peace-loving states willing to accept more specific international obligations (than those under the UN charter) in return for a greater measure of national security." Relying on Article 51 of Chapter VII (rather than Chapter VIII), this arrangement would be worldwide in scope. St. Laurent was not ready to surrender the hope that the United Nations could become an instrument of global pacification. As he reminded his audience in 1947, the provisions of the charter are "a floor under" rather than "a ceiling over" the responsibilities of UN member-states.[10] Also, during the years since, internationally minded Canadians, officials and scholars alike, have sought to preserve, logically and without hypocrisy, the integrity of multilateral institutions even while making provision for common defense.[11] And, as the leading NATO historian Lawrence Kaplan has noted, "the UN and NATO have proved to be compatible institutions; the UN provides for the Atlantic Alliance, and the Alliance carefully respects the prerogatives of the United Nations."[12]

COLLECTIVE SELF-DEFENSE AND COLLECTIVE SECURITY

Why, then, if the world's dependency on NATO has been so heavy, and the United Nations organization's de facto reliance upon it been so profound, has there often been such an aversion to the transatlantic alliance on behalf of so many in the UN community, and multilateralists generally? The basic theoretical reason presumably is that the North Atlantic Treaty, though it purports to be consistent with the UN Charter, has been considered to be fundamentally at odds with the essential, core concept of the United Nations. The opposition between NATO and the United Nations, to put it perhaps too succinctly, is between collective self-defense, or "alliance," and collective security, or "system."

Article 51 of the UN Charter, on which NATO hangs its hat, is considered by some idealistically inclined internationalists to be a throwback to the old, prewar, unenlightened balance-of-power order, conceived almost as a state of anarchy. "Nothing in the present Charter shall impair the inherent right of individual or collective self-defence if an armed attack occurs against a Member of the United Nations," the article states. In other words, the right of self-defense, in groups as well as exercised alone, is thought to be preexisting, primordial, fundamental, and not anything that derives from the new world order that emerged from World War II: that is, the charter itself is a blueprint for a new regime of collective security.

These two basic ideas, collective self-defense and collective security, have been classically and very lucidly contrasted by the political theorists Arnold Wolfers and Inis Claude and therefore need not be elaborated upon in any detail here. The basic practical difficulty is that Wolfers, who was skeptical of the idea of collective security, imagined that adherence to the UN model might lead to an obligation to take punitive action against one's own allies, as the Security Council (with the United States as a permanent member) might require. This nearly happened during the 1956 Suez crisis. Wolfers writes that "Soon after the Korean War had rekindled the hope that collective security under the United Nations would of necessity be directed against nondemocratic countries belonging to the Soviet bloc—the same countries, therefore, against which all Western collective defense arrangements were directed—the Suez crisis brought a rude awakening."[13] The somewhat more idealistic, or less realistic, Claude is inclined to credit the wisdom of collective security. But he, too, is emphatic that NATO is not an embodiment of the collective-security concept.[14]

The best expression of the essential difference between these two basic ideas perhaps still is that of President Woodrow Wilson, who said in January

1917: "There must be, not a balance of power, but a community of power; not organized rivalries, but an organized common peace."[15] In the Wilsonian view, a comprehensively organized international security arrangement, paradoxically, could actually disentangle countries from dangerous military collective self-defense alliances and alignments. That is, adherence to the League of Nations Covenant could subsume and would effectively dissolve such arrangements as the Triple Alliance or the Entente Cordiale.

Even more directly relevant to the actual institutional issue before us now—the NATO-UN relationship—is an earlier theoretical argument that raged after World War II, between the jurists Sir Eric Beckett and Hans Kelsen over whether the new NATO pact could be considered a "regional" organization or not. If it could, then its actions could come under the control of the UN Security Council, for Chapter VIII of the charter, as previously mentioned, expressly gives that body a limited authority over "regional arrangements or agencies." Article 53, paragraph 1, might even be seen to subordinate NATO were it to be considered a regional organization. It states: "The Security Council shall, where appropriate, utilize such regional arrangements or agencies for enforcement action under its authority." Sir Eric Beckett took the view that NATO, as it is a collective self-defense organization, could not be a regional arrangement in the sense of the charter. But Hans Kelsen countered that matters relating to the maintenance of peace and security appropriate for regional action must not and do not exclude self-defense, which is an inherent right that a UN member-state would surely not give up just because it belonged to what the United Nations might consider a regional arrangement or agency. Even if it were a Chapter VIII arrangement, its members still could use Article 51. His interpretation would seem to indicate that NATO could be both a collective-security entity and a collective self-defense body.[16] The Beckett-Kelsen debate, whichever side one prefers, still tends to place form before function. What is vitally important is not so much what organizations like NATO are, by definition, but what they do, and can do, throughout time; they are resilient, resourceful.

The genesis of NATO, in the context of our present discussion, is important to keep in mind. Seeds were planted that are now bearing fruit through the current growth of NATO as an organization. The U.S. negotiators of the North Atlantic Treaty in 1948 and 1949 (principally the State Department's John Hickerson and Theodore Achilles) introduced to the ongoing European discussions an important formula from the 1947 Inter-American Treaty of Reciprocal Assistance concluded at Rio de Janeiro. The text of the Rio Pact was so drafted as to include the possibility of action against aggression from within the alliance itself, as well as from an extrahemispheric source. The historical example on every Latin American mind was the chronic Chaco War between Paraguay and Bolivia (1932-1935). In 1947, when the Inter-American Treaty was signed, the possibility of aggression from outside the Western Hemisphere seemed quite remote. The twenty-one American republic partners thus stated inclusively, without specifying the direction from which aggression might come, that "an armed attack against one or more of them . . . shall be considered an attack against them all." This very familiar-sounding language is, of course, Article 5—the so-called heart—of the North Atlantic Treaty. As Hickerson pointed out at the time: "Conceived in these terms *it would be possible for the Soviet Union to join the arrangement* without detracting from the protection which it would give to its other members."[17] This logical possibility deserves to be remembered.

NATO is and has always been both an alliance and a system, with intraregional bearings and also extraregional implications. It is a hybrid creature. It also has a changeling quality. It is not at all static—as the examination of institutions in terms of such categories as "collective self-defense" and "collective security" can imply. An organization, conceived as a historically evolving entity, can turn from one thing into another and may even seem to replace itself. Consider, for comparison, how the Quadruple Alliance against Napoleonic France turned into the larger, ostensibly impartial Quintuple Alliance, which in turn eventually became the basis of the systemic Concert of Europe. Witness, similarly, how the Triple Entente plus the United States of America, then an "associated" power, became at the end of World War I the Big Four and (though without the United States) the League of Nations Council, the nucleus of the league system. Think, further, how Churchill's "Grand Alliance" or Roosevelt's "United Nations" of World War II became the United Nations organization, with the Security Council of war victors as its inner directorate.[18]

NATO is quite similar, a Cold War alliance that has, latently within it, the possibility of becoming a wider systemic entity. It is worth reflecting upon how the very existence of the North Atlantic Alliance has worked at various times during its forty-five-year history to reconcile differences between France and Germany, to control Greece and Turkey, and to chasten Great Britain and Iceland when they came to blows in their "Cod War." I contend, much more broadly, that the relationship today between Europe, as a whole, and the United States is being profoundly and subtly "managed" by the structure of the continuing, but evolving, North Atlantic Alliance relationship. To put complex organizations such as NATO into strict analytical categories "essentializes" them, depriving them and their operators, conceptually, of flexibility and a capacity for fundamental change.

NATO MEMBERSHIP AND THE "PARTNERSHIP FOR PEACE"

The "test" of whether the North Atlantic Alliance is itself a system, or UN-consistent, is whether it is inclusive, open to appropriate new members, rather than merely a self-protective, inherently exclusive arrangement. Having sought to establish the factual historical proposition that NATO has been and is both alliance-like and system-like, I offer for consideration the following hypothesis bearing on the future, on this volume's question of whether NATO "after forty-five years" has one. The proposal is this: If NATO is to maintain its broadly systemic as well as its narrower alliance-maintaining characteristics in current international circumstances, it must expand to the east progressively and rapidly, including at least the largest countries of the former "Eastern Europe." With the dismantling of the Berlin Wall, the eastward boundaries of Europe, always the main geographical focus of NATO, have suddenly shifted. Hungary, the Czech Republic, and Poland are, so to speak, "where" the Federal Republic of Germany was in 1954-55, the time when it was brought into NATO. These countries are strategically and in other ways important. They have asked to join. And if they are not included, there could be trouble, which, through the extension of NATO, might be prevented.

The more geographically remote issue of possibly including Russia as an actual member of the North Atlantic Alliance, as Boris Yeltsin at one point and Georgy Malenkov in 1954 also explicitly asked for, is much more problematic.[19] Russia usually has been on the margins of the European state system, half in or half out. Russians may not, in fact, unequivocally desire such a close, integrated security relationship with the West. The ambivalence that the Russian defense minister, General Pavel Grachev, continues to show with regard to the U.S.-designed, NATO-authorized "Partnership for Peace" (PFP) scheme would seem to support this.[20] The idea that Zbigniew Brzezinski has put forward of "a far-reaching NATO proposal for a formal treaty of alliance with Russia and a simultaneous initiative to establish a NATO-linked 'coalition for regional security' with three or four Central European states qualifying for eventual NATO membership" is grounded in understanding of the region.[21] It makes historical, political, and diplomatic sense.

The very viability of NATO today depends on it preserving its systemic character. This could be at stake if the alliance/system does not expand. The eastern part of Europe is now in an asystemic void, a danger to itself and others. So, too, is some of its southern part, particularly in the area of the former Yugoslavia. NATO is designed as an international security organization; it makes no sense for it to admit only those countries that already are secure. Its very mission is to "project stability," as Secretary-General Wörner untiringly stated. That is a main purpose of the alliance's sequence of overtures to the former Eastern bloc, from the 1991 North Atlantic Cooperation Council (NACC) through the 1994 Partnership for Peace and beyond.

NATO, THE UN, AND THE "MANDATE" QUESTION

The failure of NATO to react and to transform itself into a Europe-wide organization even more rapidly than it has done—starting in 1989 as the Cold War clearly was coming to a quick end—has meant that it now has to seek a "mandate" outside itself or, maybe, above itself. This partial loss of opportunity for independent, autonomous institutionalized action is unfortunate for NATO, though there probably are ways the organization can partially make up for it.

During the Cold War period, when the "Free World" determinedly was the free world, the leaders of the North Atlantic Alliance had a strong conception of international order of their own—a NATO ideology. The treaty's preamble, which speaks of "freedom," "common heritage," and "civilization," was taken quite seriously. As one cold warrior, the veteran Paul Nitze, wrote at the time: "It is my suggestion that a concept of world order is necessary both to hold the alliance system together and as a basis for harmonizing the relations between the alliance system as the 'coalition of free nations.'"[22] The same logic for an expansive view of NATO applies today.

What has happened, in effect, is that the North Atlantic Treaty Organization is now turning to the United Nations, or to the CSCE, for its moral charge, its commission. It has become, in a sense, ideologically decapitated. More gently stated, it has lost its halo, its aura of authority and idealism—as well as some of its international legitimacy, in a political and even juridical sense. These are indispensable to its conceiving and carrying out its military mission, including its newly acquired function of peacekeeping—which, however, according to its current doctrine, cannot be mandated by NATO itself. The NATO concept of "interlocking institutions," according to which NATO, the UN, the CSCE, the WEU, and the EU each has "a distinct role within a framework of complementary, mutually reinforcing organisations with responsibilities in the field of international peace and security," might turn out to be debilitating rather than energizing and activating.[23] "Interblocking" is the word that the NATO community has coined in self-criticism. Deadlock may well result if an idea of organizational "layering" ever takes hold: the United Nations necessarily always on top, the Chapter VIII–linked Conference on Security and Cooperation in Europe perhaps just beneath it or on the side, and NATO somewhere further below both as a "subcontractor." Manfred Wörner, for one, emphatically rejected the notion of NATO playing merely a "subcontracting" role. He was right to do so. The North Atlantic Alliance, composed of sovereign members, must be able to propose its own contracts.

This critique of the "interlocking" or layering idea might seem to imply that all international organizations are absolutely on the same level. The UN Charter did not, it should be noted, explicitly designate regional bodies as "subordinate" to the UN Security Council.[24] In theoretical terms, a case can be made for this view. In the Westphalian international system that we still live in, all states are sovereign, and they remain sovereign even when they pool a bit of their sovereignty, as members of the European Union have done. After all, virtually the same powerful states are involved whether they choose to act through the United Nations, the European Union, NATO, or another organization. A former NATO Supreme Allied Commander Europe (SACEUR), General John Galvin, reflecting upon NATO's de facto involvement in the UN Security Council–authorized Persian Gulf operation (Desert Shield and Desert Storm), referred to NATO and the UN as "fellow" organizations.[25] This is quite apt. There is much to be said for such a nonhierarchical and, also, informal idea of a NATO-UN relationship.

The United Nations and the Conference on Security and Cooperation in Europe naturally tend to look directly to their own members or signatories, some of whom happen to be parties to the North Atlantic Alliance, rather than to NATO itself, for assistance with the making and implementation of decisions and policies. It is not that they do not recognize the North Atlantic Treaty Organization (and thus fail to mention it in their reports) but, rather, that they choose to ignore it.

NATO itself, admittedly—especially as the release of Cold War tensions has reduced political coherence within the alliance—has tended to favor "selective ally participation" in important tasks. One of the risks of this new practice of discontinuing emphasis on NATO as an international legitimacy-creating organization is that the United Nations organization and even the CSCE will attempt to develop their own separate capacities when they can ill-afford to do so. To an extent, some of this expenditure is desirable, for any successful organization must be functionally competent. But at a time when material resources and moral resources are in such short supply, it makes no sense at all to ignore what NATO can do, and possibly do best. How might it be possible to assure that NATO forces and other assets will be available, when needed?

ARTICLE 43 "SPECIAL AGREEMENTS"

Notwithstanding what has been said about NATO remaining a separate, autonomous, fellow institution, independent of the UN, there is clearly a need to address this awkward double institutional aversion, this mutual allergy of the two organizations. An important key is Article 43 of the UN Charter. This relatively unknown passage provides for the conclusion of "special agreements" between UN members or groups of members—North Atlantic Alliance members or even NATO itself—and the Security Council. This is a possible political and military bridge between the world, its regions, and their nations. The article reads, in its entirety:

Article 43

1. All Members of the United Nations, in order to contribute to the maintenance of international peace and security, undertake to make available to the Security Council, on its call and in accordance with a special agreement or agreements, armed forces, assistance, and facilities, including rights of passage, necessary for the purpose of maintaining international peace and security.
2. Such agreement or agreements shall govern the numbers and types of forces, their degree of readiness and general location, and the nature of the facilities and assistance to be provided.
3. The agreement or agreements shall be negotiated as soon as possible on the initiative of the Security Council. They shall be concluded between the Security Council and Members or between the Security Council and groups of Members and shall be subject to ratification by the signatory states in accordance with their respective constitutional processes.

No Article 43 special agreement has ever been concluded, owing largely to the Cold War. Today, however, the negotiation of these connective links should be possible. As Secretary-General Boutros-Ghali himself commented in *Agenda for Peace*: "Under the political circumstances that now exist for the first time since the Charter was adopted, the long-standing obstacles to the conclusion of such special agreements should no longer prevail."[26] Surely he is correct in this assessment.[27] Some of the necessary conditions have been fulfilled by history itself. The sufficient conditions will need to be met through leadership.

Who, then, should enter into these agreements? The logical first individual UN member that should do so might be Canada, a country that has long done international military duty under various guises under UN auspices and has recently withdrawn its forces from NATO's military structure.[28] Beyond these singular arrangements, which are somewhat analogous to NATO status of forces agreements (SOFA), there should be an overarching "framework" agreement, with guidelines laid out for all North Atlantic Treaty signatories (even those not part of the integrated military structure), between NATO as an organization and the UN Security Council. One must, of course, recognize the probable lawyer's objection that the North Atlantic Treaty Organization is not a legal personality (in supposed contrast to the European Union, which has majority voting) and cannot therefore sign treaties or make comparable binding legal commitments.[29]

What I am suggesting, however, need not necessarily be in treaty form, although the language of Article 43 noting that special agreements would be "subject to ratification" would seem to require use of a treaty-related process. Should this constitutional obstacle to a commitment by NATO as such prove insuperable, a NATO negotiation with the Security Council could erect instead a kind of scaffolding for more binding bilateral agreements between individual NATO members and the council. The result would be much the same. Function, therefore, would take precedence over form.

What this mutual approach of institutions might mean, in operational terms, was articulated in a historically knowledgeable and also farsighted way by Thomas R. Pickering, when he was serving during the Gulf War period as U.S. permanent representative at the United Nations. Speaking personally, Ambassador Pickering made the following "relevant points" regarding Article 43. These merit recounting today, two years later. They are:

- First, the conclusion of such an agreement need not confer an automatic, mandatory obligation to provide troops to the Security Council, but could instead simply state their availability subject to certain terms or procedures.
- Second, Article 43 is silent on command arrangements: The phrase "on its call" does not necessarily mean "at its direction."
- Third, by specifying "assistance and facilities" the language per-

mits members to satisfy their obligations by means other than provision of combat troops—a useful flexibility.

- Fourth, Paragraph 3 specifies that agreements shall be at the initiative of the Security Council, a helpful limiting factor that ensures selectivity.
- Finally, Paragraph 3 also states that agreements may be between the Council and individual members or *groups of members,* offering a potential basis for associations between the Security Council and regionally based alliances. Since alliances offer a more functional basis for concerted military action than a chance grouping of UN member states, this too could be a useful feature.[30]

Indeed it could. Such a conception of a possible "allied" relationship between the United Nations and the "regionally based" North Atlantic Treaty Organization suggests another historical "long step," like the one of which President Truman spoke in 1949 when the North Atlantic Treaty was signed.

A NATO-UN RAPPROCHEMENT

This is probably not going to happen, however. Much more likely is a series of small steps toward that end. The NATO foreign ministers at their meeting in Brussels on 17 December 1992 confirmed the preparedness of the alliance to support, on a case-by-case basis and in accordance with its own procedures, peacekeeping operations under the authority of the UN Security Council, which would retain the primary responsibility for international peace and security. This followed, logically and somewhat incrementally, from the earlier decision of the ministers at their June 1992 meeting in Oslo, at which it was agreed that the alliance would support CSCE peacekeeping operations and also that NATO would develop practical measures to enhance the alliance's contribution in this area. It is widely believed in official circles that these decisions were and remain correct, and that NATO has an "independent" and "distinct" role to play in the future security of Europe, in "coordination" with, as appropriate, the United Nations or the CSCE.

Such a coordinated relationship is now rapidly developing, despite widely publicized decisionmaking and military command problems at the operational level, out of sheer necessity. Mainly these are between the United Nations and NATO, the two organizations that have the greatest competence in the peace and security field. Though not exactly Siamese twins, they have come to depend on each other symbiotically. As Manfred Wörner stated in October 1993:

It is because of NATO's capabilities, particularly in the field of crisis management, that the United Nations has increasingly looked to the Alliance as a partner in peacekeeping in recent years. The UN is fulfilling an extremely important and indispensable role, but it is overburdened and underfunded, today handling no less than 17 missions worldwide with over 80,000 troops at a price tag of over $3.6 billion. Under the able leadership of Secretary-General Boutros-Ghali, who enjoys my admiration, the UN has set the stage for the development of an emerging international consensus toward a broader notion of security that includes the concept of intervention for humanitarian purposes.

But even the most extraordinary dedication cannot solve the basic problem that the UN lacks the infrastructure, the logistics, and the command and control facilities for major military operations. Only NATO can offer these assets, at least in the European theatre. For NATO, in turn, cooperation with the UN facilitates the Alliance's new role in crisis management; it places our efforts in a broad, internationally accepted context. Moreover, it also increases public awareness and acceptance of crisis management. So the future may well see frequent and close cooperation between the UN and NATO.[31]

Similarly, Kofi Annan, the undersecretary-general of the United Nations for peacekeeping operations, has written in *NATO Review*, with regard particularly to UN-NATO cooperation in dealing with the situation in Bosnia: "The sheer size and complexity of peacekeeping operations makes it imperative to explore new avenues of cooperation with regional organizations such as NATO. With its existing military structure, resources and political weight, NATO has a lot to contribute to the concept of peacekeeping, particularly in its more muscular form." As the UN Security Council makes "increasing use" of its enforcement powers under the charter, UN operations have to be equipped. In this context, NATO's willingness to participate in UN operations "holds the promise of a vast qualitative as well as quantitative expansion of the means for collective action that are at the disposal of the United Nations."[32]

This wholly unprecedented cooperation between the two organizations cannot be further developed, however, without political will, similar to that manifested by President Truman in the 1940s with the conclusion of the North Atlantic Treaty. The 1990s are another time of possible international "creation." This is also, in a sense, a postwar decade. In it, as I have attempted to show, old political bodies—one large in size but physically weak and the other perhaps a bit muscle-bound—can coordinate. Though seemingly antagonistic, they can be desensitized—"de-allergized"—and induced to cohabit in the house of a newer world order.

NOTES

1. Boutros Boutros-Ghali, *Report on the Work of the Organization from the Forty-seventh to the Forty-eighth Session of the General Assembly*, September 1993 (New York: United Nations, 1993).

2. Boutros Boutros-Ghali, *An Agenda for Peace: Preventive Diplomacy, Peacemaking, and Peace-keeping*, report of the secretary-general pursuant to the statement adopted by the Summit Meeting of the Security Council on 31 January 1992 (New York: United Nations, 1992), 36. This report also mentions, with regard to Africa, the OAU, the League of Arab States (LAS), and the Organization of the Islamic Conference (OIC). With reference to Asia, it mentions the Association of Southeast Asian Nations (ASEAN). Regarding Central America, it refers to the OAS and a further unique arrangement, "The Friends of the Secretary-General."

3. Manfred Wörner, "A Vigorous Alliance—a Motor for Peaceful Change in Europe," *NATO Review* 40, no.6 (December 1992): 4.

4. For a discussion of the issue of the Atlantic Alliance's geographical scope by a participant in the drafting see Nicholas Henderson, *The Birth of NATO* (Boulder, CO: Westview Press, 1983), 101-5. See also Alan K. Henrikson, "The North Atlantic Alliance as a Form of World Order," in *Negotiating World Order: The Artisanship and Architecture of Global Diplomacy*, ed. Alan K. Henrikson (Wilmington, DE: Scholarly Resources Inc., 1986), 111-35.

5. Address of the president of the United States, Department of State *Bulletin* 20 (17 April 1949): 481-82, quoted in Alan K. Henrikson, "The Creation of the North Atlantic Alliance," in *American Defense Policy*, ed. John F. Reichart and Steven R. Sturm, 5th ed. (Baltimore: Johns Hopkins University Press, 1982), 296-322, quotation on 297.

6. Lawrence S. Kaplan, "The United States, the NATO Treaty, and the U.N. Charter," *NATO Letter* 17 (May 1969): 22.

7. Lawrence S. Kaplan, *NATO and the United States: The Enduring Alliance* (Boston: Twayne Publishers, 1988), 37; *Charter of the United Nations and Statute of the International Court of Justice* (New York: Department of Public Information, United Nations, 1945).

8. Kaplan, "The United States, the NATO Treaty, and the U.N. Charter," 23: "The upshot of these fears was the administration's decision to concentrate upon the literal rather than the spiritual compatibility of the Charter and the Treaty."

9. Dean G. Acheson, "The Meaning of the North Atlantic Pact," Department of State *Bulletin* 20 (27 March 1949): 384-88.

10. Quoted in Henrikson, "Creation of the North Atlantic Alliance," 298. A widely discussed American scheme similar to the Canadian project was the suggestion of *Foreign Affairs* editor Hamilton Fish Armstrong for adherence of like-minded states to a protocol modeled on the Geneva Protocol of 1924; this would permit collective enforcement action when and if the UN Security Council failed to act. Hamilton Fish Armstrong, "Is It Russia vs. U.S.—Or vs. U.N.?" *New York Times Magazine,* 4 September 1947; revised version in idem, *The Calculated Risk* (London: Macmillan, 1947).

11. See, for example, Tom Keating, *Canada and World Order: The Multilateralist Tradition in Canadian Foreign Policy* (Toronto: McClellan & Stewart Inc., 1993); and John Gerard Ruggie, ed., *Multilateralism Matters: The Theory and Praxis of an Institutional Form* (New York: Columbia University Press, 1993).

12. Kaplan, "The United States, the NATO Treaty, and the U.N. Charter," 22.

13. Arnold Wolfers, *Discord and Collaboration: Essays on International Politics* (Baltimore: Johns Hopkins University Press, 1962), chap. 12, "Collective Defense Versus Collective Security," quotation on 186.

14. Inis L. Claude, Jr., *Power and International Relations* (New York: Random House, 1962), 120-21. For a brief application of this distinction to some more recent events see, for example, Alan K. Henrikson, "Collective Security, the Balance of Power, and American Leadership," in *Mapping the Unknown: Towards a New World Order, The Yearbook of the Swedish Institute of International Affairs, 1992-93,* ed. Lidija Babic and Bo Huldt (London: Hurst and Company, 1993), 77-87.

15. Quoted in Arthur S. Link, *Wilson: Campaigns for Progressivism and Peace, 1916-1917* (Princeton: Princeton University Press, 1965), 265.

16. A somewhat more extended summary is given in R. A. Akindele, *The Organization and Promotion of World Peace: A Study of Universal-Regional Relationships* (Toronto: University of Toronto Press, 1976), 11-13.

17. The reference is given in Henrikson, "The Creation of the North Atlantic Alliance," 300 (emphasis added). The Soviet Union, though it had defensive arrangements of its own, considered NATO to be a conspiracy against peace—a "closed alliance" incompatible with the UN Charter. See Boleslaw Adam Boczek, "The Eastern European Countries and the Birth of the Atlantic Alliance," in *The Atlantic Pact Forty Years Later: A Historical Appraisal,* ed. Ennio Di Nolfo (New York: Walter de Gruyter, 1991), 163-75.

18. Henrikson, "NATO as a Form of World Order," 111-12.

19. Malenkov's more tendentious request was aimed at defeating the European Defense Community (EDC)—hence, German rearmament. It was contained in a note of 31 March 1954 to the American, British, and French governments announcing Moscow's "readiness to join with the interested governments in examining the matter of having the Soviet Union participate in the North Atlantic Treaty." Though intriguing, the Soviet overture was essentially a propaganda ploy, and it was treated as such by the U.S. and other Western governments. The significance of the episode has been analyzed by Robert Charles

in a series of articles: "The Soviet Union and NATO: The Would-Be Deputy," *NATO Watch*, May 1989, 14-19; "The Soviet Union and NATO: A Tale of Two Notes," ibid., August 1989, 10-18; and "The Soviet Union and NATO: 'Completely Unreal,'" ibid., December 1989, 16-23.

20. North Atlantic Treaty Organization, "Partnership for Peace: Invitation," Press Communiqué M-1 (94) 2, 10 January 1994, and Annex, "Partnership for Peace: Framework Document." On Russian and other reactions see Bruce Clark, "Grachev Calls for Wider Co-operation on Security," *Financial Times*, 26 May 1994; and "European Security: Under Whose Umbrella?" *Economist* 331 (28 May 1994): 46-47.

21. Zbigniew Brzezinski, "A Bigger—and Safer—Europe," *New York Times*, 1 December 1993. Brzezinski's idea of a formal treaty with Russia (presumably a NATO treaty with Russia) in present circumstances is reminiscent of some of the purpose of the 1887 German-Russian "Reinsurance Treaty."

22. Paul H. Nitze, "Coalition Policy and the Concept of World Order," in *Alliance Policy in the Cold War*, ed. Arnold Wolfers (1959; reprint ed., Westport, CT: Greenwood Press, 1976), 15-30, quotation on 26-27, quoted in Henrikson, "The North Atlantic Alliance as a Form of World Order," 121-22.

23. "'Interlocking Institutions': The Conference on Security and Cooperation in Europe (CSCE)," *Basic Fact Sheet* No. 6 (Brussels: NATO Office of Information and Press, September 1993).

24. Rivlin, "Regional Arrangements and the UN System," 105.

25. General John R. Galvin, remarks at The Fletcher School of Law and Diplomacy, Tufts University, Medford, Massachusetts, 16 September 1992.

26. Boutros-Ghali, *An Agenda for Peace*, 25.

27. The subject is discussed more comprehensively in Alan K. Henrikson, *Defining a New World Order: Toward a Practical Vision of Collective Action for International Peace and Security* (Medford, MA: The Fletcher School of Law and Diplomacy, 1991).

28. This recommendation was developed in somewhat more detail in Alan K. Henrikson, "The Canadian Contribution: From Word to Concept to Model," presentation to the concluding session of the 65th Foreign Policy Conference of the Canadian Institute of International Affairs (CIIA), "Does History Repeat Itself?" Ottawa, 4-5 December 1993.

29. The CSCE, it might be noted, has concluded a "framework" agreement with the United Nations organization and has observer status at the UN General Assembly. See a report by the secretary-general of the CSCE, Wilhelm Höynck, "CSCE Works to Develop Its Conflict Prevention Potential," *NATO Review* 42, no. 2 (April 1994): 16-22.

30. Thomas R. Pickering, "The UN Contribution to Future International Security," personal remarks (emphasis added) at Conference on Naval Expeditionary Forces and Power Projection, "Into the 21st Century," sponsored by The Fletcher School of Law and Diplomacy and the United States Marine Corps University, Cambridge, Massachusetts, 20-21 November 1991.

31. Manfred Wörner, "A New NATO for a New Era," speech by the secretary-general of NATO at the National Press Club, Washington, 6 October 1993.
32. Kofi Annan, "UN Peacekeeping Operations and Cooperation with NATO," *NATO Review* 41, no. 5 (October 1993): 3-7.

6

NATO and the CSCE: A New Russian Challenge

Sean Kay

Since the end of the Cold War, the North Atlantic Treaty Organization (NATO) has sought to build interlocking institutions that would allow the alliance to reach out and find new partners among the states of the former Warsaw Pact. A central element of this effort has involved the strengthening of the Conference on Security and Cooperation in Europe (CSCE, renamed the Organization for Security and Cooperation in Europe [OSCE] at its Budapest summit in December 1994). Based on the Helsinki Final Act of 1975, the CSCE is the only post–Cold War regional institution that seeks to include all of the European states. The CSCE thus can be a very successful framework for promoting fundamental values of conflict prevention, human rights, democracy, the rule of law, freedom of movement, the inviolability of borders, the peaceful settlement of disputes, and peacekeeping operations. However, its structural inability to make or enforce decisions and its cumbersome membership of fifty-three states ranging from "Vancouver to Vladivostok" makes the CSCE very weak.

NATO members had always been cautious about granting the CSCE too much authority, as this would have allowed the Soviet Union a veto over matters of direct concern to the alliance. These considerations remain valid today as the Russian Federation has embarked on a concerted effort to empower the CSCE as an alternative to NATO expansion and to codify

Russian peacekeeping in the "near abroad" region of the former Soviet Union. Despite the assertiveness in Russian foreign policy stressing the CSCE, any working security order in Europe must have NATO at its core. The moves by NATO to act under a United Nations (UN) mandate in the Balkans, to create a functioning North Atlantic Cooperation Council (NACC), and to implement the Partnership for Peace (PFP) program have all been essential steps to compensate for the weakness of the CSCE and to stress the central role of NATO in the future of European security.

All of Europe is challenged by political, economic, and military instabilities in its eastern regions that make rapid-reaction capability and peacekeeping in defense planning a high priority. NATO is the only substantive mechanism capable of meeting these demands. While movement toward building a security realm of the European Union (EU) via the Western European Union (WEU) is welcome in terms of burden sharing and strengthening integration, it does not possess the requisite capabilities, already present in NATO, to respond to international crises. States in Central and Eastern Europe have pressed for rapid admission into NATO to compensate for the weakness of the CSCE, but NATO has no working consensus for adding on new members. Expanding too soon could further encourage nationalists in Russia by conjuring up renewed concerns of encirclement, and NATO would be committed to intervene in new areas of conflict in Europe by nature of Article 5 of the North Atlantic Treaty. Rather, NATO is strengthening its own organization by reaching out to all of the East through the NACC and the PFP and by interacting pragmatically with the CSCE.

The NACC and the PFP are not designed to replace the CSCE. They are means to enhance the CSCE as a broad framework for the promotion of fundamental principles of international security in Europe. The CSCE can conceivably act as a regional mandating mechanism for NATO or PFP peacekeeping while the decision to undertake such activity and the power for command and control are retained in NATO. While its role in the former Yugoslavia is welcome, the UN is overburdened and weak. Moreover, through a close NATO relationship with Russia via the PFP and the CSCE, close scrutiny of peacekeeping in Russia's near abroad, and efforts to keep all of the former Soviet republics facing westward, can proceed. With NATO's role as the core of European security assured, the CSCE can continue to do what it has always done best: establish the standards for and ensure accountability of state behavior in Europe.

BUILDING NATO AND THE CSCE AS INTERLOCKING INSTITUTIONS

At the London summit in July 1990, NATO heads of state asserted that the CSCE and the principles it embodies should become prominent in Europe's future. Specifically, they encouraged the CSCE to endorse, inter alia, CSCE principles on the right to free and fair elections, CSCE commitments to respect and uphold the rule of law, and CSCE guidelines for enhancing economic cooperation based on the development of free and competitive market economies. To make these proposals viable, NATO leaders encouraged the CSCE to become institutionalized to provide a forum for wider political dialogue throughout Europe.[1]

Meeting in Paris in October 1990, CSCE heads of state responded to NATO's suggestions by including in the Charter of Paris a section emphasizing that "our common efforts to consolidate respect for human rights, democracy and the rule of law, to strengthen peace and to promote unity in Europe require a new quality of political dialogue and cooperation and thus development of the structures of the CSCE."[2] Pursuant to the NATO recommendations, CSCE leaders established a Secretariat in Prague, a Conflict Prevention Center (CPC) in Vienna, and an Office for Free Elections in Warsaw. Additionally, the members created a Council of Ministers of Foreign Affairs to provide the central forum for political consultation, take appropriate decisions, and prepare the biennial summits of CSCE heads of state. They also formed a Committee of Senior Officials to endow the CSCE with a standing body and a permanent structure capable of providing for regular meetings of CSCE members.

The CSCE received increased support from NATO heads of state at their Rome summit in November 1991. They called for the continued role of the CSCE Council of Ministers as the central forum for political consultation and decisionmaking on questions relating to the CSCE and for further development of new CSCE institutions. "We remain deeply committed to strengthening the CSCE process which has a vital role to play in promoting stability and democracy in Europe in a period of historic change," declared the NATO leaders. The final Rome Declaration stressed that the new CSCE institutions and structures must be "consolidated and further developed to provide the CSCE with a means to help ensure full implementation of the Helsinki Final Act, the Charter of Paris, and other relevant CSCE documents and thus permit the CSCE to meet the new challenges which Europe will have to face."[3]

In December 1991, NATO foreign ministers agreed to exchange information and documents and expressed a desire to make the collective experience of NATO available to the CSCE. To further the commitment to the

CSCE, NATO promised to contribute to several seminars sponsored by the CPC on the topics of defense conversion and the role of armed forces in democratic societies. Additionally, officers from all CSCE states were invited to attend special courses at the NATO Defense College in Rome and the NATO School in Oberammergau. Shortly after this meeting, the North Atlantic Assembly, NATO's parliamentary organization, established concrete ties with the CSCE Parliamentary Assembly by sponsoring special CSCE interparliamentary conferences on European security and by providing staff support for CSCE parliamentary meetings.

Despite such initiatives from NATO, the CSCE requirement for unanimity in all decisions remained a major obstacle to strengthening the CSCE. Convening in Prague in January 1992, the CSCE Council of Foreign Ministers amended the CSCE consensus rule, which had been the primary barrier to CSCE action in crisis prevention, management, and resolution. The council agreed that in situations in which there were clear, gross, and uncorrected violations of CSCE commitments, a majority of member-states could take "appropriate action" in the absence of the state concerned. Consensus would remain a guiding principle of the CSCE. However, this new approach, termed "consensus-minus-one," could allow the CSCE to take political action against a member-state that is in extreme violation of the CSCE's principles. While this step did not go far enough toward establishing a functional process for making or implementing CSCE decisions, it did establish a precedent for further changes in the consensus rule.[4]

Even with consensus-minus-one, the CSCE still had not assumed the ambitious role prescribed by the Charter of Paris. To compensate for the weakness of the CSCE, NATO created the NACC, which held its inaugural meeting on 20 November 1992. The NACC includes all member-states of NATO and the former Warsaw Pact and also the region's newly independent states. The NACC functions at ministerial level to provide these countries with a means to express security interests and related concerns within a NATO context. Since its inception, the NACC has become an important bridge between NATO and its cooperation partners.

The NACC could conceivably duplicate efforts of the CSCE, but in actuality it is only a forum without a mandate to make binding decisions. The NACC has functioned well as an informal mechanism for consultation through which participants might find constructive ways to fulfill their obligations as CSCE member-states. Rather than undermining the CSCE, the NACC serves as a bridge allowing the security needs of participating CSCE member-states to be raised within NATO. NATO Secretary-General Manfred

Wörner expressed the benefits of the relationship between the NACC and the CSCE: "We do not want to replace the CSCE. We want to strengthen the CSCE. We do not want to compete with the CSCE. We concentrate on security and defense related issues where NATO can offer things which the CSCE cannot."[5] The NACC thus has an important role as one of many interlocking institutions within the framework of the CSCE. Nevertheless, the creation of the NACC demonstrates the dilemma between the urgent need to have a competent mechanism for European security via NATO and the long-term goal of empowering the CSCE in a way that does not weaken the alliance.

FROM OSLO TO THE BALKANS: THE RISE AND FALL OF THE CSCE

As the fighting in the Balkans worsened during the spring and summer of 1992, both NATO and the CSCE came under increasing pressure to apply their collective resources to bring an end to the conflict. There was, however, no consensus in either body for intervention at this time. NATO foreign ministers, meeting in Oslo in June 1992, did establish a framework for future NATO out-of-area peacekeeping on a case-by-case basis under a CSCE mandate.[6] The final Oslo communiqué embodied a compromise allowing each member to draw conclusions to suit its immediate political needs. Nevertheless, NATO was instituting a significant change in the traditional approach toward out-of-area operations by declaring that

> The Alliance has the capacity to contribute to effective actions by the CSCE in line with its new and increased responsibilities for crisis management and the peaceful settlement of disputes. In this regard, we are prepared to support on a case-by-case basis in accordance with our own procedures, peacekeeping activities under the responsibility of the CSCE, including by making available Alliance resources and expertise.[7]

The key element of the compromise, the clause stating that NATO would have to consider all such activity on a case-by-case basis, divested NATO of the obligation to intervene in conflicts throughout Europe as "Europe's policeman."[8] Ultimately, the Oslo statement served two essentially symbolic roles. The first contained a veiled threat to the aggressive parties in the former Yugoslavia that the mechanisms for the possible use of force were being incorporated by NATO and the CSCE. The second provided continued impetus to the CSCE for its scheduled review conference the following month in Helsinki.

When the CSCE foreign ministers gathered in July 1992, there was much optimism that the NATO Oslo summit had established an excellent means to strengthen the CSCE by providing it with a substantive peacekeeping apparatus. The CSCE representatives welcomed the NATO offer for case-by-case peacekeeping, but failed to act upon the initiative.[9] The CSCE did take some small steps in Helsinki to enhance its infrastructure. CSCE foreign ministers called for the continued strengthening of orderly procedures for conflict prevention and crisis management by seeking the support of international institutions and organizations, the strengthening of the chairman-in-office, the establishment of a high commissioner for national minorities, and the creation of a Forum for Security Cooperation (FSC) to meet regularly in Vienna. But the failure to apply the new mechanism for NATO/CSCE peacekeeping to the growing war in the Balkans caused the CSCE to slip from serious dialogue over interlocking institutions. The Oslo and Helsinki summits did establish the principle of a political framework for a direct relationship between NATO and the CSCE but accomplished little to make the relationship operational.[10]

After the Oslo and Helsinki meetings of 1992, NATO continued to provide rhetorical support for the CSCE, yet the failure of both organizations to address the Balkan crisis forced NATO to look to the UN for an out-of-area mandate. In December 1992, NATO foreign ministers, meeting in Brussels, went beyond the CSCE by offering to make the alliance's resources available under the same arrangements for UN peacekeeping. Thus, NATO could begin immediate support of UN humanitarian efforts in the Balkans and the enforcement of a no-fly zone over the region. Although NATO leaders continued to stress the importance of the alliance's relationship with the CSCE throughout 1993, they gave it much less attention than it had previously received. At their Athens meeting in June 1993, for example, NATO foreign ministers declared that they "welcome[d] decisions taken by the CSCE to strengthen its operational capabilities through structural reforms and the appointment of a Secretary General" and would "strive to develop further the interaction and cooperation between NATO and the CSCE."[11] Clearly by this time NATO was looking toward the CSCE for much less ambitious activity than the large-scale peacekeeping operations discussed one year earlier. The continued failure of NATO and the CSCE to live up to the self-prescribed expectations for their relationship had forced the CSCE to the margins of European security by the summer of 1993.

THE RUSSIAN PROBLEMATIQUE, THE PARTNERSHIP FOR PEACE, AND THE CSCE

In Central and Eastern Europe and the former Soviet Union, an empowered pan-European CSCE in which all member-states had an equal voice was initially perceived as an attractive mechanism for filling the post-Soviet security vacuum. But the very failure of the relationship between NATO and the CSCE to fulfill that objective need forced a number of countries from Central and Eastern Europe to seek full membership in NATO. Brussels hardly viewed this as a practical solution, since premature membership would define new divisions in Europe and commit current members to intervention in a region of potential or actual instability. Moreover, early expansion would predictably diminish the existing capabilities of the alliance by diluting the ability of NATO to make decisions and act when necessary. NATO would thus follow the same route as the CSCE and indeed replace the CSCE as an important symbolic regime: in effect, a nonfunctioning pan-European organization.[12]

As the NATO members formulated what would later become the PFP in the autumn of 1993, the CSCE reentered the debate over interlocking institutions. It was now Russia that promoted the CSCE as an alternative to an expanded NATO and as a means to codify Russian involvement in its near abroad. Both before and after the dramatic events at the Russian Parliament on 3-4 October 1993, Russia had begun implementing a more assertive foreign policy by emphasizing its role as a Great Power and reexpressing its strategic interests in its former allies in Central and Eastern Europe. This policy shift reflected the cumulative influence of the Russian armed forces, intelligence services, and nationalist sentiments among the public and political leaders.[13] Having first indicated a general acceptance of expanded NATO membership in late August 1993, President Boris Yeltsin and the Russian Foreign Ministry quickly embarked on a deliberate campaign to prevent NATO expansion in favor of empowering the CSCE.[14]

At Travemünde, Germany, on 20-21 October, NATO defense ministers agreed to admit new members only in the long term and concluded that NATO would not offer security guarantees to the region's emerging democracies. Rather, NATO would support increased cooperation in the political and military sphere as well as joint training for peacekeeping tasks open to all of the members of the NACC and CSCE under the new framework of the PFP proposed by the United States. In closing comments to the press, NATO Secretary-General Wörner affirmed that the "Western Alliance would consider the legitimate concerns of Russia" and that "we do not want to isolate Moscow."[15] To critical observers in Eastern Europe, such an approach appeared to provide Russia with a de facto veto over NATO policy. Many

Russians, for their part, hailed the PFP as a brilliant and major foreign policy victory for President Yeltsin.

Russia soon turned its sights toward attaining a CSCE mandate for Russian-led Commonwealth of Independent States (CIS) peacekeeping activities, by insisting that NATO and CIS are parallel institutions. *Izvestia* reported on 11 November 1993 that Russia understood that while the CSCE is an amorphous and powerless structure,

> Moscow plays a key role in it and hopes to gradually entrust to the CSCE the responsibility for restoring peace and order on the territory of the Commonwealth of Independent States. But NATO is superfluous to Moscow in this game. Russia intends as a minimum, to receive from the CSCE a mandate for *peace-making* operations on the territory of the former USSR.[16]

When CSCE foreign ministers met on 30 November, Russian Foreign Minister Andrei Kozyrev presented a broad proposal to permit Russia to undertake special responsibility for peacekeeping in the former Soviet Union under a CSCE mandate. In his speech to the CSCE Council of Foreign Ministers, Kozyrev asked the CSCE to support (especially financially) Russian peacekeeping missions in the former Soviet Union and suggested that the CSCE should take over the political coordination of peacekeeping missions organized by the CIS, NATO, the NACC, and the WEU.[17] The proposal placed NATO states in the difficult position of trying to balance the strong opposition of the Baltic states and the Ukraine, the reality that NATO would not assume such a broad regional role, and a need not to exacerbate Russian alienation over the growing public debate about possible NATO expansion.[18]

While not endorsing the Russian proposal, the ministers did agree to strengthen the CSCE role as a pan-European and transatlantic forum for cooperative security as well as for political consultation on the basis of equality. In deference to Russia, they also agreed to pursue the possibility of enhancing capabilities to apply CSCE crisis management arrangements on a case-by-case basis to situations involving third-party forces when such arrangements are determined to be supportive of CSCE objectives.[19] The ministers also welcomed NATO's proposed PFP.

Despite Russia's continued efforts to promote an empowered CSCE, NATO had already embarked on its program of increased cooperation open to all NACC and CSCE countries through the PFP. At their summit in Brussels in January 1994, NATO heads of state reiterated the offer to undertake peacekeeping under a CSCE or UN mandate. Moreover, they stressed that the

CSCE still maintained a significant role as an interlocking institution to assist the effort to reach out to Central and Eastern Europe. Specifically, NATO leaders declared that

> Our own security is inseparably linked to that of all other states in Europe. The consolidation and preservation throughout the continent of democratic societies and their freedom from any form of coercion or intimidation are therefore of direct and material concern to us, as they are to all other CSCE states under the commitments of the Helsinki Final Act and the Charter of Paris. We remain deeply committed to further strengthening the CSCE, which is the only organization comprising all European and North American countries, as an instrument of preventative diplomacy, conflict prevention, cooperative security, and the advancement of democracy and human rights. We actively support the efforts to enhance the operational capabilities of the CSCE for early warning, conflict prevention, and crisis management.[20]

Under the Partnership for Peace, NATO will help cooperation partners prepare for joint peacekeeping activities and other areas of increased activity on a "16 plus 1" basis. However, the PFP can also enhance the CSCE. As NATO's Secretary-General Manfred Wörner wrote in the *NATO Review*: "By contributing to the further building of confidence among all European states, the Alliance hopes that PFP and the efforts that continue to be undertaken through the NACC will aid in bringing about the conditions under which the CSCE can become the core of an effective Pan-European security system."[21]

With the NACC growing and the PFP in operation, NATO does not have the pressing need for a CSCE that duplicates in many areas the bureaucratic and organizational efforts already undertaken by NATO. Rather, NATO is in an excellent position to empower its own capabilities as a means of enhancing the general principles behind the CSCE. NATO Assistant Secretary-General Gephardt von Moltke suggested at a CSCE meeting in Vienna on 13 March 1994 that the PFP is "an additional, reinforcing element to the work of the CSCE."[22] The CSCE nonetheless remains on the margins of European security and should be left to do what it has always done best: to serve as a broad regime stressing core principles of European security.

PROSPECTS FOR A PRAGMATIC PARTNERSHIP BETWEEN NATO AND THE CSCE

The best way that NATO can strengthen the CSCE is to oversee a full implementation of the PFP, especially in the area of peacekeeping. With its standing headquarters, infrastructure, command and control, airlift, and transportation capabilities, NATO possesses formidable peacekeeping potential. Successful implementation of the PFP will enhance NATO's capabilities, and more countries within the Atlantic to the Urals will be brought closer to CSCE standards. The CSCE can facilitate this process by continuing to establish and articulate the principles required for membership in the PFP.

NATO has undertaken preparations for peacekeeping through the NACC Ad Hoc Committee on Peacekeeping, which in June 1993 released an extensive report underscoring that:

1. Peacekeeping can be carried out only under the authority of the UN Security Council, or of the CSCE in accordance with the CSCE Document agreed in Helsinki in July 1992 and other relevant CSCE documentation.
2. Peacekeeping will be carried out on a case-by-case basis.
3. It is for the UN or CSCE, through consultations with contributing states and organizations, to define peacekeeping operations, including command relationships.
4. Peacekeeping requires a clear political objective and a precise mandate, as decided by the UN or the CSCE.[23]

The document asserts that any NATO peacekeeping force must be credible and based on the consent of all conflicting parties, and that all member-states of the mandating body (UN or CSCE) are eligible to volunteer forces. Finally, the report stresses that peacekeeping missions should have adequate financing and that the costs are the collective responsibility of the member-states of the mandating body (UN or CSCE) and shared on the basis of the rules applied by that body.[24]

In order to build on the initial guidelines for NATO/NACC peacekeeping accepted at the Athens ministerial meeting, the NACC Ad Hoc Group on Cooperation in Peacekeeping continued to serve as a forum for consultations on political and conceptual issues related to peacekeeping in the NACC/CSCE area.[25] Through a number of high-level seminars the group has focused on the concrete experiences by individual participants and on cooperation with other relevant institutions. The group has also received detailed studies from NATO's military authorities addressing the assets and capabilities required for the conduct of peacekeeping operations; the possibility and utility of developing a database of available resources; and the requirements for forces, procedures, and equipment to facilitate cooperation in peace-keeping operations.[26] The group also instituted its own ad hoc Technical Sub-Group (TSG) as a means of pursuing the development of practical peacekeeping measures in a coordinated manner. Currently the TSG is addressing the need to establish a NACC database in order to avoid dupli-cation with similar efforts in the CSCE and the UN.

Incorporating NATO's cooperation partners into peacekeeping training is a key aspect of the PFP, under whose terms NATO will conduct joint train-ing with its new partners on the territory of both NATO and former Warsaw Pact states. NATO military authorities in conjunction with the participating PFP partners undertake the planning for exercises. This planning is not directly related to the CSCE. Indeed, as the NACC Ad Hoc Group on Cooperation in Peacekeeping reported to the NATO foreign ministers in December 1993, key conferences designed to address the feasibility of joint and combined multinational exercises among the members of the NACC took into consideration the peacekeeping documents and practices of the UN and the CSCE. During their deliberations, however, the primary focus fell on the future activities of the NACC nations.[27]

Aside from a possible mandating or observer status, the CSCE should not have an operational role in PFP activities. The most effective way that the CSCE can assist this process is to continue doing what it does best: acting as a mechanism for establishing the guiding principles of European security. NATO heads of state explicitly declared that strict adherence to CSCE prin-ciples would be a prerequisite for membership in the PFP.[28] By requiring states to be consistent with CSCE principles in order to attain PFP mem-bership, NATO is reaffirming the values that its own members hold dear. As these states grow closer to NATO, they will reinforce the role of the CSCE as a broad framework for European security.

To further aid the CSCE, NATO must assume an active role within rele-vant CSCE structures, particularly by building on its efforts within the CSCE's Forum for Security Cooperation (FSC). Since the FSC first met on 22 September 1992 in Vienna, NATO has submitted several proposals for its activities. NATO foreign ministers stated in December 1992:

> We attach great importance to the Forum for Security Cooperation in Vienna. . . . We have put forward, in association with other participating states, a number of proposals . . . deal-ing with the harmonisation of existing arms control obliga-tions, with defense planning and with the non-proliferation of

weapons of mass destruction and conventional arms transfers. We will continue to develop further proposals. We urge all states of the CSCE to participate in the Vienna forum as well as in all other CSCE fora.[29]

NATO ministers have continued to stress the FSC as the primary area of NATO activity in the CSCE.

Given the broad mandate and agenda of the FSC, it may prove to be a primary CSCE mechanism through which NATO can participate. The FSC addresses three primary fields: arms control, security enhancement and cooperation, and conflict prevention.[30] To encourage initiatives in these issue areas, NATO has presented a harmonization paper dealing with provisions of the Treaty on Conventional Armed Forces in Europe and proposed a "Common CSCE Review on Defence Planning" to require information exchange five years in advance on plans and budget.[31] NATO has also introduced a framework proposal for "Stabilizing Measures for Localized Crisis Situations."[32]

One of the more important tasks of the FSC is to establish a "CSCE Code of Conduct in the Field of Security." With negotiations on the code under way, it is possible that upon their completion this forum could serve as a binding force on military activity within the CSCE region. To enhance this effort, NATO countries have proposed that all CSCE states should:

1. become parties to the Nonproliferation Treaty (NPT) and agree to its indefinite extension;
2. abide by the Missile Technology Control Regime;
3. ratify the Chemical Weapons and Biological and Toxin Weapons Conventions;
4. commit to full operationalization of the UN Register of Conventional Arms;
5. exchange information about national policies on arms exports and national arms export control legislation;
6. and seek agreement on common principles for arms transfers.[33]

Also, NATO has proposed educational exchanges for military personnel, on-call military and civilian experts regarding oversight and management, encouragement of observers at exercises below agreed observable levels (thirteen thousand troops), extending the precedent of air base visits to other military facilities, including major military formations to assess training, and seminars on the subject of cooperation between national military forces.[34]

Alliance efforts in this direction are positive steps toward building an appropriate relationship between NATO and the CSCE. NATO still needs to encourage the CSCE to take more pragmatic steps to rationalize its decisionmaking processes and consultative mechanisms. The CSCE therefore should not create its own security council to mandate peacekeeping. With NATO at the core of European security, it would be neither appropriate nor effective to have any direct hierarchical arrangement of interlocking institutions that would prohibit a defensive alliance from acting when its interests are threatened. However, NATO must consider the role of Russia, and thus it may be worth using the FSC or the Council of Foreign Ministers to establish an informal mechanism for consultation and dialogue on European security under a CSCE arrangement. Such a mechanism can be facilitated under CSCE auspices with a changed decisionmaking process allowing the major European powers to consult directly with each other and act in conjunction with other CSCE members and related interlocking institutions. Attained either through an informal agreement or a more formal arrangement, such a consultative device could satisfy the desire of Russia to give the CSCE a main role but also allow NATO to retain control over its own activities and decisionmaking procedures. Moreover, such an arrangement will act as a positive check against any reassertion of Russian power into the other former Soviet republics.

INTERLOCKING INSTITUTIONS AND THE CHALLENGE OF LEADERSHIP

Often referred to as having an "alphabet soup" of interlocking institutions, Europe embraces NATO, the CSCE, the UN, the EU, the WEU, and the Council of Europe, which can all play an important role in the future architecture of European security. Yet, while Europe has spent several years sorting out the letters, it has become increasingly challenged by immediate security tests, such as the fighting in the former Yugoslavia. All of Europe must share responsibility for the failures to take steps that might have averted this bloodbath in southeastern Europe. There is a strong possibility that had the NATO/CSCE relationship been mobilized in the Balkans during the summer of 1992, the process of building interlocking institutions would have been facilitated. At this crucial juncture, Europe must learn from its mistakes and take creative, bold, and practical steps to build a functioning security order for the Continent.

NATO is especially well prepared to continue its primary function: the collective defense of its member-states. But this central task now means expanding this mission to include out-of-area activities and building ties with former adversaries. Any doubts over the effectiveness of NATO as a political and military organization should have been put to rest by the effectiveness of the long-awaited ultimatum to the Bosnian Serbs to stop shelling Sarajevo or face allied air strikes. While this decision combined with enforcement of the no-fly zone and humanitarian assistance in the Balkans, NATO's response nonetheless came after an embarrassing delay that threatened the very legitimacy of the alliance.

It is very important for outside observers to remember that NATO is a collective body of sixteen member-states. Responsibility for success or failure in creating a strong future for NATO lies in the capitals of its member-states and of its new partners to the East. Within Western Europe it is essential that NATO and WEU Combined Joint Task Forces become a functional mechanism through which Europeans can assume a higher degree of responsibility for defense. More important for the future of the alliance is the charge of attaining a creative and assertive use of interlocking institutions to keep Russia facing West. Attaining a NATO-wide consensus for such goals is not an easy task, as several alliance members do not want NATO to make collective proposals to the CSCE aside from limited-issue caucuses at CSCE meetings. However, as Russia becomes more aggressive in protecting nearly twenty-five million Russians living in the near abroad and as it seeks to reestablish itself as a major power in the world, this task will be increasingly pertinent. It can best be done by enhancing the ties provided by the PFP between Russia and NATO and by utilizing the CSCE as a means of assuring accountability for any third-party peacekeeping in the CSCE region. If NATO and the CSCE take the key steps to land Russia firmly in the West, then the collective concern of all of Russia's periphery will be alleviated considerably.

When Russian Defense Minister Pavel Grachev addressed NATO defense ministers on 25 May 1994, he articulated Russia's intentions toward the PFP by stating that "it wouldn't be correct for Russia to set forth some specific conditions for cooperation or trying to say that we want to occupy a better place, a so-called warmer place under the sun, in the program." However, Grachev was also clear that Russia would request special privileges via an undefined "active mechanism" for consultation with the West over peacekeeping operations, strategic planning, and joint exercises outside of the PFP.[35]

Following the Grachev meeting, NATO political leaders felt that they had attained a significant victory in bringing Russia into the PFP and in agreeing to negotiate a "special status" with Russia so long as it would not be codified in a formal document. This policy was largely designed to meet the concerns of NATO's European members and NACC partners who feared a Yalta II. Most important, NATO has insisted that Russia not be allowed a veto over

European security. But on 10 June at the North Atlantic Council ministerial meeting in Istanbul, NATO appeared to defer to Russian sensitivities to the point of conferring a de facto veto for Russia within the alliance. At the meeting, Kozyrev restated Russia's intention to sign PFP but insisted on first negotiating a detailed and signed cooperation program that would formalize a relationship based on what Kozyrev calls "no mutual vetoes or surprises."[36]

NATO sources confirmed after the meeting that it was clear Kozyrev expected a piece of paper and a broad deference by NATO toward Russia to prove to hard-liners in Moscow that NATO had given in to Russian demands. Indeed, at a press conference in Moscow later that afternoon, President Yeltsin said with regard to Russia's special status that "NATO has agreed. And it is necessary to sign such a protocol. . . . Even if some bureaucrats reject that protocol, we will sign it anyway."[37] Even more telling, though, was the fact that, informally, Russia did have a veto over NATO and NACC activity. For five hours, the Russian delegation behaved as traditional Soviet-style negotiators by haggling over the final communiqué and over CFE (Treaty on Conventional Forces Europe) deployment levels. A senior NATO diplomat described Russia's behavior in the NACC as a "pretty bloody affair . . . an absolutely Soviet exercise, a disastrous performance by the Russians and it does not augur well."[38] After the meeting, some NATO officials openly pondered whether or not there could ever be another working NACC meeting if this was the way the Russians would behave in the future. Because of a lack of alliance consensus on how to approach Russia, Kozyrev forced NATO and its cooperation partners to drop any reference to expanding NATO membership from the communiqué. This position came despite American Secretary of State Warren Christopher's rhetorical reassurances that the United States remained committed to NATO's expansion.

Shortly after returning to Brussels, the NAC in permanent session took up the prospects of increasing the dialogue with Russia. After lengthy discussion between NATO Assistant Secretary-General Gephardt von Moltke and Russian Deputy Foreign Minister Vitaly Churkin, it was announced that a deal had been made that would act as a framework for understanding between Russia and NATO in the coming years. With such a general agreement reached, Kozyrev traveled to Brussels on 22 June and signed the PFP coupled with a joint NATO/Russia declaration stating the broad principles for the relationship. This declaration stressed that both NATO and Russia have an important role in European security and that cooperative relations of mutual respect and friendship between the alliance and Russia are a key element for security and stability within the entire CSCE area. In signing the

PFP, Russia has been accorded a special status designed to establish a far-reaching relationship both inside and outside the PFP. This relationship will be based on broad dialogue and cooperation in areas where Russia has unique and important contributions to make, commensurate with its size and role as a nuclear power, through the establishment of an extensive Individual Partnership Program. Specifically, this would be based on the sharing of information on issues regarding political-security related matters having a European dimension; political consultations, as appropriate, on issues of common concern; and cooperation in a range of security-related areas including, as appropriate, the peacekeeping field.

Following the signing of the PFP, Kozyrev stated that "we do not preclude the possibility that we or other countries should join NATO but there should be no haste."[39] There are still reasons for concern with Russia's view toward the PFP. Russia may use PFP to prevent the expansion of NATO and continue to use the CSCE to dilute NATO's effectiveness and to increase Russia's regional role. The question will be which Kozyrev and which Russia NATO will be working with. If it is the obstructionist model of the Istanbul meeting, then the emerging relationship will evolve on a rocky road. Russia must be treated as an important power. However, there are limits to what NATO can do to accommodate Russia without further encouraging nationalists.

If NATO approaches its relations with Russia in a manner that keeps Russia facing westward and consistent with CSCE principles, then the prospects for a constructive partnership may be good. Unfortunately, at a CSCE meeting of senior officials in Prague on 14 June, Russian representatives rejected conditions proposed by the CSCE for international recognition of Russian peacekeeping in the CIS. Russia would not accept a precondition stipulating that all sides in a conflict must agree to the introduction of peacekeeping forces and specifying that peacekeeping forces should not remain on a permanent basis. Russia's continued effort to use the CSCE to its will rather than to conform to its principles will create a difficult challenge for its PFP status, which requires strict adherence to all CSCE standards.

The situation became even more unclear in early July when Russia submitted a formal proposal to the CSCE that all interlocking institutions in Europe—including NATO, the NACC, and the CIS—be subordinated to the CSCE. Specifically, Russia suggested that the CSCE create a formal "Executive Committee" that would consist of ten to twelve permanent and rotating members. While an informal consultative mechanism within a CSCE framework may be in the alliance's interests, NATO and most of its cooperation partners are not likely to approve any CSCE structures that would permit

Russia a veto over key matters affecting NATO. Working through these conflicting messages from Moscow will be a central task for NATO in the coming years. One senior NATO official has opined that "to deal with Russia is not a walk in the park."[40] Ultimately, many of the core issues affecting European security may not be resolved until long-term economic, political, and military stability is attained in Russia and its near abroad.

None of these steps can be taken without strong transatlantic leadership from the United States in both NATO and the CSCE. The Partnership for Peace was an appropriate response to the political and strategic situation in Europe. However, the PFP still has to be implemented fully. Even then, the work for American leadership will not be finished, as the PFP is only an important first step. The United States must stay actively involved in the process of strengthening principles behind the CSCE by exerting continued leadership in Europe. The strong transatlantic guarantee provided by NATO is the best way to ensure CSCE principles and promote stability in Europe.

The fate of NATO and the CSCE rests with the conviction to lead among politicians in Europe and North America. The ability to change and adapt to new circumstances is an essential quality of leadership. If the goal of a new Europe is to encourage democratic institutions, competitive market economies, and the peaceful settlement of disputes, NATO and the CSCE must make their commitment to each other a functional reality that permits each organization to do what it does best. A pragmatic partnership for the future between NATO and the CSCE can enhance the positive attributes of each organization and play a central role in assisting the growth of democracy and promoting peace and stability as an unstable Europe moves toward the twenty-first century.

NOTES

1. Specifically, NATO encouraged the CSCE to adopt a program for regular consultations among member governments at the heads of state or ministerial level to meet at least once per year, a schedule of CSCE review conferences once every two years, a small CSCE secretariat to coordinate such meetings and conferences and serve as a data and information center, a CSCE mechanism to monitor elections in all the CSCE countries, a CSCE Center for the Prevention of Conflict, and a CSCE parliamentary body. See the "London Declaration," available from the NATO Office of Information and Press.
2. See the "Charter for a New Europe," available from the CSCE Secretariat in Prague.

3. From the "Rome Declaration on Peace and Cooperation," November 1991, available through the NATO Office of Information and Press.
4. The Prague meeting was also important, as it received the first significant proposal for the creation of CSCE peacekeeping forces initiated by the German delegation (with strong support from Italy and the Czech and Slovak Federal Republic). Because of opposition from the United States, Britain, and France, the proposal was tabled for a later date. However, the idea was further pursued by Dutch Foreign Minister Hans van den Broek, who suggested that NATO should have a peacekeeping role under CSCE auspices. Also at Prague, the Council of Ministers agreed to strengthen the CPC by reinforcing and increasing its role in fact-finding missions and the monitoring of disputes and in the implementation and verification of arms control agreements. For the immediate future, the ministers agreed to send an observer mission to Nagorno-Karabakh. Similar missions undertaken since Prague include providing good offices, confidence- and security-building measures, and rapporteurs and monitoring in Kosovo, Sandjak, Vojvodina, Skopje, Georgia, Estonia, Latvia, Moldova, and Tajikistan. The CSCE has also provided assistance to EU sanctions-monitoring missions in Albania, Bulgaria, Croatia, Hungary, the Former Yugoslav Republic of Macedonia, Romania, and Ukraine.
5. USIS Wireless File, No. 47, 11 March 1992.
6. Because of a lack of consensus among the NATO countries, the Oslo summit lacked a substantive operational commitment to any immediate CSCE activity. At the summit, the United States announced that it would be willing to contribute manpower to a NATO and CSCE backed peacekeeping force in the former Yugoslav republics. While the German delegation concurred with the American position, the United Kingdom and France were hesitant. Britain was especially distressed that NATO could become "Europe's policeman." For France, there was a persistent concern that any overture from NATO and the CSCE would increase the continued role of the United States in Europe. For this reason France (joined by Belgium and Spain) was adamant in its position that any peacekeeping request should be made to individual governments and not to NATO as an organization.
7. From the "Oslo Summit: Final Communiqué," available from the NATO Office of Information and Press.
8. NATO forces could be made available in response to an official CSCE request addressed to both NATO and its individual member-states, and then only in accordance with NATO procedures. Thus, a consensus would have to exist in NATO for CSCE peacekeeping. Should a NATO member wish to oppose NATO/CSCE peacekeeping, it could discourage or veto an initial CSCE request and avoid controversy within NATO. Finally, it may be possible to attain a political consensus in NATO for the principle of peacekeeping, but only those states that are willing would actually contribute forces. Without the active involvement of the major NATO powers, any such activity would be of little consequence. Moreover, it is possible that while other NATO states are com-

mitting resources to CSCE peacekeeping, those that might not contribute could free ride on participating members.

9. From "CSCE: Helsinki Summit," background document prepared by the North Atlantic Assembly, 35.

10. Further progress on building CSCE institutions was made at a meeting of CSCE foreign ministers at Stockholm in December 1992. At that meeting the CSCE established a Commission of Conciliation and Court of Arbitration to examine and rule on disputes and an Office of CSCE Secretary-General.

11. Final Communiqué: Athens Meeting of the North Atlantic Council, 11 June 1993, available from the NATO Office of Information and Press.

12. As early as 31 August, a senior NATO official told the *Washington Post* that the alliance was wary about extending membership to former members of the Warsaw Pact because such a move could antagonize Russian nationalists and arouse traditional Russian fears of encirclement. *Washington Post*, 1 September 1994.

13. Indeed, the new military doctrine of the Russian Federation completed in October-November 1993 states that the expansion of alliances to the detriment of Russian interests would be considered a threat to Russian security.

14. For example, on 14 September, *Segodnya* published an analysis by a representative of the Ministry of Foreign Affairs who wrote that "Russia opposes a bloc-oriented approach to security and would prefer to see a stronger CSCE than either a larger NATO or the creation of a 'buffer zone.'" RFE/RL Daily Reports, 20 September 1994.

15. Comments to the Press by NATO Secretary-General Manfred Wörner, 21 October 1993, available from the NATO Office of Information and Press.

16. *Izvestia*, 11 November 1993, in FBIS-SOV-93-217 (emphasis added).

17. RFE/RL Daily Reports, 1 December 1993. Foreign Minister Kozyrev has been especially clear about wanting to transform the CSCE into a regional organization and keep the NACC as a military and political cooperation organization independent from, but closely linked to, the CSCE.

18. At the meeting, Estonia acknowledged that it may be necessary to allow Russia to undertake peacekeeping operations for the CSCE in some parts of the former Soviet Union in particular cases. However, Estonian Foreign Minister Trivimi Velliste was adamant in stressing that Russia should only be permitted to do so under strict conditions and only on a case-by-case basis. He stressed that under "no circumstances should Russia be given a broad mandate to be the CSCE force." RFE/RL Daily Reports, 30 November 1993.

19. CSCE Ministerial Final Communiqué, "CSCE and the New Europe—Our Security is Indivisible," available from the CSCE Secretariat in Prague.

20. Declaration of the Heads of State and Government Participating in the Meeting of the North Atlantic Council held at NATO Headquarters, Brussels, on 10-11 January 1994, available from the NATO Office of Information and Press.

21. March 1994, available from the NATO Office of Information and Press.

22. Quoted by John Borawski, "Forging the NATO-CSCE Partnership," in *Helsinki Monitor 1994*. Borawski, who is the director of the Political Affairs Committee

of the North Atlantic Assembly, points to considerable issues that remain to be settled between the PFP, the NACC, and the CSCE. Borawski suggests that a minimum of five categories of relationships remain to be clarified by NATO:

1. States that are both NACC participants and PFP partners.
2. States that choose to remain NACC participants but not become PFP partners.
3. States as well as the representatives of the UN and CSCE that are not members of the NACC or PFP partners.
4. States that might become partners but might not necessarily participate in the NACC or the Ad Hoc Group on Peacekeeping (for example, Slovenia).
5. Russia's desire for a broader, special relationship with NATO.

23. Report of the NACC Ad Hoc Committee on Peacekeeping, June 1993, available from the NATO Office of Information and Press.
24. To contribute to the evolution of these procedures, NATO has begun to implement practical measures for cooperation in peacekeeping. NATO has articulated an objective of developing a common understanding of operational concepts and requirements for peacekeeping and exchanging experiences, ideas, and doctrines. It has also begun to examine concepts and doctrine with a view to the development of common guidelines in support of peacekeeping. Ibid.
25. "Progress Report to Ministers by the NACC Ad Hoc Group on Cooperation in Peacekeeping," 3 December 1993, available from the NATO Office of Information and Press.
26. NATO military authorities have developed a paper covering generic planning issues relating to command and control standards and procedures, standard operating procedures, and rules of engagement for peacekeeping operations at the request of the TSG.
27. The particular conference referenced by the Ad Hoc Group was a U.S.-sponsored Peacekeeping Workshop held at the Marshall Center in Garmisch, Germany, on 7-11 November 1993. The workshop was attended by 133 delegates at the colonel through major-general level and their civilian equivalents from thirty-five NACC nations, three other Ad Hoc Group participating countries (Austria, Sweden, and Finland), and five international organizations (NATO, the CSCE, the UN, the WEU, and the NAA). The workshop was designed to analyze the feasibility of joint and combined multinational exercises among the members of the NACC in four key functional areas: (1) logistics, deployment, and operational compatibility; (2) doctrine and rules of engagement; (3) command and control; and (4) civil-military relations. The findings of this workshop were intended to aid directly in planning for training and exercise programs for effective and efficient peacekeeping operations among members of the NACC. See the "Progress Report to Ministers by the NACC Ad Hoc Group on Cooperation in Peacekeeping" presented at the Meeting of the NACC at NATO Headquarters, Brussels on 3 December 1993, available from the NATO Office of Information and Press.

28. "Partnership for Peace: Invitation," available from the NATO Office of Information and Press.
29. Final Communiqué: Ministerial Meeting of the North Atlantic Council, 17 December 1992, available from the NATO Office of Information and Press.
30. The working agenda for the FSC is considerable. It includes:

> 1. Harmonization of obligations concerning arms control and development of the Vienna Document 1992 with a view to a Vienna Document 1994 (the time of the next CSCE follow-up meeting in Budapest).
> 2. The further enhancement of stability and confidence.
> 3. Global exchange of military information.
> 4. Cooperation regarding non-proliferation.
> 5. Development of provisions on military cooperation and contacts.
> 6. Regional security issues.
> 7. Security enhancement consultations.
> 8. Relevant techniques for conflict prevention.
> 9. Cooperation in the field of verification.

From the Interim Report of the NAA Working Group on the New European Security Order (1994), available from the North Atlantic Assembly International Secretariat, Brussels, 5-7.
31. Ibid., 8.
32. This proposal would create an inventory of measures for reducing tensions at regional levels. Ibid.
33. Ibid., 9-10.
34. Ibid., 10.
35. Reuters, 25 May 1994.
36. Ibid., 10 June 1994.
37. Ibid.
38. Ibid.
39. Ibid., 22 June 1994.
40. Comments of NATO Deputy Secretary-General Sergio Balanzino on 27 May 1994 following a PFP signing ceremony with Kazakhstan, available from the NATO Office of Information and Press.

7

NATO and the European Union

Claude Carlier[1]

Having dominated world affairs for so long, the European Great Powers nearly destroyed each other during this century's two world wars. After 1945 the power and influence of Western Europe significantly declined while two new superpowers, the United States and the Soviet Union, configured a bipolar world. Because of this new strategic structure, Western Europeans felt compelled to shelve old rivalries and to forge a new unity in order to reemerge as world leaders, albeit now in regional terms. Notwithstanding that desire, European unity was fraught with obstacles, for in spite of alliances, national interest too often predominated.

In the area of defense, the treaties of Dunkirk (1947) and Brussels (1948) allowed Europe to begin the creation of a security apparatus. The 4 April 1949 signing of the Washington Treaty, launching the Atlantic Alliance, completed that process through the inclusion of the United States and Canada and by establishing two structures: a political alliance and a military alliance within the framework of the North Atlantic Treaty Organization (NATO) with responsibility for the protection of Europe and North America against the Soviet Union and its allies.

While the alliance provided a successful shield against a well-defined threat, it was not always as effective in its political role. Indeed, for forty-five years Europe constituted the potential battleground for the confrontation between two ideologically opposed political and military blocs, each of which coalesced around an extra-European superpower. The collapse of the USSR has profoundly altered that geostrategic landscape.

Paradoxically, the end of the Cold War has decreased, rather than increased, stability. In fact, the Cold War, synonymous with hostility, had the advantage of bringing simplicity and stability to international affairs. The breakdown of the Soviet Union, by sweeping away that familiar situation, reinforced uncertainty and insecurity.

The successive breakups of the USSR, Yugoslavia, and Czechoslovakia dramatically asserted the difficulty of maintaining the integrity of multinational states. A return to national cultural and linguistic values is rather inevitable. In the medium term, these trends might bring about the disintegration of other states that are not based on a well-defined national identity. Several European countries have already been confronted by violent conflicts stemming from the assertive emergence of significant national minorities. Until the beginning of the 1990s, however, preoccupation with the confrontation between the superpowers had submerged those age-old conflicts that now are resurfacing at the first opportunity.

Those difficulties, as well as the fragility of democratic institutions and sentiments in generally poorer countries, can result in dictatorships for which military adventures often constitute an easy outlet. Moreover, the evolution of technology and its increasingly rapid dissemination is multiplying the destructive capacity of armaments systems and at the same time proliferating them and placing them in sometimes reckless hands.

Since 1989, Western leaders have worked feverishly—and not always together—to find and promote new instruments of security or to adapt currently existing ones to new situations. In this manner, NATO and the Western European Union (WEU) have been reorganized, the Conference on Security and Cooperation in Europe (CSCE) has been transformed and enlarged, the North Atlantic Cooperation Council (NACC) has been created, and the European Union (EU) has become increasingly concerned with European security matters. After Maastricht, the WEU has assumed a double identity in that it is now classified as the defense arm of the EU, while also reinforcing the Atlantic Alliance as NATO's European pillar.

THE THREAT

The Commonwealth of Independent States (CIS)

The disintegration of the USSR, the dissolution of the Soviet bloc, and the reunification of Germany have brought about both a geographic distancing and a quantitative and qualitative diminution of Russian military forces. While the end of the East-West conflict justified the disarmament of the

superpowers, this process in the East is being carried out in an extremely disorganized manner, leading to the creation of greater independent national
forces in Central and Eastern Europe and throughout the Commonwealth
of Independent States (CIS). The threat to the West, however, is relatively
weak because of the absence of any strong political power or will and the
accompanying weakening of its military capacity.

The recent evolution of international affairs has led to a world that is
safer from the nuclear threat. Russian military strength does remain, however, in the form of the most powerful armed forces in Europe with fifty-five
hundred aircraft, twenty-nine thousand tanks, and some twenty-two thousand nuclear warheads. But despite the impressive numbers, it is a military
diminished by serious recruitment and competency problems. The military-industrial establishment is similarly disorganized and experiencing significant financial and supply difficulties. But Russian industrial potential and
technical capabilities continue to exist, and military hardware has not in all
cases been destroyed. The armed forces may well not be immediately operational, but they could theoretically be reactivated and refurbished in a relatively short time frame—on the order of several months to several years.

The continuing economic, social, and political crisis in the former USSR
lends a certain validity to the various hypotheses about the reestablishment
of a strong, even dictatorial, central power there. The explosion of ethnic
rivalries within Russia, the aggravation of tensions in neighboring countries
with ethnic Russian minorities (twenty-five million Russians live outside of
Russia), and the conflicts that have broken out between different peoples living on Russian borders (for example, Azerbaijan and Armenia, Tajikistan,
Georgia, Moldova) could lead to political upheaval in Russia itself. The
temptation to return to old military policies, either locally or generally, cannot be dismissed. Additionally, the chances of a conflict in the near future
between Russia and Ukraine are good. There are permanent tensions
between the two states arising from a variety of sources, including the settling
of old accounts.

Insofar as nuclear arms are concerned, even though all of the tactical
arms based in Ukraine, Belarus, and Kazakhstan were transferred to Russia
on 1 July 1992, strategic weapons are still present in all four of those states.
The application of the START-II agreements, which provide for a two-thirds
reduction in the nuclear arsenals of the United States and Russia, depends
upon negotiations between these four states, and as long as that situation
remains unsettled, nuclear disarmament cannot be considered to have been
achieved. Ukraine, however, seems still to consider itself a nuclear power. If

it persists in that belief, the very bases of post–Cold War strategy will be profoundly different from those envisaged when the disarmament agreements were signed. Atomic weapons have apparently become the currency used both between the three nuclear former Soviet republics and Russia and between those republics and Western countries, notably the United States, to obtain increased economic assistance.

In the conventional arena, the problems are similar, but on a larger scale. Soviet armed forces have disappeared, as such, while the unified armed forces of the CIS have never really materialized. Much more effort, it would seem, is being devoted to the establishment of national armies.

The Treaty on Conventional Forces Europe (CFE) of 19 November 1990 stipulated a global ceiling for the USSR. Eight successor states of the Soviet Union (Russia, Ukraine, Kazakhstan, Belarus, Moldova, Armenia, Azerbaijan, and Georgia) agreed by signing the Tashkent Agreement on 15 May 1992 to divide the allocations among themselves. The dispersion of conventional forces arising from those circumstance tends to reduce the potential danger for Western Europe but underscores the instability of the CIS.

The fact is that the territory of the former USSR is a zone of instability, as demonstrated by the numerous conflicts going on there; Georgia, Nagorno-Karabakh, and Tajikistan are some of the more obvious examples. Those hostilities are at the heart of Russia's current dilemma, which manifests itself in Russia's inability to define its political line and by its reactive, rather than proactive, policies. Nevertheless, Moscow continues to demand the status of guarantor of peace and stability in those countries and seeks the blessing of NATO and the CSCE in that endeavor.

That situation gives the Atlantic Alliance a new problem. Since these are "out-of-area" conflicts, should the alliance allow Russia to confront them alone or should it try to facilitate their solution? Even though the Atlantic Alliance no longer has a designated enemy, it still has the responsibility and the duty to maintain peace. It cannot be indifferent.

Central Europe and the Balkans

For centuries, this region was at the confluence of the Russian, Austrian, Hungarian, Polish, and Ottoman empires. The innumerable wars that have ravaged this region have left their legacy in the nations, the religions, the closely related languages, and the unending rivalries that characterize it. The weight of history cannot go unnoticed.

More recently, because of the region's economic traumas and the ethnic conflicts that have brought civil war and bloodshed to the Balkans and the republics of the former Soviet Union, a very significant number of migrants and refugees have gone west. Between 1990 and 1992, more than one million people left Eastern Europe and the territory of the former USSR for the West. In 1992, the Federal Republic of Germany alone received 440,000 requests for asylum, most coming from Romania, Bulgaria, Turkey, and the former Yugoslavia.

Regional animosities and rivalries, only temporarily and artificially resolved by the post–World War I peace treaties, were contained after 1945 by Soviet force and Cold War priorities. They exploded, however, shortly after the collapse of Communist regimes. The fighting in the former Yugoslavia already has resulted in thousands of deaths, displaced more than two million people within the country, and forced more than a half million to seek refuge in other European nations. Still other points of potentially violent conflicts are clustered throughout this area of Europe.

All of these declared or potential conflicts are extremely dangerous. In Europe, France, Italy, and the Federal Republic of Germany, to mention only the European nations closest to the conflicted area, can no longer avoid an intervention that will ultimately be all the more costly because of its delay. Not to intervene would mean that others might seek to restore order, be it Russia, which might find the situation an excellent pretext for resuming a greater role in European affairs, or the United States, or the two together, which would definitely bring an end to the worldwide ambitions of Western Europe. Finally, the escalation of these conflicts and European nonintervention would constitute blatant encouragement for other states and other powers seeking glory and military victories, notably in Central Europe, but also in Africa or other regions.

The totality of these dangers illustrates the limitations of "peace dividends" and makes it necessary for the Atlantic Alliance to maintain an adequate level of defense. The number of these threats, the variety of their forms, the geographic diversity of their origins, their possible occurrence at the same time, and the level of danger attached to the destructive capacity of conventional or nuclear weapons moreover tends more to justify a reinforced, rather than a reduced, capacity for conventional military action.

CURRENT ARRANGEMENTS FOR MILITARY COOPERATION

The Western European Union (WEU)

The Western Union, formed in the aftermath of the March 1948 signing of the Treaty of Brussels, has had a lackluster career. On 20 December 1950, the

Council of the Western Union decided to merge the military organization of the Western Union with that of NATO, which after April 1951 assumed sole responsibility for planning defense policy and organizing common defense. Although the Assembly of the Western European Union first met in July 1955, years of relative dormancy followed. Belgium and France resuscitated the Western European Union in 1984 to the point that within the framework of the Treaty on European Union signed in Maastricht in December 1991, the WEU defined itself as the "European pillar of the Atlantic Alliance" and the future "armed hand of the European Union." But for its lack of experience and initiative, the WEU also currently lacks the structures, procedures, and doctrine for force deployment. It is in no position to carry out a significant military operation of any scope whatsoever and has no permanent general staff, but intends to constitute one at the appropriate time, if dictated by crises. It has at its disposal a skeletal structure with only a very small planning unit of about forty people, including twenty-eight military personnel, and a subsidiary office in Spain with about fifty people.

Nevertheless, in the public statement at Maastricht in December 1991, the member-states of Western Europe pledged to develop the WEU as the defensive component of the European Union and as a means for reinforcing the European pillar of the Atlantic Alliance. The WEU demonstrated an operational organization for the first time by making military plans and carrying out operations as required in the circumstances of the Gulf and Yugoslav crises. The WEU, however, has not prejudged the question of whether it constitutes a regional agreement or organization as foreseen in Article 8 of the United Nations (UN) Charter. It is arguably a collective defense organization and not a regional one. Indeed, if it were a regional organization, it would only be able to take action, in accordance with Articles 53 and 54 of the UN Charter, with the authorization of the Security Council.[2] Be that as it may, it is in the WEU's political interest to act in concert with the United Nations; however, political interest is not completely compatible with legal obligation.

While Belgium and France are agreeable to the redevelopment of the WEU, other countries, such as the Federal Republic of Germany, which fears being drawn into a conflict outside its area of interest, are far less enthusiastic. As a matter of fact, the WEU has been in no position to contest the technical superiority of NATO and has only a political role in the Yugoslav conflict and in the Adriatic. In all events, while the WEU certainly has a future in European unification, it has no substantive operational existence. Providing it with one—assuming that members were willing to do so—

would amount to creating redundant military structures and procedures parallel to those of NATO.

The Conference on Security and Cooperation in Europe (CSCE)

In Helsinki in 1975, the Conference on Security and Cooperation in Europe recognized the permanence of the borders resulting from World War II. Within the framework of that conference, the thirty-four countries of the European continent participated in a dialogue on peace and security in Paris in 1990. And on 10 July 1992, in Helsinki, the CSCE declared itself to be a regional organization under Chapter VII of the UN Charter. It followed from the Helsinki Declaration that the CSCE would only intervene with the agreement of all parties to a conflict and after the establishment of a viable cease-fire. As a matter of fact, it has no real resources for solving differences or avoiding crises. Since it lacks mechanisms for making effective political decisions and for mounting peacekeeping operations, its organizational structure will require considerable reinforcement if it is to fulfill its missions.

The United Nations

The UN could and will without doubt ultimately be forced to equip itself with more efficient means of crisis management. While the UN is clearly the political arena for many politico-military operations, the political conditions necessary for its intervention, the possibilities for preventing it from taking action (through exercise of the veto), the necessarily limited role that any single country can take in it, and the imperatives specific to the defense of peace in Europe make it difficult to envisage an effective operational role for the UN in all cases. In all events, this organization, as presently constituted, has no military strength of its own, although it does have pretensions of maintaining international peace and security in order to forestall and eliminate dangers to the peace (Article 1 of the UN Charter).

The authors of the UN Charter, aware of that weakness, provided that the Security Council could have at its disposal a General Staff Committee, which would be responsible, under the authority of the Security Council, for the strategic management of all the armed forces put at the council's disposal. Nonetheless, as its authors were aware of the difficulties of establishing such a committee, the charter limits itself to stating that matters relating to the command of those forces would be settled at a later date (Article 47.3). The Cold War and the political realities of a bipolar world prevented that from ever happening.

NATO

Under the terms of this alliance, the United States gave its Western European allies a security guarantee; in return, the allies agreed to cooperate in matters of politics, economics, and security and to recognize the supremacy of the United States in the alliance. NATO, the military component of the Atlantic Alliance, is essentially a mutual defense pact. Its mission lost much of its raison d'être with the end of the bipolar confrontation between East and West. Its very existence was even called into question after the fall of the Berlin Wall and the disintegration of the Soviet Union. Although it is clearly suffering in a sense from the disappearance of the Warsaw Pact, it has existed for forty-five years and has proven itself. Drawing its inspiration from the methods of the American armed forces, it has put into place procedures, structures, and norms that have the merit of existing and of working.[3]

The crisis in the former Yugoslavia spurred the development of a new policy. Thus, in June 1992 in Oslo the North Atlantic Council decided to act out-of-area only at the request and under the aegis of the CSCE. On 2 September, NATO offered its support to the UN in order to protect humanitarian aid and control heavy weapons in Bosnia. NATO's Airborne Warning and Control System (AWACS) aircraft flew surveillance missions over Bosnian airspace, and the permanent naval forces of NATO in the Mediterranean helped to impose the Security Council's embargo in the Adriatic. On 17 December 1992, the allies decided to increase their participation in peacekeeping and declared themselves ready to act, on a case-by-case basis, under the aegis of the UN.

During the January 1994 NATO summit, the Atlantic Alliance confirmed its determination, under the authority of the UN Security Council, to launch air strikes in order to prevent the strangulation of Sarajevo and other endangered zones in Bosnia-Herzegovina. Nevertheless, the secretary-general of the United Nations announced that he did not favor such intervention, thus highlighting the divergent conceptions of the perceived roles for the UN, NATO, and the WEU.

Indeed, while the UN views NATO and the WEU as regional organizations, these alliances have never declared themselves as such under the provisions of Articles 52 and 53 because they believe that such a declaration could prevent them from exercising their rights of legitimate collective self-defense under the terms of Article 51. In fact, given the absence of appropriate structures within the United Nations and the impossibility of delegating such military responsibilities to NATO or to the WEU, it is likely that one of the five permanent members would be asked to take the initiative in the event of future UN interventions. That state would have to have strong support, both at home and in the international community, in order to act.

However, beyond the function of limiting its zones of intervention, which is not a real difficulty, NATO suffers from two weaknesses: It was conceived for massive military operations in Central Europe and is thus not well adapted to smaller-scale interventions, and it was conceived to react to military aggressions on short notice and under the undisputed leadership of the United States. Consequently, it does not have the necessary political structures and procedures for the kinds of action foreseen in Europe in a necessarily more flexible and cooperative framework.

It is possible to remedy those difficulties, in large part through negotiations aiming to bring France back into NATO decisionmaking councils without necessarily reintegrating French forces directly into the permanent, integrated military structure of the organization. French political and military leaders would prefer not forcing their way on a case-by-case basis into NATO-led operations. They would favor being directly associated with the decisionmaking process and, to the maximum extent possible, being part of the command structure. Such a reorganization can only take place if France's allies wish it to occur and if they create conditions favorable for a return with dignity. The principle of closer relations with NATO is no longer disputed in France, even if some questions are raised about specific issues, such as the perception that the United States and occasionally Great Britain wield excessive influence in the alliance's military structures.

American supremacy in the distribution of responsibilities raises some serious short-term difficulties. On the one hand, the maintenance of an American presence in Europe would seem to presuppose the retention of American leadership in the command of forces for strategic reasons, so that America's military commitment to the defense of Europe can be retained at a credible and dissuasive level. On the other hand, though, American public opinion and the U.S. Congress consider their country's presence in Europe to be both costly and risky.

While the constitution of a European defense mechanism seems to be a long-term objective, the evolution of the Atlantic Alliance is responsive to short-term factors. The question for the alliance is not so much the war of ten years from now as the war of today or of tomorrow. Indeed, after the disappearance of the Warsaw Pact, the dangers facing Europe have been of an entirely different nature and have led NATO to redefine its strategy. The meeting of the North Atlantic Council held in Rome on 7-8 November 1991 established a new mission for NATO as one of the indispensable bases for the maintenance of security in Europe. NATO then opened itself up to the states of Central and Eastern Europe by creating, in December 1991, the North Atlantic Cooperation Council (NACC).

In its new strategy, the alliance gives equivalent importance to the changes in Eastern Europe and to those in the West, resulting notably from initiatives for the development of the European Union. Thus, in Oslo in June 1992, the alliance agreed to enlarge the area of responsibility of NATO so that the CSCE could call on it to maintain peace outside of its traditional zone of action. Henceforth, NATO was to be responsible for enforcement of the aerial exclusion zone over the former Yugoslavia and for any necessary air strikes in Bosnia-Herzegovina. That evolution of events was dictated by emergencies—the crises in Croatia and in Bosnia-Herzegovina—but emergencies can still be expected to endure for another few years, at least until the economic and political stability of Europe can be assured.

THE BEGINNINGS OF A EUROPEAN SECURITY AND DEFENSE POLICY

Since the end of the Cold War and of East-West confrontation, the necessity for security policy has fundamentally changed. War in the Balkans has suddenly made Europeans increasingly aware of their responsibilities, and they have stepped up efforts to implement an effective strategy for preventing war and for managing crises. Even so, Europe has shown itself incapable of reaching agreement on the steps to be taken, and that failure has opened the door to serious situations. War has once again become possible in Europe.

For its part, the United States was unable to form a coalition for military action because of the lack of unity and resolution on the part of the Europeans. Consequently, it was only possible to implement partial measures, such as the establishment of the no-fly zone over Bosnia and its monitoring by allied air power. When all is said and done, the war is still going on because the West has been unable to send a clear message to the belligerents to bring an end to the fighting. In view of that situation, the European pillar of the Atlantic Alliance should be strengthened and should have at its disposal foreign and security policies independent from, but complementary to, those of NATO. The WEU appears to be the European agency best able to fulfill that role.

Nevertheless, at present, the Europeans are incapable of carrying on a protracted military campaign in a distant location without the help and material support of the United States. Certain military resources, such as satellite surveillance information, air and sea transport, and embarked fleet air power, either do not exist or are available in insufficient numbers. The arms systems used by NATO's European member-states are very different from each other, so the states cannot use each other's munitions and spare parts. Soldiers from one country are, in most instances, unable to use the armaments and equipment of their allies. Consequently, their combat effectiveness is limited. Costs are also higher because it is necessary to maintain separate stocks and logistical systems. To those shortcomings must be added the considerable difficulties arising from the multiplicity of languages and of training methods.

In the future, it will be imperative for European armed forces to adopt as great a level of standardization as possible, as well as an extensive program of cooperation. The idea of a European army is at present not a realistic one. Because of the difficulties just cited, current forms of military integration do not go beyond the level of army corps. The size of the force necessary for a large-scale operation is such that it can only be envisioned in the context of a multinational effort. The question of military alliances highlights the necessity for a fundamental discussion about the need for a European defense instrument, especially in view of the long-term perspective of an American withdrawal.

In order to deal with the known perils in Eastern Europe and the Balkans and taking into account the strength in men and matériel of the states in those regions, a viable, active intervention capacity will require land forces with a strength exceeding one hundred thousand soldiers. No European country is at present able to supply that many troops on its own. The same is true of fleet air-power actions, which, however, would be facilitated by the support of most countries located near the zone of operations.

In the case of the conventional Russian threat to Eastern Europe, the disproportionate nature of forces is such that it would surely entail an American military presence in Europe in order to create an essential and significant dissuasive force (both nuclear and conventional) for the short and medium term. It is, therefore, essential to avoid too rapid a disengagement by the United States, because of the overwhelming military inferiority of Western Europe, as economically prosperous as it may be, with respect to Russia, as troubled by advanced economic and social crises as it may be.

In terms of conventional armaments, the relationship between Russia, on the one hand, and French, German, and British forces, on the other, is 4:1 for heavy tanks, 1.5:1 for light tanks, 2:1 for armored vehicles, 3.75:1 for towed or self-propelled guns, 7:1 for multiple-warhead rocket launchers, and 2.6:1 for combat aircraft, using the most generous definitions. Only the addition of American military equipment, both conventional and nuclear, guaranteed by the presence of at least minimal troop complements, can reestablish equilibrium. But because the United States no longer wishes to play the role of planetary policeman, Europeans must take the initiative and contribute more to their own security.

For obvious political reasons, European contributions to peacekeeping operations must remain within the framework of the United Nations. Nevertheless, it is appropriate to note that since at present the United Nations has no operational military capability, the largest actions are in fact taking place under the aegis of NATO (as in the case of Yugoslavia) or more or less directly under that of the American military (as in the case of the Persian Gulf). When confronted with these realities, France altered its previous stance and supported the alliance's new strategic concept.

The Franco-German Proposals

On 12 and 13 November 1987, the fiftieth Franco-German summit created the Franco-German Brigade, independent of NATO military structures. After a two-year trial, it was formalized on 1 October 1989. On 14 October 1991, President François Mitterrand and Chancellor Helmut Kohl informed the president of the Council of Europe that in order to contribute to greater European responsibility for security and defense, the two countries were going to form an army corps in which the armed forces of other WEU member-states would be able to participate. At that time, the Franco-German Brigade became a component of the new army corps.

The United States initially feared that this Franco-German initiative in the areas of security and defense would divide the allies and compromise America's influence and interests in Europe. The thought of a German alliance with France, the country that had withdrawn from NATO's unified military structure in 1966, also troubled the United States.[4] Notwithstanding these apprehensions, President George Bush on several occasions expressed the desire to see a "European security identity" created, and General Colin Powell had, during the summer of 1992, declared that a European defense identity was politically and militarily suited to the management of inter-regional crises, humanitarian operations, and maintaining the peace.

The agreement reached between the Supreme Allied Commander Europe (SACEUR) and the chiefs of the general staffs of the participating countries in the European Corps (Eurocorps) on 21 January 1993 dispelled American objections. That agreement spelled out the following issues: the missions of the Eurocorps within the framework of NATO; the conditions under which the Eurocorps would be put under the command of the SACEUR; and responsibilities for planning and liaisons between the SACEUR and the commanding general of the Eurocorps.

By virtue of the principle of dual command structure, the Eurocorps can be assigned within the framework of European institutions either to NATO or to national authorities. This arrangement favors the Atlantic Alliance, as NATO was given assignment priority. In fact, it brought France much closer to the NATO military fold. By subordinating the operational command of French troops participating in the Eurocorps, France contributed to the establishment of a European security component and to a reform of NATO that went far beyond day-to-day politics.

The Franco-German Agreement of La Rochelle, concluded on 22 May 1992, established a calendar for the organization of a Eurocorps with a strength of some thirty-five thousand troops by 1995.[5] Belgium decided to participate, while Spain and the Netherlands sent liaison officers. On 1 October 1993, the general staff was constituted with a German general officer as the first corps commander.

The organization of the Eurocorps, worked out in collaboration with the Atlantic Alliance, is a complement to the alliance and provides for sharing tasks and responsibilities with the United States. Such cooperation facilitates adaptation to the changes that have resulted from new geopolitical circumstances. Given the wide variety of the Eurocorps' missions, it could be used within the framework of a UN action and also be deployed within the framework of the WEU, both in its role as an instrument of the WEU and as a special European contribution to NATO.

THE JANUARY 1994 NATO SUMMIT

The future of the Atlantic Alliance necessarily involves a rethinking of its missions and structures, taking into account the establishment of a European defense capability, the emergence of democratic countries in Eastern Europe, the clarification of its relationship with the United States, and the implementation of a negotiated solution to the conflict in the former Yugoslavia. The United States seems to be in agreement with the principle of a European defense mechanism, as well as with that of putting certain NATO assets at the disposal of the WEU for peacekeeping operations.

Relations with the Eastern European countries are quite complex. The former satellites of the USSR are asking for admission into the Atlantic Alliance in order to protect themselves against possible Russian imperialism, especially in light of the increased influence of the extreme nationalist right in that troubled country. Confronted with that potential threat, the Eastern European countries have confidence only in the United States and, consequently, in NATO. Nevertheless, their expressed desire is running into two major objections: It reawakens the old "encirclement complex" so dear to the Russian extreme right and could weaken the position of reformers; and it runs counter to the expressed wishes of the U.S. Congress and the American public to reduce American involvement in Europe.

All of this has given rise to an American project, the Partnership for Peace (PFP), which, at least for the present, excludes any expansion of NATO membership but proposes as an alternative military cooperation between NATO and the former members of the Warsaw Treaty Organization, including republics of the former Soviet Union.

The thirteenth NATO summit, held in Brussels on 10-11 January 1994, was the occasion for the formal implementation of the PFP proposed by the United States. The objective of the PFP, in view of recent political and security developments within Europe, is to keep the democratic states of Eastern Europe, desirous of attaining NATO membership, waiting. At the same time, it allows members of the alliance the leisure to watch the evolution of the Russian situation while establishing closer military relations with the countries of Eastern Europe as compensation for certain conditions, such as respect for democratic values and more open defense budgets. The PFP can be seen as a delaying tactic that does not satisfy the candidates for NATO membership. It does, however, appear to be the most reasonable solution.

Members of the alliance have publicly supported the development of a European defense and security identity. They support the reinforcement of the European pillar of the alliance through the vehicle of the WEU, which is to become the security component of the European Union. During discussions within the North Atlantic Council, they announced that they were prepared to put the collective facilities of NATO at the disposal of the WEU for operations decreed by the European allies. The development of separable, but not separate, forces will be encouraged in order simultaneously to satisfy both European and alliance security needs.

CONCLUSION

The end of the Cold War brought about the disappearance of the Soviet empire and the reappearance of truly independent states in Eastern and Central Europe, as well as within the former Soviet Union. Those countries are seeking to generate both democratic forms of government and market economies. Because of these new developments, internal European security no longer depends solely on military power and ability. Political, economic, social, and cultural factors are also important.

While Western European countries are cooperating with each other at an unprecedented level, the eastern half of the continent is in the process of disintegrating. While in the West the idea of settling every intraregional conflict by force is unthinkable, that is not the case in the East, where, from the Balkans to Central Asia, a significant number of groups have taken up arms to support their arguments or to reach their political objectives.

It is evident that an effective European security policy must, in cooperation with the United States, help Central and Eastern European states develop democratic institutions, provide those states with the financial and economic aid necessary for their transformation from demand to free-market economies, and provide cultural assistance in order to help the states, the peoples, and the minorities of the area to calm the historic rivalries that had until recently been repressed.

It is also clear that the institutional infrastructure necessary to accomplish those goals goes beyond Cold War-era NATO. It is in the common interest to protect Europe from the danger of a return to the old geopolitics, characterized by competition for national power, competition for influence among the European states, and essentially national defense policies. Either the failure of the European Union or the breakdown of collective defense structures could bring about such an undesirable development.

The virtual disappearance of the military threat from the East has brought about a shift of interest in relations between Western Europe and the United States. Whereas the relationship between the two previously centered on military matters, it is now more concerned with economic issues, thus revealing fundamental, but previously overshadowed, differences of opinion.

As a response to the new situation, Western Europe is attempting to bring about economic and political integration, including the development of common foreign, defense, and security policies. It is thus affirming the common desire of the Western European nations to assume greater responsibility for Europe and to strengthen European identity. The formerly vital importance of the vast American nuclear and conventional arsenal has diminished. Recent agreements on nuclear and conventional arms reduction have opened up the prospect of a reasonable conventional equilibrium in Europe while in principle allowing British and French nuclear forces to fulfill the indispensable residual role of dissuasion. Western Europe wants to be the equal partner of the United States; but to attain that status, it will have to assume greater responsibility for, and pay the price for, its own security. For its part, the American government is increasingly under pressure to cut military spending. Its troop strengths in Europe are to be cut to one hundred thousand men by the end of 1996. Moreover, the United States is making it perfectly clear that there is an area in Europe in which it prefers not to become involved, leaving the initiative to the Europeans while at the same time retaining its influence and leadership.

Nevertheless, close relationships between America and Europe must be maintained in the interest of European security. Western Europe and the United States must carry out a thoroughgoing overhaul of the contract that they signed in 1949, replacing it with a new construct that will define the role and responsibilities of each with respect both to the other and to the rest of the world. Such an agreement would modify institutional relations and institute mechanisms to implement new policies and new common objectives. If it does not move in that direction, the Atlantic Alliance will surely decline, as none of the allies will succeed in attaining its goals. Such an outcome portends serious consequences for European security and, consequently, for that of the United States.

NOTES

1. Mark R. Rubin of Kent State University translated this article from the original French text.
2. Another problem remains to be solved. How can the parliamentary oversight required by Article 9 of the modified Treaty of Brussels be brought to bear in the context of the WEU's increasingly extensive commitment to the UN, since that organization does not have a parliamentary structure?
3. The NATO "culture" is completely integrated into the mentalities of the officer corps of member-states and into the way that their general staffs function. Sometimes, as is the case for the Bundeswehr, they know no other.
4. Spain has never joined the NATO military organization, and Greece withdrew from 1974 to 1980.
5. It should be pointed out that this well-manned European unit has benefited from the experience of the Franco-German Brigade, which was created on 1 October 1988.

PART 4

NATO and Its
Anglo-American Members

■ ■ ■

8

NATO and
the United States

Stanley R. Sloan[1]

"Why NATO?" is an old question in search of a new answer. Over the course of four decades, the Soviet threat provided an answer that sustained transatlantic cooperation and rationalized defense spending to questioning parliaments and publics. When the Warsaw Pact collapsed and the Soviet Union disintegrated, the alliance appeared not only to have won the Cold War but, in so doing, to have finished its work. Today, this perception of the North Atlantic Treaty Organization's (NATO) irrelevance is changing, moving toward a new assessment of its role in the post–Cold War world. One thing has not changed: The judgment of the United States on the alliance's utility will be critical to NATO's future.

This chapter begins with a survey of the rationale for NATO that sustained the U.S. commitment to the alliance throughout the Cold War. The analysis then moves on to look at the United States and NATO in the early stages of the post–Cold War era, tracking developments in U.S. policy, particularly during the Clinton administration. It concludes with speculation about what NATO might mean to the United States in the future. The presentation argues that, from the perspective of U.S. values, interests, and policies, NATO was more than simply a way of responding to Soviet power in Europe and, in spite of the end of the Cold War, could remain an important part of the way that U.S. foreign and defense policy copes with the emerging new international order.

WHAT HAS NATO MEANT TO THE UNITED STATES?

Lawrence S. Kaplan, NATO's leading historian, has called NATO "the enduring alliance."[2] Indeed, the alliance has endured far longer than many of its critics predicted or even than its founding fathers expected. Why has it enjoyed such staying power?

Until the 1990s, the easiest, historically most potent answer had been: the Soviet threat. The perceived need to counter the power and expansionist designs of the Soviet Union provided common ground for a very diverse grouping of nations to remain more or less united under the NATO banner until the Cold War ended, the Warsaw Pact disbanded, and the Soviet Union disintegrated.

From the U.S. perspective, surely this was the most important reason for the alliance. Had NATO not been established, Soviet power might have carried Communist ideology and control into Western Europe. At the very least, the Soviet sphere of influence would have grown, to the long-term detriment of U.S. political, economic, and security interests. At the worst, unchecked Soviet expansionism in Europe could have led eventually to U.S.-Soviet nuclear war.

In spite of the overwhelming importance of the Soviet threat, one suspects that NATO was more to the United States than just a way of countering Soviet power. It could be argued that simple inertia has kept NATO from closing down its shop at the end of the Cold War. But the fact that the alliance has continued into the mid-1990s suggests that there are some reasons beyond inertia for NATO's refusal to join the Warsaw Pact in the dustbin of history.

Without necessarily placing reasons in rank order of importance, it might be instructive to list some of the other considerations that have given NATO a special place in U.S. foreign policy. A major consideration, beyond the Soviet threat, has been the question of internal European stability. For over forty years, U.S. leaders have generally accepted that the U.S. presence in Europe has played a constructive stabilizing role within Western Europe as well as between East and West. Just as the United States sought to block Soviet domination of Western Europe, it hoped to prevent a revival of the internal Western European conflicts that already had led to World Wars I and II. The U.S. presence in NATO provided a secure framework for former adversaries to begin to build new patterns of cooperation. As those patterns developed in the form of European unification, the importance of the U.S. stabilizing factor diminished but did not entirely disappear.

NATO also provided a vehicle for U.S. leadership in the world. The alliance's heavy reliance on U.S. conventional forces and nuclear weapons gave the United States a decisive voice in decisions about European security. Within Europe, the United States exercised extraordinary influence. This influence did not automatically carry over to foreign and defense policy issues outside Europe (witness European attitudes toward the U.S. role in Vietnam, just to mention the most obvious case). But Washington's leading position in NATO was the foundation for the U.S. claim to leadership of the Western world.

In recent years, the domestic U.S. debate has tended to emphasize the financial costs of the U.S. leadership role. But the U.S. role in NATO carried with it some economic benefits as well. European reliance on the United States sold more than a few weapons systems to allied nations, often in competition against indigenously developed products. More important, the United States benefited from the trade and investment opportunities that existed in part because of the security envelope that U.S. military forces provided for the process of European economic unification.

NATO also created a direct link between the military power of the United States and the ideals that underlay the U.S. role in the world. A Kissingerian view of the world argues that balance-of-power considerations are the most reliable foundation for U.S. foreign and defense policy. Such an approach views ideals or morality as unwelcome intrusions into the foreign policy-making process. But the nature of U.S. democracy, including the substantial constitutional role played by the U.S. Congress in shaping foreign and defense policies, ensures that those policies cannot be carried out successfully without reference to goals that are broader and more complex than those implied with reference to balance-of-power considerations alone. The American people want to believe that their foreign commitments draw on and support the American way of life. This link between democratic principles and foreign policy imposes a set of conditions on any American presidency that can be ignored only at an administration's peril.

The Treaty of Washington gave voice to U.S. ideals and a view of a world that would be compatible with those ideals, as did the United Nations (UN) Charter. Because NATO included a much narrower, more like-minded, mostly democratic set of nations than did the United Nations, it was possible to see the relationship as some sort of community of common values as well as shared interests—more than just an alliance. As Kaplan has noted, "what distinguishes the alliance from others is not just longevity, or even the military balance, but the promise of a genuine community as outlined in the treaty's preamble."[3]

For the United States, then, NATO has been an affirmation of its values as well as an instrument of diplomacy, leadership, and defense against threats both military and ideological. How much of this remains relevant at the end of the Cold War?

WHAT DOES NATO MEAN TO THE UNITED STATES TODAY?

Since the end of the Cold War, Americans have increasingly asked of NATO, "What have you done for us lately?" By mid-1994, neither Washington nor Brussels had answered the question with complete success. The emphasis on defense burden sharing that tended to dominate intra-alliance discussions in the waning years of the Cold War left a strong residue in the U.S. Congress and among the American people. NATO came to be seen as a way that the Europeans managed to extract a free ride on defense from their sucker cousins across the big lake. (To many in the United States, NATO means "those Europeans," just as to many Europeans NATO translates into "those Americans.")

The Bush administration worked diligently to attempt to justify the alliance in terms of future "risks" to U.S. security. It began the process of adapting NATO to the emerging post–Cold War world, but the task was barely under way when Bush left office, discredited for paying insufficient attention to mounting social and economic problems at home.

Bush administration officials apparently did understand that if NATO's mission were not broadened to include more than defense against a disappearing threat, the alliance would go out of business. Meeting in Copenhagen in June 1991, NATO's North Atlantic Council issued a statement on "NATO's Core Security Functions in the New Europe." This statement affirmed that the allies, under Article 4 of the treaty, would use the alliance as a forum for consultations on "any issues that affect their vital interests" and for "appropriate coordination of their efforts in fields of common concern."[4]

Building on the foundation established at Copenhagen, the allies in 1992 began developing concepts for NATO contributions to international peacekeeping missions, first agreeing that NATO could entertain requests from the CSCE for peacekeeping forces and then accepting that requests from the United Nations would also be entertained. The voyage toward NATO's future had begun.

Advent of the Clinton Administration

The Clinton administration inherited the responsibility for continuing the process of redefining the alliance in terms of U.S. values, interests, and goals for the post–Cold War world. The new administration made virtually no progress toward establishing its own approach to NATO in its first six months, as it made virtually no progress in defining its foreign and defense policy objectives more generally.

The results of the 1992 elections were widely interpreted as a message that the electorate wanted its political leaders to concentrate on getting the domestic house in order. But did the electorate at the same time reject all the assumptions that have motivated the U.S. role in the world over the last four-plus decades? The answer, of course, is no. The electorate made no clear statement on the U.S. role in the world other than to say, by inference at least, that the United States could not carry all the burdens of defense and foreign policy leadership as it has in the past.

The rhetoric of candidate Clinton tended to support most of the goals that traditionally have motivated U.S. foreign and defense policies and placed an increased emphasis on the promotion of human rights. Candidate Clinton argued for a broader sharing of global security burdens but did not deny a special international responsibility for the United States, the sole surviving superpower and a force for global stability.

It did not surprise most observers when the Clinton administration devoted top priority to domestic economic and social issues in its early months in office. President Clinton's aides reportedly said that he had delegated foreign policy formulation to the secretaries of state and defense and the national security adviser. According to press reports, White House sources said that on domestic policy issues, "Mr. Clinton is personally absorbed in the give and take," but on foreign policy issues, "he has basically asked these aides to work out solutions and then submit them to him to be approved or rejected."[5]

Former President Bush's image as a political leader consumed by his interest and involvement in foreign and defense policy had helped open the door to the White House for Bill Clinton, and the new president and his administration appeared to want to make their mark on the domestic affairs of the nation as quickly as possible. As the new administration took office, public opinion polls showed that Americans were much more concerned about the economy, unemployment, the deficit, health care, and other domestic issues than they were about any foreign policy problem visible at the time.[6] NATO was a very small blip on the radar screen of U.S. priorities.

In addition, during his first several months in office, President Clinton appeared much more comfortable dealing with the details and designs of domestic policy, and less sure of himself in the foreign and defense policy arenas. One press report based on interviews with administration officials suggested that "the best way of describing Mr. Clinton's approach to the world is that he comes to it very much as a governor, and not a grand geo-political theoretician. He keeps asking on every issue, 'How will it change things on the ground? How will it change people's lives?'"[7] One critic observed that "curiously, the Clinton Administration, bristling as it is with academic talent, has been content to live hand to mouth on foreign policy. . . . Despite Clinton's campaign criticism of President George Bush's lack of vision, and despite promises of 'a fresh assessment' of U.S. foreign policy, the President, it seems, either doesn't comprehend or doesn't wish to grapple with the fact that in foreign policy he stands at a historic crossroads."[8] In their public statements, President Clinton and Secretary of State Warren M. Christopher, for the most part, emphasized continuity in traditional U.S. alliances and bilateral relationships. However, in one major change of emphasis, while the Bush administration had been reluctant to lead on behalf of aid to the former Soviet Union to support democratic development there until certain conditions were met, the Clinton administration made early aid a primary focus of its foreign policy.

During the 1992 campaign, Bill Clinton had suggested that he favored a greater U.S. military role in the former Yugoslavia. In office, however, the administration's attempts to develop policy initiatives that responded to humanitarian as well as geostrategic concerns were failures, both for the international community's attempt to promote a peaceful solution to the conflict and for the leadership image of the United States abroad. The new administration found it exceedingly difficult to produce coherent and polit-ically sustainable options for dealing with the conflict in the former Yugoslavia, perhaps reflecting not only the complexity of the challenge but also the administration's lack of a philosophy concerning the use of force on behalf of foreign policy objectives.

The "Tarnoff Doctrine"

Of all the administration's foreign policy statements in its first six months, none had more impact than some not-for-attribution comments taken from a May 1993 press background briefing by a "high-ranking administration official." That official was subsequently identified as Undersecretary of State for Political Affairs Peter Tarnoff, the third-ranking official in the State Department.

According to press reports, Tarnoff said that "it is necessary to make the point that our economic interests are paramount." He added that, with limited resources, the United States must "define the extent of its commitment and make a commitment commensurate with those realities." With regard to the use of force, Tarnoff said, "We simply don't have the leverage, we don't have the influence, we don't have the inclination to use military force, we certainly don't have the money to bring to bear the kind of pressure which will produce positive results anytime soon."[9] Such an approach, leading the United States toward the position of a self-deterred power, would imply fundamental changes in the U.S. role in the world generally and, more specifically, in NATO.[10]

White House officials and Secretary of State Christopher immediately disavowed the Tarnoff statements.[11] In a speech at the University of Minnesota, Christopher said that "the need for American leadership is undiminished. . . . Where collective responses are more appropriate, we will lead in mobilizing responses. But make no mistake, we will lead."[12] To emphasize the point, the Clinton administration called for a NATO summit meeting to set a new course for America's principal alliance.

The Tarnoff comments, even after the high-level denials, seemed to reflect a genuine desire in the new administration to share the costs, and a consequent willingness to share the leadership, with other countries in meeting global problems. But Tarnoff's remarks, which came before the administration had developed any coherent philosophy or framework for its foreign policy, were not bounded by policy definitions and were left wide open for interpretation.

Following the Tarnoff remarks, a torrent of op-ed commentaries appeared challenging the wisdom of pursuing his stated vision, and its implied drift toward a diminished U.S. leadership role. Brent Scowcroft, former national security adviser in the Bush and Ford administrations, wrote that "[a] better world can emerge only as a result of strong and enlightened leadership. Whether we like it or not, the U.S. alone can provide that leadership."[13] Likewise, Michael Mandelbaum, who had been a foreign policy adviser to candidate Bill Clinton, wrote that if the Clinton foreign policy architects do not "rally public support for leadership . . . what has come to be known as the Tarnoff doctrine, with its connotation of American weakness and retreat, could become a self-fulfilling prophecy, with tragic consequences for the whole world."[14]

NATO's Place in a New Foreign Policy Network

In September 1993, the administration reacted to growing criticism that it had no foreign policy. President Clinton's national security adviser, Anthony Lake, proposed a strategy that would seek to enlarge the area of democracy abroad to replace the policy of containing communism, making it clear that the administration would resist "isolationist" temptations. According to Lake, "Geography and history always have made Americans wary of foreign entanglements. Now economic anxiety fans that wariness. Calls from the left and right to stay at home rather than engage abroad are reinforced by the rhetoric of the neo-know-nothings."[15]

But Lake cautioned that a policy seeking to engage the United States in support of democracy worldwide did not mean that the United States would become involved in every conflict or source of instability around the globe. Lake said that the United States would attempt to bring diplomacy to bear "always," but that "there will be relatively few intra-national ethnic conflicts that justify our military intervention. Ultimately on these and other humanitarian needs, we will have to pick and choose, although we will always do our best."[16]

With regard to the balance between unilateralism and multilateralism, Lake said that the administration believes that "We should act multilaterally where doing so advances our interests—and we should act unilaterally when that will serve our purpose."[17] This comment may have reflected the fact that when the administration began translating a more multilateral approach into operational decisions, it ran into complications. The crises in Somalia and the former Yugoslavia had raised concern in Congress and throughout the country about any open-ended commitment to participate in internationally organized multilateral military operations, particularly if the United States would not be able to shape and control such operations. For example, the House Committee on Appropriations approved restrictions on spending for international missions that would require the administration to give at least fifteen days' notice before approving the deployment of U.S. troops for such missions and to specify the financing arrangements and the likely duration of the commitment.[18]

Responding to such concerns, U.S. Ambassador to the United Nations Madeleine Albright, in a major address to the National War College in September 1993, backed away from earlier administration enthusiasm about multilateral operations.[19] While still supporting increased multilateralism, she said that the United States would want several questions answered before deciding whether to support UN peacekeeping or peace-enforcement operations. The questions included: Does the mission have clear definable objectives? Is a cease-fire in place, and have the parties agreed to a UN presence? Are the necessary financial and human resources available? Can an "end point" to the operation be identified?

When President Clinton went before the UN General Assembly later in the month, he confirmed a more circumspect administration attitude toward the role of the United Nations in international security operations, observing that "the United Nations simply cannot become engaged in every one of the world's conflicts."[20]

This policy approach appeared to mollify domestic critics of multilateralism, but it raised new questions about the willingness of the United States to act at all unless vital U.S. interests were directly threatened. Criteria intended to produce financial and time limits on U.S. military commitments may seem quite reasonable, but they are difficult or impossible to meet with strong certitude for many situations. Using this set of criteria for affirming U.S. support therefore might result in false projections, policy paralysis, or protracted decisionmaking while a crisis worsened or was resolved unfavorably in terms of U.S. interests.

The statements by the administration appeared to create an important opening for NATO. The president and his top advisers had called on traditional American values, attempted to translate them into a policy designed for the post–Cold War world, and acknowledged the continuing need to bring power to bear in a way that would deter potential aggressors. At the same time, the administration was backing away from reliance on the United Nations as the venue of choice for multilateral military operations. The speeches affirmed the importance of NATO but failed to identify what new role the alliance would play in the "enlargement" strategy.

Meanwhile, other dynamics in the U.S.-European relationship were running away from cooperation and toward confrontation. The Clinton administration remained irritated that Great Britain and France had not accepted the U.S. proposal in the spring of 1993 to lift the arms embargo and use airpower to strike Bosnian Serb forces. The allies remained skeptical about the U.S. approach as long as their peacekeeping forces on the ground did not have a mandate to participate in more active military operations and could be the target for retaliation by Serbian forces. In addition, the U.S. position lacked credibility in their eyes because the administration was unwilling to commit any ground forces to Bosnia until a peace settlement had been reached.

The NATO Summit Agenda[21]

When the Clinton administration proposed that a NATO summit be held late in 1993 or early in 1994, there apparently was no consensus in the administration concerning what the summit should accomplish. As the summit approached, however, three issues dominated transatlantic discussions of the summit agenda: mission, membership, and U.S. and European roles in the alliance.

NATO's Mission.

The most basic issue was NATO's mission: What purpose should the alliance serve in the absence of a single overwhelming threat to allied security? The answer to that question had been emerging over the preceding few years. When NATO governments in 1992 agreed to offer NATO cooperation and assets to support peacekeeping operations in response to requests from the CSCE or the United Nations, they did not decide what priority NATO should give to such tasks. Different schools of thought implied varying approaches to the summit.

- Stand-pat: One approach held that NATO could concentrate on preserving the core of consultation and defense cooperation focused on defense of the vital interests of the members in Europe. According to this approach, adding peacekeeping and peace-enforcing tasks beyond NATO's borders would be divisive and undermine the cooperation that has developed over the last four-plus decades.
- Evolve: Another approach suggested that the summit continue the evolutionary process of the last few years and enable the alliance to adjust to new tasks progressively over several years. This option implied a process of adapting NATO practices and procedures, first in Europe and then perhaps beyond, but in an incremental manner.
- Renew: According to another perspective, unless the summit strongly impressed U.S. and allied public and parliamentary opinion about the need for cooperation on "crisis management," including peacekeeping and peace-enforcing missions outside as well as within Europe, support for the alliance—the rationale for European defense spending and for the U.S. troop presence in Europe—would decline dramatically. This approach suggested radical changes in the structure and armaments of NATO forces, as well as NATO planning, training, and exercises to prepare allied forces for new missions.

NATO's Membership.

The membership issue was created by the proclaimed interest of virtually all former Warsaw Pact and Soviet successor states in joining NATO. In response, the allies in December 1991 had created the North Atlantic Cooperation Council (NACC), a consultative process without structure or staff, to develop military ties with these states without satisfying their desire to join NATO.

Poland, the Czech Republic, and Hungary energetically pursued the case for expanding NATO. These governments saw membership as a guarantee against future Russian influence, a source of psychological support for their new democratic systems, a token of acceptance into the community of democratic nations, and a direct link to the power and influence of the United States. These arguments made sense to many in the West who saw an expansion of NATO to the East as consistent with the goals articulated in the Treaty of Washington. The German government had been more supportive of expanding NATO to the East than other allies, but even it was divided internally concerning modalities. The British and French and some other allies had serious reservations about expanding NATO membership.

Several issues gave pause to many allied governments. Some U.S. and allied officials were concerned that early membership for the three leading contenders would strengthen the hand of Russian hard-liners who said the West was taking advantage of Russia's weakness. Recent electoral gains of former Communists in parliamentary elections in Poland and the risk of weakening alliance cohesion by opening the door to new members were also argued as reasons to move slowly. There were three broad perspectives on this question.

1. Preserve core membership: This approach was based on the belief that adding new members to the alliance would weaken alliance cohesion and make decisionmaking much more difficult. This implied developing military cooperation with former Warsaw Pact nations and successor Soviet states but keeping the membership issue off the agenda. Variations included creating new security structures to accommodate the Central and Eastern Europeans, or strengthening the NACC and/or the CSCE to respond to their concerns.

2. Begin process of expansion: This approach acknowledged the difficulties associated with expanded membership but accepted that the alliance must respond to the entreaties of the Central and Eastern European states as well as take into account Russian concerns. This option implied a strategy that would open the door to membership but pursue expansion carefully and incrementally.

3. Support early expansion: This approach called for early acceptance of the bids by Poland, the Czech Republic, Slovakia, and
Hungary to join the alliance, while keeping the option open for
other former Warsaw Pact states, Russia, and other former Soviet
republics. This perspective suggested the need to avoid a security
vacuum in Central Europe, to support the spread of democracy,
and to promote longer-term benefits of military cooperation
with these states.

U.S. and European Roles in the Alliance.

The relationship between U.S. and European roles in the alliance was given
new prominence when the members of the European Community (EC) (in
the Treaty on European Union, completed in December 1991 in Maastricht,
the Netherlands) agreed to work toward a "European security and defense
identity" by expanding their political cooperation into the area of defense.
They also decided that the Western European Union (WEU) would become
the EC's defense arm, within the overall framework of the transatlantic
alliance. Since Maastricht was signed, however, the EC countries had run
into a variety of obstacles to rapid implementation of the treaty, including its
defense aspects. Although EC members remained committed to the long-term
goal of a European defense identity, they had more recently concentrated on
making the various elements of European defense cooperation—for example,
the Franco-German Eurocorps—compatible with NATO.

The Bush administration had worried that European defense cooperation would undermine NATO unity and had criticized most proposals
aimed at strengthening the European defense identity, moderating its stance
only toward the end of its term in office. The Clinton administration, by
contrast, said that it supported the goals adopted by the Europeans at
Maastricht, but the American discussion nonetheless still included a variety of perspectives:

- Preserve U.S. role: This approach argued that the alliance still
relied on U.S. leadership, particularly within the integrated military structure, and that the United States could not depend on
the Europeans to provide effective leadership, even under
reduced threat conditions. This option implied retaining an
American as NATO's Supreme Allied Commander (SACEUR) as
well as active U.S. leadership in political consultations and consensus building.

- Encourage greater European role: This approach was based on the perceived need to shift defense burdens from U.S. shoulders to those of the Europeans as well as on the European desire to have more say in alliance decisionmaking. It implied greater European self-reliance for defense in Europe as well as more contributions to global security requirements. This option, pursued by the Clinton administration, nonetheless accepted that change would be gradual and that the United States could not make Europe more united than European governments were willing and able to do on their own.
- Europeanize the alliance: This approach implied an urgent need to let the Europeans manage their own security affairs while the United States refocused its energies on domestic issues and other security problems. It assumed that Western Europe would only take on responsibility for its own security if the United States left the European countries no other choice.

U.S. Tilt Away from Europe?[22]

Late in 1993, as preparations for the NATO summit approached a critical juncture, statements by Clinton administration officials appeared to tilt U.S. policy away from the traditional close partnership with Western Europe. This policy tilt created the impression that the administration was taking a zero-sum approach to relations with Asia and Europe, requiring that U.S. policy shift its focus away from Europe in order to construct a more profitable relationship with Asia. The tilt was seen in:

- President Clinton's renewed recriminations aimed at France and the United Kingdom for opposing the administration's proposal for a "lift (the arms embargo) and strike (Serbian targets)" policy toward Bosnia;
- Secretary of State Christopher's assertion that "Western Europe is no longer the dominant area of the world" and that Washington had been too "Eurocentric" for too long;
- The publicity hype preceding the Asia-Pacific Economic Cooperation (APEC) summit meeting that included unnamed "senior administration diplomats and trade officials," implying that APEC relationships were becoming more important to the United States than those with Europe.

European diplomats in Washington, who had been reassured that the United States could pursue an activist Asian policy without sacrificing good relations with Europe, asked what had changed. Some sought to dismiss the appearance of a tilt toward Asia as a tactic to win concessions in the endgame of the global General Agreement on Tariffs and Trade (GATT) negotiations. They hoped that the United States had not turned away from a unifying, global approach toward a new, divisive, region-vs.-region tack.

A Successful Summit

Fortunately for transatlantic relations, the GATT negotiations reached a compromise solution, removing one apparent stimulus for administration charges aimed at Europe and eliminating one possible obstacle to a successful transatlantic summit meeting.

The NATO leaders faced the considerable challenge of "renewing" the alliance and reconciling a variety of conflicting views on most issues. They responded with decisions that solved few problems but did provide coping mechanisms that could help adjust NATO to the evolving European and international security scene. The Partnership for Peace program provided an artful compromise allowing all European states that wished to move closer to the alliance to do so at their own pace. The program postponed decisions that, sooner or later, would be required to respond to the strong desires of several new democracies to become full NATO members. It promised to buy time that could be used to prepare countries for eventual membership and to convince Russia that its interests were not being threatened in the process.

The summit declaration's support for the process of European security and defense cooperation helped move the allies toward compromising a Franco-American debate that had unnecessarily handicapped transatlantic cooperation. The agreement to restructure NATO forces to facilitate formation of Combined Joint Task Forces (CJTF) (discussed later in more detail) would allow a more versatile application of NATO forces to military requirements in and outside of Europe. The leaders also strengthened NATO's commitment to use force in Bosnia to stem the brutality being inflicted on innocent civilians. Most important, the summit further consolidated the rapprochement in U.S.-French security relationships.

The progress was facilitated by changed attitudes in Washington and Paris toward some long-standing philosophical differences over transatlantic relations. In Paris, the French government had taken a more pragmatic attitude toward military cooperation with NATO, becoming directly involved in NATO preparations for peace missions and also regarding NATO's response to the Bosnian conflict. In Washington, the Clinton administration did its part by rejecting the Bush administration's skepticism about

European security and defense cooperation. This hallmark of the administration's policy toward Europe yielded multiple references in the summit declaration to the importance of such cooperation and the constructive role played by the Western European Union (WEU). (The declaration included no fewer than eight references to the WEU, seven references each to the European Security and Defense Identity and European Union, and two each to the Maastricht Treaty on European Union and the Union's Common Foreign and Security Policy goal.) This warm embrace of European unity goals and institutions overcame the split that had previously blocked areas of security cooperation that appeared otherwise to be in the interests of France and the United States.

The summit therefore not only avoided open acrimony but also helped ameliorate some bad feelings raised by the administration's seemingly anti-European strategy. In spite of this progress, difficult challenges lie ahead.

Gap between Rhetoric and Reality

The constructive trends in U.S.-French relations, in and of themselves, did not guarantee that Europe would be more capable of assuming security burdens than it was before. All the summit references to European unity were essentially bouquets presented by the United States rather than new accomplishments or goals offered by the European Union members. In fact, the post–Cold War cuts in defense spending of most European allies (except France) were rapidly eroding military capabilities available for cooperative European or NATO missions.

Further, the current progress in U.S.-French relations may have reached its limit, at least for a while. Following the summit, French President François Mitterrand appeared unwilling to allow France to move any closer to NATO. Further progress may have to wait until after presidential elections scheduled for 1995 determine Mitterrand's successor.

In addition, NATO would not benefit if the Clinton administration's greater tolerance for European security and defense cooperation became simply a way for the United States to reduce its role in Europe at a time when the alliance still does not work particularly well without U.S. leadership.

Shifting Relationships among Major Allies

Ironically, the positive developments in U.S. relations with France may have stimulated less encouraging dynamics in U.S. relations with the United Kingdom and Germany. The political balance in transatlantic relations since France left NATO's integrated command structure in the mid-1960s was heavily influenced by France's independent and, from an American perspective, difficult position. The French position created special roles as well as problems for the United Kingdom and Germany.

After France's departure, Germany became the dominant continental partner for the United States in the alliance. U.S. and German cooperation on policy issues inevitably guaranteed alliance consensus. Germany also began to carry more water for the United States in relations with France. This special role of trying to work out compromise solutions between often-differing French and U.S. policy lines was uncomfortable for Germany, but it also bestowed on it a certain status. To the extent that the United States resumes a more direct dialogue with France, Germany may find itself playing a less conflicted but also a less important role in the alliance, particularly given the limitations on Germany's military contributions to security operations beyond its borders.

There may be implications for British-American relations as well. The extent to which the United States can deal effectively with France calls into question the special role that the United Kingdom had played as an interpreter of U.S. views to Europe and of European perspectives to Washington. The aid that British officials reportedly provided to George Bush's unsuccessful reelection campaign already had made John Major's Conservative government suspect in the eyes of the Clinton administration. The U.S. rapprochement with France and U.S.-British differences over policy toward Bosnia and Northern Ireland apparently created a sufficiently large gulf between the United States and the United Kingdom to lead some U.S. diplomats to complain that the British had gone from being the most helpful to one of the most difficult partners in the alliance. Prime Minister Major's successful visit to Washington early in 1994, crowned by an invitation to stay in the White House, seemed to smooth over some Anglo-American difficulties, but longer-term trends may still be troublesome.

NATO'S POST–COLD WAR RATIONALE AND U.S. INTERESTS

Perhaps the most underappreciated wild card in the transatlantic equation after the Brussels NATO summit is the role of the U.S. Congress and its perception of the future utility of NATO. Early in 1994, many members of Congress appeared ready to judge NATO based on what the allies could do about Bosnia. Against this difficult measure, members of Congress may find little reason to support continued U.S. investments in the alliance. And yet, irrespective of what can or cannot be done about Bosnia, there are substantial arguments for sustaining NATO cooperation. Without continuing military cooperation in NATO, the United States and its allies would find it very difficult to conduct the kind of coalition military operations that were so key to the success in the war against Iraq. Military units from different countries, variously equipped, with unique military traditions and practices, are not capable of working together effectively unless they have thoroughly practiced communicating and operating with one another. Ongoing military cooperation in NATO creates the potential for cooperative military intervention in situations that threaten peace, whether in or beyond Europe.

By mid-1994, NATO governments had not been willing or able to articulate those reasons in a fashion that communicated the message clearly to Congress—or for that matter to European parliaments, where, in the absence of a compelling mission for NATO, there is strong pressure to reduce contributions to the alliance. The key to NATO's ability to sustain its relevance may be found in the agreement at the NATO Brussels summit on a new way to organize NATO military cooperation.

Combined Joint Task Forces (CJTF) and NATO's Future [23]

The January 1994 NATO summit meeting in Brussels approved a U.S. proposal that would help restructure NATO command arrangements and forces to meet the more varied military security demands of the post–Cold War era. The allied decision to create Combined Joint Task Forces (CJTF), if successfully implemented, could give the United States and NATO more flexible military options for dealing with contingencies in and beyond Europe, for example when intervention capabilities are needed to support a UN peace operation. CJTF could become the main way for the United States to develop more effective sharing of global military burdens with its European allies. The plan would accommodate joint U.S.-European missions as well as operations mounted by the Europeans with little or no direct U.S. involvement. In addition, the new command arrangements could accommodate participation of forces from non-NATO allies: the new democracies that aspire to NATO membership, for instance.

What is a CJTF?

The term *Combined Joint Task Force* is composed of a string of specific, but relatively straightforward, concepts of military organization. A *force* is any grouping of military capabilities, manpower and equipment, construed in organized units. A *task force* is such a grouping that has been organized to achieve a specific mission or task. A task force usually is disbanded as soon as that mission is accomplished, and the units return to their parent commands. (A *standing* task force is organized to deal with what is viewed as an ongoing military requirement.) The addition of the term *joint* means that two or more military services (army, navy, air force, or marines) are part of the task force. The term *combined* means that the forces of two or more nations are involved.

Origins of the CJTF initiative.

The CJTF initiative is the latest step in the process of adapting NATO military cooperation to the post–Cold War world. The road leading to the concept began with the review of NATO's strategy mandated at the NATO summit meeting in London on 5-6 July 1990. The review produced a "new strategic concept," approved at the NATO summit in Rome in November 1991, that described the risks to allied security as "multifaceted . . . and multidirectional." The NATO leaders agreed that forces "will be developed to permit measured, flexible and timely responses" to crisis situations. According to the concept, NATO defenses "will rely increasingly on multinational forces," because multinational units reinforce alliance solidarity and "provide a way of deploying more capable formations than might be available purely nationally."

CJTF Purposes.

The United States, led by then–Secretary of Defense Les Aspin, proposed CJTF in 1993 as the way to make NATO's military structure more responsive to post–Cold War military and political conditions.[24] The intent was to provide flexible command arrangements within which U.S. forces and those of allied and other nations could be grouped to take on a wide variety of missions beyond the borders of alliance countries. The proposal had three goals:

1. to give NATO's force and command structure sufficient flexibility to respond to alliance security requirements and new missions beyond Article 5 contingencies (in other words, beyond defense of allied nations from direct attack), including requests from the United Nations or the Conference on Security and Cooperation in Europe (CSCE) for NATO to provide military intervention capabilities;[25]
2. to facilitate the dual use of NATO forces and command structures for alliance and/or Western European Union (WEU) operations, encouraging European nations to undertake missions with forces that are "separable but not separate [from NATO]" in the context of an emerging European Security and Defense Identity (ESDI);[26]

3. to permit non-NATO partners to join NATO countries in operations, exercises, and training as envisioned in the Partnership for Peace, a U.S.-proposed program of military cooperation open to all non-NATO European states that was also initiated at the January 1994 summit.

The first steps.
The first step in any restructuring of military capabilities is normally to provide the necessary command and control arrangements. This is essentially where the NATO leaders started in Brussels. They gave broad direction to NATO's senior governing authority, the North Atlantic Council (NAC), with the advice of NATO military authorities and in coordination with the Western European Union, to "develop this concept and establish the necessary capabilities." NATO officials began working to implement the decision.

The French government, which participates selectively in NATO military cooperation, required that the project remain under the direct sponsorship of the NAC to ensure that French officials would have a full say in the development of CJTF arrangements. In fact, the first problem encountered was the need to create a new committee to take into account the French requirement for NAC political control and the desire of the United States and other allies that NATO military authorities be represented in the shaping of CJTF plans.

According to the U.S. proposal, the Supreme Allied Commander Europe (SACEUR) should direct his three Major Subordinate Commands (MSC)—Allied Forces Northwest, Center, and South—to designate from within their headquarters a general officer and a staff to serve as a standing contingency CJTF headquarters for their region. One or any combination of the three CJTF headquarters units could be assigned forces to conduct missions. The CJTF would normally be available for missions accepted and conducted by NATO as a whole, including the United States. But the CJTF could also be used for missions taken on by the NATO European allies who are members of the Western European Union. In such a case, the CJTF commander, instead of receiving guidance from and reporting through NATO channels, would wear a WEU hat and report through a WEU command structure, ultimately under the political direction of the WEU Council of Ministers. If NATO assets (for example, NATO's Airborne Warning and Control System aircraft) were to be used by WEU, those assets could be placed under the operational control of the WEU commander when supporting a WEU operation. This would require regularized liaison and effective communications between NATO and WEU political and military authorities.

Currently, the Europeans lack the full range of airlift, command and control, and intelligence capabilities to take on most missions beyond their national borders. In the U.S. concept, if the WEU were to take the lead on a CJTF mission, the United States would not transfer operational control of strategic assets to WEU command but would provide services to WEU, such as transporting forces and providing intelligence support. CJTF therefore would facilitate U.S./NATO provision of capabilities for European-led operations, while at the same time meeting U.S. pressures for allies to carry a larger share of global military burdens. For some time, the need for U.S. support will likely give the United States decisive influence over the choice of missions.

Once a command structure with operational procedures is in place, the allies could start identifying national units that could be combined to constitute a task force. Command post and planning exercises could be conducted, and eventually field exercises to test the complete range of cooperation that would be required to make the CJTF concept operational. But for now, the CJTF is little more than the acronym itself. The headquarters have not been established, no forces have been identified for CJTF missions, and most of the procedures for political, financial, and operational control remain to be agreed.

The long-term potential.
The CJTF concept has the potential to revolutionize military cooperation within the NATO framework. If the idea were carried to its logical conclusion, NATO countries would plan, equip, and designate forces to join in CJTF missions. Allied political authorities would have at their disposal a variety of "Lego Legions" that could be mixed in force packages tailored for specific missions.

Preparing for CJTF missions, U.S. forces would plan, train, and operate with units from NATO countries and from nations that have joined the Partnership for Peace program. Individual countries—particularly smaller allies and financially limited peace partners—could take responsibility for specialized capabilities, limiting unnecessary duplication and making the most out of scarce defense resources.

The fact that the NATO countries would have such flexible capabilities at hand could help deter aggressive behavior in and beyond Europe. NATO countries would be better positioned to make key contributions to UN peace operations, particularly those requiring more active enforcement activities than is usually contemplated in traditional peacekeeping missions.

Potential implementation problems.

For the CJTF concept to work, a number of demanding conditions would have to be met, including:

- The CJTF approach will not work without continued U.S. leadership and force contributions. The United States would be required to keep significant military resources committed to NATO and to restructure those forces away from their traditional roles in Central Europe (defending against a Soviet/Warsaw Pact threat) toward more coalition-oriented missions outside Europe.
- European allies would have to stem the decline in defense spending of recent years and reorient and equip some of their forces to be able to contribute to the varied coalition-style task force missions envisioned in the CJTF plan. Each European ally would have to develop a domestic political consensus in favor of taking on military missions beyond national borders. This will be a particularly difficult process in Germany, where political and attitudinal constraints may limit Germany's military contributions for some time to come.
- The United States and France would have to sustain and deepen the more pragmatic cooperation of recent years that has opened the way for a program like the CJTF. France has the potential to be the most important European contributor to CJTF operations. If French policy reverted to more nationalistic ways or the United States qualified its support for the European Security and Defense Identity, progress in establishing CJTF capabilities would be seriously hampered.
- Even with the best intentions in Washington, Paris, and other allied capitals, making the CJTF concept work will be very demanding. To make allied forces capable of working effectively together as envisaged in the CJTF concept, further progress would be required in promoting standardization, or at least interoperability, of military equipment, supplies, and operating procedures. Such cooperation as has been developed among the participants in NATO's integrated command structure would have to be extended to include France and Spain, which are not in that structure, and to any peace partners who might wish to make significant contributions to the CJTF.

In sum, making CJTF work in practice will require political commitment, resources, and goodwill on all sides. Otherwise, it will remain a nice idea that never makes it from the planning tables to the battlefield.

Implications for NATO's future.
The CJTF has been chosen as the way to transform NATO's role for the post–Cold War world and to accommodate a more cohesive European role in the alliance. If the program is implemented, NATO will progressively develop military capabilities that could be used in a wide variety of contingencies. This would not guarantee that the United States or its allies would make the political decisions to use such capabilities, but if multilateral military force capabilities are available (as they were not at the outset of the Yugoslav crisis), policymakers would at least have the option to use them.

The creation of credible multilateral military intervention capabilities could play the same kind of constructive deterrent role that was played by NATO defense cooperation in the Cold War. Maintaining a credible defensive posture against potential aggression by the Soviet Union helped ensure that Soviet leaders were never seriously tempted to test NATO's capability to respond. It is not known how effective a deterrent the CJTF capability might prove to be against the lesser threats for which it is designed, but it presumably would be better for the interests of the United States and its allies than if no such capability existed.

If the United States and its allies cannot implement the CJTF concept, then NATO will appear increasingly irrelevant to security requirements, at least as seen from the United States. In such circumstances, the U.S. commitment to participate in European defense arrangements would continue to weaken. European nations might then be left to choose between making the large investments necessary to build stand-alone European defense capabilities or allowing defense efforts to decline further in the absence of a credible rationale for their national forces.

WHAT WILL NATO MEAN TO THE UNITED STATES?[27]

The questions of mission, membership, and methodology place a heavy burden on NATO's agenda. None of the issues at play is likely to be solved easily, and many will tend to create divisions among the allies. Under these circumstances, a strategy for the further evolution of transatlantic relations might beneficially include the following considerations:

- The allies, having set out a program for associating other states with the alliance, now need to pay closer attention to the relationship among themselves. New political and economic dynamics in the relationship, if not channeled constructively, could create troublesome splits among current NATO members.

- In particular, the allies need to put more emphasis on the purpose and missions of the alliance as a force for peace beyond as well as in Europe. The absence of any clearly compelling rationale, at least as perceived by publics and parliaments, is already reflected in rapidly declining defense capabilities in Europe and diminishing support for NATO expenditures in the U.S. Congress.

- Even in the absence of a Soviet threat, the allies share an interest in making their economic relationships as free from conflict as possible, as urged in the NATO Treaty. The free market system to which all the allies are committed, however, requires competition in order to function. The continuing challenge, therefore, is to ensure that such competition is accepted as part of the relationship, and that resolution of economic conflicts is seen as the tool that channels that competition in mutually beneficial directions.

- In order for allied military authorities to construct the interchangeable "Lego Legions" that are envisioned by the Combined Joint Task Force initiative, NATO nations will have to make a more serious commitment than before to standardizing military equipment and ensuring interoperability of forces. Without a serious effort, the CJTF concept will fail.

- The summit compliments for the process of European political and security cooperation will remain empty promises unless the European allies give them some content. Recognizing that European unification is a long and difficult historical process, it might be important in the near term for the European allies to look for small but symbolically important steps to reflect their commitment. For example, the WEU members could establish at their expense a Peace Operations Training Center on German territory, open for training of units from all NATO and peace partner nations. Most important, however, the European allies may have to develop some conceptual framework for the future structure and capabilities of European forces as a way of building a floor under the decline in defense efforts.

- The allies stiffened the backbone of their position on Bosnia at the summit, and their move appeared to encourage some progress toward peace. The chances for a lasting peace, however, remain in question. At some point, it might be wise for the allies to acknowledge that they all failed to intervene in the situation at a point when NATO might have been able to play a decisive role. Such an admission of failure would help set the stage for developing crisis management options and military intervention capabilities that NATO states could choose to use to deter or limit future threats to peace.

None of this will happen without clear but flexible American leadership. If the United States hopes to share responsibility and burdens with other countries in trying to maintain a semblance of order in the post–Cold War world, NATO remains an important instrument of policy toward that end. The alliance offers the only working international framework for effective organization of multilateral military operations and a set of tried-and-true consultative forums.

New formulas for sharing both burdens and responsibilities clearly need to be developed in the alliance. But neither a Europe that does not yet possess the unified military capability nor individual European nations on their own are capable of assuming the critical catalytic role played by the United States in transatlantic relations during this period of history following the end of the Cold War. The Clinton administration has made a start at the Brussels summit toward providing that essential leadership. Whether the administration, Congress, and the American public are prepared to sustain that role remains to be seen.

NOTES

1. The author is the senior specialist in international security policy for the Congressional Research Service of the Library of Congress. His views are not necessarily those of CRS or the Library of Congress.
2. Lawrence S. Kaplan, *NATO and the United States: The Enduring Alliance* (Boston: Twayne Publishers, 1988).
3. Ibid., 184.
4. In April 1991, a CRS report concluded that NATO's strategy review could logically lead to agreement that "the allies will consult actively concerning security issues arising outside the NATO area under the mandate provided by Article 4 and will make such arrangements as necessary to respond to such problems." This was the approach chosen by the allies a few months later. See Stanley R. Sloan, "The NATO Strategy Review: Negotiating the Future of the North Atlantic Alliance," CRS Report for Congress 91-379 RCO, 30 April 1991, 6.
5. Thomas L. Friedman, "Clinton Keeping Foreign Policy on a Back Burner," *New York Times*, 8 February 1993.
6. Doyle McManus, "Military Ouster of Iraqi Leader Favored by 60%," *Los Angeles Times*, 21 January 1993.

7. Thomas L. Friedman with Elaine Sciolino, "Clinton and Foreign Issues," *New York Times*, 22 March 1983.

8. Jonathan Clarke, "The Conceptual Poverty of U.S. Foreign Policy," *Atlantic Monthly*, September 1993, 54.

9. See Terry Atlas, "White House: U.S. Not Abdicating Global Role," *Chicago Tribune*, 27 May 1993.

10. See the author's thesis on the tendencies of the United States toward self-deterrence summarized in Stanley R. Sloan, "From US Deterrence To Self-Deterrence," *Christian Science Monitor*, 3 May 1994.

11. Daniel Williams and John M. Goshko, "Reduced U.S. World Role Outlined but Soon Altered," *Washington Post*, 26 May 1993.

12. Steven A. Holmes, "Christopher Reaffirms Leading U.S. Role in World," *New York Times*, 28 May 1993.

13. Brent Scowcroft, "Who Can Harness History? Only the U.S.," *New York Times*, 2 July 1993.

14. Michael Mandelbaum, "Like It or Not, We Must Lead," *New York Times*, 9 June 1993.

15. Daniel Williams, "Clinton's National Security Adviser Outlines U.S. Strategy of Enlargement,'" *Washington Post*, 22 September 1993.

16. Ibid.

17. Ibid.

18. David Rogers and Thomas E. Ricks, "Congress Is Uneasy With Peacekeeping As General Urges U.S. Role in Bosnia," *Wall Street Journal*, 23 September 1993.

19. John M. Goshko, "U.S. Lists Stiff Conditions for Troop Role in U.N. Peace Keeping," *Washington Post*, 24 September 1993.

20. Ruth Marcus, "Clinton Seeks Limits On Peace Keeping," *Washington Post*, 28 September 1993.

21. This analysis of the NATO summit agenda was originally developed in Stanley R. Sloan, "The NATO Summit: Transatlantic Relations at a Crossroads," CRS Report for Congress 93-939S, 28 October 1993.

22. The following discussion is based on analysis originally developed in Stanley R. Sloan, "Transatlantic Relations in the Wake of the Brussels Summit," *NATO Review* 42, no. 2 (April 1994): 27-31.

23. The discussion of Combined Joint Task Forces was developed originally in Stanley R. Sloan, "Combined Joint Task Forces (CJTF) and New Missions for NATO," CRS Report for Congress 94-249S, 17 March 1994.

24. There currently is little published material on NATO's CJTF initiative. Discussions with U.S. and NATO officials provided background for this report. The analysis also draws on "Trans-Atlantic Security and the Development of a European Security and Defense Identity: A View from the U.S." by Col. S. Nelson Drew, published as a special issue of The Alliance Papers by the United States Mission to NATO, Brussels, Belgium.

25. Such missions could include a wide range of operations requiring the use of military forces in and around Europe, in the Middle East, or elsewhere.

26. The goal of developing a European Security and Defense Identity—a European pillar for the transatlantic alliance—was set in the Treaty of Maastricht among the members of the European Union.
27. This discussion is based on an analysis originally published in Sloan, "Transatlantic Relations in the Wake of the Brussels Summit."

9

NATO and the "Special Relationship"

Phil Williams and Gary Schaub, Jr.

The Anglo-American "special relationship" has long been the subject of memoirs, press commentary, and scholarly analysis. Judgments have varied about both its nature and its importance. Supporters of the special relationship believe that it was one of the keys to Western success in winning the Cold War, providing the foundation on which the Atlantic Alliance was built and maintained. Yet the special relationship has also had its detractors: President Charles de Gaulle resented the Anglo-Saxon domination of the North Atlantic Treaty Organization (NATO) and withdrew French forces from the integrated military command structure partly as a protest against the close relationship between London and Washington; proponents of greater European defense cooperation have regarded the special relationship as a major obstacle; and critics on the British left have seen the special relationship as little more than British dependence on the United States. Moreover, there have been occasions—the Suez crisis; the lack of British support for the United States in Vietnam; Margaret Thatcher's failure to persuade the United States to purchase the British battlefield communication system, Ptarmigan, rather than its French competitor, RITA; and the Clinton administration's decision to allow Gerry Adams into the United States—when the special relationship seemed anything but "special." Yet, in each case the damage was temporary. Close cooperation between London and Washington on nuclear matters followed Suez. Vietnam did not preclude subsequent British support for the United States in other out-of-area contingencies. The RITA sale did not dampen the mutual enthusiasm of Reagan and Thatcher for one another's policies. And the Gerry Adams visit was succeeded fairly rapidly by John Major's visit to the United States and, on the public level at least, a reconciliation between President Clinton and the British prime minister.

This suggests that the relationship is both resilient and enduring. Moreover, it is clearly a cozy and comfortable relationship. With the end of the Cold War, however, it is both necessary and opportune to reconsider the special relationship and its impact on the evolution of European security arrangements. Accordingly, this essay will elucidate the nature of the special relationship, delineate the historical connections between NATO and the special relationship, assess the impact of the end of the Cold War on the special relationship and NATO, and determine whether the continuation of this relationship is advantageous for Britain and the United States in the post–Cold War world.

THE NATURE OF THE SPECIAL RELATIONSHIP: STYLE AND SUBSTANCE

If the special relationship is both enduring and important, it remains amorphous and difficult to encapsulate: It is an asymmetrical relationship both in terms of the relative power of the two states and its salience in their calculations. The special relationship is more special and more important to the United Kingdom than it is to the United States. Indeed, "the United Kingdom has only one special relationship, whilst the United States enjoys a number of such relationships."[1] Even so, the Anglo-American connection is not insignificant for the United States, as it is far deeper than most alliance relationships. It involves shared attitudes and expectations, cooperative working arrangements, well-established patterns of consultation at all levels, and both informal and institutionalized linkages across a wide range of foreign policy and security issues. It is based on a broad congruence of outlook and interest on most security issues and an expectation on the part of both Britain and the United States that, on any issue of mutual concern, each government will have ample opportunity to make its views and preferences known to the other—and can generally expect a sympathetic hearing.

Shared Assumptions, Common Interests, and National Interests

This congruence of assumption and outlook stems from a cultural and historical affinity rooted partly in geopolitical considerations. Britain and the United States have shared an interest in preventing a single hostile power from dominating the European Continent. This was evident during 1917-18 and again during World War II, a conflict that cemented long-standing ties between Britain and the United States. Moreover, the patterns of cooperation established in the first half of the 1940s were maintained and strengthened.

Geopolitical considerations continued to foster highly convergent interests between Britain and the United States throughout the Cold War. The U.S. policy of containment both coincided with and was crystallized by British efforts to restore and maintain the balance of power in Europe. These geopolitical underpinnings provided a sound basis for cooperation in spite of differences of emphasis. Both Washington and London were concerned about Soviet power and Soviet ideology, but for Britain, ideology was secondary: The Soviet Union was seen primarily as the latest in a series of acquisitive states attempting to establish hegemony in Europe and overturn the balance of power. For the United States, in contrast, the ideological dimension was central to the Cold War. In practice, though, this difference of emphasis did little to disturb a fundamental common interest in maintaining a strong and effective bulwark against Soviet power in Europe.

To present the special relationship only in terms of shared interests, however, would be a mistake. The special relationship also facilitated the pursuit of individual national interests by the United States and Britain. For London, the special relationship provided a means of maintaining global influence in spite of diminished resources. Close cooperation with the United States was seen, sometimes implicitly and sometimes explicitly, as a way of slowing down Britain's decline as a Great Power and mitigating the consequences of this decline, allowing London to retain "the avuncular good will of . . . an ancient family that has seen better times but still is able to evoke memories of the wisdom, dignity, and power that had established the family name in the first place."[2] Britain has been far more willing than any other European ally to cooperate with the United States on out-of-area issues. The "global partnership" eased the pain of disengagement from empire and enabled Britain to exercise incommensurate influence. In addition, the precedents of support allowed Britain to call on the United States for assistance in the Falklands conflict, in spite of the costs for the United States in its relationship with Argentina and other South American countries. London has also benefited from the assistance of the United States in maintaining its nuclear status, even though, at certain junctures, key U.S. officials had serious reservations about this assistance. In many ways, then, Britain has used its links with the United States to elevate its own standing and influence, a tactic similar to that used by France in its relationship with Germany.[3]

Britain also adopted a conciliatory style that enhanced subtle efforts to shape U.S. policy in directions congenial to London. By cooperating with the United States and formally acquiescing in policies that were not entirely palatable, Britain believed that it could moderate and modify the U.S. stance to accord with British preferences. "One feature of the Anglo-American relationship was the degree to which diplomatic subtlety overcame substantive disagreements" on particular issues such as NATO strategy.[4] Such an approach was in marked contrast to that of France, which, lacking Britain's conception of the need to be a good ally, took great pride in confronting the United States much more overtly. Even though the policy of influence through cooperation did not always succeed—if only because the policy debate in Washington is often highly insular and impervious to external influences—arguments that Britain unfailingly adopted an uncritical stance toward American policies oversimplify a subtle diplomacy designed primarily to advance British interests that were not synonymous with those of the United States.

The special relationship was also exploited by Washington vis-à-vis Western Europe. As Kenneth Waltz noted in the early 1960s, the United States "wanted a Europe united and strong and thus able to share . . . burdens . . . but a Europe at the same time docile and pliant so that it would agree on which burdens are to be assumed and how duties should be shared."[5] Britain helped the United States to maintain this delicate balancing act. On the one hand, Britain has been a good ally in terms of its own burden-sharing efforts and its exhortations to other Europeans to fulfill their obligations to NATO. Responding to congressional pressures for troop reductions in Western Europe during the late 1960s, for example, Britain played a pivotal role in the creation of the Eurogroup, a European caucus in the alliance that coordinated European defense efforts and made clear that the allies were bearing a fair share of the burdens of the common defense. On the other hand, London opposed any forms of defense cooperation that excluded the United States or could be construed as ganging up on Washington. In this sense, the French comment that Britain was America's Trojan horse in Europe was valid (although Germany also played this role, albeit in a less overt fashion).

The argument that Britain was the U.S. representative in European deliberations and institutions, preventing them from becoming too critical of the United States or too independent of Washington, suggests only a negative quality. In fact, the British role was one of facilitation as well as obstruction. Britain acted as intermediary between the United States and Western Europe, ensuring that the relationship remained intact through periods of transatlantic discord.

Sometimes, however, the role of the "good ally" meant that Britain incurred costs, particularly when Washington used London's support to legitimize U.S. out-of-area ventures. In the U.S. attack on Libya in April 1986, for example, F-111s from U.S. bases at Upper Heyford and Lakenheath were used as part of the strike force. The justification for the use of planes based in Britain was cast largely in terms of their capacity for precision strikes, but this was less important than the political considerations: The tacit support of at least one European government helped the Reagan administration win domestic support and rebut the criticisms of other European allies. Even if the United States exploited the special relationship in this way, however, such episodes had only transitory costs for Britain, while yielding large dividends in terms of deepening the special relationship during a period of dwindling British resources.

Consultative Arrangements

The special relationship is exceptional not only for the overt areas of congruence between the United States and Britain but also for the means whereby cooperation is sustained. Successive British governments were able to establish what Henry Kissinger described as

> a pattern of consultation so matter-of-factly intimate that it became psychologically impossible to ignore British views. They evolved a habit of meetings so regular that autonomous American action somehow came to seem to violate club rules. Above all, they used effectively an abundance of wisdom and trustworthiness of conduct so exceptional that successive American leaders saw it in their self-interest to obtain British advice before making major decisions. It was an extraordinary relationship because it rested on no legal claims; it was formalized by no document; it was carried forward by succeeding British governments as if no alternative were conceivable.[6]

This is not to ignore occasional stresses and strains in the London-Washington connection. Like all relationships, the special relationship is subject to short-term fluctuations. These seem to depend in large part on the relationship between the British prime minister and the U.S. president. When their personal rapport is good, the relationship appears to be strong (for example, Macmillan and Kennedy, Thatcher and Reagan); when rapport is absent, the relationship appears more fragile. This is not surprising since much of the process of wielding influence is done on a personal level. Close and continuous contact between prime minister and president, British foreign secretary and the U.S. secretary of state, and between the U.K. minister of defense and the U.S. secretary of defense has been at the heart of the Anglo-American relationship. But the special relationship cannot be accounted for simply by the warmth of the personal relations at the top of the governmental hierarchies. Frictions over lack of consultation (as, for example, over the American intervention in Grenada) have been rare, largely because the practice and procedures of cooperation have been institutionalized at a variety of levels. "Beyond the diplomatic and political links, an intricate network has, over the years, been established" in which British and American policymakers and officials work closely together.[7] This is evident in a variety of forums, including NATO, where British and American officials attempt to coordinate their approaches on a variety of issues.[8]

In fact, the bilateral institutional arrangements on issue areas of enduring common interest—what might be termed the "substance" of the special relationship—have provided long-term stability in spite of changing circumstances and occasional divergences of interest and approach. The key areas of this institutional linkage are intelligence cooperation, collaboration on nuclear issues, and cooperation between U.S. and British conventional forces.

Intelligence Cooperation

One of the most substantive areas of Anglo-American cooperation during the Cold War was intelligence acquisition and, to a lesser extent, intelligence assessment. This grew out of collaborative efforts during World War II and was formalized in a concordat in 1947—the UKUSA Treaty (the UK-USA Agreement or Secret Treaty)—which also includes Canada, Australia, and New Zealand. Under this agreement, the signatories shared signal intelligence (SIGINT) collection responsibilities. "The world was divided into areas of responsibility, with each nation having the primary responsibility for SIGINT collection in a particular area" where it could obtain the maximum intercept coverage.[9] This basic agreement was supplemented not only by other bilateral and multilateral accords but also by "unwritten agreements based on convention and working practice, which in many cases are just as important as the written agreements."[10] Indeed, it is these conventions and practices that help to make the relationship special.

The balance of effort, the mutuality of dependence between the parties involved, and the distribution of benefits from this vast network of cooperation are all difficult to assess precisely. It is clear, however, that the United

States is the linchpin of this system—and reportedly pays for much of the hardware and the satellites on which Britain depends. The Falklands campaign highlighted this dependence on the United States for satellite information, although the sharing of information with Britain during the conflict was more routine than many commentaries suggested. Britain itself has extensive capabilities in the SIGINT business. In addition to the Government Communications Headquarters (GCHQ) in Cheltenham, there are GCHQ listening posts in Cyprus, Hong Kong, and Ascension Island. The United Kingdom has also made a variety of facilities available to the United States, including access to the British Indian Ocean territory of Diego Garcia. Agreement was reached in 1970 on the creation of a communications facility on the island (which subsequently became a forward pre-positioning area for the U.S. Central Command). In addition, the United Kingdom has acted as host to four major U.S. bases that are part of the global network of the National Security Agency. In the mid-1980s, the United States constructed several dish aerials at a GCHQ outstation near Bude in Cornwall as part of an Anglo-American agreement for monitoring private and commercial communications as well as international military and diplomatic traffic. Extensive cooperation also took place in ocean surveillance.

Although some of these activities may have been reduced as a result of the end of the Cold War, the cooperative apparatus remains extensive. Collaboration in collection is complemented by bilateral arrangements between Britain and the United States for pooling information gleaned through their various facilities. Such exchanges help to cross-check information and enable Britain to provide an independent European analysis of events that on occasion may help to balance and correct that of the United States. These patterns of cooperation were so well established that rather than being terminated at the end of the Cold War, they have been extended to new areas of concern, such as transnational crime and drug trafficking.

Nuclear Cooperation

The second area where the special relationship has been particularly impressive in both the depth and extent of cooperation is the nuclear link. Cooperation here is manifest in regular consultations between British and American leaders as well as close and continuing ties at the working levels. Furthermore, the individual military services of both countries have established their own patterns of collaboration. During the 1950s, for example, the Royal Air Force (RAF) and the Strategic Air Command (SAC) maintained close links. "SAC encouraged the RAF to build the V-Bomber Force . . . provided substantial assistance in inter-departmental and inter-service disputes, and took part in many interesting and useful discussions on operating procedures and future developments."[11]

In the aftermath of Suez, and with Harold Macmillan as British prime minister, the United States amended the Atomic Energy Act to allow the sharing of nuclear technology and expertise with states that had developed a nuclear capability on their own. In practice this policy applied only to Britain. In 1960, Macmillan received assurances that the U.S. air-to-surface missile currently being developed, the Skybolt, would be shared with Britain in order to extend the life of the V-bomber force. With this agreement in hand, the British canceled their Blue Streak missile program, hence becoming dependent upon the United States for a nuclear delivery system.[12]

Skybolt did not fare well in internal budget battles in the Pentagon, however, and was eventually canceled in 1962—in spite of intervention on the part of British Minister of Defense Peter Thorneycroft. While most of the U.S. government wanted to provide a replacement for Skybolt, the State Department, preoccupied with the idea of West European integration and seeing the special relationship as an obstacle to this process, opposed a deal on Polaris, opting instead for more modest alternatives that would extend the life of the British deterrent to 1969 at the latest.[13] State hoped that this would effectively end Britain's membership in the nuclear club and encourage Britain's entry into the European Economic Community. However, "McNamara evidently had conceived that were he in the other's shoes he probably would opt for Polaris. And although he was counting on the British to take thought, he could not resist doing some of their work for them."[14] Here was the special relationship at work.

After a series of acrimonious exchanges prior to and at the U.S.-British summit meeting at Nassau in December 1962, President Kennedy overrode his State Department advisers and reached an agreement with Macmillan to provide Britain with Polaris missiles. The British force was "assigned as part of a NATO nuclear force and targeted in accordance with NATO plans" produced by the Joint Strategic Target Planning Staff of the United States Strategic Air Command.[15] Britain received access to deliberations previously denied it and an opportunity to influence U.S. and NATO targeting doctrine at the operational level. At the same time, Britain insisted on an escape clause and retained operational independence for its deterrent force in circumstances where vital interests were at stake.

The Nassau agreement also had the effect of deepening the relationship between the U.S. and British navies. Such ties remained strong. They were evident in the Polaris Improvement Program that began in 1967 and were consolidated by the British decision to acquire Trident. Agreement in principle on this acquisition was reached during Prime Minister Thatcher's first visit to Washington in December 1979. Negotiations over the precise terms of the agreement continued in the first half of 1980, and the Trident deal was announced on 15 July of that year.

The Anglo-American agreement over Trident extended existing patterns of cooperation and took place within the framework of previous assumptions and policies. Indeed, in considering the options for a follow-on system to Polaris, one of the key considerations for Britain was that both the SLBM (submarine-launched ballistic missile) option and the American link had proved very successful. The government continued along this well-trodden path. Even though the United Kingdom was clearly the junior partner, the acquisition of Trident offered both "technical guarantees and financial security compared to an independent programme."[16] Moreover, the Trident deal strengthened the close working relationship that had developed between the leading British laboratory in Aldermaston and the Los Alamos and Lawrence Livermore national laboratories in the United States.[17]

While it could be argued that this pattern of cooperation was not unique—in that the United States also assisted France with the modernization of its strategic nuclear forces—cooperation with Britain proved more extensive and sustained. It was also overt, whereas that with France was covert.

The nuclear link also extended into areas in which the British benefited less directly or where they had serious reservations about the U.S. approach—such as the Strategic Defense Initiative (SDI). British reactions to SDI ranged from ambivalent to hostile, yet the British participated in SDI research, in a mixture of opportunism and damage limitation. The research program would go ahead whether Britain was involved or not, and it therefore made sense to obtain some of the economic benefits expected to accrue to collaborating states. In addition, participation would allow Britain to assess the state of the art in defensive technologies and obtain a clearer picture of the problems that Britain's strategic deterrent force might encounter in the future. Most important of all, it would provide an opportunity to influence the direction and scope of the SDI program from inside. Public criticism was traded for private influence—at least, that was the hope. How much influence Britain actually had, of course, remains uncertain. Even if the special relationship did not give Britain a veto over U.S. policies that London disliked, it did provide opportunities for efforts to influence those policies.

Conventional Cooperation

Although the nuclear relationship is the most salient aspect of Anglo-American defense cooperation, it is far from the only element. Cooperation at the conventional level occurs for the most part within NATO, but there are areas in which Britain and the United States cooperate extensively in a relationship based on experience, confidence, and trust between individual services of the two countries. Perhaps the most obvious of these is at the naval level, where throughout the Cold War there was joint planning for operational tasks such as protecting the sea-lines of communication. The relationship between the British and American air forces was also close, with considerable cross-fertilization of ideas about doctrine and operations. The links between the armies of the two countries have been less extensive and direct during this period, although a common concern with contingencies in Europe has helped to ensure a continuing and positive dialogue.

THE SPECIAL RELATIONSHIP AND THE COLD WAR

Throughout the Cold War, the special relationship played a crucial role in maintaining the vitality and cohesion of the Atlantic Alliance. Although Britain's close relationship with Washington occasionally created resentment in Paris and exacerbated tensions in Franco-American relations, by acting both as a "good ally" and as an intermediary between the United States and the Western Europeans, Britain helped to maintain the transatlantic linkage that it had done much to bring about.

The special relationship was closely bound up with the creation of NATO—although, ironically, an Atlantic alliance was not the first choice of either the United States or Great Britain for securing Western Europe. For the United States, the hope and expectation was that by reinvigorating Western European economic development, an indigenous balance of power in Europe would be restored. It is ironic that the Marshall Plan led to a security guarantee (in order to provide a more secure environment in which economic recovery could come to fruition) when in fact it had been intended to limit the American commitment to Western Europe.

There is also irony in Britain's role in the creation of the Atlantic Alliance. As John Baylis has noted, "Although NATO was the result of a consistent British attempt to secure American assistance for West European defense, it also owed a great deal to the collapse of previous policies, particularly the search for an independent role for Britain."[18] Ernest Bevin worked extremely hard to obtain a U.S. commitment to Western Europe—and was instrumental in pursuing a degree of West European cooperation that proved to Washington that the European allies were serious about security and capable of self-help—but did so only after the initial British preference for the establishment of a third force had fallen through.

Even if both the U.S. and British roles in the creation of the Atlantic Alliance were tinged with irony, the special relationship subsequently played a key role in maintaining the health and vitality of the Atlantic Alliance. Britain was acutely sensitive to Washington's historical resistance to entangling alliances and was anxious to prevent any reappraisal of the American commitment to NATO. Starting from the assumption that Western Europe lacked the resources to maintain an indigenous balance of power vis-à-vis the Soviet Union, Britain worked to ensure sustained and substantial American involvement in European security affairs.

In the mid-1950s, for example, it was Britain that took the lead in promoting the Western European Union as the framework for West German rearmament and ensuring that there was no U.S. disengagement in response to the failure of the European Defense Community. Similarly, Britain was wary of developments likely to prove divisive in Atlantic relations and displayed a cautious, not to say skeptical, attitude toward Western European defense cooperation, especially when it was presented as an alternative to the American security guarantee.

Another manifestation of the desire of Britain to be a reliable and effective ally of the United States and a loyal member of NATO was London's willingness to take the lead in fulfilling its alliance obligations. As far as was possible within financial constraints, Britain made great efforts to meet the agreed NATO targets for defense spending. Indeed, there were periods when Britain was willing to accept more than a "fair" share of the defense burden, in the hope that this would help to contain pressures for a reduction in the American military presence in Western Europe that were fueled by frustration and resentment over the lack of burden-sharing by the European allies. This willingness was perhaps most evident in the late 1970s and the first half of the 1980s, when NATO agreed to a 3 percent per annum real increase in defense budgets. The British performance in meeting this target was better than that of most of the other European allies, and as the 1986 White Paper noted, "The defence budget in 1985-86 was some three billion pounds higher in real terms than it had been in 1978-79; this was the longest period of sustained growth in defence expenditure in more than 30 years."[19]

Acceptance of the need to reassure the United States about the seriousness of the European contribution to the common security was also evident in British activities beyond the NATO area. "Out-of-area" issues became a major source of discord in the early 1980s, with the United States demanding compensation, facilitation, and even participation by the Europeans in contingencies outside NATO's formal area of responsibility. Recognizing that the European response to these demands was a highly symbolic political issue in Washington, Britain was prepared to accede to American demands in order to shore up American domestic support for the commitment to Europe. This sometimes placed London at odds with its European allies, especially France, which contended that since the United States was in Europe out of self-interest, the Europeans could reject American demands with impunity.

Ironically, although Britain always appeared subservient to the United States, British policy has always had a more muted theme that complemented reliance on Washington with a simultaneous desire to maintain ultimate responsibility for British national security. In the final analysis, Britain, no less than France, was unwilling to depend exclusively upon another state for the provision of security. The British nuclear deterrent, although partly an embodiment of concerns over status, also reflected a continuing desire for independence and a recognition that under some conditions British and U.S. interests might diverge. Britain was never as explicit as France about the dangers of excessive dependence on Washington for security, yet its nuclear policies were based on Gaullist logic without the accompanying rhetoric. However, this was obscured by cooperation with the United States in the acquisition of the strategic nuclear force that seemed to underline Britain's dependence rather than its independence.

Part of the answer to this apparent contradiction can be found in the distinction between acquisition dependence and operational independence. Perhaps even more important was the fact that British policy implicitly rested upon a two-tier concept of security, involving both structure and strategy. The structure was a set of security arrangements in Europe based on the division into two military blocs and the U.S. willingness to underwrite the security of Western Europe. At the level of structure, Britain regarded the U.S. connection as particularly important if potentially fragile; at the level of strategy, however, Britain attempted to play a more European and more nationalistic role. Not only did successive British governments prefer alliance strategies that emphasized deterrence through threats of escalation rather than through conventional defense or denial, but they also maintained the independent nuclear deterrent as a weapon of last resort in addition to its broader role as a contribution to deterrence in Europe. In one sense, the nuclear component of

British strategy fortified and sustained the security structure; in another, it acted as a hedge against the collapse of that structure through a divergence of U.S. and European interests in a crisis, an American reappraisal of its commitment, or the collapse of the Cold War security structures.

Important as this hedging strategy was, it was implemented in a way that never challenged the basic tenets of the special relationship. Indeed, the British tended to the structure with such care that they sometimes succeeded in obfuscating and diluting some of the differences between the United States and Western Europe. The fact that Britain was often, although not invariably, on the side of the United States in intra-NATO disputes meant that transatlantic disputes lost some of their sharpness and political symbolism: They were not simply disputes between an isolated United States on the one side and a united Western Europe on the other. Blurring confrontations in this way was essential to the continued cohesion and effectiveness of the Atlantic Alliance. In a curious way, however, the Anglo-American relationship provided more opportunity for France to give full vent to its opposition to the United States: Any damage Paris did to transatlantic relations would be balanced and compensated by British efforts. The special relationship allowed France to pursue independent—and irresponsible—policies with impunity. Had Britain not been there as a counterweight, the consequences of French policies would have been much more serious.

The Anglo-American relationship, of course, was not the only pillar that maintained NATO. Perhaps of even greater importance was the Bonn-Washington connection. The Federal Republic of Germany was the front-line state during the Cold War, and its dependence for security on the United States gave Washington a degree of influence in Bonn that surpassed its influence in London. Moreover, although Germany sometimes sympathized with France, when forced to choose it was ultimately unwilling to side with Paris against Washington. French efforts to mobilize Germany against the United States were thus doomed to fail. In a sense, Germany, even more than Britain, was the U.S. Trojan horse in Europe.

None of this is meant to diminish the role of the special relationship between London and Washington in maintaining the cohesion and vitality of the Atlantic Alliance. With the end of the Cold War, however, there are insistent and inescapable question marks about the future of both Anglo-American relations and the Atlantic Alliance. The symbiotic relationship between the Atlantic Alliance and the Anglo-American connection ensures that their future is also bound up together. The key question is whether the special relationship and NATO can endure beyond the particular historical era that provided both their raison d'être and constant reinforcement. Discussions of post–Cold War security architectures for Europe impinge directly on the structural underpinnings of British postwar security policy and the relationship between Washington and London. The way in which Britain and the United States have responded to the new situation is the theme of the next section.

THE END OF THE COLD WAR AND ITS IMPLICATIONS FOR NATO AND THE SPECIAL RELATIONSHIP

New Challenges, Old Responses

The post–Cold War environment has brought both new problems and new opportunities for Britain, the United States, and Western Europe in terms of securing peace and stability on the European continent. The primary common interest underlying both Anglo-American relations and the transatlantic partnership—the need to maintain a balance of power against the Soviet Union—has disappeared, and the main preoccupation is no longer threats to be balanced, but risks to be managed. New challenges—such as ethnic conflict in the former Eastern bloc, economic and political migration from the East and North Africa, threats to essential resources such as oil, the proliferation of technologically advanced weaponry, and "instability" in general—are intractable and complex, involving as they do the breakdown of authority and legitimacy structures that were enduring features of the Cold War system. At the same time, the incentives to get involved in new kinds of conflict are very limited.

The change in the security environment has had somewhat paradoxical consequences for moves toward a Western European defense identity. On the one hand, the demise of the Soviet Union has made it possible to contemplate greater European self-reliance in the security field with a degree of equanimity inconceivable during the Cold War. On the other hand, the removal of the threat has also removed some of the incentives for more concerted European action. These cross-pressures are reflected both in the progress that has been made toward greater Western European defense cooperation and in the very modest nature of the steps that have been taken. The Western European Union has been given a more solid institutional role and has undertaken substantial—if low-risk—missions on its own, such as enforcing the blockade on the former Yugoslavia.[20] Overall, however, the impression is that at least in relation to the conflict in the former Yugoslavia, Western Europe is more concerned with evading responsibility than with decisive action.

The United States, in spite of occasional exasperation with its allies, has effectively connived in this situation. Although the United States has gone from being the indispensable guarantor of European security to a prudent insurer against unlikely contingencies and the supplier of logistical support to European enterprises, it still sees its role in Europe as crucial—a conclusion that Britain meticulously and systematically encourages.

Indeed, Britain and the United States, for different reasons, have been reluctant to engage in a fundamental reevaluation of the institutions, policies, and relationships that prevailed during the Cold War. Moreover, there is a negative synergy in the sense that London and Washington now play to each other's weaknesses and fuel each other's anxieties instead of playing to one another's strengths. The creative statesmanship of the early Cold War has been replaced in the post–Cold War era by a stultifying conservatism that clings (consciously or unconsciously) to the power relations of the Cold War, lacks a sense of vision for a new European security order, and hinders the progression toward a self-sufficient European security order that does not depend on the United States.

U.S. policy toward post–Cold War Europe seems to have been designed primarily to minimize the loss of the influence that Washington enjoyed during the Cold War as a result of its role as alliance leader. Britain has not only encouraged this goal but has provided valuable and irreplaceable assets for U.S. policymakers in their efforts to achieve it.

In order to maintain its influence, the United States has sought to retain the institutions that helped to maintain peace, security, and stability during the Cold War—and that Washington dominated. NATO is the most obvious example. Even though the alliance is unlikely to be transformed from a collective defense organization aimed against a clear enemy to a collective security system upholding international order, the principle of peaceful change, and other norms of international society, the United States has regarded it as the only real institution for security matters. The main reason is that the NATO framework offers the United States a crucial seat at the table on European affairs—a seat that, even if it does not enable Washington to exert as much influence in the future as in the past, is irreplaceable. The habit of leadership is difficult to kick: Although David Calleo's argument that Europe was America's protectorate was greatly overdrawn, patterns of dominance and subordination in the alliance could not be entirely obscured by the language of Atlantic partnership. The United States may have become the leader of the Western alliance with some reluctance, but it came to relish a role that gave it immense political influence in Europe.

The demise of the Soviet Union has eroded much of this influence. No longer dependent on Washington, the Europeans are less susceptible to American direction. As the United States attempts to maintain at least a residual leadership role and commensurate influence, close bilateral relationships with particular countries are likely to be crucial. In this connection, it has been argued that Germany now provides the best access point for the United States, given Bonn's power and its central position in the European Union, as well as its close relationship with the United States during the Cold War.[21] Britain, the argument goes, is not nearly as influential in European affairs and cannot preserve U.S. influence or promote U.S. interests as effectively as Germany.

The difficulty with this argument is that it prescribes a role for Germany that Bonn is unwilling to play. It is also based on a misunderstanding of the U.S.-German relationship during the Cold War. Germany was a front-line state and was therefore dependent upon Washington for its security. "Germany did not choose to foster ties to the United States in the postwar period; this arrangement was thrust upon Germany. Few historical or cultural factors exist to make such cooperation between America and Germany inevitable. . . . Moreover, instances in which Bonn has brushed off serious U.S. concerns are numerous . . . [and] such incidents collectively tend to undermine the possibility of a special relationship between the United States and Germany."[22] With the end of the Cold War and the removal of the security imperative, Germany is much more willing to cooperate with France, even if this incurs Washington's disapproval. In addition, Germany has demonstrated an independence on out-of-area issues that has raised concerns in Washington. The German decision to recognize the breakaway Yugoslavian republics of Slovenia and Croatia in January 1992, and to force this decision on its European Community partners, not only clashed with U.S. policy but also brought forth the consequences that Washington feared: ethnically fueled civil war. At the same time, Germany has not displayed a willingness to incur sacrifices commensurate with its new assertiveness. During the Gulf War, for example, "Germany was even reluctant to accept a proposal to use its air force in Turkey against Iraq if Turkey (a NATO member) was attacked by Iraqi missiles."[23] All of this suggests that while Germany and the United States may continue to enjoy a cooperative relationship, "Germany is no replacement for Britain as the United States' key partner in Europe."[24] And to the extent that Washington wants or needs a Trojan horse in Europe, Britain has become more important than ever.

For its part, Britain is eager to play this role, partly because of an innate conservatism and partly because of a reluctance to give up the benefits that it enjoyed under Cold War arrangements. These benefits include entrenched positions in existing security institutions, including "a disproportionate share of NATO command appointments . . . and over-representation in the NATO international staff," continuing status as a modernized nuclear power, and influence on global affairs through the special relationship with Washington.[25] It is not in Britain's interest to give up such influence by submerging itself in a French-led European security structure. The formation of an independent European security organization would also lend strength to the argument in favor of a single European Union seat on the UN Security Council, further disenfranchising Britain.

Another inhibition to casting its lot with the other Europeans is that although Britain has had a tradition of extensive cooperation with Germany, albeit in broader forums rather than on a purely bilateral basis, its relationship with France has been characterized by mutual suspicion and antipathy. There have recently been some signs of French and British interest in greater collaboration, such as the creation in the fall of 1992 of the Franco-British Joint Commission on Nuclear Policy and Doctrine. Its objective is to coordinate "deterrence, nuclear doctrines and concepts, anti-missile defenses, [and] arms control and nonproliferation" policies.[26] It is not inconceivable that this objective might eventually result in attempts to cooperate more extensively, especially in the sequencing of patrols to ensure that the maximum number of SSBNs (nuclear-powered ballistic missile submarines) is always on station. Such steps do not demand any cessation of sovereignty or any sharing of information that would complicate Anglo-American relations. To the extent that French and British strategic nuclear forces come to be viewed as being held in trust for the rest of Europe, they could appear very attractive. Nevertheless, there is still considerable concern in London that France has downgraded the American connection and envisages the future security framework very differently than the United Kingdom does. Consequently, security cooperation with France would be very much a second-best alternative to a continuation of the primary collaboration with the United States, a collaboration that is currently providing Britain with modern and accurate SLBM (submarine-launched ballistic missile) systems that will ensure the life of its nuclear deterrent for at least another thirty years.[27] Despite fears that the United States might cut off its nuclear collaboration with the British in the pursuit of other arms control goals, a repeat of Skybolt is very unlikely. The Trident deal is a decade and a half old, and the United States has no interest in alienating Britain, which remains its major representative and spokesman in European councils.[28]

Finally, the special relationship still enhances British influence over global events, as was demonstrated during the Gulf War. President Bush's reaction to the Iraqi invasion of Kuwait was strengthened very significantly as a result of his meeting with Prime Minister Margaret Thatcher.[29] Close cooperation continued into the tenure of John Major. In fact, there was hardly a news conference during Desert Shield in which President Bush failed to state that he had "just talked to" the British prime minister; he referred to no other European leader as often.

In many ways this was a great success for British diplomacy, and it came at a time when such a success was much needed. In July 1990, in the aftermath of the London summit, which had been largely a triumph for the Bonn-Washington axis, British defense policymakers and planners were resigned to the fact that the real special relationship was now between Germany and the United States. Not only did Britain appear to be marginalized in Western Europe, but it also seemed to be losing its position as the United States's most important European ally. With its support for the United States in the Gulf, however, and its commitment of substantial forces to Desert Shield and Desert Storm, the United Kingdom attempted to reestablish its position, an effort facilitated by the constraints on German military action beyond the NATO area. This attempt to revitalize the "special relationship" was successful: "The Gulf war provided the United States with a unique opportunity to gain insight into the reliability of its European allies in times of crisis. . . . Britain stood out yet again as the most committed and trustworthy ally."[30] Germany, in contrast, was a great disappointment in this campaign.

Fiddling over Architecture

The other area in which Britain's role has major importance for the United States concerns the post–Cold War European security architecture—and in particular the future role of NATO vis-à-vis a more independent West European defense identity. While Britain has recognized that the Western European Union (WEU) provides a necessary hedge against the departure of the United States from Europe, London has also insisted that the WEU should work within, and be compatible with, the existing NATO framework: Nothing should be done to hasten or provoke a U.S. departure. Britain, far from being a cheerleader for change in European security arrangements, has forestalled efforts to demote NATO from its position as institution of first resort. London has opposed efforts to develop an independent European structure or concerted security policy and has been critical of the Franco-

German axis at the core of the movement toward greater European security cooperation. The U.S. stance complemented and reinforced this hostility, especially during the Bush administration. After all, a single European voice on security matters, along with an organizational vehicle for expressing it, would further erode the United States's dominance over European security matters.[31] Consequently, the prevailing conception of the WEU in Washington visualized it as institutionalized within the NATO framework, not as an independent or semi-independent body that would act separately from the United States. It was to be the European pillar of the Atlantic Alliance rather than a separate entity.

These tensions have their origins in old arguments about Atlantic Europe versus European Europe that were symbolized most dramatically in the clash between the Gaullist vision of an independent or third force Western Europe and the Kennedy administration's grand design based around the notion of a twin pillar Atlantic Alliance. If the tensions are familiar, however, the context is very different. In 1991, Bonn no longer felt compelled to side with the United States in Washington's long running, if often muted, dispute with France over the future shape and role of a Western European defense identity. This made Britain even more valuable to Washington, as London was sympathetic to American concerns about the increasingly exclusive direction of European defense cooperation. Britain was supported by the Netherlands, Portugal, and Italy, all of whom were hostile to the idea that the European Community would control the Western European Union. These nations preferred that the WEU form the European pillar in NATO and provide the bridge between the European Union and NATO.

A compromise was worked out and enshrined in NATO's Rome Declaration (November 1991) and the European Community summit at Maastricht (December 1991). The result was that the WEU would be simultaneously the defense component in the process of European unification and a way of strengthening the European pillar of the Atlantic Alliance. Although this formulation did little to clarify the position of the WEU, it postponed a fundamental choice, partly by ignoring the latent tensions between two very different conceptions of the role of the Western European Union. It also prepared the way for a series of working compromises that were made easier by the pervasive problems of European Union and lukewarm support for Maastricht in European electorates. If the Anglo-American vision of the WEU is not invariably accepted, working compromises have been achieved. The independent WEU naval operation in the Adriatic, for example, merged with a similar NATO operation in June 1993.[32] Furthermore, the "new French government has indicated its intention of playing a greater role in NATO without altering its policy of not putting its armed forces under the integrated military command. . . . France has already agreed to participate in peacekeeping operations organized and commanded by NATO."[33] A decision has also been made that the Eurocorps, which was to be the heart of a European defense capability outside of NATO consisting primarily of French and German armored divisions, "could be made available to NATO for peacekeeping missions or should one of its members be attacked."[34] In spite of these compromises, however, the architectural issue is far from settled.

Against this background of dispute over the role of the United States in the European security system, the Anglo-American relationship can be assessed either positively or negatively. On the positive side, the special relationship has helped to maintain Atlantic unity and slowed moves toward a separation of Western Europe and the United States. Moreover, Britain, recognizing the U.S. desire for a global partner with the resources and will to fulfill that role, has demonstrated both enthusiasm and skill for maneuvering the WEU into playing this role. Britain's traditional role as intermediary between Europe and the United States has once again been revived to great effect.

An alternative interpretation suggests that the continuation of the special relationship has had a negative impact on European security. In the first place, it has perpetuated and intensified the gap between the progress toward European Union in other areas and forward movement in the security policy space. By obstructing the Franco-German axis, Britain has helped to take the dynamism out of the movement toward greater self-reliance. At the same time, the inconclusive debate over the proper security framework has diverted attention from substantive challenges. Wrangling over the proper institutional framework for post–Cold War European security has left real problems unsolved and real challenges unmet—a case of fiddling over architecture while Yugoslavia has burned. More attention to solutions rather than means would have enhanced the capacity to manage the post–Cold War security system.

The debate over architecture has led the United States and Britain to postpone a serious reassessment of their interests and the best means of achieving them in Europe. The danger is that the debate could effectively have scuttled a European capability to ensure its own security while doing little or nothing to discourage U.S. disengagement from Europe. By not acceding to the Europeanists in its foreign policy, Britain may finally fail in the balancing act between European docility and responsibility that it has performed for over four decades.

The final paradox is that NATO may be unsuitable for meeting the new challenges. Although NATO has redefined its purposes at a rhetorical level, in terms of actual policy the debate over whether NATO can or should be transformed from a collective defense to a collective security organization has not been resolved. Genuflections toward collective security—most obviously in the emphasis NATO has placed on crisis management as part of its revised strategic concept—have been accompanied by a reluctance to extend membership eastward in ways that would entangle NATO more deeply in the problems of Eastern Europe. The Partnership for Peace is a compromise between the competing impulses for extension on the one side and nonentanglement on the other. But the compromise reflects an underlying catch-22. If the states of Eastern Europe and the former Soviet Union exhibit the norms associated with democracy, market economies, and the peaceful conduct of foreign policy, NATO membership itself would be unnecessary. Their failure to maintain these norms would create a situation where NATO involvement would most likely be needed but least likely be forthcoming.

For NATO to be effective as a collective security organization requires not only a broad consensus on what needs to be done to maintain international order but a commitment to peacekeeping and peace enforcement in spite of the costs and casualties that might be incurred. This commitment is lacking. Unless all of the states potentially involved in a peacemaking enterprise place a high premium on what Arnold Wolfers called "milieu goals" as opposed to the "possession goals" that generally dominate the calculations of national interest, then it is unlikely that they will be prepared to accept a high level of sacrifice.[35] In this connection, the Clinton administration's efforts during 1993 and the first half of 1994 to redefine the U.S. role and responsibilities in the United Nations were very important. The efforts to set limits to the cost of peacekeeping and peace enforcement and the requirement that military intervention not take place unless specific national interests are at stake, while understandable in the context of the U.S. debate over Somalia and Bosnia, were antithetical to notions of collective security in Europe.

As the alliance addresses Europe's post–Cold War security agenda, the same problem of interest emerges. Bosnia, for example, has been defined primarily as a humanitarian issue rather than a security one. Indeed, security interests have not been defined in terms of order, stability, and norms of behavior. Although this is not surprising given the potential costs of military involvement in the former Yugoslavia, it does underline the dependence of collective security endeavors on a general recognition that the only real choices are between short-term costs and a long-term deterioration of the security environment that will ultimately impose more serious costs.

Ultimately, the issue boils down to a question formulated by Paul Hammond in relation to the traditional burden-sharing issue in NATO: Who owns the problem? The difficulty with problems that are owned by everyone is that they are also owned by no one. Inaction or asymmetrical sacrifices can easily generate acrimony. The Yugoslav experience reveals at least two crucial problems: varying degrees of commitment and divergent assessments of the challenges. In a sense, this is a new variant of the old debates in NATO over the Soviet threat. The difference is that the old divergences actually occurred within a relatively narrow band, whereas the new divergences cover a much broader spectrum. As threats are more diffused, assessments of these threats become more disparate.

If this implies some gloomy conclusions about the capacity of NATO to meet the new challenges of European security, it also suggests that the British position has encouraged the evasion of responsibility by Western Europe. By helping to perpetuate European reliance on Washington, Britain has encouraged the Europeans to deny—at least implicitly—that they, and not the United States, own the problem of European security. Indeed, British policy toward European defense cooperation has had a pernicious effect. Britain has hindered the movement toward a new set of security arrangements that are more in keeping with the distribution of power in the postwar world; has pandered to the American desire to maintain its influence in Western Europe in spite of the demise of the Soviet Union; and has allowed old habits and outmoded assumptions to drive its policy and prohibit creativity. This has led to an uncritical support for NATO and an unwillingness to ask whether a European security institution responsible to the European Union might not be a more appropriate instrument for dealing with the new security challenges in post–Cold War Europe. The challenges that are on the agenda are Europe's challenges and not primarily those of the United States. Even a resurgent Russia that is more assertive in the "near abroad" does not pose a threat to the balance of power that requires U.S. involvement.

The British argument is that there is no ready alternative to NATO and to continued reliance on American power; British policy, however, consists largely of an attempt to ensure that no alternative is developed. Moreover, by pandering to Washington's baser instincts, Britain also makes it more difficult for the United States to engage in the reappraisal of its commitment to Western Europe that is long overdue. George Kennan, writing in the

1940s, had a vision of a pluralist world in which Western Europe was an independent power. That world is not as close as it should be—and a major reason for this is the special relationship between London and Washington.

NOTES

1. Wyn Rees, "The Anglo-American Security Relationship," in *British Security Policy: The Thatcher Years and the End of the Cold War,* ed. Stuart Croft (London: HarperCollins Academic, 1991), 143.
2. Henry A. Kissinger, *White House Years* (Boston: Little, Brown and Company, 1979), 89.
3. On the French use of this tactic see Stanley Hoffmann, "De Gaulle, Europe and the Atlantic Alliance," *International Organization* 18 (Winter 1964): 1-28.
4. Kissinger, *White House Years,* 90.
5. Kenneth A. Waltz, "The Stability of a Bipolar World," *Daedalus* 93 (Summer 1964): 905.
6. Kissinger, *White House Years,* 90.
7. David Newsom, "US-British Consultation: An Impossible Dream?" *International Affairs* 63 (Spring 1987): 228.
8. Ibid., 229.
9. Jeffrey T. Richelson and Desmond Ball, *The Ties That Bind,* 2d ed. (Boston: Unwin Hyman, 1990), 5.
10. Ibid., 135.
11. Colin McInnes, *Trident: The Only Option?* (London: Brassey's, 1986), 38.
12. John Newhouse, *War and Peace in the Nuclear Age* (New York: Alfred A. Knopf, 1989), 183.
13. Richard E. Neustadt, *Alliance Politics* (New York: Columbia University Press, 1970), 46.
14. Ibid.
15. Lawrence Freedman, "British Nuclear Targeting," in *Strategic Nuclear Targeting,* ed. Desmond Ball and Jeffrey Richelson (Ithaca: Cornell University Press, 1986), 119.
16. McInnes, *Trident,* 40.
17. Rees, "The Anglo-American Security Relationship," 155.
18. John Baylis, *The Diplomacy of Pragmatism: Britain and the Formation of NATO, 1942-49* (Kent: Kent State University Press, 1992), 124.
19. *Statement on Defence Estimates 1986, Volume 1. Cmnd. 9763-I* (London: Her Majesty's Stationery Office, 1986), 6.
20. This operation was later combined under a NATO command with a parallel NATO effort. See International Institute for Strategic Studies (IISS), *The Military Balance, 1993-1994* (London: Brassey's, 1993), 31.
21. See William E. Odom, "The German Problem: Only Ties to America Provide the Answer," *Orbis* 34 (Fall 1990).

22. B. Vivekanandan, "Washington Must Rely On London, Not Bonn," *Orbis* 35 (Summer 1991): 421.

23. Ibid.

24. Ibid., 422.

25. Philip A. G. Sabin, *British Strategic Options in the 1990s, Adelphi Paper 254* (London: International Institute for Strategic Studies, Winter 1990), 37.

26. *Survey of Current Affairs*, August 1993, 192-93.

27. *The Progress of the Trident Program, Defence Committee, Sixth Report* (London: Her Majesty's Stationery Office, 16 June 1993), vii.

28. See David H. Dunn, "President Clinton and the Anglo American 'Special Relationship': Time For Change?" *Politics* 13, no. 1 (1993): 46-47, for arguments to this effect.

29. Bob Woodward, *The Commanders* (New York: Simon & Schuster, 1991), 230-31.

30. Vivekanandan, "Washington Must Rely On London, Not Bonn," 422.

31. For earlier concerns on this see Henry A. Kissinger, *Years of Upheaval* (Boston: Little, Brown and Company, 1982), chap. 5.

32. IISS, *Military Balance, 1993-1994*, 31.

33. Ibid., 34.

34. Ibid., 32.

35. See Arnold Wolfers, *Discord and Collaboration* (Baltimore: Johns Hopkins University Press, 1962).

PART 5

NATO's Regional Challenges

10

NATO and the Former Warsaw Pact States

Boleslaw A. Boczek

A mong other consequences, the dramatic developments in Central and Eastern Europe since 1989 brought an end to the division of Europe, thereby marking the conclusion of the Cold War confrontation between the North Atlantic Treaty Organization (NATO) and the Warsaw Pact. Concurrently, questions emerged over the continued need for NATO in the completely transformed political and strategic conditions on the European continent: The nature of the risks faced by the West changed completely with the demise of the Soviet state, against whose threat the alliance had so successfully protected the security of its members since its creation in 1949. Yet, as it soon became obvious, the end of the Cold War did not automatically produce an era of peace and stability on a continent no longer divided by ideological confrontation. While the security environment of the West improved radically, the collapse of communism unleashed new dynamics in some parts of post–Cold War Eastern Europe. Long-suppressed nationalist conflicts, ethnic rivalries, and territorial disputes reemerged, creating zones of violence and instability in the successor states of the Soviet Union and Yugoslavia. In most cases, economic hardship and the instability of nascent political institutions not all firmly on a democratic path have compounded the risks of domestic chaos and international conflict. And, of course, there is the critical but uncertain role of Russia, which still remains a nuclear superpower with a large, though reduced and greatly weakened, conventional capability.[1]

From the point of view of the Western alliance, the probability of a resurgent and nationalistically assertive Russian threat to the West appears extremely negligible at this time. Yet prudence requires that it ought not to be ignored completely as long as Russia is going through a period of transformation fraught with risks and uncertainties. The Central and Eastern European perception of Russia, however, is much less optimistic. This is especially true of the three Baltic republics and Poland, and among the "near abroad" states.[2] Following the end of the Cold War, the countries of Central and Eastern Europe found themselves in a security vacuum without any institutionalized international defense arrangement, and they desperately strove to obtain security guarantees from NATO, preferably as full-fledged members of the alliance, against a possible threat of Russian neo-imperialism. Subsequent sections of this chapter will elaborate various aspects of these Central and Eastern European concerns.

From this very cursory survey of the strategic picture in post–Soviet Europe, one can conclude that the end of the Cold War did not eliminate the need for some kind of credible security system designed to maintain stability on the Continent. The uncertainties that surfaced in Eastern Europe have since had the potential of spilling over into NATO countries and directly affecting the security of alliance members.

Theoretically, a number of security structures could be suggested to manage the challenges of post–Cold War Europe, especially those generated by the developments in its eastern part.[3] These structures are:

1. the Atlantic Alliance;
2. a European structure based on the Western European Union (WEU);
3. a continent-wide collective security system based on the Conference on Security and Cooperation in Europe (CSCE),[4] in which each member undertakes to oppose any aggressor from within the system;
4. a worldwide collective security system of the United Nations;
5. a revived concert of Europe in which the major powers, through consultations, would minimize potential conflict;
6. a more polycentric system in which member countries would limit their military capabilities to defensive purposes.

Some of these options could be applied in a complementary fashion as "interlocking" systems, for example, NATO and CSCE, NATO and WEU, or United Nations (UN) and CSCE.[5]

A detailed analysis dealing with the question of which of the above-listed security systems is most appropriate for dealing with the multifaceted challenges facing post–Cold War Europe transcends the scope of this study. Suffice it to say that most analysts agree that, realistically, NATO offers the only security structure that can credibly and effectively cope with these challenges. This is a conclusion arrived at without prejudice to the mainly preventive role of such structures as the CSCE or the UN system. The CSCE would be especially helpful in the areas of confidence-building measures, peaceful settlement of disputes, and arms control. But as one leading security analyst has asserted, "NATO is the best matched to the full spectrum of challenges the West faces in the post–Soviet era."[6]

This conclusion, in essence upholding the continued validity of the security functions of the Atlantic Alliance, needs to be complemented by the essential proviso that, in order to cope with the challenges of the day, NATO must accommodate itself to the new geopolitical and strategic situation in two respects. First, it must adapt its strategic concept—including its military doctrine, force posture, and other components necessary for the preservation of the strategic balance in Europe—to the new environment;[7] second, it must perform the equally important but more complex and difficult task of revising its relationship to the countries of the former Warsaw Pact. In the process, it must project stability and security to a region that has become the focus of tension in Europe following the end of the Cold War. The Western alliance has to take up this challenge in a bold and innovative fashion or simply become irrelevant and wind up its activities like the Warsaw Pact itself. As events have unfolded, in practical terms, and especially in light of the Russian factor, the most difficult decision for NATO to make has been whether to provide security guarantees to the countries of Central and Eastern Europe and, if so, whether and how to differentiate among various aspirants. In the latter instance, the alliance would have to determine what substantive criteria to apply and within what temporal framework to proceed toward a successful stabilization of the European security structure.

FROM THE LONDON DECLARATION
TO THE NORTH ATLANTIC COOPERATION COUNCIL

In retrospect, the reaction of the Western alliance to the historic changes that have occurred in Eastern Europe hearkens back to the philosophy of the 1967 Harmel Report, which emphasized a strong defense, on the one hand, and relaxation of tensions by building bridges to the countries of the Warsaw

Pact, on the other. The Harmel Report's vision of a stable settlement in Europe, which would end the unnatural barriers between Eastern and Western parts of the continent and provide appropriate security guarantees, could not be fulfilled until after the Cold War. It is in this sense that the NATO document on the New Strategic Concept in November 1991 actually referred to the report.[8]

The alliance took up the challenge of reaching out to the East even before the formal dissolution of the Warsaw Pact when the June 1990 NATO foreign ministers meeting in Turnberry in Scotland issued a message extending an offer of friendship and cooperation to the Soviet Union and other Eastern European countries. This "Message from Turnberry" foreshadowed the most far-reaching declaration of NATO since its founding in 1949, namely the London Declaration on a Transformed North Atlantic Alliance, issued by the heads of North Atlantic Council in London in July 1990.[9]

The London Declaration represents a watershed in the history of NATO and a turning point in its relations with the member countries of the then still formally existing but moribund Warsaw Pact. The declaration proclaimed a new concept of Europe as one geopolitical and cultural entity no longer divided by hostile blocs, concluding: "The democratic countries of Central and Eastern Europe form part of the political structures of the new Europe." Consequently, NATO leaders proposed to the Warsaw Pact a joint declaration in which they solemnly stated that they were no longer adversaries and reaffirmed their loyalty to UN Charter principles banning the threat or use of force in international relations. In that spirit, NATO leaders extended offers to the Soviet Union and the Central and Eastern European countries to establish regular diplomatic liaison with NATO. Furthermore, leaders and representatives of these countries were invited to the NATO headquarters in Brussels. NATO Secretary-General Manfred Wörner then visited Moscow to convey to Soviet leaders the declaration's proposals. Soon visitors from Eastern Europe began a series of regular contacts that developed from initial high-level diplomatic visits into a stream of intensifying military and political exchanges of expertise in a number of fields, thereby laying the foundation for the rapidly expanding relationship between NATO and the countries of Central and Eastern Europe.[10]

The principles of the London Declaration were reaffirmed in the wider forum of the CSCE summit in Paris in November 1990, which—in addition to signing the landmark agreement limiting the Conventional Forces in Europe (CFE) and the Charter of Paris for a New Europe (the latter signed by all thirty-four CSCE states)—adopted a Joint Declaration of Twenty-Two States (NATO and Warsaw Pact), pledging that these states were no longer adversaries. The signatories also committed themselves to building new partnerships for a new era of European relations. All other CSCE states were invited to join this commitment. It is worthwhile to add that the declaration also reaffirmed the right of every state "to be or not to be a party to a treaty of alliance." Although the declaration does not impose strictly legal obligations, this provision certainly created a political commitment that continues to bind the signatories, including Russia, which by its own choice assumed the rights and obligations of the Soviet Union after it ceased to exist on 20 December 1991.[11]

The North Atlantic Council took further steps to build up the evolving "partnership" with the countries of Central and Eastern Europe when it met in ministerial session in Copenhagen in June 1991, by which time the Warsaw Pact had formally ceased to exist. The Copenhagen meeting resolved to strengthen contacts with the former Warsaw Pact states by:

1. organizing meetings of officials and experts on security policy issues;
2. intensifying military contacts by organizing discussions at NATO Headquarters and major commands;
3. inviting officers from Central and Eastern Europe to NATO training facilities;
4. establishing contacts with experts from these countries to participate in NATO "third dimension" scientific and environmental programs;
5. encouraging greater contacts between the parliaments of these countries and the North Atlantic Assembly.[12]

While referring to a substantial increase in the security of all European states, the North Atlantic Council noted in Copenhagen that concerns about security remained in some countries. No names were mentioned, however, with the alliance adopting a noncommittal posture toward the recently formed Visegrád group of countries (the Czech and Slovak Federal Republic, Poland, and Hungary), which, alarmed at the security gap in their region, already dreamed of finding shelter under the secure umbrella of the Western alliance.[13]

NATO's determination to continue implementing the agenda of the London Declaration received a further incentive from the attempted anti-Gorbachev coup in August 1991. In its reaction to the events in Moscow, the North Atlantic Council, noting the enhanced concern of the Central and Eastern European states, reiterated its conviction that "its own security is inseparably linked to that of all other states in Europe, particularly to that of the emerging democracies."[14] It need not be emphasized that the failure of the anti-Gorbachev coup was welcomed with relief in NATO's headquarters. Throughout this period, however, no specific guarantees were forthcoming for these emerging democracies beyond vague expressions of concern and expectation that the Soviet Union would respect the integrity and security of all states in Europe. As Secretary-General Wörner openly stated, "the Alliance has made it clear that it cannot for the foreseeable future invite these countries to become members nor offer them security guarantees."[15]

In November 1991 the North Atlantic Council's Rome Declaration on Peace and Cooperation initiated the next stage in the evolution of the relationship between NATO and the former Warsaw Pact countries. This declaration inaugurated a more institutionalized relationship for consultation and cooperation in political and security matters with the Central and Eastern European countries. More specifically, the foreign ministers of these countries were invited to attend the forthcoming Brussels meeting of their NATO counterparts in December 1991 to issue a joint political declaration on the way to developing further the process of regular diplomatic liaison and to building a genuine partnership. The Rome Declaration proposed annual meetings at the ministerial level of the NATO members with the five Central and Eastern European countries (Bulgaria, the Czech and Slovak Federal Republic, Hungary, Poland, and Romania), the already free Baltic republics (Estonia, Latvia, and Lithuania), and the Soviet Union (whose life expectancy at the time was barely one month), to be held in a North Atlantic Cooperation Council (NACC). Still other contacts would come in the form of periodic meetings with the North Atlantic Council at the ambassadorial level, additional meetings as warranted by circumstances at the ambassadorial and ministerial levels, and regular meetings with the NATO Military Committee and other alliance committees.[16]

As proposed in Rome, the NACC held its inaugural meeting in Brussels on 20 December 1991, a date that coincided with the dissolution of the Soviet Union. The Statement on Dialogue, Partnership and Cooperation, adopted by the NACC, in effect endorsed the proposals put forward by the preceding month's Rome Declaration.[17] Upon the demise of the Soviet Union, participation in the NACC was expanded to include, by January 1992, all the successor states of the Soviet Union, with Georgia the last to join. When Albania signed in April 1992 and then the Czech Republic and Slovakia as separate states on 1 January 1993, the number of members in this NATO-inspired consultative forum reached thirty-eight countries (NATO's sixteen plus twenty-two).

THE NACC

Consultations and cooperation within the framework of the NACC proceeded in accordance with the jointly elaborated annual "Work Plan for Dialogue, Partnership and Cooperation," of which four have been adopted since 1992. The annual work plan identifies a broad spectrum of topics and activities in security and defense planning fields where consultation and cooperation could be most relevant. The number of undertakings generated under the plans grew significantly between the initiation of the program in 1992 and 1994. In the opinion of the late Manfred Wörner, the creation of the NACC had affected NATO more than any other decision during his tenure as secretary-general, as a substantial portion of the alliance's time, energy, and resources had been spent on NACC work-plan activities and other forms of cooperation with Central and Eastern European states.[18]

Besides consultations, the first work plan in 1992 encompassed a wide range of cooperative activities focusing on security and related issues, such as arms control and disarmament, defense planning, strategy, force and command structures, civilian-military relations, national defense programs and budgets, training and education methods and concepts in the defense field, conversion of defense production to civilian purposes, scientific and environmental affairs ("Challenges to Modern Society"), civil-military coordination of air traffic management, and dissemination of information about NATO in the former Warsaw Pact countries. The more expanded work plans for 1994 and 1995 added all kinds of high-level seminars on defense policy and management, exchange of visits, civil emergency planning, economic issues, and other topics and cooperative activities. Peacekeeping, conducted primarily in the Ad Hoc Group of Cooperation in Peacekeeping, became a central component of the NACC cooperative effort, with education, training, and joint peacekeeping exercises scheduled for 1994 and 1995.[19]

While within a relatively short period of time the NACC made considerable progress in institutionalizing NATO's cooperation with its former adversaries, there was evidence of difficulties encountered in its work. For example, there was no special NACC budget or central management with a clearly defined concept or strategy, and there was also no qualified secretariat. Further criticism of the NACC pointed to the need for a fundamental reorientation to focus on more concrete forms of cooperation in such activities as implementation of arms control agreements, systematic consultation during crises, defense conversion, and participation in a common air defense and ground surveillance network, among other activities. It has also been noted that if confidence between NATO and its Eastern partners is to deepen, the cooperation between their military personnel, which consisted mostly of exchanges and workshops at the general staff and other senior levels, should be extended to include junior officers and even noncommissioned officers, as well as practical exercises with the ultimate goal of combined training.[20] Finally, contrary to the NACC principle of nondifferentiation between the participating states, there was a perception that the NACC was actually "sixteen and twenty-two" rather than thirty-eight equal participants and even that "not all NATO allies take the NACC seriously."[21]

Still, despite all this criticism, the NACC has served a useful purpose, and its annual work plans have at least provided some focus and direction to its labors. In addition, by giving its cooperation partners from the East "a common security anchor" through creation of the NACC, NATO helped to prevent the formation of competing alliances in Central and Eastern Europe.[22] In general, the NACC has played a constructive role in the transition from the old Cold War confrontational and bipolar structure of European security to a new pattern of dialogue and cooperation between the Western allies and their erstwhile adversaries. The NATO declaration of July 1990 inaugurated the transformation of the alliance, initiating the process of reaching out to the former Warsaw Pact states. The creation of NACC marked a further advance in the evolution of the relations between NATO and its cooperation partners in the East by developing an institutional basis for consultation and cooperation in political and security matters. However, in Central and Eastern Europe the initial perception of the NACC was by far more optimistic, as this NATO body raised hopes there that cooperation within its framework might only be a waiting room on the way to full NATO membership in the not-too-distant future.

TOWARD THE PARTNERSHIP FOR PEACE

Among the former Warsaw Pact members in Central and Eastern Europe, the "northern tier" states—Poland, the Czech and Slovak Federal Republic (which in January 1993 split up into two independent states), and Hungary—were especially eager to establish cooperative ties with NATO. Moreover, membership in Western military as well as in economic and political structures became their principal strategic goal even before the formal dissolution of the Warsaw Pact. The Visegrád group countries began to operate in April 1990 within an informal structure of consultation and summit meetings and within a very limited institutional framework of a "process" rather than an "organization" in order to avoid creating an impression of building up an alternative to NATO and the European Union in their area.[23] The Visegrád states perceived NATO as the only credible security arrangement in the conditions of the security vacuum produced by the Cold War's end and the unstable environment in the successor states of the Soviet Union. They pointed out that, historically, Central Europe belonged to the sphere of Western civilization whose values they endorsed and to whose creation they had contributed over the past thousand years. Admission to NATO and the European Union would only mean a return to the European system from which they were "artificially separated."[24]

While recognizing that the possibility of aggressive action by Russia is negligible at this time, Poland, which borders on three successor states of the Soviet Union in the east (Belarus, Lithuania, and Ukraine) and—through a bizarre twist in history—on Russia in the northeast because of the Kaliningrad enclave on the Baltic Sea, is concerned about the possibility of a revived Russian imperialist policy at some time in the future. Within a more immediate time frame, the Russian threat is perceived there in terms of Russia's propensity to resume thinking in imperial categories of spheres of influence and utilizing subtle political and economic pressures. The impact of such Russian policy moves would be enhanced and helped by the Poles' sense of being abandoned by the West. Moreover, these concerns are not alleviated by the fact that the latest military doctrine of the Russian Federation includes the development of mutually advantageous military cooperation with foreign states, "above all with states belonging to the Commonwealth of Independent States *and countries of Central and Eastern Europe,*" among the main guidelines for ensuring the military security of Russia.[25] Poland has also identified additional dangers in regional conflicts and mass migration from the not-yet entirely stabilized eastern areas of the European continent.

In Hungary, anxiety about Russia is not so strongly felt as in Poland. Still, membership in NATO remains the major objective for a country acutely aware of the resurgence of nationalist conflicts in its immediate neighborhood. The Czechs originally opted for a pan-European security structure, but soon rejected any security alternative to NATO. In principle, Slovakia's goal is to join NATO, but support for this policy is not so firm there as in the other three Visegrád countries.[26]

Initially, when membership in the NACC was limited prior to the dissolution of the Soviet Union, the four Visegrád countries still entertained the hope that the NACC could lead to membership in NATO or at least some sort of improvised associate status (otherwise unknown under the Washington Treaty) with a guarantee in substance equal to that under Article 5 of the treaty. However, with the influx of all the ex-Soviet republics the number of the NACC cooperative partners reached the unwieldy number of thirty-eight, mostly heterogeneous states, and it became evident that the NACC was not the right vehicle to achieve NATO membership. Also, while useful as a forum for dialogue and consultation, the NACC could not deal effectively with problems resulting from the strategic vacuum in the East.

Prior to the emergence of the Partnership for Peace (PFP) in October 1993, the West had not done much explicitly to discourage the hopes of the Visegrád states concerning their desire to join NATO. Within the alliance itself there was no consensus among the more important allies on the issue of expanding NATO. In general, Germany was a more vocal sponsor for the Visegrád group, and its defense minister, Volker Rühe, advanced arguments for admitting the four countries. France, Italy, and the United Kingdom were not so positive, displaying caution on the issue of extending the alliance eastward but not necessarily ruling out the possibility.[27] In any case, European members of the alliance found it convenient to leave the matter largely in the hands of the United States.

For the four leading candidates for NATO membership, the position of the alliance leader was decisive, and they were to be disappointed in their pleas. Unlike the Bush administration and, in general, the Republican foreign policy establishment, the Clinton administration was reluctant to commit itself to early admission, pursuing a more cautious course that eventually led to the adoption of the compromise idea of the PFP. But even within the Democratic administration there was sharp division and debate over how to deal with the calls for membership. As late as early October 1993, U.S. Secretary of State Warren M. Christopher strongly leaned toward the idea of expanding the alliance by admitting the four Visegrád candidates or at least covering them by some sort of security guarantee. But Strobe Talbott, the administration's coordinator of policy on issues involving relations with Russia and the other post–Soviet states and later deputy secretary of state, persuaded Christopher to change his view. Apparently it was Talbott who became the prime mover behind what was criticized as the administration's "Russia-first" policy on NATO's enlargement and other issues. Accepting Talbott's argument that admission of the four countries would play into the hands of Russia's anti-Western ultranationalists, thereby undermining the prospects for reform and democracy, the U.S. administration decided to propose to the allies the postponement of NATO expansion for the indefinite future and to opt instead for the evolutionary but vague program of PFP, devoid of any clear-cut criteria or timetable for admitting new members. This option, in essence a rejection of the applications for admission, was a compromise between antagonizing Russia by admitting the four Central European countries and doing nothing about the desire of these states to find security as members of their alliance covered by the guarantee of Article 5 of the Treaty of Washington.[28]

The Talbott approach prevailed, and Christopher and Secretary of Defense Les Aspin submitted it to the allies at the meeting of NATO defense ministers at Travemünde in October 1993, where the future of defense-related cooperation with the Central and Eastern European states was a major subject. The PFP program was further discussed at the meetings of the North Atlantic Council and the NACC in December 1993 and presented at the NATO summit in Brussels in January 1994.[29]

THE PFP

Two NATO documents set out PFP principles and objectives: the Invitation issued by the heads of state and government participating in the meeting of the North Atlantic Council held at NATO Headquarters, Brussels, on 10-11 January 1994; and the accompanying Framework Document further spelling out the rules governing the partnership.[30] The PFP was established within the framework of the NACC, but the relationship between the two will have to be worked out and clarified in the actual practice of the partnership's activities.

Concerning the sensitive issue of alliance expansion, it is clear that although the PFP was not conceived as a substitute for NATO membership, active participation in it "will play an important role in the evolutionary process of the expansion of NATO."[31] The Invitation implies that such involvement will be an essential prerequisite for any future membership of a participant. It reaffirms that "the Alliance, as provided for in Article 10 of the Washington Treaty remains open to the membership of other European states in a position to further the principles of the Treaty and to contribute to the security of the North Atlantic area."[32] In order to provide at least some encouragement to the four Visegrád candidates, but without referring to any specific countries, the NATO members assure the invited countries that they "expect and would welcome NATO expansion that would reach to democratic states to our East, as part of an evolutionary process, taking into account political and security developments in the whole of Europe."[33] However, just as the PFP was not conceived as a substitute for membership in NATO, participation in the partnership would not necessarily result in eventual membership or be regarded as a vehicle for competition for such membership. As phrased by NATO's leading spokesmen, the PFP puts the question of NATO membership where it belongs, namely, at the end rather than the beginning of the process of drawing closer to NATO.[34] Still, the implication is that active and constructive participation in such activities as planning, training, and exercises, as well as regular political consultation, are among the essential conditions for future membership.

In order to allay any security concerns of the partners and to encourage active participation in the partnership, the Invitation pledges NATO consultation with any *active* participant in the PFP, if that partner "perceives a direct threat to its territorial integrity, political independence, or security." This promise, in substance reiterating Article 4 of the NATO treaty, does not provide any security guarantee. Such a guarantee is extended only to the members of the alliance by the treaty's Article 5.

The North Atlantic Council's invitation to join the NATO members in a Partnership for Peace is addressed to the other states participating in the NACC (that is, twenty-two states) and other CSCE states able and willing to contribute to the program. Slovenia became the first non-NACC state to join the PFP by signing the Framework Document in March 1994. Two other non-NACC countries, Finland and Sweden, joined in May 1994.[35]

As the first step, all partners sign the Framework Document, which sets out the principles and objectives of the partnership. In addition to the otherwise binding principles of international law as laid down in the UN Charter and that are reiterated in the Framework Document, the partners must reaffirm their commitment to the Helsinki Final Act and all subsequent CSCE documents and to the obligations in the field of disarmament and arms control. Respect for existing borders, protection and promotion of fundamental freedoms and human rights, safeguarding freedom, justice, and peace through democracy, and preservation of democratic societies and their freedom from coercion and intimidation are the shared values and principles of the partnership.

Countries joining the PFP are to pursue, in cooperation with NATO, five categories of objectives:

1. transparency in defense budgeting;
2. democratic control of defense forces;
3. readiness to contribute, subject to constitutional considerations, to operations under the authority of the United Nations and/or the responsibility of the CSCE;
4. development of military cooperation with NATO in peacekeeping, search and rescue, humanitarian operations, and other activities;

5. over the long term, development of forces better able to operate with those of NATO members.[36]

Theoretically, all signers of the Framework Document are equal from the start on the way toward possible NATO membership, and no distinction is made between "European" states, the only category of state that under Article 10 of the Washington Treaty may be invited to join NATO, and other "non-European" states, such as the Transcaucasian and Central Asian republics (with the possible exception of Kazakhstan, part of whose territory is in Europe), which are ineligible for NATO membership under the treaty's present text.

By 11 January 1995, when Belarus signed the Framework Document, twenty-four countries had joined the PFP. They included all the Central and Eastern European states, Albania, Slovenia, Finland, and Sweden, and all the successor states of the Soviet Union except Tajikistan.

While providing the partners with equality of opportunity at the start of their participation—the signature of the Framework Document—the PFP goes beyond the NACC nondifferentiation principle by taking into account the varying interests and differing potentials of the individual partner countries. These various political and military aspects of individual partnerships are spelled out in each presentation document, which provides the steps that a partner will take to achieve the policy goals of the PFP and lists the military and other relevant assets that might be used for partnership activities. Each presentation document also indicates a program of exercises and other activities proposed by NATO and of special interest to the partner. By 14 October 1994, most partners had submitted their presentation documents to the NATO authorities; Poland was the first partner to do so on 25 April 1994, followed by Romania three days later.[37]

The third step in the NATO-partner cooperation starts with the subscribing state's development of an individual Partnership Program, which is first submitted to the Political-Military Steering Committee (PMSC), a NATO body established to work with the partners in preparing and implementing their individual programs. The final draft program then passes through the stages of discussion with a NATO team, approval of the redrafted text by the PMSC and the NATO Council, and disclosure to the alliance members. In order to assist partners in developing their individual programs, NATO prepared a currently updated Partnership Work Program listing all kinds of cooperative activities that could be included in such programs. Poland was the first subscribing country to have its individual program approved by the council and accepted by alliance members on 5 July 1994. As of 1 December, in addition to Poland, the individual partnership programs of Finland, Sweden, Romania, the Czech Republic, Hungary, Lithuania, Slovakia, and two more partners had been approved and entered the implementation phase. Several more programs were also close to completion.[38]

In anticipation of an increase in the intensity of PFP activities, the Framework Document invited the partners to establish—at their own expense and in agreement with NATO and, as necessary, Belgium—their own liaison offices at NATO headquarters in Brussels to facilitate their participation in NACC/PFP meetings and other activities. Except for a few countries with well-established diplomatic representations in Brussels, the PFP subscribing countries took up NATO's offer of permanent facilities at NATO headquarters. In addition, the partner countries were invited to send permanent liaison officers to a separate Partnership Coordination Cell at Mons that would carry out the military planning necessary to implement the partnership program. By 1 December 1994, eleven partner countries had appointed liaison officers at the cell. The legal status of the partners' missions and other representatives to NATO will be regulated by a convention to be drafted by the council.[39]

ARGUMENTS AGAINST NATO MEMBERSHIP

As already noted, the idea of the PFP originated closely linked to the problem of expanding NATO's membership to countries of Central and Eastern Europe, in particular the four Visegrád states that NATO considered the only realistic candidates for admission to the alliance. But concerned that such a move "would risk creating new divisions in Europe, which ultimately would harm rather than aid the security of the Central and Eastern European states and of Europe as a whole,"[40] the Western allies reached a consensus in October 1993 that there should be no immediate enlargement of the alliance. While various arguments surfaced against expansion, the major one reflected the concern that Russia could interpret admission of the four Central European countries to NATO as a threat to its security and an attempt to isolate it. This would alarm Russian public opinion, play into the hands of the ultranationalists and Communists, and undermine the position of Yeltsin and prospects for reform and democracy. "Swift expansion of NATO eastward could make a neo-imperialist Russia a self-fulfilled prophecy," warned Secretary of State Christopher. President Clinton, while firmly believing that "at some point in the future" the alliance would be expanded and include only certain Eastern European states, admitted that such action "possibly would appear threatening to Russia, Ukraine, and other former Soviet republics" and "would be a critical mistake."[41]

In Russia itself, the question of NATO's expansion into Central Europe became hostage to the interplay of domestic pressure groups, among which the armed forces appeared to play a decisive role. In August 1993, Yeltsin waived any objections to the admission of Poland to NATO; but in an attempt to cultivate the support of the military in the wake of the bloody October events in Moscow, he cautioned Western leaders against allowing the Central and Eastern European countries to join NATO.[42] Later, the strong showing of the nationalist forces in Russia's parliamentary elections in December 1993 provided Yeltsin and the military with a welcome argument to intensify their campaign against extending NATO's membership. In reaction to Lithuania's rash and unexpected application for admission into NATO, the Russian government warned sternly that expanding NATO could evoke a "negative reaction in Russia's public opinion," play into the hands of the country's extreme nationalists, and eventually lead to "military and political destabilization in a key region for the fate of the world."[43] Russian Foreign Minister Andrei Kozyrev advanced similar arguments when he warned that Russian extremists were ready to restore the Russian empire in reaction to "an illusory Western attack." While admitting that "Russia has no right to dictate who is to join NATO and who is not," he pleaded Russia's right to be sure that NATO "will take into consideration the peculiarities of the transition period which inevitably has to be long."[44] Kozyrev's position remained basically unchanged following Russia's joining the PFP. The Russian military, in general not a friend to NATO, also moved strongly against NATO expansion, which—especially if it should include the Baltic states—"could be taken as an attempt to isolate us and create a *cordon sanitaire* along our western borders." Moreover, in the military's view, NATO's enlargement would require rethinking Russia's "defense conceptions" and "the redeployment of armed forces."[45] This position of the Russian military found expression in the newly adopted "Military Doctrine of the Russian Federation," which, among the main existing and potential military threats outside Russia, includes "expansion of military blocs and alliances to the detriment of the interests of the military security of the Russian Federation."[46]

While some other, more legitimate reasons can be invoked against an immediate enlargement of NATO, the contention relative to the fear of antagonizing Russia is not convincing on a number of grounds.[47] First, it would be supreme irony if Russia could influence NATO membership policy from a position of weakness whereas no Soviet threats had been able to dissuade the Western alliance from admitting new members—especially West Germany—at a time when the Soviet threat to the West was realistically much greater than the Russian threat is now, after the collapse of Soviet power. As a matter of fact, NATO should take account of the favorable strategic reality and extend eastward at a time when Russia does not appear to be in a position to prevent it.[48]

Second, the argument that the enlargement of NATO would pose a threat to Russian security interests fails to distinguish between Russia's legitimate security concerns and interests conceived in the old imperialist mold. Claiming the right of veto over NATO's membership policy or the security policy of the Central and Eastern European states cannot be counted among Russia's legitimate concerns. Responsible Russian leaders themselves have recognized the defensive nature of the Western alliance, which for decades contributed to peace and stability in Western Europe and which Russia ceased to view as an adversary following the Cold War, as pledged at the CSCE Paris Summit in 1990. And if the very existence of an alliance were to imply an adversarial relationship, then the Commonwealth of Independent States would have to be seen in that light as well.

Third, extending NATO to the Central and Eastern European states would be in the interest of Russia rather than against it. These countries find themselves in the gray zone of a security vacuum and an area of potential political instability. Quite rationally, they have the right to be concerned about unforeseen developments in Russia or elsewhere in the former Soviet Union. Extending the alliance to the four candidates in Central Europe would in fact strengthen the stability of the area rather than destabilize it, as claimed by the Russian government, and stability and feelings of security in Central Europe certainly are in the interest of a democratic Russia. It would provide the best guarantee that the countries of this area would pursue a friendly policy toward Russia. If these countries are integrated into NATO, the alliance can appropriately accommodate the security concerns of Russia that would be legitimate only if, as a result of NATO's enlargement, the West were to pose a military threat to Russian security. Apart from arms control agreements, Russian concerns could satisfactorily be met by applying the precedents of Denmark and Norway, whereby the new members in the East would renounce the right of peacetime stationing of foreign troops and nuclear weapons on their territory, among other possible obligations. More recently, a similar agreement was arranged for the territory of the former East Germany.[49]

Fourth, in view of what was stated above, admitting the four Visegrád states to NATO would not be tantamount to "drawing a new line" across

Europe, but actually to moving the already existing line between the NATO-protected Western democracies and the non-NATO democracies eastward in the interests of the security and stability of East and West alike.[50] It is also unrealistic to claim that enlarging NATO would "isolate" Russia, by far the largest country in the world. Moreover, the expansion of NATO could be coupled with reassuring Russia by developing with it a treaty-based cooperative relationship that would recognize Russia's status as a pivotal member of a wider European or even Eurasian security order.[51]

Finally, the argument that the expansion of NATO would adversely affect the prospects for democracy in Russia is equally untenable. Ultimately, democracy's fate depends on sustained economic progress and political stability and culture rather than on the outcome of the issue concerning NATO's expansion. Additionally, NATO's apparent reluctance to admit the Visegrád states may embolden conservative elements in Russia rather than bring comfort to the democratic elements. In any case, Russian public opinion is by far more preoccupied with the domestic agenda, especially the country's economic situation, than with the expansion of NATO. The process of internal transformation in Russia is likely to take a long time and, in the meantime, NATO must shape its policy in light of the objective strategic reality and its own perceived broader interests, since "to hold the future of NATO hostage to the outcome of Russian politics is a recipe for the demise of the alliance."[52]

Still other points have been raised against the enlargement of NATO by admitting the four Central European aspirants. It has been argued that their admission would trigger applications from other states participating in the PFP.[53] A glance at the roster of the participants reveals a considerable degree of heterogeneity in terms of their geography; political culture and tradition; progress in implementing economic reform and democratic principles of government; the context of their foreign policy; and their military strength; as well as their potential to further the principles of the NATO treaty and to contribute to the security of the North Atlantic area and, thereby, to their chances for alliance membership.

Setting aside Finland and Sweden, the other PFP participants, all of them, except for Albania and Slovenia (former Warsaw Pact members) can in general be divided into the following groups in terms of their chances for membership in NATO. First, as discussed above, the four Visegrád countries—the Czech Republic, Poland, Hungary, and perhaps, also, Slovakia—are realistically the only serious candidates at this time. Compared with these four aspirants, Bulgaria and Romania are more distant prospects for membership. Bulgaria, while interested in joining NATO, perceives the alliance as only one structure that can guarantee European security "in its entirety and indivisibility." Romania's interest in becoming a member of NATO is much keener. It makes an effort to present itself as historically part of the Western world and is more explicit in its desire for full integration in the alliance. Romania was the third partner to have its individual partnership program approved and accepted by NATO. Slovenia and Albania are the other members of the Balkan group of PFP signatories whose chances for qualifying for admission to the alliance are quite remote.[54]

Among the Soviet Union's successor states, the three Baltic states, concerned about the Russian threat, are most eager to join NATO. Without coordinating its action with the other two Baltic states, Lithuania became the first ex-Soviet republic to apply for NATO membership. Although unsuccessful, this attempt nonetheless provoked a strong rebuff from a Russia opposing any idea of such membership for the three Baltic states. Subsequently, Lithuania adopted a more cautious approach, underscoring an evolutionary process of integration into the NATO structure. Latvia and Estonia are also determined to become NATO members in due time, but according to opinion prevailing in the West, the prospects of the three Baltic countries joining NATO are realistically quite distant, with at least half a dozen candidates in line ahead of them.[55]

Apart from Russia, which represents a special case in the relations between NATO and the former Warsaw Pact countries and will be addressed in this chapter, is a group of other European successor states of the Soviet Union: Belarus, Moldova, and the rather sensitive case of Ukraine, whose chances of qualifying for NATO membership are exceedingly remote. Finally, the Transcaucasian and Central Asian states, which are situated in Asia (except for a small part of Kazakhstan), are not eligible for membership under Article 10 of the Washington Treaty. Except for Tajikistan, all have signed the PFP Framework Document, but none aspires to NATO membership.[56]

It may be that, if the Visegrád countries were admitted to NATO, their entry would set off a series of requests for further admissions and possible charges of discrimination in case of rejection. However, NATO has the right to regulate the pace of expansion according to its own criteria and the discretion to determine whether a candidate state is in a position to further the principles of the NATO treaty and contribute to the security of the alliance.

Another argument raised against the admission of the four Central European states to NATO concerns the fear that the alliance might thereby become entangled in ethnic and irredentist nationalist conflicts between the states of Central and Eastern Europe. In reality the ethnic composition of

Poland, the Czech Republic, and Hungary is among the most homogeneous in Europe, and only Slovakia has a fairly sizable Hungarian minority whose treatment has caused friction in its relations with Hungary. For its part, NATO has long been familiar with the conflict between members Greece and Turkey, potentially more dangerous than any minority-related conflicts in Central Europe. Furthermore, it could be argued, as was done in the Greece-Turkey situation, that local conflicts could be managed more easily within the context of a security structure such as the NATO alliance. In addition, a lasting settlement of any territorial and minority-related disputes of a candidate for NATO membership could be included among other stability-enhancing criteria of admission. This proviso would apply to Hungary in its relations with Slovakia and Romania, and possibly to other states of the Visegrád group and to the Baltic states.[57]

Economic issues are also invoked as reasons to bar Central and Eastern European states from NATO, especially in the United States, where some see NATO's possible commitment for the security of these states as a major new financial burden at a time of declining defense budgets in all NATO members, except perhaps France.[58] It could be argued, however, that enlargement of the alliance would not require any significant new expenditures, given the greatly reduced risk of aggression from the East. What the countries aspiring to NATO membership need at this time is psychological rather than military security. For them, such membership represents not just security against any future Russian threat but also an institutional affirmation of their return to the West.

The final argument raised against offering immediate membership to the Visegrád countries concerns their state of preparedness to take up the responsibilities of NATO membership in political, economic, and military terms. In particular, it has been claimed that in their current condition these states are not yet ready to integrate into the alliance and need to adapt their military and defense establishment to the standards and procedures prevailing in the Western alliance.[59] Yet such obstacles to membership as a lack of democratic control over the armed forces and inadequate transparency in defense planning and budgeting were not disqualifying elements in the earlier cases of Portugal or Turkey. Moreover, interoperability of weapons and equipment is still to be fully realized by the alliance. There is, however, some validity in the readiness argument, and the leaderships of the Visegrád states have recognized the merit of the PFP as a useful preparatory stage toward making their military assets compatible with NATO standards and eventually integrating them into the Western alliance.

NATO ASPIRANTS IN THE PFP

Following the Travemünde meeting but prior to the January 1994 summit, the U.S. administration embarked upon an intensive diplomatic campaign to persuade the four Central European governments to embrace the partnership idea. President Clinton himself met in Prague with the leaders of the Czech Republic, Poland, Hungary, and Slovakia, and special envoys were sent to their capitals to convince the four NATO aspirants to accept the PFP invitation. The four countries were assured that it was no longer "a question of whether, but of when and how" they would be integrated into NATO.[60]

In view of the fact that the PFP Invitation makes only a general reference to an evolutionary expansion of the alliance, specifying neither the timing nor precise criteria for admission to NATO, the four countries initially met the partnership concept with little applause but much skepticism and disappointment. However, having no other choice if they ever hoped to join the alliance and recognizing that the PFP at least met their minimum demands of association with NATO, the four Visegrád countries grudgingly endorsed the partnership as a step in the right direction. But, at the same time, they insisted that the PFP "must lead to full membership of NATO."[61] Despite this reluctant endorsement of the PFP as "too little but in the right direction," the four disappointed candidates appreciated the significance of the partnership as a necessary step on the way to NATO membership and were ready to cooperate within its framework to the best of their resources and abilities. They were, however, somewhat confused about the relationship between the NACC and the PFP and the role of the WEU in the European security structure. It can be added in this context that, soon after the four Visegrád countries had joined the PFP, the WEU Council created a status of association with these Central European Consultation Partners of the WEU.[62]

Since each country is evaluated on its own merits, the PFP introduced an element of competition among the Visegrád states, exacerbated by uneven availability of resources, with the Czech Republic claiming to be more advanced on the way to NATO than the other three first-line candidates. Under the Framework Document, the states subscribing to the PFP are to fund their own participation in partnership activities. Furthermore, they will "endeavor" otherwise to share the burdens of mounting exercises in which they take part. The Czech Republic offered to accept a 1 percent deficit in its budget for 1994 to bring its armed forces up to NATO standards. The defense budget was to rise 12 percent. For the Czechs, political compatibility is the primary condition for NATO membership, but they are prepared to achieve technical compatibility within about two years after the signing of the PFP. Slovakia allocated 1 percent of its defense budget to the partnership and offered to make available to NATO training groups at the battalion level a new military school for PFP training purposes and production of new weapons. Poland's estimate was that its commitment to the PFP would require about $22 million out of a total defense budget of $1.9 billion. The United States and Germany made commitments to contribute to funding the partnership programs of the Visegrád states.[63]

Command and control structures, communications, and air defense are on the top of Poland's priority list in adapting its defense system to NATO standards. Defense procurement and interoperability are also important objectives. Hungary, which coordinated its presentation document not only with NATO but also with Austria, envisages developing training programs with NATO and a regional peacekeeping center in Budapest. All the Visegrád countries emphasize in their PFP programs the need to bolster civilian control over their armed forces and transparency of their defense planning and budgeting.[64]

The Central and Eastern European states consider peacekeeping operations an important instrument for integration into the Western security structure. Each of them offered a variety of sites, centers, and other facilities for peacekeeping within the framework of the PFP. To promote closer military cooperation and interoperability, the PFP Invitation proposed peacekeeping field exercises beginning in 1994, but in fact various aspects of peacekeeping training and education, including seminars, the exchange of instructors, and courses for staff officers and unit commanders, had already been addressed by the NACC Ad Hoc Group on Cooperation in Peacekeeping, which also envisaged joint exercises in 1994.[65]

Both the Visegrád group and other Eastern European states have been very much interested not only in joint planning of field exercises with NATO but also in hosting them on their territories. About a dozen land exercises at the company or platoon level were scheduled for 1994, now involving members of the NACC Ad Hoc Group. As far as land exercises within the framework of the PFP are concerned, Poland in October 1994 became the first partner country to host a peacekeeping exercise. Code-named Cooperation Bridge '94, it involved some 650 troops from 13 countries (Bulgaria, the Czech Republic, Denmark, Germany, Italy, Lithuania, the Netherlands, Poland, Romania, Slovakia, Ukraine, the United Kingdom, and the United States). Cooperative Spirit '94 in the Netherlands and Cooperative Venture '94, a maritime exercise in the Norwegian Sea, followed this exercise. A number of other maritime exercises in the Baltic Sea were scheduled under the auspices of the NACC. The joint U.S.-Russia staff exercise in Russia was delayed for internal political reasons but finally took place in September 1994. The three Baltic states also appreciate the importance of peacekeeping operations within the PFP and for this purpose agreed to set up a joint military unit, BALT-BAT, to participate in such operations.[66]

In general, field exercises to promote interoperability and cooperation in peacekeeping became a major focus of the PFP programs of the Central and Eastern European countries, and a number of progressively more complex exercises were planned for 1995. By October 1994 the process of implementation of the partnership had been well under way, helping these countries to develop, with NATO's aid, a common defense culture and habits of cooperation on the road—as they hoped—to full integration in the Western alliance. On this route, however, the position of Russia loomed as the major obstacle for these candidates and the most difficult challenge for the alliance itself.

RUSSIA AND THE PFP

No discussion of the PFP and, more generally, the relationship between NATO and the former Warsaw Pact countries can avoid raising the sensitive issue of Russia and its role in the post–Cold War European security structure. The Western allies recognized that as a transcontinental Eurasian power, Russia offered a unique case. But at the same time, they realized that it somehow had to be drawn into the emerging partnership program. As a state participating in the NACC and, of course, the CSCE, Russia was invited to subscribe to the PFP Framework Document and start participating in partnership activities on an equal footing with the other partners. However, since the very launching of the partnership idea it became evident that, as a condition for subscribing to the PFP, Russia would insist on special treatment befitting its status as a major nuclear power.[67]

In Russia, whether or not to join the NATO-affiliated partnership became a subject of intense domestic debate during which Moscow sent confusing and contradictory signals about Russia's intentions concerning the PFP. It appears, however, that the "special status" argument involved Russian national pride suffering from the lost empire syndrome and disillusionment with, and rising antagonism against, the West, especially among extreme nationalists and Communists.[68]

In negotiating Russia's accession to the PFP, Russian Defense Minister General Pavel S. Grachev acted as the chief exponent of his country's position in Brussels. He called for the creation of a "full-blooded strategic rela-tionship" between Russia and NATO, to be formalized in a separate instru-ment, additional to any documents used in relations with the other prospective partners. Such a special relationship would, in fact, go far beyond partnership rules and entail a broad consultation mechanism between Russia and NATO on all kinds of major problems of European and global security.[69] In substance, Grachev's proposal was tantamount to Russia's becoming vir-tually a full-fledged member of the alliance, with a voice in its decisions, including those pertaining to enlargement. In this respect, Russia strongly opposed any expansion of the alliance to embrace its former satellite states in Central and Eastern Europe.

In its PFP negotiations, Russia once again revealed its strategic goal to elevate the CSCE, which Kozyrev credited with winning the Cold War, into an umbrella security system and alternative to NATO that would extend, in Kozyrev's NACC-borrowed phraseology, "from Vancouver to Vladivostok."[70] In this system, the CSCE would coordinate the activities of NATO, the European Union (EU), the WEU, and the Russian-led Commonwealth of Independent States (CIS). Parallel with a progressive dilution of NATO and its NACC, Russia's other major strategic goals are to maintain and strengthen its preeminence in the "near abroad," that is, the CIS, and obtain CSCE legit-imation for its military presence in other CIS states through peacekeeping operations, in reality peacemaking operations or simply sheer coercive mil-itary measures against insurgents or other troublesome political groups. In Brussels, Grachev acknowledged Russia's objective of strengthening the CIS but insisted that Russia's military presence in some "near abroad" states should be viewed only in terms of "peacekeeping objectives posing no secu-rity threat to its neighbors" and rejected as groundless claims that "Russia is trying to realize imperial goals."[71]

There are, however, indications that Russia's goals are at least "proto-imperial,"[72] as its leaders have stated that the reintegration of the former Soviet space (less, ostensibly, the three Baltic states) is the country's "para-mount task."[73] Also, the fact that the main guidelines for ensuring the mil-itary security of Russia list the task "to develop mutually advantageous military cooperations with foreign states, above all, with states belonging to CIS and countries of Central and Eastern Europe"[74] is a reminder that not only the "near abroad" but also the former Warsaw Pact countries still belong to an area of special Russian interest and influence.

NATO found Russian demands for a special status in the PFP with the consequent ability to influence NATO's decisionmaking and for recognition of Russia's hegemony in the CIS unacceptable. While each country planning to subscribe to the PFP, including Russia itself, is in a way special, the Russian conception of being "special" far exceeded the PFP principles articulated in the Invitation and the Framework Document. In fact, the "broad consultative mechanism," suggested by Russia, could be perceived as a NATO-Russia condominium reminiscent of the 1945 Yalta accord that determined the division of Europe for more than four decades. Indeed, NATO's PFP negotiations and Russia's references to a strategic partnership between the United States and Russia with joint security guarantees for the Central and Eastern European countries did not fail to cause serious concern in Central Europe and the Baltic states.[75]

Keen to bring Russia into the partnership, NATO confronted a dilemma between somehow meeting halfway Russian demands for a special status and reassuring Central and Eastern European countries that Russia's position in the PFP would not portend a deal at their expense. A face-saving diplomatic formula was needed that, without compromising the NATO position, would take into account Russia's stature but would concurrently soothe the anxieties of these concerned countries. After protracted bargaining, such a formula was devised, and Russia joined the PFP when Kozyrev signed the Framework Document at a meeting of the North Atlantic Council on 22 June 1994. In this sense, the treatment of Russia did not differ from that accorded any other prospective partner signing this document. However, the treatment of Russia was symbolically unique in that, first, the United States was represented by Secretary Christopher at the signing ceremony and, second, at Russia's insistence, an unsigned summary of conclusions between the NATO Council and the Russian representative, Kozyrev, accompanied the endorsed Framework Document.[76]

Without mentioning the term "special" to describe Russia's ties to NATO and in substance falling short of Russia's maximum demands, the four-point summary conveys the message that Russian participation in the partnership carries more weight than that of any other subscribing state. Emphasizing friendly relations between NATO and Russia as a key element for security and stability in the CSCE area, the two sides agree to develop an extensive Individual Partnership Program "corresponding to Russia's size, importance and capabilities." In the major reference to the new partner's stature, they pledge to pursue, through sharing of information, political consultations, and cooperation in a range of security-related areas, "a broad, enhanced dialogue and cooperation in areas where Russia has unique and important contributions to make, commensurate with its weight and responsibility as a major European, international and nuclear power." At the same time, in an attempt to reassure the Central and Eastern European countries, the summary promises that the "far-reaching, cooperative NATO/Russia relationship, both inside and outside Partnership for Peace," which they agreed to set in operation, "is not directed against the interest of third countries." To emphasize that no secret deals are involved, the summary adds that the NATO/Russia relationship "is transparent to others."[77]

Both NATO and the Russian representative welcomed Russia's accession to the PFP as the beginning of a new chapter in the era of cooperation in post–Cold War Europe. But each side had different hopes and expectations concerning Russia's presence in the headquarters of an alliance created to keep it out of Western Europe in the first place. By bringing Russia into the partnership, NATO hoped to ease Russia's fear of isolation and gradually have it adopt a less suspicious and more cooperative posture toward the West. It also desired that contacts between defense professionals from the two sides would develop habits of cooperation and mutual reassurance excluding any thought of resort to violence and eventually leading to integration of Russia into a wider European collective security system. For his part, the Russian foreign minister, upon signing the PFP document, expressed the hope that NATO would no longer be an alliance aimed at Russia. At the same time, however, simply echoing Grachev's pre-signature bargaining position, he continued calling for NATO to serve as a vehicle for integrating East and West into a single security space, from Vancouver to Vladivostok.[78] Obviously, Russia's joining the NATO-sponsored partnership has in no way changed the main outlines of the Russian strategy calling for a progressive diluting of NATO by subordinating it to the loosely conceived fifty-three nation CSCE. In Kozyrev's view, the top priority of NATO and Russia was "to avoid confining military-political cooperation . . . to a geographically limited area," which in practice meant opening the partnership to as many countries as possible and not treating it as a pre-NATO station for just a few countries and especially the Visegrád group.[79]

At the June 1994 NACC meeting in Istanbul, shortly before Russia joined the PFP, Kozyrev had opposed endorsing the entry of the Central and Eastern European countries into the WEU, a move Russia viewed as bringing them into NATO through the back door.[80] In Brussels, on the day of accession to the partnership, he was careful expressly not to oppose admission of these countries to NATO. However, contrary to misleading press reports, neither he nor any other Russian leader expressed agreement to such admission. When, upon signing the Presentation Document, Kozyrev admitted to the possibility of enlarging NATO, he meant the Visegrád countries *and* Russia as equally viable candidates. He also urged that the potential of the PFP process be fully exhausted and found it quite possible that "the dynamic development of the partnership, as well as the cooperation within the CSCE and NACC framework, will make less pressing . . . the eastward expansion of the NATO zone."[81]

Russian opposition to any expansion of NATO that would exclude Russia itself became quite clear in December 1994 when its foreign minister objected to the NATO decision to initiate a process to define the criteria for alliance membership and then to present them to interested PFP participants by the end of 1995. Although the alliance named neither specific eligible countries nor the time frame for enlargement, and although the Russian government had been fully briefed in advance about the plan, Kozyrev found the one-year schedule too short and demanded clarification before Russia would sign its Individual Partnership Program and commence participating in the partnership's activities.[82] It appears, however, that access to NATO through the PFP offers Russia advantages that it would not like to miss, and the Russian foreign minister's reaction has to be regarded as only one bargaining move in Russia's campaign against an eastward expansion of NATO that ignores its perceived national interests.

Russia's presence in the heart of NATO ("the fox in the henhouse") could provide it with the opportunity to exploit to its best advantage the possibilities of "enhanced dialogue" through political consultations to which reference is made in the summary of the NATO-Russia PFP discussions. As hoped by the Russian foreign ministry, participation in the partnership would enable Russia "to sway the future evolution of this program according to Russia's national interests."[83] As a matter of fact, in late 1994 Russia's foreign minister again proposed establishing a consultation mechanism that would operate not only in emergencies but on a regular basis, even though NATO had rejected such an institutionalization of the Russia-NATO political ties at the PFP negotiating stage. It is in the interest of the alliance to retain its ability to decide whether an issue is of "common concern" and whether political consultations on such an issue are "appropriate" under the circumstances—the terms used in the June 1994 summary of conclusions. Expansion of the alliance is not among such issues, and—as categorically stated by President Clinton at the Budapest CSCE conference—cannot be subject to any country's veto.[84]

SUMMING UP AND SUGGESTIONS

In quick reaction to the end of the Cold War, the Atlantic Alliance embarked upon a process of transformation, adapting itself to the fundamental political and strategic changes in Europe and general international relations. Beginning with the watershed London Declaration of 1990 that proclaimed the end of the division of Europe, a series of high-level decisions guided the alliance's transformation and redefined its mission in the new Europe. In this agenda, the establishment of a fresh cooperative relationship with the countries of Central and Eastern Europe, formerly allied against NATO, became an integral part of the alliance's strategy and a virtual raison d'être for its continued existence after the Cold War. Very soon, diplomatic liaison was established between NATO and the former Warsaw Pact countries, including the successor states of the defunct Soviet Union, and the rapidly increasing contacts and consultations on political and defense matters contributed to an evolving positive relationship based on dialogue and cooperation. In December 1991, the North Atlantic Cooperation Council institutionalized this relationship, and by early 1993 it had grouped the sixteen members of NATO and all the former Warsaw Pact countries, including the successor states of the Soviet Union. Among the Central and Eastern European states, the so-called Visegrád group—the Czech Republic, Hungary, Poland, and Slovakia—and the Baltic states came to perceive NATO as the key to their security against a possible revival of Russian imperial ambitions. As their contacts with NATO intensified, pressures grew in those countries for a NATO security guarantee or, preferably, membership in the alliance now ostensibly committed to enhancing security and stability in the whole of Europe. In January 1994, in response to these pressures, NATO launched a Partnership for Peace program that—while in principle committing NATO to an evolutionary expansion to democratic states in the East—essentially deferred the issue of admitting new members to the alliance. The prime reason for this posture involved concern about a negative reaction from Russia, which strongly objected to extending NATO to the democracies in Central and Eastern Europe and regarded the plans for such expansion as a potential threat to Russian security. Still, NATO, and especially the United States, reassured the first-line candidates for membership that their admission some time in the future was certain.

In a first move toward expansion, NATO at its December 1994 meeting decided to begin an extensive study designed to establish specific criteria for membership and to present them to interested partners by the end of 1995. It is noteworthy that, in a reversal of early positions, America's allies only reluctantly and with reservations endorsed this U.S. initiative. In particular, France and Germany appeared concerned, as the United States had been at an earlier stage, about Russia's reaction and were not very eager to extend defense commitments at a time of the confused NATO response in Bosnia. It must be added that no country's name or admission timetables accompanied the NATO announcement on initiating a membership study, probably to allay Russian suspicions of an early expansion of the alliance. But, as already noted, even a modest step beyond the PFP toward NATO membership of the Central European democracies provoked a strong Russian reaction. Russia's foreign minister failed to sign his country's Individual Partnership Program, and President Yeltsin sternly warned CSCE participants in Budapest that NATO plans for expansion eastward threatened to split Europe and plunge it into a "cold peace."[85]

As stressed previously, the Russia-focused argument against integrating the Central European democracies into NATO is untenable. No country is automatically excluded, and each candidate for membership ought to be considered on an individual basis in strict adherence to NATO criteria, which are likely to be quite demanding and stringent.

If NATO's vision is a pan-European security structure—and this, ostensibly, is the case—then this collective defense organization may gradually undergo a metamorphosis into a wider security structure combining the features of both collective security and collective defense, and Russia, if otherwise meeting the criteria, could not be excluded from membership. But in this early post–Cold War period it is difficult to envisage such an organization. At this point, NATO still remains an alliance, under Article 10 of the North Atlantic Treaty, open to accession by other European states sharing its values and principles and otherwise able and willing to meet the specific criteria of membership. In this respect, the capacity and desire of the individual PFP participants varies considerably. The Visegrád states, with Slovakia perhaps less than the other three, have advanced more than the other partners on the way to meeting the criteria that the alliance is expected to develop in 1995.

In addition to the requirements of Article 10 (for being in a position to further the principles of the North Atlantic Treaty and contributing to the security of the North Atlantic area) and the commitment to NATO's fundamental values, a prospective member is expected to have reasonably achieved the objectives named in the PFP Framework Document. They include: transparency in defense planning and budgeting; democratic control of defense forces; capability and readiness to contribute to operations under the authority of the United Nations or the responsibility of the Organization for Security and Cooperation in Europe (the renamed CSCE); ability to undertake missions in the field of peacekeeping, search and rescue, humanitarian, and any other missions under NATO auspices; and development of forces better able to operate with those of the members of the alliance. In all these military matters, specific standards will have to be determined for each applicant state.

It would also be appropriate to establish certain substantive criteria and requirements designed to enhance peace and stability in the region and to contribute to strengthening the position of democratic governments. They should cover such matters as acceptance by the candidate country of the existing borders, renouncing any territorial claims, and, in general, settling outstanding territorial disputes. Protection of minorities without discrimination could also be included among the prerequisites for admission.

Parallel with disclosing the membership criteria, the alliance should designate the Czech Republic, Hungary, Poland, and possibly Slovakia as the closest to reaching the defined standards and fix a reasonable date for joining the alliance, possibly within three years. Where appropriate, the required standards should specify as exactly as possible the financial and military commitments of each candidate.

The expansion of NATO is conceived as an ongoing evolutionary process that takes account of political and security developments in the whole of Europe. Logically, Russia cannot be excluded as a potential candidate should it really meet the required NATO criteria. Realistically, however, Russia's road to achieving the high standards of political culture envisaged in the PFP Framework Document and other possible criteria defined by the alliance will be long and uncertain. Hence, in recognition of Russia's legitimate security interests and its status as a major power, special treaty arrangements should accompany the eastward expansion of NATO. First, the membership model of the new members should follow that of Denmark and Norway, more recently applied to the eastern part of Germany, in which nuclear weapons and foreign troops are not allowed to be stationed in peacetime in the territory of the state concerned. Second, a concert-like arrangement in the form of a treaty of friendship and cooperation between NATO and Russia could meet Russia's claims to major power status and provide a basis for its participation in coordinating security within a wider European framework.

In a more general perspective, the topic discussed in this chapter touches upon some fundamental issues confronting the Atlantic Alliance in the post–Cold War era, and especially its current role, its cohesion, and the willingness of the United States to remain engaged in European affairs. Hence, in the final analysis, the problem of the relations between NATO and the former Warsaw Pact countries is bound to become an inquiry into the future of the Western Alliance itself.

NOTES

1. A summary of security challenges facing NATO in the post–Cold War era is found in "The Alliance's New Strategic Concept—Agreed by the Heads of State and Government Participating in the Meeting of the North Atlantic Council in Rome on 7-8 November 1991," *NATO Review* 39, no. 6 (December 1991): 25-32. For discussion of nationalist, ethnic, and territorial conflicts see Jacques Rupnik, "Europe's New Frontiers: Remapping Europe," *Daedalus* (Summer 1994): 91-114; and Jeffrey Simon, "Central Europe: 'Return to Europe' or Descent to Chaos?" in *European Security toward the Year 2000* (Washington: National Defense University, 1993), 31-52.

2. This pessimistic view is shared by Zbigniew Brzezinski, "The Premature Partnership," *Foreign Affairs* 72, no. 2 (March-April 1994): 67-82; and Steven Erlanger, "East Europe Watches the Bear Warily: Five Years Later," *New York Times*, 21 October 1994. Russian defense minister Pavel S. Grachev in November 1993 defined the term "near abroad" as including only the other states of the Commonwealth of Independent States (CIS); Brigitte Sauerwein, "Visiting Switzerland: Grachev Defines 'Near Abroad,'" *IDR International Defense Review* 27 (January 1994): 5.

3. For an excellent systematic analysis of possible security arrangements for Europe see Charles Glaser, "Why NATO Is Still Best: Future Security Arrangements for Europe," *International Security* 18 (Summer 1993): 5-50; Nanette Gantz and James B. Steinberg, *Five Models for European Security: Implications for the United States* (Santa Monica, CA: RAND Corporation, 1992) (N-3446 A); and Adrian Hyde-Price, "Alternative Security Systems for Europe," in *European Security—Towards 2000*, ed. Michael C. Pugh (Manchester: Manchester University Press, 1992), 124-39.

4. The CSCE renamed itself the Organization for Security and Cooperation in Europe (OSCE) at its Budapest meeting in December 1994.

5. William van Eekelen, "Building a New European Security Order," *NATO Review* 38, no. 4 (August 1990): 18-23; Sir Michael Alexander, "European Security and the CSCE," ibid. 39, no. 4 (August 1991): 10-14; Werner Bauwens et al., "The CSCE and the Changing Role of NATO and the European Union," ibid. 42, no. 3 (June 1994): 21-25; Victor-Yves Ghebali, "The CSCE in the Post–Cold War Europe," ibid. 39, no. 2 (April 1991): 8-11; William Höynck, "CSCE Works to Develop Its Conflict Prevention Potential," ibid. 42, no. 2 (April 1994): 16-22; Max van der Stoel, "Preventing Conflict and Building Peace: A Challenge for the CSCE," ibid. 42, no. 4 (August 1994): 7-12; and Hans Binnendijk, "The

Emerging European Security Order," *Washington Quarterly* 14 (Autumn 1991): 71-81.

6. Glaser, "Why NATO," 50.

7. See "The Alliance's New Strategic Concept Agreed by the Heads of State and Government Participating in the Meeting of the North Atlantic Council in Rome on 7-8 November 1991," *NATO Review* 39, no. 6 (December 1991): 25-32. For some analysis see Michael Legge, "The Making of NATO's New Strategy," ibid. 39, no. 6 (December 1991): 9-14; and Eckhard Lübkemeier, "The Political Upheaval in Europe and the Reform of NATO Strategy," ibid. 39, no. 3 (June 1991): 16-21.

8. The Harmel Report, named after its initiator, Belgian Foreign Minister Pierre Harmel, was published in December 1967 under the title "The Future Tasks of the Alliance"; for its philosophy see Joachim Brockpähler, "The Harmel Philosophy: NATO's Creative Strategy for Peace," *NATO Review* 38, no. 6 (December 1990): 17-21. See also "New Strategic Concept," 25.

9. The Warsaw Pact was officially dissolved on 1 April 1991, and the protocol on its dissolution was signed on 1 July 1991; on its final days see Otto Pick, "The Demise of the Warsaw Pact," *NATO Review* 39, no. 2 (April 1991): 12-16. On the Turnberry message see *NATO Handbook* (Brussels: NATO Office of Information and Press, 1992), 60; the London Declaration is reprinted in *NATO Review* 38, no. 4 (August 1990): 32-33.

10. For a review of the military contacts see Angus Watt, "The Hand of Friendship—The Military Contacts Programme," *NATO Review* 40, no. 1 (February 1992): 19-22. On the role of the NATO Defense College in these contacts see Richard J. Evraire, "The NATO Defense College Reaches out to the East," ibid. 41, no. 6 (December 1993): 15-18.

11. "The CSCE Summit—Paris, 19-21 November 1990," *NATO Review* 38, no. 6 (December 1990): 26-31. The Joint Declaration is not a treaty and is therefore not eligible for registration with the United Nations under Article 102 of the UN Charter.

12. "Partnership with the Countries of Central and Eastern Europe. Statement Issued by the North Atlantic Council Meeting in Ministerial Session in Copenhagen on 6 and 7 June 1991," *NATO Review* 39, no. 3 (June 1991): 28-29; Manfred Wörner, "NATO Transformed: The Significance of the Rome Summit," ibid. 39, no. 6 (December 1991): 4; Paul C. Rambaut, "Environmental Challenges: The Role of NATO," ibid. 40, no. 2 (April 1992): 24-27; Deniz Yuksel-Beten, "CCMS: NATO's Environmental Programme Is Expanded and Opened to the East," ibid. 39, no. 4 (August 1991): 27-32; Simon Lunn, "The Hands of Friendship—The Parliamentary Contribution," ibid. 39, no. 4 (August 1991): 10-14.

13. The group is named after the Hungarian town in which its second meeting took place in February 1991.

14. "North Atlantic Council, Statement Issued at NATO Headquarters, Brussels, on 21 August 1991," *NATO Review* 39, no. 4 (August 1991): 9.

15. Wörner, "NATO Transformed," 4. On NATO's reaction to the collapse of the coup see "Secretary General Welcomes Restoration of Constitutional Order in Soviet Union," *NATO Review* 39, no. 4 (August 1991): 9.
16. "Rome Declaration, 7-8 November 1991," *NATO Review* 39, no. 6 (December 1991): 19-22.
17. Adopted on 20 December 1991 and reprinted in *NATO Review* 40, no. 1 (February 1992): 29-30. During the NACC session, the Soviet ambassador requested that in accordance with his instructions from Moscow all references to the Soviet Union be excluded from the statement.
18. For the First Work Plan (issued on 10 March 1992) see *NATO Review* 40, no. 2 (April 1992): 34-35; for the 1993 plan see ibid. 41, no. 1 (February 1993): 30-31; for the 1994 plan see ibid. 41, no. 6 (December 1993): 30-33. For the revised 1994 plan, valid also for 1995, see NATO Press Service, Communiqué M-NACC-2 (94) 121, 2 December 1994. On the work of the NACC see Henning von Ondarza, "Pillar of the New European Security Architecture—The North Atlantic Cooperation Council," *NATO's Sixteen Nations* 38, no. 5/6 (1993): 41-43.
19. "Meeting of the North Atlantic Cooperation Council—NATO Headquarters, Brussels, 3 December 1993. Progress Report to Ministers by the NACC Ad Hoc Group on Cooperation in Peacekeeping," *NATO Review* 41, no. 6 (December 1993): 27-30. See also John Kriendler, "NATO's Changing Role—Opportunities and Constraints for Peacekeeping," ibid. 41, no. 3 (June 1993): 16-22. For cooperation in defense conversion see NATO, "Basic Fact Sheet," no. 10 (June 1994).
20. A critical review of the NACC was part of an intensive study of NATO in 1993 conducted by the North Atlantic Assembly Presidential Task Force, *America and Europe: The Future of NATO and the Transatlantic Relationship—Final Report* (Brussels, 1993). See also Bruce George, "The Alliance at the Flashpoint of a New Era," *NATO Review* 41, no. 5 (October 1993): 7-11; Warren Christopher, "Towards a NATO Summit," ibid. 41, no. 4 (August 1993): 6; and Ondarza, "Pillar," 42-43.
21. George, "Alliance," 8.
22. Manfred Wörner, "A Vigorous Alliance—A Motor for Peaceful Change in Europe," *NATO Review* 40, no. 6 (December 1992): 6.
23. Paul Latawski, "On Converging Paths? The Visegrád Group and the Atlantic Alliance," *Paradigms* 7 (Winter 1993): 79. See also the Cracow Declaration of the three states adopted on 6 October 1991 in *European Security* 1 (Spring 1992): 104, referred to in ibid., 78. On the Visegrád group see also Joshua Spero, "The Budapest-Prague-Warsaw Triangle: Central European Security after the Visegrád Summit," *European Security* 1 (Spring 1992): 58-83; and Rudolf L. Tökés, "From Visegrád to Krakow: Cooperation, Competition, and Coexistence in Central Europe," *Problems of Communism* 40 (November 1991): 100-114.
24. German Defense Minister Volker Rühe used this phrase in his argument for integrating the Visegrád states into the European Union and NATO. "NATO's Membership for Russia Doubted," *New York Times,* 10 September 1994.

25. "Basic Provisions of the Military Doctrine of the Russian Federation," *Jane's Intelligence Review* 6 (January 1994): 8 (emphasis added).
26. Geza Jeszenszky, "Nothing Quiet on the Eastern Front," *NATO Review* 40, no. 3 (June 1992): 7-13; idem, "Our Wish to Be Firmly Anchored," *NATO's Sixteen Nations* 39, no. 2 (1994): 29-31; Vaclav Havel, "Address to the NATO Council," *NATO Review* 39, no. 2 (April 1991): 31-35; idem, "Central Europe Belongs in NATO," *NATO's Sixteen Nations* 38, no. 5/6 (1993): 2-3; Jiri Dienstbier, "The Future of European Security. Prague Conference Confirms Agreement on Basic Ideas," *NATO Review* 39, no. 3 (June 1991): 3-6; Jaromir Novotny, "The Czech Republic—An Active Partner with NATO," ibid. 42, no. 3 (June 1993): 12-15; Josef Zieleniec, "Partnership for Peace—The Perspective from Prague," *NATO's Sixteen Nations* 39, no. 2 (1994): 14-15; Michal Kovác, "Slovakia and the Partnership for Peace," *NATO Review* 42, no. 1 (February 1994): 15-18; Eduard Kukan, "Slovakia—Cooperation with NATO," *NATO's Sixteen Nations* 39, no. 2 (1994): 54-55; "Slovakia —Wrong Turning," *Economist*, 12 November 1994.
27. Michael R. Gordon, "U.S. Opposes Move to Rapidly Expand NATO Membership. But Officials Are Divided," *New York Times*, 2 January 1994. Latawski, "On Converging Paths?" The United Kingdom would not like an expansion of NATO that might dilute its Atlantic character and its special relationship with the United States. France, believing that the enlargement would entail enhanced American influence in Europe, would rather opt for a European security scheme. Howard LaFranchi, "Europeans Share US Aim to Stall Eastern Europe's Entry into Alliance," *Christian Science Monitor*, 7 January 1994. For Italy see Giovanni Januzzi, "NATO's Outlook: A Perspective from Italy," *NATO Review* 41, no. 6 (December 1993): 11-15.
28. Gordon, "U.S. Opposes Move"; Daniel Williams, "Summit Weighs Alliance's Future, Looks for Leadership," *Washington Post*, 9 January 1994; Carla Anne Robbins, "Talbott's Abiding Passion for Russia Shapes His Career and Clinton's Administration Policy," *Wall Street Journal*, 7 January 1994; Robert B. Zollick, "Strobe Talbott on NATO: An Answer," *Washington Post*, 5 January 1994. Departing Defense Secretary Les Aspin drafted the American compromise. Steven Erlanger, "NATO Issue: Rightist Vote Helps Russia," *New York Times*, 29 December 1993.
29. "Meeting of NATO Defence Ministers—Travemünde, 20-21 October 1993," "Communiqué Issued by the Ministerial Meeting of the North Atlantic Council. NATO Headquarters, Brussels—2 December 1993," and "Statement Issued at the Meeting of the North Atlantic Cooperation Council. NATO Headquarters, Brussels—3 December 1993," *NATO Review* 41, no. 6 (December 1993): 24-27. "Declaration of the Heads of State and Government participating in the Meeting of the North Atlantic Council Held at NATO Headquarters, Brussels, on 10-11 January 1994," ibid. 42, no. 1 (February 1994): 30-33.
30. Reprinted in *NATO Review* 42, no. 1 (January 1994): 28-29.
31. Ibid.
32. Ibid.

33. Ibid.
34. Les Aspin, "New Europe, New NATO," *NATO Review* 42, no. 1 (February 1994): 7; Manfred Wörner, "Partnership with NATO—The Political Dimension," *NATO's Sixteen Nations* 39, no. 2 (1994): 7.
35. NATO, "Progress Control Table for PfP Milestones—Updated as of 14/10/1994," (PFP/SC-N(94)8).
36. "Partnership for Peace: Framework Document," sec. 3.
37. NATO, "Progress Control Table."
38. "Ministerial Meeting of the North Atlantic Council, 1 December 1994—Final Communiqué," NATO Press Service, Press Release M-NAC-2 (94) 116:2; NATO, "Progress Control Table." As part of the gradual de facto merger of the NACC tasks with those of the PFP, military cooperation in the area of peacekeeping, conducted mainly in the NACC Ad Hoc Group on Cooperation in Peacekeeping, became a major focus of PMSC attention, with the NACC Ad Hoc Group merging with the PMSC. "Statement Issued at the Meeting of the North Atlantic Cooperation Council. Istanbul, Turkey, 10 June 1994," *NATO Review* 42, no. 3 (June 1994): 30. Gebhardt von Moltke, "Building a Partnership for Peace," ibid. 42, no. 3 (June 1994): 6-7. See also "NATO Encourages Technology Transfer as PfP Develops," *IDR International Defense Review* 27 (September 1994): 5.
39. Accommodations for the partners' missions were found in the Manfred Wörner Wing at NATO headquarters. On logistical difficulties of the PFP program see "NATO Infrastructure Ill-Prepared for Partnership for Peace," *IDR International Defense Review* 27 (March 1994): 9.
40. Manfred Wörner, "Shaping the Alliance for the Future," *NATO Review* 42, no. 1 (February 1994): 6.
41. Warren Christopher, "NATO Plus," *Washington Post,* 9 January 1994; Daniel Williams and Lee Hockstader, "NATO Seeks to Reassure East as Russia Warns against Expansion," ibid., 6 January 1994. For seven arguments against enlargement see Trevor Taylor, "NATO and Central Europe," *NATO Review* 39, no. 5 (October 1991): 17-22.
42. Latawski, "On Converging Paths?" 87-88.
43. Statement by Yeltsin's spokesman, Vyacheslav Kostikov, quoted in Williams and Hockstader, "NATO Seeks to Reassure." See also Alexei Pushkov, "Russia and the West: An Endangered Relationship?" *NATO Review* 42, no. 1 (February 1994): 19-23.
44. Andrei Kozyrev, "Foreign Minister Pleads for Partnership," *Washington Times,* 11 January 1994.
45. Statement by Lt. General Dmitri Kharchenko in *Krasnaya Zvezda,* the official organ of Russia's Ministry of Defense, quoted in Williams and Hockstader, "NATO Seeks to Reassure."
46. "Basic Provisions of the Military Doctrine," 7.
47. For criticism of this argument see, for example, Ronald D. Asmus, Richard F. Kugler, and F. Stephen Larrabbee, "Should NATO Go East—II. Building a New NATO," in *Foreign Affairs—Agenda 1994: Critical Issues in Foreign Policy* (New

York: Council on Foreign Relations, 1994), 201-13 (reprinted from *Foreign Affairs* September/October 1993); Brzezinski, "Premature Partnership"; Frank Gaffney, Jr., "Who Gets the Last Laugh? Policy Jackstraws at State," *Washington Times*, 5 January 1994; Latawski, "On Converging Paths?" 86-88; Janusz Onyszkiewicz, "Why NATO Should Expand to the East. A Polish View," *Washington Post*, 6 January 1994; Richard Perle, "The Charade in Brussels," *New York Times*, 11 January 1994; and Edward L. Rowny, "NATO and the Difference between Eastern and Central Europe," *Washington Times*, 15 March 1994. Henry Kissinger called the chances of antagonizing Russia a "false dilemma," adding that throughout history Russia had always wanted a veto over its neighbors; Williams, "Summit Weighs Alliance's Future."

48. In response to this argument, President Clinton, while admitting the risk of forfeiting the chance at the time of Russia's weakness, argued that the West would have sufficient warning to react against a potentially expansionist Russia. *Washington Times*, 9 January 1994.

49. See Boleslaw A. Boczek, *Scandinavia: New Focus of Soviet Pressures* (London: Institute for European Defense and Strategic Studies, 1989), 17, 43-44. Regarding the territory of the former East Germany see Treaty on the Final Settlement with Respect to Germany, concluded by the two Germanys, France, the USSR, the United Kingdom, and the United States, 12 September 1990, reprinted in *International Legal Materials* 29, no. 5 (September 1990): 1186-1931. It is also significant that according to Russian military doctrine, deployment of foreign troops on the territory adjacent to the Russian Federation is included among "factors which facilitate the escalation of a military danger into a direct military threat to the Russian Federation," unless it is done as part of a UN-approved collective security action by agreement with the Russian Federation. "Basic Provisions of the Military Doctrine," 7.

50. Poland's foreign minister stated that "we reject the simplistic and incorrect interpretation of the envisaged enlargement of the Alliance as an exercise in 'drawing new division lines on the continent.' On the contrary . . . widening of the Alliance to the East would meaningfully project stability in that region." Andrzej Olechowski, "From Partnership to Membership," *NATO's Sixteen Nations* 39, no. 2 (1994): 44. See also Maciej Kozlowski, "Poland Is Ready for NATO Membership," *New York Times*, 12 December 1994; Piotr Kolodziejczyk, "Poland: A Future NATO Ally," *NATO Review* 42, no. 5 (October 1994): 7-10.

51. Asmus et al., "Should NATO Go East?" 210; Brzezinski, "Premature Partnership," 82.

52. Asmus et al., "Should NATO Go East?" 210.

53. For example, see Taylor, "NATO and Central Europe," 18-19.

54. Stanislav Daskalov, "Bulgaria and NATO—Partnership for Stability in a Changing World," *NATO's Sixteen Nations* 39, no. 2 (1994): 12; Victor Valkov, "Partnership between Bulgaria and NATO: A Promising Development," *NATO Review* 39, no. 5 (October 1991): 13-17. For the Romanian position see Teodor Viorel Melescanu, "The Partnership for Peace—A Way out of the Past," *NATO's*

Sixteen Nations 39, no. 2 (1994): 46-47; and idem, "Security in Central Europe: A Positive Sum Game," *NATO Review* 41, no. 5 (October 1993): 12-18. Albania's goal is to integrate into the Western political and military structures; see Alfred Serreqi, "Albania, the Partnership for Peace and the Democratic Process," *NATO's Sixteen Nations* 39, no. 2 (1994): 8-9 and Adam Copani, "The Democratic Process and Albanian Security Policy," *NATO Review* 40, no. 5 (October 1992): 20-26. Albania was a nominal member of the Warsaw Pact until 1968, when it withdrew its membership.

55. Deborah Sewaro, "Lithuania Seeks Membership in NATO; Russia Not Happy," *Washington Times,* 6 January 1994; Povilas Gylys, "Lithuania's Partnership with NATO," *NATO's Sixteen Nations* 39, no. 2 (1994): 41-42. For Latvia see Georgs Andrejevs, "Search for Security in Common Structures," ibid. 39, no. 2 (1994): 35-36; and Andrei Martov, "Baltic States Emerge from Cold War Shadow," *IDR International Defense Review* 27 (May 1994): 9. For Estonia see Juri Luik, "The Right Step in the Right Direction at the Right Time," *NATO's Sixteen Nations* 39, no. 2 (1994): 17-19; Lennart Meri, "Estonia, NATO and Peacekeeping," *NATO Review* 42, no. 2 (April 1994): 7-9; and "Estonia: In a Bear's Paw," *Economist,* 19 November 1994, 60.

56. For Georgia see Alexandre Chikvaidze, "On the Way to Partnership," *NATO's Sixteen Nations* 39, no. 2 (1994): 27-28; George Shevardnadze, "Georgia's Security Outlook," *NATO Review* 41, no. 4 (August 1993): 7-10. For Kazakhstan see H. E. Kanat Saudabayev, "Kazakhstan and NATO—Towards an Eurasian Security System," *NATO's Sixteen Nations* 39, no. 2 (1994): 33-34.

57. Taylor, "NATO and Central Europe," 19; Asmus et al., "Should NATO Go East?" 209; Latawski, "On Converging Paths?" 89. Latvia and Estonia have large Russian minorities, and Estonia has a territorial dispute with Russia involving roughly 5 percent of its territory, making Estonia's NATO membership highly unlikely as long as the dispute remains unsolved. "Estonia in a Bear's Paw."

58. See, for example, Taylor, "NATO and Central Europe," 18; and Walter Russell Mead, "No Cold War Two: The United States and the Russian Federation," *World Policy Journal* 11, no. 2 (Summer 1994): 12. Warren Strobel, "Smaller Budgets Stand in Way of a Bigger NATO," *Washington Times,* 7 January 1994.

59. See, for example, statements by Aspin in Williams, "Summit Weighs Alliance's Future," and by Christopher in Christopher, "NATO Plus."

60. Ann Devroy and Daniel Williams, "U.S. Sees Security Problems in Quick Expansion of Alliance," *Washington Post,* 5 January 1994; Craig R. Whitney, "NATO Plight: Coping with Applicants," *New York Times,* 4 January 1994; Daniel Williams, "Shalikashvili to Lobby Ex-Soviet Bloc Nations: U.S. Opposes Bids for Immediate NATO Seats," *Washington Post,* 4 January 1994. David B. Ottaway, "War Games in Poland Proposed: E. European Officials Reluctantly Endorse NATO 'Partnership'," ibid., 8 January 1994.

61. Ottaway, "War Games in Poland"; Daniel Williams, "U.S. Trying to Sell NATO Partnership: Ex-East Bloc Countries Want Full Seat," *Washington Post,* 1 January 1994; Whitney, "NATO Plight."

62. For the Czech Republic see Zieleniec, "Partnership for Peace"; for Hungary, Jeszenszky, "Our Wish Is to Be Firmly Anchored"; for Poland, Olechowski, "From Partnership to Membership"; and for Slovakia, Kukan, "Slovakia— Cooperation with NATO." NATO noted the status of association of the WEU with the Central European States in the final communiqué of the ministerial meeting of the North Atlantic Council in Istanbul on 9 June 1994 and in the statement issued at the NACC meeting on the following day. See *NATO Review* 42, no. 3 (June 1994): 27, 30.

63. For the Czechs' claims to be more advanced on the way to NATO see Jane Perlez, "4 Countries in Audition for NATO," *New York Times*, 11 January 1995; "Central European Security, 1994," 1, 3; "Czechs Pursue Integration into NATO Structure," *IDR International Defense Review* 27 (April 1994): 9-10. On Slovakia see Kukan, "Slovakia—Cooperation with NATO," 55. On Poland see "NATO Encourages Technology Transfer as PfP Develops," *IDR International Defense Review* 27 (September 1994): 5. The United States promised to seek $100 million for bilateral programs in fiscal year 1966 to support PFP, with Poland to receive $25 million.

64. For the Czech Republic see "Czechs Pursue Integration NATO Structure," *IDR International Defense Review* 27 (April 1994): 9; for Hungary, Jeszensky, "Our Wish," 30; for Poland, Olechowski, "From Partnership to Membership," 46-47; for Slovakia, Kukan, "Slovakia—Cooperation with NATO," 55.

65. Under the NACC Plan for 1994, "exploration of options for joint training and joint exercises" was included among the numerous activities in the area of defense planning issues and military matters. See "Work Plan for 1994," *NATO Review* 41, no. 6 (December 1993): 31.

66. For the exercises in Poland see "Exercise Cooperative Bridge 94," NATO Press Service, 26 August 1994, Press Release (94) 71. For the Baltic states see Andrejevs, "Search for Security," 36; Luik, "The Right Step," 17.

67. See, for example, Kozyrev, "Russia Plans Leading Role"; Alessandra Stanley, "Russia Seeks Link to NATO but Nationalists Are Bitter," *New York Times*, 18 March 1994; idem, "Russian Aide Voices Doubts on joining NATO Group," ibid., 1 April 1994; John F. Harris, "U.S. Seeks Special Role in NATO for Russians," *Washington Post*, 20 March 1994; Elaine Sciolino, "NATO Rejects Russian role in Decision-Making," *New York Times*, 10 June 1994; idem, "Russia Pledges to join NATO Partnership," ibid., 11 June 1994.

68. On 17 March 1994, Grachev told U.S. Defense Secretary William Perry that Russia would be ready to join the PFP by the end of March 1994. Fred Hiatt, "Russia Speeds Plans for Link to NATO," *Washington Post*, 18 March 1994. But on 31 March, a spokesman for Yeltsin, Vyacheslav V. Kostikov, announced that the decision on joining was being reconsidered and could take six months. Stanley, "Russian Aide." Allegedly, Yeltsin made the decision to postpone entry into the PFP to win backing from Russian nationalists. Michael Specter, "Yeltsin Wins Peace Accord in Parliament," *New York Times*, 29 April 1994. Then on 24 May Grachev brought to Brussels assurances from Yeltsin that

Russia would join the Partnership, but did not set any date. William E. Schmidt, "Russia Tells NATO It Is Ready to Join Peace Partnership," *New York Times*, 25 May 1994. However, he demanded for Russia a special status going beyond that applying to the other partners. William Drozdiak and John F. Harris, "Russia Asks Fuller Ties with NATO," *Washington Post*, 26 May 1994; Daniel Sneider, "Russia Prepared to Join NATO," *Christian Science Monitor*, 27 May 1994. On 10 June, Kozyrev reaffirmed Russia's commitment to join. Elaine Sciolino, "Russia Pledges to Join NATO Partnership," *New York Times*, 11 June 1994. And on 22 June Kozyrev signed the PFP Presentation Document. Daniel Williams, "Russia Joins NATO Plan," *Washington Post*, 23 June 1994.

69. See the accounts in Drozdiak and Harris, "Russia Asks Fuller Ties," and Sciolino, "NATO Rejects Russian Role in Decision-Making."

70. Andrei Kozyrev, "Russia and NATO: A Partnership for a United and Peaceful Europe," *NATO Review* 52, no. 4 (August 1994): 4. The term "from Vancouver to Vladivostok" was first used in the statement issued at the NACC meeting in Oslo on 5 June 1992, ibid. 40, no. 3 (June 1994): 32.

71. Drozdiak and Harris, "Russia Asks Fuller Ties." For an excellent review of Russia's policy toward the "near abroad" states see "Russia and the Near Abroad: A Teddy Bear, After All," *Economist*, 10 December 1994.

72. Brzezinski, "Premature Partnership," 76.

73. Statement by the Russia's deputy foreign minister in *Moscow News*, 13 May 1994, quoted in Sneider, "Russia Prepared to Join NATO." See also the analysis in Dimitri K. Simes, "The Cold Peace: Don't Expect the New Russia to Be Our Ally," *Washington Post*, 17 July 1994.

74. "Basic Provisions of the Military Doctrine," 8.

75. For NATO's position see Sciolino, "NATO Rejects Russian Role." NATO Deputy Secretary-General Sergio Balanzino categorically stated that no outsider could have a "*droit de regard*" (right of inspection or overruling) over NATO. For concern in Central Europe and the Baltic states see Ryszard Malik, "Polish Fears of a Russian-U.S. Axis," translated from *Rzeczpospolita* (Warsaw) in *World Press* 41, no. 4 (April 1994): 10; Meri, "Estonia, NATO and Peacekeeping," 7-8.

76. Williams, "Russia Joins NATO Plan." The summary is reproduced in *NATO Review* 42, no. 4 (August 1994): 5.

77. Some of the wording referring to Russia essentially paraphrases the text found in the final communiqué of the Istanbul meeting of the North Atlantic Council, 9 June 1994, in *NATO Review* 42, no. 3 (June 1994): 26.

78. Williams, "Russia Joins NATO Plan"; Steven Greenhouse, "Russia and NATO Agree to Closer Military Links," *New York Times*, 23 June 1994.

79. Kozyrev, "Russia and NATO," 6.

80. That is how U.S. officials interpreted the Russian objection. See Daniel Williams, "Western Envoys Wary of Russia's Entry into NATO," *Washington Post*, 25 June 1994.

81. Kozyrev, "Russia and NATO," 6. Charles Goldsmith, "Russia Enrolls in Partnership with NATO: Moscow Drops Opposition to Alliance's Expansion into former Soviet Bloc," *Wall Street Journal*, 23 June 1994.

82. Sciolino, "U.S. and NATO Say Dispute on Bosnia War Is Resolved"; Williams, "Russian Minister Balks." For NATO's decision to begin a study of membership see "Ministerial Meeting on 1 December 1994," 3.

83. Alessandra Stanley, "Russia Seeks Link to NATO but Nationalists Are Bitter," *New York Times*, 18 March 1994; Hiatt, "Russia Speeds Plan."

84. Elaine Sciolino, "Yeltsin Says NATO Is Trying to Split Continent Again: Calls U.S. Domineering," *New York Times*, 6 December 1994.

85. Sciolino, "Yeltsin Says." Ten days following the Budapest meeting Vice President Al Gore's visit to Moscow seemed to have reassured the Russians. He reportedly explained that the decision on enlargement would be made after 1995 and in close consultation with Russia. See Zbigniew Brzezinski, "NATO—Expand or Die?" *New York Times*, 28 December 1994.

NATO
and the Balkans

S. Victor Papacosma

THEY'RE STILL THE BALKANS, glared the cover of the 20 April 1985 issue of the *Economist*. The lead article referred to "trouble again stirring in the Balkan pot" and asserted that "trouble in the Balkans has a habit of causing trouble elsewhere." Bearing in mind that the Warsaw Pact and Communist regimes were then still intact, the article's warning—"Do not underestimate the Balkans' capacity for turmoil"[1]—must be labeled quite prophetic in light of subsequent events.

Southeastern Europe, positioned at a strategic geographic crossroads and now comprised of Albania, Bulgaria, Greece, Romania, the republics of the former Yugoslavia, and European Turkey, has a long record of volatility. This peninsula has for millennia attracted numerous invaders and conquerors, and the more modern versions of regional and Great Power rivalries dominated much of European diplomacy during the nineteenth and twentieth centuries. Because of the heavy involvement of stronger outsiders, Balkan inhabitants have infrequently been in the position to determine their own destinies.

A closer look at the longer historical record, not to be attempted in this study, will reveal that despite almost constant European preoccupation with which powers controlled or exerted influence in the Balkans (and if the Ottoman Empire, already located in the region, is not categorized as a European Great Power), since the close of the Napoleonic Wars, direct military confrontation between rival Great Powers in this area has been minimal. In this century, although the immediate origins of World War I are to be found in the ferment of Balkan nationalism, the region essentially served as a secondary front until the last months of the war, particularly after the Entente's abortive Dardanelles campaign. During World War II, Hitler's forceful diplomacy toward Romania and Bulgaria and then the quick victories of his military against Yugoslavia and Greece in the spring of 1941 consolidated Axis control over the Balkans prior to the invasion of the Soviet Union. Apart from extensive anti-Axis resistance activity in Yugoslavia and Greece, the Balkans did not surface as a significant military front for more than three years. By then, the Germans were in full retreat.

The Balkans, though, were a European corner that played an important role in Allied planning and policy. Whereas strategic considerations had earlier predominated in British decisionmaking for the eastern Mediterranean, by the spring of 1944 Winston Churchill increasingly evaluated the political impact of policy and military campaigns. With Stalin's army approaching the Romanian frontier in the early spring of 1944, London apprehensively viewed the likelihood of the Soviet Union filling the power vacuum created by the German military retreat from Eastern Europe. Churchill sought to prevent challenges to Britain's traditional interests in the Mediterranean from expanding Soviet influence and attempted to arrive at an agreement with Josef Stalin allowing the British to take the lead in Greece in return for a Soviet lead in Romania. London and Moscow arrived at a tentative agreement in May 1944. Thus began a process whereby allies sought to avoid conflicting interests in the Balkans.

To advance this approach, Churchill traveled to Moscow in October 1944 and with Stalin produced the momentous "Percentages Agreement," a "naughty document" according to one Foreign Office account. With the Red Army well positioned in Romania and Bulgaria for campaigns southward and westward and with limited British forces about to land in Greece, the prime minister sought an agreement with Stalin to secure British interests and avert future disputes. Churchill stressed London's particular preoccupation with Greece and that Britain "must be the leading Mediterranean Power and he hoped that Marshal Stalin would let him have the first say about Greece in the same way as Marshal Stalin about Roumania." Stalin acknowledged these British interests in Greece and the Mediterranean. Having quickly established the broader guidelines of their understanding, Churchill and Stalin delegated their foreign ministers to work out relative percentages.[2] Overall, British efforts at Moscow produced a seemingly workable, albeit controversial, guide for distributing Allied influence in the Balkans during the remainder of the war that had potentially much longer-range implications.

While Stalin was consolidating Soviet influence to the north, Churchill proceeded to solidify British interests and efforts to restore the monarchy in Greece by supporting militarily the weak units of the Greek government against the leftist-led forces of EAM/ELAS, the main wartime resistance organization, from December 1944 to January 1945. Churchill expressed his appreciation of Stalin's nonintervention in support of the Greek Communists, who ultimately yielded and agreed to stop fighting. Despite growing Western concerns over Soviet methods, Churchill and Roosevelt accomplished little in a substantive manner at Yalta in February 1945 to curb expanding Soviet domination over other Balkan states and Eastern Europe. Although the relative importance of some of the roles would shift in the following four decades or so, the strategic lines of division had been drawn for the regional protagonists.

NATO AND THE COLD WAR BALKANS

To reverse the increasingly apparent inability of Britain to blunt Soviet gains and to thwart further moves, the United States redefined its world role. Among the Truman administration's first serious disputes with Moscow would be the latter's policies in Eastern European states. In the Balkans, attention centered on Soviet tactics in Romania and Bulgaria. Early in 1946 the Joint Chiefs of Staff had concluded that Eastern Europe was not vital to the United States but that "control over strategic points within these states and over their resources would represent a significant addition to the war potential of an adjacent great power."[3] The Soviet Union would be in an advantageous position to expand its influence southward and westward. Such concerns heightened as Moscow, now firmly consolidating its control over most of Eastern Europe, proceeded to place pressure on Turkey for revision of international agreement on access to and defense of the Turkish Straits. Concurrently, the Communists in Greece launched an armed campaign in mid-1946 to overthrow the British-backed government. The United States, in reaction to general world challenges from the Soviets, embraced a containment policy and, in response to specific regional conditions in Greece and Turkey, adopted the Truman Doctrine.

Issues in the Balkans had helped shape Cold War fault lines by 1947-48, but unlike the relative stability of the rigid East-West divide in the more

northern areas of Eastern Europe, altered regional dynamics would contribute to their modification there in subsequent years. Stalin did not directly
support the Greek Communists, partly out of recognition of spheres-of-
influence realities emanating from his 1944 agreement with Churchill and
partly out of the Greek Communists' initially close association with the
independent-minded Marshal Tito, who extended important aid to them.
Tito's several attempts to augment Yugoslavia's influence in the southern
Balkans met with the disapproval of Stalin, who resolved to use the forum
of the Cominform to issue a resolution on 28 June 1948 expelling Yugoslavia
and castigating its leadership. Tense months followed, but Tito's regime
held up against the Soviet bloc's political, economic, and military pressures.
The West reaped unsolicited and quick benefits from Yugoslavia's plight: The
thirty-three divisions of the Yugoslav army were neutralized and no longer
associated with the Soviet bloc. And when the Greek Communists sided with
Stalin in the rift with Tito, Yugoslavia closed its frontier to them in July
1949—an action that, along with extensive Truman Doctrine aid, contributed to the formal end of the Greek civil war by October.

Despite professed strategic concern over the distribution of power in the
Mediterranean and Balkans, this area did not play a major role in the 1948-
49 negotiations leading to the formation of NATO. It was largely in response
to French demands that Washington and London even agreed to Italy's
inclusion in the founding membership. Policymakers were placing a priority on securing the central front, the Atlantic approaches to continental
Europe, and the northern approaches to the British Isles. Nonetheless, Greece
and Turkey, which had improved relations since 1930 and which had now
become outposts against Soviet expansion in the eastern Mediterranean,
applied for inclusion into the Atlantic Alliance in April 1950.

At the September 1950 meeting of the North Atlantic Council in New
York, it was decided that Greece and Turkey would be accorded associate sta-
tus and could participate in defense planning relative to the Mediterranean.
Opposition to full membership decreased in the following months, largely
in reaction to the Korean War and unsettling developments in the Middle
East. Moreover, the United States increasingly backed their joint entry in
order to secure the southern flank of the SHAPE (Supreme Headquarters
Allied Powers Europe) command and to establish American air bases in
Turkey. In May 1951, Washington formally proposed that full membership
be granted to Greece and Turkey. The worsening Middle East situation, and
particularly the Iranian crisis, convinced the British in July to add their backing. The prospect of adding twenty-five divisions to lean NATO ranks proved

attractive. The Atlantic Council unanimously recommended the inclusion of Greece and Turkey into NATO at its September 1951 session in Ottawa, although Denmark and Norway gave only reluctant approval. Formal entry came at the Lisbon meeting in February 1952.[4]

NATO powers also acted to capitalize on Yugoslavia's split with Moscow and started providing aid in 1950. In a 29 November 1950 letter to Congress, President Harry S. Truman emphasized that the continued independence of Yugoslavia was of great importance to the security of the United States, adding: "We can help preserve the independence of a nation which is defying the savage threats of the Soviet imperialists, and keeping Soviet power out of one of Europe's most strategic areas."[5] Tito also set about to improve relations with non-Soviet bloc neighbors. Yugoslavia and Italy, both in a more accommodating spirit now, resolved their thorny dispute over Trieste in October 1954. To the south, Yugoslavia signed a Treaty of Friendship and Mutual Aid with Greece and Turkey on 28 February 1953, followed by a military alliance on 9 August 1954. Aligned with the two newest members of NATO, Yugoslavia became a de facto member of this organization via a back door. The cohesion of the trilateral arrangement buttressing NATO interests in the Balkans wilted rather quickly, however. Belgrade's links with Moscow improved in response to Nikita Khrushchev's de-Stalinization policies, Tito began forging a policy of nonalignment, and Greek-Turkish relations soured.

During the 1950s, the Greek majority population on British-controlled Cyprus intensified its agitation for *enosis*, or union, with Greece. London opposed such a change in the island's status, as did Ankara, which did not wish to see its Turkish minority on Cyprus subjugated to Greek rule. The Cyprus question aggravated Greece's relations with two NATO allies, Britain and Turkey, and became an international issue whose impact would be felt beyond the eastern Mediterranean. This conflict glaringly revealed that, whereas the United States and most of its NATO allies might share a strategic worldview and strong commitment to collective defense during the Cold War, the two members of the southeastern flank too easily shifted attention to divisive regional issues.

The compromise solution in 1960 of an independent Cyprus with a fault-ridden constitution provided only a short hiatus in the strained ties between Athens and Ankara. Cyprus persisted as a multinational problem and did not shrink into the diplomatic background, as two crises in 1963-64 and 1967 brought Greece and Turkey nearly to the brink of war. The two states separately sought backing and moral support from the United States and NATO, which at best contained, but contributed little to resolving, the dispute. Consequently, relations between Greece and Turkey have never resumed the civil character evident at the time of their joint NATO entry, and their individual ties with NATO and the United States have experienced troubled periods.

Greek internal politics became increasingly turbulent after the spring of 1965, only to be stabilized with the imposition of a harsh military dictatorship on 21 April 1967. While public opinion and some governments in Western Europe regularly criticized the Greek junta, it never experienced serious pressure from NATO or the United States. During a period of constant turmoil in the Middle East and of an augmented Soviet presence in the Mediterranean, the stability offered by the dictatorship appeared to serve NATO and American interests. The signing of a home-port agreement in 1972 for the stationing of U.S. Navy carrier forces near Athens provided another example to the dictatorship's critics of America benefiting from the authoritarian regime's existence.

The Greek junta, realigned in November 1974 and now even more extremely nationalist in composition than its predecessor, sought to rid the Greek world of the independent-minded Archbishop Makarios, Cyprus's president, and plotted his ouster with the island's national guard (dominated by junta allies) on 15 July 1974. Concerned for its people in a Cyprus controlled now by apparently pro-*enosis* interests, Turkey distorted its rights as a guarantor state in the 1959 Zurich-London agreements to suit its specific interests and landed forces on the island in the dawn hours of 20 July 1974. Athens responded with a call for general mobilization, which rapidly became a fiasco. Totally discredited and diplomatically isolated, the junta, under pressure from fellow officers, quickly exited on 23 July, hoping to avert national catastrophe through the creation of a civilian government under Constantine Karamanlis.

Despite the initial exhilaration of the Greeks over the dictatorship's downfall, the hangover of Cyprus remained with its continued bloodshed and thousands of refugees. The Turks violated cease-fires, methodically increased their troops on the island to forty thousand, and on 14 August sabotaged the Geneva peace talks with a broad offensive, taking over nearly 40 percent of the island within two days. Barely four hours after Turkey launched its invasion, Karamanlis announced the withdrawal of Greece's armed forces from the NATO military command. Karamanlis later disclosed that only two options lay before him: to declare war against Turkey or to limit links with NATO. He chose the lesser evil. The government had to somehow appease public opinion, which was inflamed by NATO's evident indifference to Turkey's actions on Cyprus and by allegations that NATO acted to limit Greece's response to the Turkish invasion.[6]

The hostile relations between Greece and Turkey over Cyprus, which had almost resulted in full-scale war, also furnished the occasion for Turkey to challenge Greek rights on still another front. Ankara sought to exploit the regional disarray to advance its interests in the Aegean Sea by challenging established practices or internationally recognized sovereign rights of Greece. Thus, Turkey contested Greece's mineral exploitation rights in the Aegean continental shelf, disputed Athens's prerogatives in the Aegean Flight Information Region (FIR) and its long-standing policy of a ten-mile territorial airspace for its Aegean islands, and tried to take advantage of Greece's withdrawal from the NATO military command to promote Ankara's role in the area's operational control. Greek security interests focused on the perceived threats from Turkey and led the new government to make appropriate shifts in defense and foreign policy.[7] In a period of regional détente between neighboring NATO and Warsaw Pact states, the Greeks and Turks concentrated their strategic concerns and militancy on each other. NATO solidarity inevitably suffered.

Karamanlis reached out to diversify Greece's foreign policy by speeding up Greece's entry into the European Community and by improving relations with countries in Eastern Europe and the Third World, particularly with the Arab states. Enhanced and more cordial ties with Greece's neighboring Balkan states received priority as an obvious counterweight to Turkish pressures. Greece now attempted to gird its security outside of NATO for a conflict not covered, according to Greece's allies, by a strict interpretation of the alliance's articles. Enough had been achieved in developing better ties with Yugoslavia, Bulgaria, and Albania that Defense Minister Evangelos Averoff in 1979 declared in the Greek parliament that Greece was in no way menaced by its northern neighbors. The implication of a Turkish threat from the east, of course, registered.[8] It was only after considerable haggling and American mediatory efforts that Turkey withdrew its opposition to Greece's reintegration into the NATO military command in October 1980.

One year later, the election victory of Andreas Papandreou and his Panhellenic Socialist Movement (PASOK) did not augur well for the interests of NATO and the United States in Greece. The former Berkeley economics professor had harped persistently on their generally negative roles and influence in Greek security affairs. Stridently nationalistic, Papandreou, as an opposition spokesman, had ceaselessly taunted the conservative governments for stiffer positions against Turkey. Despite this prelude and the subsequent tone of his policy statements and abrasive methods, Papandreou's eight-year tenure brought no major shifts in Greece's broader relations with NATO, the European Community, or the United States. By cutting through the political rhetoric and posturing, one can conclude that despite sharper language and different tactics, Papandreou extended policies launched by the putatively pro-West and more moderate Karamanlis.

Papandreou repeatedly stated to Athens's NATO allies that the threat to Greece's security came from Turkey to the east, not from the Soviet bloc to the north, and that NATO should extend a security guarantee for Greece's frontier against potential Turkish aggression. Such a request was denied on several occasions, and a Cold War atmosphere continued to blanket relations between the two states. The January 1985 Athens announcement of a new defense doctrine affirming that Greece's primary threat came from the east confirmed what had been actual policy since the Turkish invasion of Cyprus. In spite of these and what NATO saw as other unpopular stances by Athens, Papandreou's governments kept Greece within NATO and maintained relatively close defense ties with the United States. The socialist leader yielded to certain realities. A falling-out with the United States and, consequently, with NATO would only improve Turkey's diplomatic and military muscle in the Aegean and Cyprus and accentuate Greek weaknesses. America consented to maintain a military balance between the two feuding allies, thereby providing the support that Greece could not expect to find from other sources. Papandreou had cogently declared that Greece's relations with the United States and NATO passed through Ankara. Concurrently, the socialist governments continued their predecessors' policy of working for improved relations with Greece's three northern neighbors.

THE SOVIET UNION AND THE COLD WAR BALKANS

Maintaining control over developments in the Balkans also proved troublesome for the Soviet Union, which had to accept diminished strategic capabilities in the region. A first major setback came when Yugoslavia's ouster from the Cominform and Tito's ability to maintain power despite Soviet bloc pressures cast a debilitating blow to the perception of the Communist monolith. The Yugoslav leader's subsequent success in developing a nonaligned role for Belgrade deprived Moscow of important security positioning in the western Balkans and access to Adriatic ports. Initially, Albania found the opportunity to free itself of domineering Yugoslav influence by siding with

Moscow in 1948 at the time of its break with Belgrade. But when Nikita Khrushchev embarked on his de-Stalinization program and moved to normalize relations with Tito in the mid-1950s, Enver Hoxha perceived threats to his continued Stalinist-style leadership and to Albania's national interests. Tirana began its incline toward China in the budding Sino-Soviet dispute and in 1961 openly broke with Moscow, terminating diplomatic and other relations. In the process, the Soviets lost important naval bases for their submarines at this critical entryway into the Adriatic. Nominally still a member of the Warsaw Pact, Albania formally withdrew after the Soviet invasion of Czechoslovakia in the summer of 1968.

Romania, for its part, began to express an independent foreign policy in 1963 and held its last joint exercises with the Soviet Union and Bulgaria in 1964. That same year the Romanian Communist party plenum declared that Romania was to put its national interests before those of the Soviet Union and that nations had a right to determine their own destiny as well as rights of national sovereignty. Nicolae Ceausescu assumed power in 1965 and for more than two decades implemented independent policy positions and dallied with the West in a manner annoying for Soviet interests. Bulgaria remained the only relatively trouble-free and continuously loyal state for Moscow and Warsaw Pact interests in the Balkans.

Regional rivalries and bilateral issues predating the Cold War also inhibited Moscow from forming a solid security bloc. For example, Hungary protested Romania's treatment of the large Hungarian minority in Transylvania. Romania's concern over Moscow's domination in Soviet Moldavia contributed to its independent-minded foreign policy. Bulgaria and Yugoslavia continued their prewar dispute over Macedonian issues. Other potentially volatile regional feuds included Bulgaria's treatment of its Turkish minority during the 1980s, Serbia's policies toward the large Albanian minority in the Kosovo province, and Albania's oppressive measures against its Greek minority. Among bordering states in the Balkans, only Romania and Yugoslavia maintained consistently cordial relations.[9]

Ultimately, both superpowers maneuvered prudently in their respective shares of the Balkans and implemented strategy relegating the land region to one of secondary importance. From the beginnings of NATO, analysts stressed the overriding significance of the Central Front and the need to defend it against a massive attack of Soviet-bloc forces. Most planners believed the Warsaw Pact would direct its assault against the core of NATO's political and military presence in West Germany. NATO strategy for the southern region during the Cold War was driven by conventional warfare requirements, and nuclear weapons located there were to be directed over-whelmingly to the deterrence of the Soviet threat to the centers of economic and political importance in Central rather than Southern Europe. Little wonder that Ian Lesser has concluded that "the defense of Frankfurt and Athens were never really equivalent in NATO strategy."[10]

NATO and, arguably, even the Warsaw Pact can be seen to have benefited from Yugoslavia's nonalignment and Albania's essentially semi-isolationist policy. Such orientations meant that neither bloc could exert overriding influence in or militarily exploit these strategically located countries against its rival in an area that neither side wished to see become a primary front. Denial of access to critically located Balkan real estate on the flanks of the two blocs thus diminished the possibility of provocative posturing in the Balkans and contributed to regional stability. The strategic value of Balkan territory for each opposing bloc would obviously increase if the other attempted to augment its military presence or influence there. That Belgrade appreciated this situation and sought to remain a beneficiary was reflected in a Yugoslav foreign minister's candid appraisal: "As Yugoslavs, we need the Americans to protect us from the Russians. As Communists, we need the Russians to protect us from the Americans."[11]

But because of its frontier positioning for the superpower blocs, south-eastern Europe never lost its potential to become an area of confrontation. Thus, the Soviet invasion of Czechoslovakia on 20-21 August 1968 and the proclamation of the Brezhnev Doctrine raised concerns about further Soviet moves. In the Balkans, Yugoslav fears heightened, and after some delay the Johnson administration in mid-October announced that America had a "clear and continuing interest in Yugoslavia's independence, sovereignty, and economic development." The NATO Council in its November meeting gave warning signals to the Soviet Union that it should not act against Yugoslavia, and American Secretary of State Dean Rusk referred to a "gray zone," including Yugoslavia, that was to be shielded by NATO. Having received necessary assurances, Tito nonetheless sensed that the Soviet threat was receding and that too close an association with the West might be counter-productive. In late November he noted publicly that he believed the Soviet Union had no reason to attack Yugoslavia and that his country would not call on anybody for aid, specifically not the Americans.[12]

Moscow was able to offset some of its diminished capacity on the Balkan land mass when it increased the size of Soviet naval forces in the Mediterranean. At the time of Greek and Turkish entry into the Atlantic Alliance, the Mediterranean had been a veritable NATO lake. Such would not be the case after the Soviet buildup began in the mid-1960s. The critical advantage, however, still appeared to remain with NATO, which, apart from sustained superiority in the numbers of naval units, could also maintain vital porting and support facilities in Greece and Turkey. The Soviets did not have such options on a consistent basis in the eastern Mediterranean.

Neither the United States nor the Soviet Union effectively deflected the overriding nationalist concerns and strategic attention of allied states in the Balkans toward broader alliance objectives in the superpower confrontation. NATO stepped cautiously and with few accomplishments in trying to reconcile the differences between Greece and Turkey and, obviously, alliance solidarity and planning suffered. And when one considers the broad sweep of the post–World War II era, the Soviet Union moved warily and suffered even greater setbacks in maintaining what was initially and briefly a solid Communist wall of four states in southeastern Europe. Moscow never responded in the Balkans with military force to assert its interests as it did in Hungary in 1956 and in Czechoslovakia in 1968. "The potential cost of military intervention as a Soviet policy tool in the Balkans [had] simply been perceived as too great."[13] The 1944 Churchill-Stalin "Percentages Agreement" had essentially held, with neither superpower directly challenging the influence of the other, even when local Balkan conditions offered opportunities to exploit.

NATO AND THE POST–COLD WAR BALKANS

As the 1980s drew to a close and the new decade began, dramatic developments in the Soviet Union and Eastern Europe combined to topple Communist party domination and to bring an end to the Cold War. Soviet hegemony in Eastern Europe crumbled, the Warsaw Pact officially ended its existence on 1 July 1991, and the Union of Soviet Socialist Republics formally died in December 1991. Superpower rivalry ceased, and NATO had justified its existence handsomely by defending Western interests and deterring aggression from the East for four decades. But whither NATO's post–Cold War calling?

Balkan problems, fundamental to the origins of the Cold War and laterally to the consequent founding of NATO, would also contribute, in a tortuous manner, to the Atlantic Alliance's evolving mission after 1989. The proclaimed "new world order" proved short-lived and, if anything, not very "new" for southeastern Europe. Many old problems, with pre-1939 origins, revived vigorously along with new variables to create an updated Balkan morass. Nationalism was replacing communism as the dominant ideology, and the world was reminded once again of the durability and regenerative volatility of ethnic hatreds and regional rivalries. Communism and the superpower confrontation had simply muted these sentiments in certain areas but, as the above comments imply, had nonetheless plagued policy-makers in both blocs.

The fall of communism in and rapid superpower retreat from Eastern Europe essentially left the region's peoples to their own devices, a rare condition with good and bad consequences. The region no longer served itself up as an area of contention between rival Great Power interests. Hostilities in the Balkans, if they did not directly involve neighboring Greece and Italy, both NATO states, could ostensibly remain localized between the disputants. But the balkanization of Yugoslavia compelled governments in Europe and America to reevaluate such initially optimistic assumptions. Despite the absence of superpower confrontation, the energy of the Balkan whirlpool, as before in history, has been hard to contain, and its drawing power can be felt beyond the confines of southeastern Europe.

The complex process of transition from communism to regimes and institutions more resembling those of democratic and free-market Western Europe has not been smooth and has encountered, dependent upon the country, varying degrees of political, economic, and social difficulties. In the Balkans, as in some republics of the former Soviet Union, ethnic issues have dominated and given direction to post–Communist developments. Yugoslavia, which had implemented a moderate form of Communist rule and which had played with its nonaligned foreign policy a positive role in maintaining regional stability, has had a bloody post–Cold War life. Tito's creative manipulation of Communist power and federalism had managed to hold together a multiethnic state. Cold War dynamics and a viable economy also contributed to the maintenance of this regime. But potential difficulties manifested themselves even before Tito's death in 1980. The highly decentralized system formed in the 1970s granted major authority to the constituent republics. The Yugoslav economy began experiencing serious problems with rising inflation, decreased competitiveness, heavy indebtedness, and increased regional inequalities in income distribution. Ethnic problems, which the decentralized federal structure sought to contain but which were never eliminated, became even more complicated with the addition of a newly mobilized group for agitation, the Albanians in Serbian-dominated Kosovo. Conditions worsened during the 1980s, and the fall of Communist regimes elsewhere intensified centrifugal separatist forces in Yugoslavia. Attempts to dismantle Communist hegemony and to maintain the federal structure faltered and then failed, as each national group had its own agenda. The Yugoslav People's Army (JNA), with its Serbian-dominated officer corps, remained the only important organization still committed to the maintenance of the federation.[14]

Tensions within Yugoslavia increased in 1990-91, and widespread fighting erupted after the JNA moved to counter the secessions of Slovenia and Croatia, proclaimed on 25 June 1991. Slovenia, largely because of its very small Serbian minority and geographic position, saw its struggle with the JNA end rather quickly, but fighting in Croatia, with its relatively large and concentrated Serbian population, increased in intensity. The Federal Republic of Macedonia voted to assert its sovereignty in September, but no bloodshed resulted from this pronouncement. Such would not be the case following a referendum in early March 1992, boycotted by its Serbian population, when the Federal Republic of Bosnia-Herzegovina declared its independence. Bosnian Serbs, in turn, proclaimed the Serbian Republic of Bosnia-Herzegovina later that month and began to shell Sarajevo, the Bosnian capital, on 5 April.

On NATO's doorstep, Yugoslavia with its declining state of affairs attracted attention, but the United States and its allies during the late summer of 1990 began concentrating on a response to Iraq's invasion of Kuwait. EC member-states appeared preoccupied with advancing European integration. The future of the Soviet Union also concerned Western policymakers, who hoped to take advantage of pending opportunities to downsize defense budgets. Just a few years earlier, Yugoslavia's disintegration, with the accompanying shock to the regional status quo, probably would have created a Cold War crisis and might well have invited the intervention of one superpower—with an inevitable counterresponse from the other. Stakes such as these did not exist now, and consequently broader security issues beyond the borders of the former Yugoslavia that threatened the territorial integrity of NATO members did not appear to be involved. An alliance based on collective defense and conceived for the different international challenges of the Cold War, NATO thus had no prescribed charge in the Yugoslav situation— a redefinition of its mission had to be proposed and accepted to justify its existence. With its structure, forces, equipment, and overall military capabilities, NATO was, however, the organization that could doubtlessly produce the most conclusive results if it were called on to act assertively by its members. Notwithstanding many differences and the utilization of intra-alliance pressures and compromises in arriving at a common policy, the Soviet threat had provided the crucial unifying focus for NATO allies for four decades.

New criteria for determining threats to security and accompanying responses had to be established for the alliance that had succeeded so well in another era and that generated few calls for its dissolution in the present.[15]

NATO was by no means ready or willing to involve itself in the worsening Yugoslav situation when fighting broke out in mid-1991. The constraints were many and included the reluctance of the United States to intervene and its preference to have Europe respond to the crisis.[16] As just one early example, this phenomenon of a lack of unity among allies plagued policymaking and the determination of common strategy in NATO and in what have come to be termed NATO's interlocking (by some analysts interblocking) institutions. The European Community (EC), the Conference on Security and Cooperation in Europe (CSCE), the Western European Union (WEU), and the United Nations all entered into the diplomatic campaign to arrange an end to the Yugoslav fighting before the close of 1991.

At first, too, Europeans and Americans expressed the hope that some form of reconstituted Yugoslavia, amenable to all parties, could be formed. During the fall of 1991 Germany, in particular, drifted away from this position and eventually persuaded its EC partners in December to grant diplomatic recognition to former Yugoslav republics meeting certain conditions. The United States, among other states, and prominent international figures labeled the subsequent recognition of Slovenia and Croatia as premature, believing that instead of containing the crisis it actually contributed to its extension into Bosnia-Herzegovina during the early spring of 1992. The situation then became even more complicated, as a triangular conflict involving Muslims, Serbs, and Croats in shifting alliances further plagued those actively seeking resolution to the conflicts. By the summer of 1992, world opinion generally singled out the Serbs as the prime culprits in a war of aggression that viciously and deliberately claimed thousands of innocent civilians among its victims.

Western diplomatic initiatives, chronically reactive to worsening conditions and increased bloodshed, lacked adequate evidence of armed force and will to reinforce them, largely because governments considered the political, military, and financial stakes too great. European and American leaders deliberately avoided the prospect of consigning the large numbers of troops believed to be necessary to impose peace in such a hostile setting. The American attitude toward the formidable military challenges in the rugged terrain of Bosnia was rather puckishly embodied in the judgment: "We do deserts—we don't do mountains."[17] General Colin Powell, chairman of the U.S. Joint Chiefs of Staff, wrote a widely read op-ed page article warning of pitfalls if America became engaged, stating that military force had to match political objectives and that in Bosnia there were no clear political goals.[18] Traditional appraisals of the Balkans as a quagmire dominated military-political assessments in Western capitals, and the Serbs understandably became emboldened by the prospect of a continued tepid response by the world community.

Within the context of the reordered Europe, the major decisionmaking states did not perceive their national interests to be directly threatened by this otherwise dreadful war in the nasty Balkans. But the press and television diligently exploited the news-making developments and horrors so that neither voters nor their leaders could ignore them. The bloodshed was not ending, and if aggressors remained unchallenged and successful, the use of force to change borders, condemned so recently under the terms of the Paris Charter of November 1990, and the genocidal practice of "ethnic cleansing," reminiscent of Hitler's policies, were establishing grim precedents for others to emulate. Moreover, the mushrooming numbers of refugees in Europe, at unprecedentedly high numbers for the period since the late 1940s, portended sensitive domestic problems for European states. This Balkan war, therefore, had a potential impact on developments in other regions and for continued instability.

Shortly after the outbreak of fighting in Yugoslavia in late June 1991, the EC brokered its first cease-fire and sent observers to monitor conditions. Many other mediated cease-fires followed, only to be broken by the belligerents. Brussels reacted to the ongoing crisis by dispatching EC observers to the area of fighting, establishing a peace conference for the conflicting parties, imposing an arms embargo, and freezing EC aid to Yugoslavia. The EC then called upon the United Nations in September to join in the peacemaking process. The UN responded with a succession of Security Council resolutions, with peacekeeping forces, sent first to Croatia (March 1992) and then to Bosnia, with a smaller monitoring force to the Former Yugoslav Republic of Macedonia (FYROM), and with humanitarian aid to relieve suffering in Bosnia-Herzegovina. The CSCE also participated in the manifold initiatives to end the fighting. The deployment of UN peacekeeping units to Croatia did facilitate the establishment of relative quiet, although Croats were hardly ready to accept the militarized occupation of about one-third of their territory by Serbs as a permanent condition.

NATO, for its part, had begun the process of mission redefinition for the post–Cold War era in June 1990 at its London summit and continued it at the Rome summit in November 1991, several months after fighting had broken out in Yugoslavia, and in subsequent meetings. Adopting a new strategic concept and calling for associated new force structures, NATO was reorganizing and reorienting itself for changes occurring in Europe. Importantly, provision was made for the new force structures to assume a greater role for multinational formations in support of UN or CSCE peacekeeping missions. The Atlantic Alliance now had the authorized capability to operate out-of-area and not solely in response to a direct threat to one of its member-states. The North Atlantic Council resolved at Oslo in June 1992 that NATO would be prepared to support CSCE peacekeeping activities on a "case-by-case" basis, a position declared jointly with the WEU at the Helsinki CSCE summit the following month. At its ministerial meeting in Brussels in December 1992, NATO confirmed its readiness to support on a case-by-case basis peacekeeping operations under the authority of the UN Security Council, which had the primary responsibility for international peace and security. Underlying this approach was the evident reality that "NATO is not prepared to undertake a peacekeeping operation on its own initiative; it is unlikely that such an approach would find consensus among the Allies."[19]

With the greatest capabilities at its disposal but essentially sharing many of the same policymakers participating in the other involved institutions, NATO in July 1992 began its slow and incremental participation in efforts to contain and end hostilities in the former Yugoslavia.[20] Even before its December 1992 decision regarding support for UN peacekeeping operations, NATO joined with the WEU in air and sea operations to enforce UN Security Council Resolutions 713, 757, and 787 preventing unauthorized shipping from entering the territorial waters of the reconstituted and downsized Federal Republic of Yugoslavia (that is, Serbia and Montenegro). Initially, there was no authorization to stop, board, and search vessels suspected of breaking sanctions, but in November the decision was made to uphold UN Security Council resolutions imposing an arms embargo on all republics of the former Yugoslavia and an economic embargo on Montenegro and Yugoslavia.[21] The alliance in early April 1993 responded with Operation Deny Flight to UN Security Council Resolution 820 allowing NATO aircraft to shoot down planes violating the no-fly zone imposed on Bosnian airspace in October 1992 and monitored since then by NATO aircraft. The first flights by American, French, and Dutch fighter jets on 12 April 1993 represented a momentous act, if only in symbolic terms, in that the alliance assumed a combat mission in a nondefensive capacity and out-of-area. The North Atlantic Council in early July adopted plans offering close air support to UN troops and other personnel in Bosnia if they were attacked and requested air strikes. Concurrent with these developments, NATO also agreed in early June to back with air power the UN Security Council resolution for the creation and securing of six safe areas (in Sarajevo, Tuzla, Zepa, Gorazde, Bihac, and Srebrenica). Bosnian Serb forces were required to leave these cities and to allow UN peacekeepers unrestricted access. As the strangulation of besieged Sarajevo tightened, NATO on 2 August threatened to bomb Serb forces unless they relented. A barely nominal retreat followed.[22]

Despite all the attention directed toward peacekeeping units, even larger numbers of peacemaking forces appeared necessary to create the conditions appropriate for the effective disposition of peacekeepers, whose mission was limited and constantly threatened. But with no coherent political strategy to unify the disparate positions of NATO members, truly effective military measures could not be implemented to influence the warring parties—primarily the Bosnian Serbs—to end their fighting and to arrive at a lasting settlement. The complex situation had become even more so when Croats began fighting Bosnian Muslims, their former allies, in early April 1993. The concern of the international community translated into diplomatic, economic, and humanitarian approaches. Ultimately, the Band-Aid regimen of NATO and its interlocking institutions in dealing with hemorrhagic conditions did little for the region's acute ailments, other than to contain the distress from spreading beyond its existing confines and to ameliorate some of the suffering through humanitarian relief. Britain's John Major capsulized the sentiments of those opposing full-scale war when he remarked in late May 1993: "People are not prepared to put 200,000 troops in Bosnia to force them [that is, the Serbs] back by armed force, but we will maintain a diplomatic pressure and we will not accept the land gains by force."[23]

The quest for an honorable diplomatic solution to the multifaceted crisis also fell victim to the passing of time. In particular, UN mediator Cyrus Vance and European Community negotiator Lord David Owen worked tirelessly but unsuccessfully to draft a plan for peaceful resolution of outstanding issues and for a restructured Bosnia-Herzegovina. Alliance measures to reinforce UN resolutions for pressuring the Bosnian Serbs, who controlled about 70 percent of the countryside, fell far short of their intended purpose. Pursuing brutal tactics essentially directed at creating an ethnically divided Bosnia associated or federated with Serbia, the Bosnian Serbs were succeeding in their attempts to carve out the largest share for themselves, although they comprised only about one-third of Bosnia's prewar population. The original Vance-Owen plan, focusing on the cantonization of Bosnia into ten units, died during the late spring of 1993, and the new strategy, drafted by

Owen and Norway's Thorvald Stoltenberg, who had replaced Vance, shifted toward the creation of a new Bosnian union of three ministates. Despite the condemnation of world opinion, aggression had provided rewards for the Serbs, even as they refused to accept the share of about half of Bosnia's territory allotted to them as too small. Borders were being changed by force, the principle of partition seemingly had been accepted, and thousands of refugees would never be able to return to their ancestral homes.

It was becoming increasingly evident by the end of 1993 that the configuration and extent of the partitioned portions provided the main points of contention among the disputants. In the meantime, the horrors continued unabated, and humanitarian relief efforts confronted numerous obstacles. Decisive military action to force an end to these patterns, advocated by many politicians and journalists, found few supporters among decisionmakers. Apart from the general unwillingness of NATO allies to supply the extensive commitment of troops considered necessary to implement effective ground strategy, Britain and France, which provided the largest contingents for UNPROFOR (UN Protection Force) in Bosnia, opposed measures such as widespread air strikes, fearing that their lightly armed peacekeeping units would become easy victims or hostages of the Bosnian Serbs. Generally advocating increased air activity, the Clinton administration, at times erratic in its own positions, experienced difficulties arriving at some sort of consensus with European allies. Moreover, Washington maintained that it would provide American troops for peacekeeping purposes only after a definitive cease-fire and peace had been agreed to. The three Western members of the UN Security Council also had to consider the concerns of Russia, in the process of developing post–Soviet foreign policy, in an area of its traditional interest, southeastern Europe. Some analysts argued that President Boris Yeltsin's policies, generally nonconfrontational toward NATO positions, would be challenged by and add to the support of extreme Russian nationalists and old Communists if the West aggressively sought to defeat the Serbs.

While a number of measures to bolster the image and mission of NATO predominated at the Brussels summit of 10-11 January 1994, the Bosnian imbroglio was approached carefully so as not to disrupt unity. NATO leaders confirmed all previous decisions and reaffirmed the alliance's readiness to execute air strikes to prevent the strangulation of Sarajevo and other threatened areas in Bosnia. By the end of the month, intensive discussions in Brussels centered increasingly on utilizing air attacks against Serb forces to relieve UN peacekeepers in captive areas and to help free designated safe havens from the suffocating grip inflicted upon them.[24]

A challenge to demonstrate NATO's resolve came shortly afterward in formulating a response to the mortar-shell attack of Sarajevo's marketplace on 5 February that resulted in sixty-eight dead and more than two hundred wounded. Blamed on the Serbs, this carnage heightened outrage in Western capitals and forced an emergency meeting of the North Atlantic Council, which announced its ultimatum on 9 February. It condemned the ongoing siege of Sarajevo, called for the Serbian withdrawal of or placing under UN control by 20 February all heavy weapons located in an area within twenty kilometers of Sarajevo's center, and sanctioned NATO support for UNPROFOR in carrying out its task of identifying heavy weapons that were not withdrawn or regrouped in conformity with the listed demands. NATO also authorized air strikes, to be in response to UN requests, against targets in violation of these terms. NATO's quickly fashioned firmness appeared to work, as virtually all heavy weapons in and around Sarajevo—including those of the Muslims—were withdrawn or placed under UNPROFOR control by the deadline.

When six Serbian aircraft violated the no-fly zone over Bosnia on 28 February, NATO planes shot down four of the intruders. This brief encounter not only provided another opportunity to display NATO's stiffened posture but also corresponded to a veritable "baptism in the Balkans": These were the first shots ever fired in combat by NATO forces in the alliance's forty-five years of existence. Coupled with the announcement in late February of a U.S.-brokered cease-fire between the Bosnian Croats and Muslims, these developments raised hopes for a lasting solution.

Such prospects dimmed quickly. Although conditions in Sarajevo eased, the Bosnian Serbs resumed provocative actions on several fronts to confront the Muslims, to harass UNPROFOR, and to test the resolve of NATO. In the process, divisions glaringly reappeared in the ranks of those seeking peace. In one instance, when Serb forces attacked French peacekeepers on 12 March, the UN called for NATO planes, only to cancel the attack at the last minute. Both sides offered conflicting public statements on why the mission was terminated, with NATO also complaining of the indecisiveness of UN authorities and the slowness of UNPROFOR procedures. In the meantime, the Serbs withdrew unscathed from their positions.

Western apprehensions over Russian sensitivities, along with Serb insistence during the February crisis, had led to the introduction of Russian units into the UN peacekeeping forces in Sarajevo. Considerable uncertainty surrounded Russia's augmented military and diplomatic role in the Bosnian crisis. Some analysts ventured that Bosnia could now become the setting for a proxy war reminiscent of Cold War scenarios.[25] Concurrently, UN officials expressed concern in March that the momentum for peace was faltering and that countries were unwilling to provide strong military and political support and, especially, the thousands of troops necessary for policing cease-fires throughout Bosnia. One UN official volunteered: "If the momentum dissipates, they [the Bosnian Serbs] will go back to their old manipulative ways, back to the Balkan way of doing things."[26]

A pattern of sorts did seem to set in, with little progress toward establishing conditions for a final peace. NATO continued to involve itself in combat activity on a highly selective basis and at the request of UN authorities. Thus, on 10-11 April, NATO planes, technically to protect UN units, struck positions of Bosnian Serbs near Gorazde after they had renewed their attacks against the designated Muslim safe haven. The Serbs held their positions, and the Russians condemned the attack, complaining that they had not been consulted. UN and NATO leaders defended the decision as one falling under the existing guidelines of UN resolutions. The North Atlantic Council on 22 April followed with an ultimatum for the Bosnian Serbs to cease their onslaught against Gorazde and to move their heavy weapons to twenty kilometers from the city's center. If the Serbs refused, NATO threatened air strikes against Serb heavy weapons and other military targets within this area. The council also asserted its resolve to respond similarly for the five other safe areas. After a slow Serb response to the demands and the hesitancy of the UN—much to the chagrin of NATO leaders—to authorize the bombing runs, the Serbs did finally retreat in large part. NATO aircraft next struck on 5 August against Serb heavy weapons violating the Sarajevo exclusion zone after Serbs removed arms from a UN weapons depot. The Serbs relented and returned the stolen equipment. Seven weeks later, on 22 September, three NATO planes fired on an unmanned Serb tank within the Sarajevo exclusion zone as a retaliation against a Serb attack on a UN armored vehicle manned by French soldiers.

These pinprick actions contributed little to change the course of the battlefield struggle or to influence diplomatic maneuvers for arranging peace. During the spring a "contact group" of Britain, France, Germany, Russia, and the United States formed to forward new peace proposals. The terms, announced on 5 July, allocated 51 percent of Bosnia-Herzegovina's territory to the nascent Muslim-Croat federation and the remainder to the Serbs, with both parts remaining in a single state. The former begrudgingly accepted the provisions, but the Bosnian Serbs balked, claiming that the plan called for an inequitable slashing of the 70 percent land area controlled by them and that it denied them the right to form a separate state or to join Serbia.

Importantly, Russia backed the proposal, as did Serbia's Slobodan Milosevic, who urged the truculent Bosnian Serbs to accept. When they did not, Belgrade imposed a trade embargo on the Bosnian Serbs in August. In return for this reversed stance toward its Bosnian compatriots, Serbia's leadership hoped for an easing of the UN-imposed economic sanctions that had taken their toll on its economy.

Among the contact group states, the United States alone outspokenly advocated the lifting of the arms embargo for the Bosnian Muslims as a means of eliminating the Serbian superiority in weapons and creating conditions for a more equal confrontation. The Clinton administration also pushed for more extensive and intensive NATO air strikes against Serb targets. These positions, seen as a means also to compel the Bosnian Serbs into accepting the contact group's peace proposals, ran counter to the views of other group members. As the countries providing the largest numbers of troops to the UN peacekeeping units in Bosnia, Britain and France contended that lifting the arms embargo would only intensify and broaden the conflict and endanger their lightly armed forces. Rather than face such a prospect, London and Paris would pull out their troops before they became battlefield casualties or hostages. Such a move also augured a vital setback to the critical humanitarian and relief aid engineered locally by the UN detachments, whose replacements from other UN member-states would be hard to produce.

In late September, NATO defense ministers meeting in Seville tangled with these variant positions within NATO and over the constraints on its uncomfortable mission as a subcontractor to the United Nations. Britain's Lieutenant General Sir Michael Rose, commander of the UN forces in Bosnia, emphatically stated: "We cannot bomb our way to peace. Increased use of force, to my mind, is not a solution at the moment." He instead advocated continued step-by-step negotiations. U.S. Secretary of Defense William Perry did manage a stronger NATO statement on a tougher air strikes policy against the Bosnian Serbs, but the likelihood of convincing UN authorities to adopt a harder line seemed dim. One UN official summed up the situation: "If NATO or the United States were to send in ground troops to fight a war here they would be in a better position to dictate policy. Until that happens NATO here is in support of a peacekeeping mission. It's not time for the big stick yet."[27]

The Russian factor had also to be considered. Despite a number of differences, Russia had worked reasonably well with its four partners in drafting the contact group's peace proposal. But because of professed traditional links with the Serbs and a potential nationalist backlash at home, Moscow's leadership could not advocate stepped-up attacks against the Bosnian Serbs, the lifting of the arms embargo on the Muslims, or the granting of a relative free hand in policymaking for the Balkans to the United States. The Russians, therefore, shared with their British and French colleagues a reluctance to support a dramatic shift in UN policy.

On the diplomatic front, the UN responded to the relative faithfulness of Belgrade in enforcing its embargo on trade and communication with the Bosnian Serbs by revoking economic sanctions. In turn, the Bosnian government, subjected to pressures and concerns on several fronts but also yielding to the grim reality that the short-term gains from the lifting of the weapons embargo would be limited, if not outweighed by greater losses, called for a compromise measure on 27 September. The Muslims proposed a postponement of the call for lifting the weapons embargo against them for six months, but in return asked for stronger international protection. In the meantime, the Bosnian Serbs continued to demonstrate in varied ways that they controlled important lifelines for Sarajevo and other designated safe havens.

The impasse persisted on the battlefield, among decisionmakers, and between institutions. The clarification of objectives mutually agreed on by all involved parties seeking peace was not in sight. General Rose voiced a major element of this continuing difficulty from the perspective of the UN peacekeeping forces, under whose restraining direction NATO had to operate: "If someone wants to fight a war here [in Bosnia] on moral or political grounds, fine, great, but count us out. Hitting one tank is peacekeeping. Hitting infrastructure, command and control, logistics, that is war, and I'm not going to fight a war in white-painted tanks."[28]

NATO's redefined role as a subcontractor in support of UN peacekeeping missions on a case-by-case basis had become increasingly awkward, and the precarious UN-NATO relationship worsened during the fall of 1994. With NATO openly critical of UNPROFOR's reluctance to use air strikes by alliance warplanes against the Serbs, General Bertrand de Lapresle, French commander of UN forces in former Yugoslavia, spoke of "cultural differences" between the two organizations. He added: "NATO wants to identify an enemy, demonstrate its military effectiveness and win victories. The mission of U.N. protective forces is to keep the peace."[29] Meeting in New York in late October, NATO and UN negotiators drafted an accord for a tougher policy in Bosnia. NATO air strikes were now to be conducted on a "timely basis," and "while general warning may be given to an offending party, tactical warning of impending air strikes, in principle, will not." Under normal circumstances, several targets were to be authorized for each air strike to be carried by NATO in close coordination with UNPROFOR. The joint statement also referred to "dual key" arrangements remaining in effect to ensure that "decisions on targeting and execution will be taken jointly by UN and NATO military commanders." In an unconvincing public relations statement, the concluding section affirmed "once again the excellent cooperation of the two organizations in the implementation of the relevant UN Security Council resolutions."[30]

One alliance source candidly remarked in the accord's aftermath: "What we have here is an agreement papering over the cracks between two bureaucracies with fundamentally different views on peacekeeping and on how to implement broadly the same mandate." Another source volunteered that precisely because the new measures might be more effective, "U.N. commanders on the ground could be more hesitant in calling in NATO support." *Die Zeit's* diplomatic correspondent, Christoph Bertram, concluded: "In short, NATO has made an organization unwilling to use force the guardian of its ability to use force." But the same analyst also pointed out that the inability of NATO states to agree among themselves on a strong policy from the beginning brought them into this imperfect association with the United Nations. "The recent protest by their defense ministers contains, therefore, a good deal of hypocrisy. NATO can huff and puff, but it still lacks the will to act decisively on its own." Russia voiced its own criticism of the late October agreement by stating that if any organization apart from the United Nations had the final word on the use of force it would signal a fundamental shift in peacekeeping operations. If NATO gained ultimate control over whether to use force in the Balkans, Russia would withdraw its peacekeeping troops.[31]

Battlefield and diplomatic developments during November would contribute to significant policy shifts on the part of the outside powers. Bosnian Muslim-Croat forces had launched an offensive in late October against the Bosnian Serbs and made important gains. Initially cheered by this turn-around, groups sympathetic to the Bosnian Muslim cause soon became disheartened when the Bosnian Serbs regrouped and succeeded in their counteroffensive against Muslim fighters and civilians in the Bihac enclave of northwestern Bosnia—an officially designated UN safe area whose status was to be secured with NATO support. Then on 11 November the United States announced that it had ordered American forces in the Adriatic to stop enforcing the arms embargo against the Bosnian Muslims. U.S. ships participating in NATO/WEU's Operation Sharp Guard would only divert or delay ships carrying arms bound for the Bosnian Muslims. Although decisions from the preceding August had mandated this altered stance if breakthroughs toward peace had not occurred by November and although the actual impact on the course of the fighting was largely symbolic, the move, taken in the aftermath of the Democratic defeat at the polls, nonetheless fomented further disarray in the ranks of allies. Willy Claes, who had taken over as secretary-general after the death of Manfred Wörner, stated that "NATO will continue to enforce fully and totally all U.N. Security Council resolutions which form the basis of our involvement in former Yugoslavia." Another NATO official tersely remarked: "What is happening is that contradictions which have existed for a long time within NATO with regard to Bosnia are now being exposed as a consequence of U.S. domestic policies."[32]

The impact of "contradictions" intensified. The UN on 21 November authorized NATO air strikes on the Udbina airfield in Serb-occupied Croatia, from which Serb planes attacked Muslim positions in nearby Bihac. UN officials, however, limited the choice of targets. The mission's thirty-nine aircraft, constituting the biggest military operation by NATO in its forty-five-year history, fired only on the runway, a taxiway, antiaircraft guns, and a surface-to-air missile site. UN commanders argued against targeting Serb planes on the airfield in order to avoid casualties, but ultimately they sought to avert Serb reprisals against UN troops, particularly the ill-equipped Bangladeshi contingent trapped in Bihac. When NATO planes followed on 23 November with two more raids against Serb antiaircraft systems, the Serbs did retaliate by rounding up UN personnel, spurring additional fears that UN soldiers might be killed.[33] Despite public protestations of UN-NATO resolve in executing these air strikes, it had become evident that Bosnian Serb forces recognized, and appreciated, the missions for what they were: pinprick strikes with pinprick consequences for their side by stronger powers unable to agree upon common, decisive, and forceful measures.

With allies sharply criticizing each other and with NATO solidarity fraying markedly, the Clinton administration undertook sharp modifications in American policy in late November. In a confidential memorandum to the president, National Security Advisor Anthony Lake noted: "Bihac's fall has exposed the inherent contradictions in trying to use NATO air power coercively against the Bosnian Serbs when our allies have troops on the ground attempting to maintain impartiality in performing a humanitarian mission. . . . The stick of military pressure seems no longer viable." Limited bombing had failed to pressure the Serbs into accepting the contact group's peace plan. Unsuccessful in budging Britain and France from their policy positions toward the Bosnian conflict, Washington now concluded that it was more important to reestablish NATO unity, albeit at a potential price for America's leadership role. The United States had been unable to impose its will on allies with troops in Bosnia, in large part because of its own unwillingness to commit soldiers to the region until after the cessation of fighting. A number of commentators referred to the worst crisis within NATO ranks since Suez nearly four decades earlier. To stress America's concerns about NATO, Secretary of State Warren Christopher on 29 November baldly pronounced: "The crisis in Bosnia is about Bosnia and the former Yugoslavia. It is not about NATO and its future. The United States is staying in Europe . . . and so NATO remains the foundation for our American role in Europe."[34]

In determining that a diplomatic route toward arranging peace in the thirty-two-month Bosnian conflict should now be increasingly emphasized, Washington, in conjunction with other contact group members, offered the Bosnian Serbs the possibility of a "special relationship" with Serbia. The Serbs first had to accept Bosnia's sovereignty "in principle" and the group's original proposal for territorial division (which had 51 percent falling under Muslim-Croat control). There were no evident assurances that this new tack would provide better results or, for that matter, contribute to vastly improved relations among the allies. In playing their hand boldly, the Bosnian Serbs by early December stalled the entire UN military and aid delivery operation in the most vulnerable Bosnian regions with hostage-takings, beatings of UN troops, and blockades of overland fuel and food convoys. The Serbs, concerned about possible NATO air attacks, declared that they could not assure the safety of any aircraft flying in Bosnian airspace and informed UN sources that they linked the release of UN peacekeepers to NATO. Despite continued Serb provocations and violence against UN units, UN commanders refused to call on NATO for countermeasures and protection.[35]

Concurrent with these developments and the increasingly untenable conditions for UNPROFOR, officials projected a possible UN withdrawal from Bosnia with the participation of NATO. The impact of such a move on the warring parties and region would be manifold, with no side reaping great benefits. If withdrawal of the UN's approximately twenty-three thousand troops were to occur, the United States committed itself to provide up to half of the personnel of the projected NATO support force of fifty thousand. At this critical juncture the Bosnian Serb side contacted former president Jimmy Carter to assume a mediatory role. In a mission fraught with controversy, Carter agreed, flew to Sarajevo, and succeeded in arranging a temporary cease-fire between the Bosnian Serbs and Muslims that began on 23 December. UN mediators then took over and worked out a subsequent agreement for a four-month cessation of hostilities starting on 1 January 1995.[36] Since nearly ninety cease-fires (one estimate) had preceded this latest arrangement, realistic observers could hardly be anything but skeptical about the prospects for peace through mediation. The divisions between the belligerents were still great, and shaky unity characterized ties between the outside powers and institutions seeking peace.

OTHER BALKAN CONSIDERATIONS

To return to the broader regional picture, it is critical to note, albeit briefly, that the southern flank is an area of critical concern for NATO and not solely for the volatile Yugoslav situation, which for the moment is contained geographically. With the demise of the Soviet Union, Communist regimes in Eastern Europe, and the Warsaw Pact, the threat to NATO's traditional primary front, the central region, is by no means what it had been for four decades. There is a necessary shift of attention elsewhere, particularly to the strategic environment of the Mediterranean with an accompanying out-of-area of focus on Middle Eastern and North African problems and challenges, including those of terrorism, radical Islamic fundamentalism, and militant states with advanced weapons capabilities. The eastern Mediterranean also serves as a vital link with the Caucasus and Central Asia.[37]

The importance of NATO's southeastern members and the land, sea, and air communications that they can offer was reinforced during the Gulf War. But the ongoing contentious relations between Greece and Turkey persist in creating problems for allied solidarity as they continue their feuds over Cyprus and conflicting claims to territorial airspace and waters and mineral exploration rights in the Aegean. They also found themselves supporting divergent positions and sides during the Yugoslav crisis. Ominously, and despite the strains on their economies, Greece and Turkey were among the world's biggest arms importers in 1992 (Greece with about $2 billion and Turkey with about $1.5 billion). The pattern continued in 1993 and 1994. The largest part of these deliveries fell under the "cascade" program whereby smaller NATO states qualified to receive free heavy weaponry from allies obligated to slash their arsenals under the terms of the Treaty on Conventional Armed Forces in Europe (1990).[38] There is no assurance that these weapons will be used exclusively for alliance missions. Alliance concerns heightened in the autumn of 1994 over the Aegean's potential volatility when Turkey challenged Greece's right to extend its territorial waters to twelve miles, as provided for in the International Convention on the Law of the Sea that went into effect on 16 November 1994.

Moreover, Greece perceives itself as the only NATO state to have its security directly threatened by the breakup of the former Yugoslavia and other Balkan developments. Greek strategists had long appreciated the stabilizing role played by a politically unified, nonaligned, and economically viable Yugoslavia in the Balkans. Its dissolution predictably upset the regional strategic balance, unleashing national rivalries and hatreds. Utmost in Greek considerations was the fate of Yugoslav Macedonia, whose extremists had long been held in relative check by federal authorities. To Greece's evident despair, the Macedonian question did rear its historically ugly head to challenge Greek interests in the months immediately before and after the citizens of Yugoslav Macedonia voted to assert their sovereignty in September 1991. Although there was no question of FYROM's armed forces being in the position to effectively challenge Greece's military, Greeks vociferously expressed concern over the usurpation of the Macedonian name and history by their northern neighbors for expansionist claims to Greece's northern region. Greece's grievances also included Skopje's hostile propaganda, flag (with the sun of Vergina, perceived as part of Greek patrimony, on it), and constitutional articles that betrayed irredentist objectives. Greece also saw relations with post–Communist Albania sour because of Tirana's harsh policies toward its sizable Greek minority in the country's south.

Although less vocally supportive of Serbian policies as 1994 advanced, Greece, in large part due to historically good ties, remained the only European Union (EU) member to maintain relatively cordial relations with Belgrade. For its stiff positions toward FYROM (including an economic embargo imposed in February 1994) and its friendly demeanor toward the Serbs, Greece attracted considerable criticism from its NATO and EU allies. Ironically, what has gotten lost in all the rhetoric is that the main tenet of Greek diplomacy, haplessly expressed in the years since 1991, is defensive and calls for the maintenance of current borders. Historically too much has happened around and in Greece with the consequence that Greece nurtures a chronic hypersensitivity to and nervousness about real and perceived threats. In the minds of many Greeks reflecting on Turkey's invasion of Cyprus and continued Turkish challenges in the Aegean, NATO membership was not the total guarantor of Greek national security interests.

In the resulting security vacuum created by the end of the Cold War and the demise of the Soviet Union, Eastern European states have actively sought full membership in NATO. Among other reasons, concerns about dealing with troubled relations between allies—as those between Greece and Turkey—have doubtlessly influenced alliance thinking on expanding NATO membership, particularly in the Balkan region, and on offering alternative status under the terms of the Partnership for Peace (PFP).[39]

CONCLUSION

The complexities of the Balkans have long captured the diplomatic attention and incited the involvement of outside powers, many of whose policymakers, were it feasible to do so, would gladly have espoused the sentiment behind Otto von Bismarck's oft-quoted statement before the German Reichstag at the time of another Bosnian and Balkan crisis in 1876: "I see in it [the crisis] for Germany no interest . . . worth the healthy bones of a single Pomerainian musketeer." Bismarck's recognition that an aloof attitude toward this volatile corner of the European continent was a luxury is reflected in his later observation to Albert Ballin, the German diplomat, who recounted it to Winston Churchill on the eve of war in July 1914: "I remember old Bismarck telling me the year before he died that one day the great European War would come out of some damned foolish thing in the Balkans."[40] Even though some new variables are evident, there are also enough historical examples before us to confirm the hardly cautious judgment that a new European security order will not be ensured as long as one area of the continent remains ablaze. Simply containing a conflict and pursuing policies to stem its expansion—basic to current tactics in the Balkans—is inadequate.

NATO's role in fashioning a secure Europe is critical, but the Atlantic Alliance can be only as strong as the collective will and objectives of member-states allow it to be. If the current Balkan situation is providing an important test, the NATO performance has been uneven, indecisive, and still in process. If the crisis in the former Yugoslavia somehow comes to a peaceful close in the near future, the consequences for NATO—and other involved institutions—might not be grave. If it continues and if there are other violent breakdowns in the region, then the cumulative effect on NATO and its whimpering solidarity might be debilitating. Superpower confrontation has yielded its overbearing and domineering role on the world's strategic stage to ethnic, tribal, religious, and territorial wars on many regional stages. New responses to check the disruptive and bloody conflicts must be devised. If older institutions, such as NATO, fail in meeting these newer challenges, it is hard to believe that new, more effective ones can be established in their place. In such a context, NATO, despite its capability of responding with dominating force, will not be taken seriously, even by its own members, who will probably maintain the alliance but in an enfeebled state.[41] Thus, instead of asking, "Does NATO have a future?" one might better ask, "What kind of future does NATO have?"

NOTES

1. *Economist,* 20 April 1985, 15.
2. The official record of the Moscow talks is found in Joseph M. Siracusa, "The Meaning of TOLSTOY: Churchill, Stalin and the Balkans in Moscow, October 1944," *Diplomatic History* 3 (Fall 1979): 446-62. After considerable haggling and with some revision of Churchill's original proposals, Anthony Eden and Vyacheslav Molotov worked out relative percentages. Britain would have 90 percent influence in Greece with 10 percent influence for the Soviet Union. The percentages in reverse would hold for Romania. Yugoslavia would see a 50-50 distribution while Bulgaria and Hungary would have 80 percent influence for the Soviets and 20 percent for the British. Nothing was recorded regarding Albania.
3. Quoted in Melvyn P. Leffler, *A Preponderance of Power: National Security, the Truman Administration, and the Cold War* (Stanford: Stanford University Press, 1992), 50.
4. Douglas T. Stuart, "Introduction," in *Politics and Security in the Southern Region of the Atlantic Alliance,* ed. Douglas T. Stuart (Baltimore: Johns Hopkins University Press, 1988), 1-2; S. Victor Papacosma, "Greece and NATO," in *NATO and the Mediterranean,* ed. Lawrence S. Kaplan, Robert W. Clawson, Raimondo Luraghi (Wilmington, DE: Scholarly Resources Inc., 1985), 191-92; Lawrence S. Kaplan and Robert W. Clawson, "NATO and the Mediterranean Powers in Historical Perspective," in ibid., 5-6; Monteagle Stearns, *Entangled Allies: U.S. Policy Toward Greece, Turkey, and Cyprus* (New York: Council on Foreign Relations Press, 1992), 74-5; Jed C. Snyder, "Proliferation Threats to Security in NATO's Southern Region," *Mediterranean Quarterly* 4 (Winter 1993): 105-6.
5. Quoted in George W. Hoffman and Fred W. Neal, *Yugoslavia and the New Communism* (New York: Twentieth Century Fund, 1962), 148.
6. C. M. Woodhouse, *Karamanlis: The Restorer of Greek Democracy* (Oxford: Clarendon Press, 1982), 217-19; Demetris Bitsios, *Pera apo ta synora, 1974-1977* [Beyond the frontier, 1974-1977] (Athens: Hestia, 1983), 203-5; Theodore Couloumbis, *The United States, Greece, and Turkey: The Troubled Triangle* (New York: Praeger, 1983), 101-2, n. 52.
7. For details on Greece's post–1974 security problems see Jonathan Alford, ed., *Greece and Turkey: Adversity in Alliance* (London: Gower, 1984); Papacosma, "Greece and NATO," 189-213; and Christos Rozakis, "An Analysis of the Legal Problems in Greek-Turkish Relations 1973-1988," *Year Book 1989* (Athens: Hellenic Foundation for Defense and Foreign Policy, 1990), 193-251.
8. Details on Greek policy in the Balkans after 1974 can be found in Evangelos Kofos, *Greece and the Balkans in the '70s and '80s* (Athens: Hellenic Foundation

for Defense and Foreign Policy, 1991); and C. Svolopoulos, *He hellenike politike sta valkania, 1974-1981* [Greek policy in the Balkans, 1974-1981] (Athens: Evroekdotike, 1987).

9. For details on Soviet and Warsaw Pact roles and problems in the Balkans consult individual chapters in Robert W. Clawson and Lawrence S. Kaplan, eds., *The Warsaw Pact: Political Purpose and Military Means* (Wilmington, DE: Scholarly Resources Inc., 1982); and Jonathan Eyal, ed., *The Warsaw Pact and the Balkans: Moscow's Southern Flank* (London: Macmillan, 1989). See also Daniel N. Nelson, "The Warsaw Treaty Organization and Southeast European Political-Military Security," in *The Warsaw Treaty Organization and Southeast European Political-Military Security,* ed. Paul S. Shoup (Washington: Wilson Center Press, 1990), 123-50.

10. Ian O. Lesser, *Mediterranean Security: New Perspectives and Implications for U.S. Policy* (R-4178-AF) (Santa Monica: RAND Corporation, 1992), 15. See also F. Stephen Larrabee, "Long Memories and Short Fuses: Change and Instability in the Balkans," *International Security* 15 (Winter 1990-91): 59; Snyder, "Proliferation Threats to Security in NATO's Southern Region," 102; and Marten van Heuven, *How Will NATO Adjust in the Coming Decade?* (RAND Note N-3533-JS) (Santa Monica: RAND Corporation, 1992), 1.

11. Quoted in Pierre Hassner, "Western European Perceptions of the USSR," *Daedalus* 108 (Winter 1979): 137.

12. Tito also criticized the "grey zone" concept by stating: "We have not recognized any spheres of interest since 1943. The spheres of interest stop at our borders. What sort of zone they have and whether it is grey, I do not know. Here in Yugoslavia it is a bright zone, and we have nothing to fear." Quoted in Adam Roberts, *Nations in Arms: The Theory and Practice of Territorial Defense* (New York: Praeger, 1976), 127; Stevan K. Pavlowitch, *Yugoslavia* (New York: Praeger, 1971), 224; and Dennison Rusinow, "Yugoslavia and Stalin's Successors, 1968-69," *American Universities Field Staff: Southeastern Europe Series* 16 (August 1969): 4.

13. Phillip A. Petersen and Joshua B. Spero, "The Soviet Military View of Southeastern Europe," in *Problems of Balkan Security: Southeastern Europe in the 1990s,* ed. Paul S. Shoup (Washington: Wilson Center Press, 1990), 230.

14. For a succinct analysis see Steven L. Burg, "Why Yugoslavia Fell Apart," *Current History* 92 (November 1993): 357-63.

15. F. Stephen Larrabee has concluded: "The idea that the only real security threat is an attack on the members of N.A.T.O. is outdated now." "Recent Developments in the Balkans: External and Security Aspects," *The South East European Yearbook 1992* (Athens: Hellenic Foundation for Defense and Foreign Policy, 1993), 91.

16. One U.S. official reportedly stated in late June: "After all, it's not our problem, it's a European problem." Quoted in James R. Steinberg, *The Role of European Institutions in Security after the Cold War: Some Lessons from Yugoslavia* (RAND Note N-3445-FF) (Santa Monica: RAND Corporation, 1992), 13.

17. Quoted in John Fenske, "The West and 'The Problem from Hell,'" *Current History* 92 (November 1993): 354.

18. Colin Powell, "Why Generals Get Nervous," *New York Times*, 8 October 1992.

19. John Kriendler, "NATO's Changing Role—Opportunities and Constraints for Peacekeeping," *NATO Review* 41, no. 3 (June 1993): 18.

20. Unless otherwise cited, basic information on NATO's involvement in the former Yugoslavia in the following section is drawn from newspaper accounts and several sources available electronically from NATO: Henk Vos, "Co-operation in Peacekeeping and Peace Enforcement" [cited 21 October 1993], available from NATO Public Data Service, NATODATA%BLEKUL11.BITNET@PSUVM. PSU.EDU; Sir Russell Johnston, "The Yugoslav Conflict—Chronology of Events from 30th May 1991-8th November 1993" [cited 29 November 1993], ibid.; idem, "Lessons Drawn from the Yugoslav Conflict" [cited 5 December 1993], ibid.; Bruce George, "After the NATO Summit" [cited 26 May 1994], ibid.; and Henk Vos and James Bilbray, "NATO, Peacekeeping and the Former Yugoslavia" [cited 15 July 1994], ibid.

21. During the period from 22 November 1992 to 28 December 1994, NATO and WEU forces challenged 44,513 merchant vessels, boarded 3,431, and diverted 895 to a port for inspection. After 15 June 1993 the mission was called "Operation Sharp Guard." "NATO-WEU Operation Sharp Guard—6 Oct 94" [cited 29 December 1994], available from NATO Public Data Service, NATO-DATA%BLEKUL11.BITNET@PSUVM.PSU.EDU.

22. "Operation Deny Flight," [cited 29 December 1994], available from NATO Public Data Service, NATODATA%BLEKUL11.BITNET@PSUVM.PSU.EDU.

23. *International Herald Tribune*, 29 May 1993.

24. The chairman of the North Atlantic Military Committee during the winter of 1994 stated that the NATO integrated forces made the single largest contribution to the international involvement in the former Yugoslavia. Apart from the forces serving directly under UN control, there were over one hundred aircraft, more than a dozen ships, and around ten thousand men and women from alliance states conducting NATO integrated maritime and air operations in support of the UN effort. Alliance members also directly contributed an additional fifteen thousand personnel to UNPROFOR operations. Field Marshal Sir Richard Vincent, "The Brussels Summit—A Military Perspective," *NATO Review* 42, no. 1 (February 1994): 10.

25. "The only victors from the air strikes episode were the Serbs, who finally managed to draw the Russians into the conflict." Jonathan Eyal, "How Bosnia Could Become a Proxy War," *Wall Street Journal Europe*, 3 March 1994, quoted in George, "After the NATO Summit." The Associated Press on 22 February 1994 cited three Russian views on Moscow's involvement. A spokesman for Boris Yeltsin stated: "Without firing a single shot or threatening anyone, without putting the life of one of our soldiers in danger or spending a single ruble, Russia in fact won the most important battle for its world status. Not only has Russia returned to its roots in its historical policy and role in the Balkans . . .

but it firmly defined the parameters of its influence in Europe and the world." An *Izvestia* commentator added: "Averting the air strikes, Yeltsin and Kozyrev avoided an attack from their political opponents at home which seemed inevitable." Yeltsin's chief of staff offered: "No major decisions concerning the world's security can be made without Russia."

26. *New York Times*, 8 March 1994.
27. "U.S. Increasingly Isolated on Bosnia," Reuters, 30 September 1994; "NATO-Yugoslavia," Associated Press, 30 September 1994; "NATO Sound and Fury on Bosnia—Will It Work?" Reuters, 30 September 1994; "Perry-Yugoslavia," Associated Press, 3 October 1994.
28. "U.N. General Opposes More Bosnia Force," *New York Times*, 29 September 1994.
29. "Moslems Leave DMZ but Serb Blockade Continues," Reuters, 24 October 1994.
30. NATO, "Press Statement Issued Jointly by UN and NATO," Press Release (94) 103 (28 October 1994).
31. "U.N.-NATO Accord Masks Differences—NATO Sources," Reuters, 28 October 1994; Christoph Bertram, "Irreconcilable Partners: The U.N. and NATO at Cross Purposes in the Balkans," *Washington Post*, 2 November 1994; "Russian Peace-keepers Could Withdraw— Kozyrev," Reuters, 30 October 1994.
32. "NATO Retains Embargo, Europe Dismayed by U.S. Move," Reuters, 11 November 1994; "Pentagon Details Bosnian Embargo Plans," ibid.
33. "Serb Planes Could Fly Again Despite NATO Strike," Reuters, 21 November 1994; "Bombed Croatian Serb Airfield Repaired and Possibly in Use," *Washington Post*, 5 December 1994.
34. "In Policy Switch, U.S. Puts Bosnia Aside to Preserve Alliance," *Washington Post*, 30 November 1994; "U.S. and Bosnia: How a Policy Changed," *New York Times*, 4 December 1994; Michael Kelly, "Surrender and Blame," *New Yorker*, 19 December 1994, 50.
35. "Not Quite the End in Bosnia," *Economist*, 10 December 1994, 46.
36. "What Happens to Bosnia after the U.N. Withdraws?" *Boston Globe*, 16 December 1994; "The Consequences of Pulling Out," *Economist*, 17 December 1994, 53; "Bosnia Cease-Fire to Start Today," *Washington Post*, 24 December 1994; "U.N. Says Bosnia Is Quiet as Cease-Fire Starts," *New York Times*, 25 December 1994; "And so to Belgrade," *Economist*, 24 December 1994, 48; "Bosnian and Serb Commanders Meet as Cease-fire Begins, *New York Times*, 2 January 1995.
37. Among the many publications on this subject are William T. Johnsen, *NATO's New Front Line: The Growing Importance of the Southern Tier* (Carlisle Barracks, PA: Strategic Studies Institute, 1992); Lesser, *Mediterranean Security: New Perspectives and Implications for U.S. Policy*; and Snyder, "Proliferation Threats to Security in NATO's Southern Region," 102-19.
38. *Defense News*, 17 May 1993; *Washington Post*, 30 September 1993; *Financial Times*, 7 June 1994. An updated report stated: "For the second consecutive year, Turkey and Greece appeared to be the biggest importers of tanks in 1993, according to the latest U.N. arms register published [13 October]." Reuters, 13 October 1994.

39. Romania was the first state to sign the Partnership for Peace Framework Document on 27 January 1994. Other Balkan states signed in the following months: Bulgaria on 14 February, Albania on 23 February, and Slovenia on 30 March.

40. Alan Palmer, *Bismarck* (New York: Scribner's, 1976), 188; Winston S. Churchill, *The World Crisis* (New York: Scribner's, 1931), 103.

41. NATO Secretary-General Claes acknowledged certain lessons from NATO's uncomfortable Balkan involvement in a 9 December 1994 interview with a Belgian newspaper. He denied that NATO was paralyzed and stressed that if NATO was losing part of its credibility, it was because UN authorities refused to authorize a military solution. He also projected that NATO would not in the future accept working conditions that paralyzed the alliance. "NATO Claes," Voice of America, 9 December 1994.

12

NATO and the Middle East: The Primacy of National Interests

Mary Ann Heiss

The North Atlantic Treaty provided for alliance intervention in what were termed "out-of-area events," a phrase that could conceivably be used to cover a multitude of sins but that ostensibly meant areas—such as the Middle East—that fell outside the North Atlantic Treaty Organization's (NATO) geographic parameters. The Middle East, located at the juncture of Asia, Africa, and Europe, borders NATO's southern flank and was considered geographically and strategically important to the Western alliance. Despite agreement on its importance, however, NATO countries never really formulated a coherent strategy for the Middle East. Western European partners approached Middle Eastern problems more from a perspective that protected their own local interests, while the United States tended to view the region through the lens of the Cold War and emphasized the Communist threat. Because of their different priorities and conflicting threat perceptions, the NATO nations found it impossible to replicate in the Middle East the kind of cooperation that characterized their policies in Europe. Instead, they often worked at cross-purposes, formulating Middle Eastern policy on an ad hoc, national basis rather than developing a coherent alliance strategy. On numerous occasions throughout the Cold War, the United States and its NATO allies even split publicly over how to address Middle Eastern problems, including the possibility that regional differences might escalate into superpower confrontation. Although the end of the Cold War has removed the specter of superpower intervention in the region, challenges to the Western alliance's Middle Eastern interests remain, as does the potential for intra-alliance disagreement.

ANGLO-AMERICAN COOPERATION IN IRAN

One of the first Middle Eastern problems to divide the NATO nations, particularly Great Britain and the United States, was the Iranian oil dispute of the early 1950s. For the British, the nationalization crisis threatened their traditional control over Iranian oil and imperiled their other international investments as well. To counteract these dangers, British officials pursued a hard-line policy that would limit Iranian gains and ensure continued British control of Iranian oil. For the Americans, the main danger in Iran centered around the possibility that the oil dispute would destabilize the Iranian economy and lead to Soviet advances throughout the Middle East. To prevent such an eventuality, the Americans initially advocated a moderate course that would assuage Iranian nationalism without surrendering that country to Communist control. Over time, though, they abandoned that strategy in favor of a joint Anglo-American front that quashed Iranian nationalism, ensured continued Western control of Iranian oil, and protected important NATO interests. Although the British and the Americans ultimately joined forces, the nationalization crisis revealed the different priorities that motivated policymakers in London and Washington. It also presaged more serious disagreements that would divide the Atlantic Alliance during the 1956 Suez debacle.

Iran's nationalization of the Anglo-Iranian Oil Company (AIOC) in 1951 stemmed from fifty years of dissatisfaction with the company's near domination of that country's economy and society. In 1949, the Iranians had tried to better their financial return from the AIOC by negotiating a new concession agreement with the company. Although the Supplemental Oil Agreement, as it was called, would dramatically increase Iran's oil receipts, it did not go far enough to suit Mohammed Mossadegh and his followers in the National Front, a multifaceted quasi-party that objected to foreign control of Iran's oil. They believed that Iran's oil revenues should be used to benefit the Iranian people, not to line the coffers of a foreign corporation. With this goal in mind, they launched successful campaigns to defeat the supplemental agreement and, after Mossadegh became prime minister, to nationalize the AIOC's Iranian holdings.[1]

The British reaction to these developments illustrated the concerns that would shape London's policy throughout the Iranian imbroglio. The AIOC's

Iranian operations and its refinery at Abadan provided oil-starved Britain with twenty-two million tons of oil products and seven million tons of crude oil per year. They also generated £100 million in foreign exchange annually, which the British sorely needed during the financial crisis of 1951. Nor do these calculations tell the whole story. As Britain's largest overseas investment, the AIOC's Iranian operations stood as a symbol of British power in the Middle East. If those operations were nationalized, Great Britain's worldwide prestige would suffer and its vital assets elsewhere, such as the Suez Canal, would be jeopardized. Under these circumstances, the British were determined to do what they could to safeguard the AIOC's position in Iran. Initially, the AIOC and the British government, which owned a controlling share of the company's stock, offered cosmetic and financial inducements that created the appearance if not the substance of Iranian control. When Mossadegh rejected these inducements, they instituted a worldwide boycott of Iranian petroleum sales that had support from the U.S. government and the major U.S. oil companies. The boycott crippled Iran's economy but failed to moderate its policy. In October 1951, the AIOC withdrew from Iran and the country's oil exports ground to a halt; a year later, Iran severed diplomatic relations with Great Britain.[2]

If the British took an "empirical" approach to the Iranian oil dispute, U.S. policymakers emphasized the "higher" dangers involved.[3] As the only direct land barrier between the Soviet Union and the Persian Gulf, Iran served as a vital link in the Western alliance's Middle Eastern security chain; Soviet control of its territory would make the defense of Greece, Turkey, and the eastern Mediterranean all but impossible. Compounding Iran's importance were its rich oil reserves, which the United States considered crucial to the reconstruction and rearmament of the Western European NATO nations. Loss of these reserves would have dire consequences. In the short term, it would create serious shortages of aviation gasoline and other fuels needed for the military effort in Korea and raise the specter of civilian rationing. In the long term, it might compromise NATO's ability to fight a protracted war with the Soviets, force augmentation of its military establishments, and result in an expansion of Soviet military bases in the Middle East. "Events in Iran," warned U.S. officials in an articulation of the domino theory that would dominate their thinking during the Cold War, "cannot be separated from the world situation," especially from developments in such strategically vital nations as Egypt and Turkey.[4] With so much resting on Iran's continued alliance with the West, the United States could not "take the chance of seeing [it] surrender to communism" or "fall into the Soviet orbit."[5]

Initially, at least, American policymakers favored a negotiated Anglo-Iranian settlement that paid lip service to the idea of nationalization but also recognized the contractual rights of the AIOC. Such a settlement, they maintained, would preserve world peace and the global balance of power while still safeguarding both British and Iranian interests. In order to facilitate such a settlement, the U.S. government adopted a policy of benevolent neutrality that favored neither party in the oil dispute but advised both to act with caution and restraint.[6]

As the Iranian crisis dragged on, however, U.S. policymakers grew increasingly concerned about its potentially disastrous impact on Western security and began to recognize that preserving British oil interests in Iran would go a long way toward defending NATO interests there and throughout the Middle East. To this end, they decided to abandon their initial middle-of-the-road stance in Iran and to ally instead with traditional British interests. In late 1952, President Harry S. Truman joined Prime Minister Winston Churchill in a last-ditch effort at a compromise solution. Although this effort failed to resolve the Anglo-Iranian imbroglio, it signaled the culmination of Washington's transformation from an honest broker in the Iranian dispute to a full-fledged British partner and set the stage for closer Anglo-American cooperation in the future.[7]

By the time Dwight D. Eisenhower took office in early 1953, the Iranian situation was fast approaching a crisis point. The British-led boycott of Iranian oil sales had decimated Iran's economy, and U.S. officials were more concerned than ever that mounting economic instability would lead to a Communist takeover. Prime Minister Mossadegh did nothing to allay their fears. During the spring and summer, he entered into a tacit alliance with the Communist Tudeh party, failed to stop mass public demonstrations that U.S. officials feared would grow into a full-scale revolution, and appeared ready to sell oil to the Soviet Union in order to prop up the Iranian economy. According to the shah, such actions threatened to turn the prime minister into "the Dr. Benes of Iran."[8] The Eisenhower administration agreed, and to keep Iran from going the way of Czechoslovakia, it decided to move against Mossadegh. In August 1953, a coup supported by the British and American governments replaced him with Fazlollah Zahedi, who went on to negotiate an oil agreement that ensured continued Western domination of Iran's oil industry (including a 40 percent share for U.S. companies) and provided the economic foundation for the long rule of Mohammad Reza Shah. In October 1955, Iran joined the Baghdad Pact, and from that point until the Iranian Revolution in 1978, it served as NATO's staunchest ally in the Middle East.[9]

Washington's concern with saving Iran from communism finally compelled it to abandon its efforts to work with Mossadegh and to side with London instead. Preserving Iran's Western orientation and preventing Soviet control of its oil reserves ultimately doomed all thought of a compromise settlement. In the end, Cold War considerations proved overriding. U.S. officials came to believe that the only way to protect NATO interests in Iran was to support Britain's position and remove Mossadegh, and their action ushered in twenty-five years of Iranian friendship with the West. But if the Iranian nationalization episode ended in a triumph for the NATO allies, the Anglo-American differences that characterized its early stages served as a harbinger for the more serious transatlantic split that would come over Suez.

ALLIED DIVISION OVER SUEZ

Only three years after Anglo-American cooperation helped to resolve the Iranian oil dispute, the crisis that began when Egyptian Prime Minister Gamal Abdel Nasser nationalized the Suez Canal tore the two allies apart. The British Foreign Office saw the conflict with Nasser as a reprise of the earlier struggle with Mossadegh.[10] Like the battle for control of Iranian oil, the fight over the Suez Canal threatened Britain's economic stability and worldwide prestige. Facing basically the same threat as in Iran, British officials adopted the same hard-line attitude as well, even resorting to military action in concert with France and Israel to achieve their aims. Any other course, they feared, would be fatal to their position throughout the Middle East. U.S. officials disagreed. Convinced that military action would only drive Nasser into Moscow's arms, thereby endangering NATO interests in the eastern Mediterranean and Middle East, they advised caution instead. Unlike the Iranian crisis, however, in which the Americans had abandoned moderation for a more pro-British stance as the crisis wore on, in the case of Suez there was no shift in U.S. policy. Washington remained resolute in opposing a militant posture and ultimately forced London to reverse course.

The details of the Suez crisis have been well covered in the literature, so only the barest outline need detain us here. After becoming prime minister in April 1954, Nasser negotiated an end to British military presence in the Suez Canal Zone, eschewed membership in the failed Middle East Command and Middle East Defense Organization and in the NATO-modeled Baghdad Pact, and laid plans for the construction of a hydroelectric dam at Aswan that would help to modernize the Egyptian economy. Although U.S. officials initially saw Nasser as a moderate nationalist with whom they could work and were quick to promise financial aid for the Aswan Dam, his subsequent support for pan-Arab nationalism and his cozying up to the Soviet bloc alienated officials in both Washington and Tel Aviv. In July 1956, the Eisenhower administration withdrew its offer of aid for the Aswan Dam, whereupon Nasser nationalized the Suez Canal to make up the financial shortfall. Three months later, Britain, France, and Israel initiated a military operation designed to retake the canal, satisfy Israeli territorial designs, and remove Nasser from power.[11]

British officials believed that only firm action against Nasser could protect their considerable interests in the Suez Canal.[12] As the largest single shareholder in the Suez Canal Company, an enterprise that had generated a profit of $100 million in 1955, the British government stood to lose financially if Nasser took control of the canal, even if he did make good on his pledge to compensate its shareholders. But the canal was more than just an economic asset. It was also the transitway for 25 percent of Britain's (and over 60 percent of Western Europe's) oil, and British officials did not relish the thought of entrusting "an integral part of the Middle East oil complex" to the capricious and anti-British Nasser.[13] Finally, there was the matter of prestige. At a time when British power was declining throughout the Middle East, and so soon after losing their monopoly over Iranian oil, the British saw the Suez Canal as the last remaining symbol of their once-great empire and were determined not to surrender it without a fight.

Britain was joined in its hard-line stance by France and Israel, which had their own grievances against the Egyptian prime minister. The French, of course, were partners with the British in the Suez Canal Company and wanted to retain control of their valuable property. They were also unhappy about Nasser's support for Algerian rebels who were then fighting for independence from French control. For their part, the Israelis feared that Nasser planned to launch another Arab war against their country with arms he had acquired from the Soviet Union. They were also incensed over Nasser's announcement that the nationalized Suez Canal would remain open to all nations save Israel. Given their individual complaints against Nasser, Paris and Tel Aviv were thus more than willing to join London in a military operation that would at once restore Anglo-French control of the Suez Canal, protect Israel, and with any luck eliminate the troublesome prime minister from the scene.[14]

U.S. policymakers considered the Anglo-French-Israeli operation a serious error; President Eisenhower called it "'the damnedest business [he] ever saw supposedly intelligent governments get themselves into.'" Nasser had a legal right to nationalize the canal, the Americans argued, so long as he compensated its former owners and kept it open to international traffic. Military intervention to retake it could lead to all sorts of difficulties. Egypt might retaliate by blocking Western access to the canal, a development that would not only have serious military implications for NATO's position in the Middle East but also pose problems for Western European oil consumers during the upcoming winter. Moreover, a military operation in Egypt would draw French and British troops away from NATO's European theater and thus diminish the alliance's readiness at a time of global tension. It was not clear, after all, whether the Soviet Union's recent intervention in Hungary was to be a jumping-off point for a larger assault against the West. Beyond these tangible dangers, intervention held some intangible ones as well. It would inflame anti-Western sentiment in the Arab world, push Nasser deeper into the Soviet camp, and allow Moscow to step in as the defender of small nations against Western imperialism. According to Eisenhower, military action "'might well array the world from Dakar to the Philippine Islands against [the NATO nations]'" and generate hostility that "'could not be overcome in a generation and, perhaps, not even in a century.'"[15]

When asked to sanction the intervention beforehand, U.S. officials had demurred. After the allies struck anyway, they condemned the operation that made it impossible for the West to launch a propaganda attack against Soviet heavy-handedness in Hungary, and worked through the United Nations to arrange a cease-fire. But when Anglo-French troops were slow to withdraw, Washington resorted to economic and financial—particularly oil—sanctions to speed things along. The power of such sanctions stemmed from the fact that by the winter of 1956-57, Britain and France were facing a severe shortage of oil. Nasser had blocked the Suez Canal during the initial days of the confrontation, saboteurs had cut oil pipelines across Syria, and Saudi Arabia had halted oil sales to Britain and France. Only oil from the United States could make up the shortfall, but Eisenhower refused to make that oil available until the allies pulled out of Suez. The importance of these oil sanctions cannot be overestimated. British officials themselves were certainly well aware of the effect that U.S. sanctions would have on their Suez operation; upon learning of Washington's intentions, Chancellor of the Exchequer Harold Macmillan exclaimed, "'Oil sanctions! That finishes it.'"[16]

As in the Iranian crisis, Anglo-American differences over Suez revealed the array of fears and concerns that motivated officials in London and Washington. Policymakers in the Foreign Office were again concerned about Britain's global position and sought to preserve at least a modicum of its

former influence in Egypt. They saw the battle over Suez as part of the struggle between the developed and developing worlds, between what world systems scholars call the core and the periphery.[17] As the core nation responsible
for Egypt and the rest of the Middle East under the postwar Anglo-American
division of labor, Britain alone should determine how to protect what it saw
as the Western core's interests in that region. And for officials in London, those
interests could best be protected by a firm stand at Suez, even if that stand
risked war. Giving in to Nasser, they maintained, would lead to the complete
expulsion of "'all western influence and interests from [the] Arab countries'"
and elsewhere.[18] Closer to home, and perhaps more to the point, Harold
Macmillan feared that it would turn Britain into "'another Netherlands.'"[19]

U.S. officials agreed that Suez was part of the world struggle between the
developed and developing countries. But for them the real danger lay not in
a victory for the forces of nationalism but in the triumph of communism.
As policymakers in the State Department saw things, British bellicosity
would only confirm Egyptian impressions of Western imperialism, steel
Nasser's determination to rid his nation of Western influence, and cement
his ties with the Soviet Union. It might also lead to an Arab embargo of oil
sales to the NATO nations, a development that would have serious economic and strategic consequences for the alliance, or to a complete Soviet
takeover of the Middle East, which would completely reconfigure the East-
West balance of power.[20]

For the United States, the goal of preventing the spread of communism
dictated the adoption in Egypt of the opposite strategy from the one pursued
in Iran. There the need to stop a possible Soviet advance had led Washington
to subordinate the needs of Iranian nationalism to traditional British interests: Containment in Iran could best be accomplished by propping up the
British position and using London as the bulwark of Western power. In
Egypt, the situation was reversed. Now it was the British position that had
to be subordinated, even at the risk of undermining Britain's global position
and precipitating a split in the NATO alliance. During the three years that
separated the Iranian and Suez disputes, U.S. officials had come to realize
that they could no longer hope to contain Soviet influence in the Middle East
by backing the British and crushing indigenous nationalism. On the contrary, backing the British would only inflame nationalist sentiment, threaten
to tar the United States with the brush of British imperialism, and make a
Soviet takeover of the region all the more likely. Thus, in order to prevent a
Communist advance into Egypt, the United States had to abandon its British
ally and instead pursue a course that assuaged Egyptian nationalism. This did

not necessarily mean that U.S. officials shared Nasser's goals; they did not. It simply meant that mollifying Egyptian nationalism became the preferred U.S. tactic for achieving the goal of containment. The overriding anti-Communist orientation of U.S. policy remained the same. What changed in the case of Suez, as Peter L. Hahn has noted, was that the United States had to choose between two interests that in the past had coincided: support for the British and containment of the Soviets. Given the state of Cold War tensions at the time, the choice was a foregone conclusion.[21]

In many respects, the Suez crisis was a turning point in the postwar history of Eastern and Western relations with Egypt and the Middle East. For the East, the crisis initiated a new spirit of amity between Moscow and Cairo; by the 1960s, the Soviets counted Nasser as one of their closest allies in the Middle East and, in fact, in all of the Third World.[22] For the West, the crisis had less auspicious results. It marked the last gasp of British imperialism in the Middle East and, much as France's defeat at Dien Bien Phu thirty months earlier, served as painful confirmation that Britain was no longer a great global power.[23] It also caused a serious rift in the Atlantic Alliance and engendered British and French animosity toward the United States that was soon papered over but not completely ameliorated. Finally, the Suez crisis pushed the United States to play a greater role in trying to stabilize the Middle East and hold the line against Communist expansion there. The Eisenhower Doctrine codified this new policy in January 1957, and U.S. aid to Jordan later that year and intervention in the Lebanese civil war in 1958 put that policy into practice. The decades after the Suez crisis would see a sharpening of all of these trends, as Middle Eastern events—particularly the escalating Arab-Israeli conflict and the consequences of the West's growing dependence on imported oil—exacerbated existing U.S.-European differences and ultimately reshaped the NATO alliance itself.

CONTINUED CONFLICT OVER OIL AND THE ARAB-ISRAELI DISPUTE

The relative calm that characterized the Arab-Israeli conflict during the decade following the Suez crisis was shattered in June 1967, when Israel locked horns with Egypt, Syria, and Jordan during the Six-Day War. Although American support for Israel and Soviet support for the Arabs was widely known, neither side really intervened in the conflict, and Israel secured a tremendous military victory on its own, capturing control of the Sinai, the West Bank of the Jordan, the Golan Heights, and East Jerusalem. If the superpowers largely refrained from influencing the course of the war, however, both used the conflict to enhance their own positions in the Middle East, with the United States cementing its special relationship with Israel and the Soviet Union strengthening its ties with the Arab states. The short-lived June war also affected the Western alliance. French President Charles de Gaulle, who in 1966 had withdrawn France from NATO's integrated military command, further split with his Western allies by condemning Israel for firing the first shot in the conflict and by halting French arms sales to Tel Aviv. These developments signaled de Gaulle's determination to pursue a more independent course in international affairs and opened the door for the significant American arms sales to Israel that would characterize the post-1967 period. They also portended the more serious cracks in the Western alliance that would appear during the 1973 Yom Kippur War.

The Arab oil embargo that accompanied the October 1973 war exacerbated the intra-NATO differences that had characterized the Six-Day War. For the Western Europeans, who received two-thirds of their oil from Arab countries, the embargo threatened their energy security and economic well-being. But instead of confronting it together, they worked individually to protect their own supplies, even to the point of undercutting each other with the Arabs in order to gain access to oil. For U.S. officials, the embargo was an effort to blackmail them into abandoning Israel and allowing the Soviet-backed Arabs to control the Middle East. To prevent such an outcome, they tried to effect a diplomatic solution to the Yom Kippur War that gave each side some, but not all, of what it wanted and prevented the superpowers from intervening on behalf of their respective regional clients. They also tried to forge a common consumer response to the embargo that would negate its divisive effects for the Atlantic Alliance and defuse its usefulness as a political weapon. Although the United States was able to keep the Yom Kippur War from becoming a superpower conflict, it was less successful on the oil front. By the time the embargo ended, NATO's oil security policy lay in tatters, as did the solidarity that had constituted its cornerstone.

Ostensibly, the oil embargo was aimed at weakening U.S. support for Israel. In the years since the Six-Day War, and particularly since the 1970 Jordanian crisis, Washington had provided Jerusalem with extensive military aid—$1.2 billion in credits from 1971 to 1973 alone. It had also tacitly supported Israeli occupation of territories seized in 1967, namely the Sinai, the West Bank, the Golan Heights, and East Jerusalem.[24] Israel's occupation of these areas was anathema to all of the Arab states, but none more than Egypt, which was determined to avenge its humiliating 1967 defeat at all costs. Hence President Anwar Sadat's decision for a joint Egyptian-Syrian attack in October 1973.[25] To provide a united Arab front in the conflict and to pressure the West into abandoning Israel, Sadat had convinced Saudi Arabia's King Faisal to institute the embargo. As the Arab world's largest oil producer, Saudi Arabia was the key to an embargo's success. And although Faisal initially resisted the idea, preferring instead to lead a (successful) campaign for higher oil prices on world markets, visible U.S. support for Israel during the Yom Kippur War changed his mind.[26]

From its beginning, the embargo strained relations among the NATO nations, which the Arabs divided into three categories based on their support for Israel. The United States and the Netherlands, considered Israel's biggest supporters, would be completely cut off from Arab oil; Britain and France, seen as "friendly" to Arab interests, would receive the same amount of Arab oil as in the past; and the other European NATO nations (along with Japan), strong supporters of neither side, would see their oil imports decline monthly until the Yom Kippur War was settled. But those countries that would continue to receive Arab oil would pay significantly higher prices: During the last three months of 1973 alone, the posted price of Middle Eastern crude doubled, from $5.12 per barrel to $11.65.[27]

To circumvent the supply dislocations posed by the embargo, the major oil companies adopted an "equal suffering" policy under which all countries would endure the same percentage decrease in normal oil supplies regardless of their status on the Arab list. For the companies, this was the only "'equitable and practical'" way to handle the embargo: It ensured that no nation received better treatment than any other and safeguarded the integrity of their international contracts.[28] For the Western Europeans, however, and especially for the French and the British, it was an unfair policy that penalized them in favor of the pro-Israeli Americans.[29]

When it proved impossible to alter the companies' policy, the Western Europeans decided to curry favor with the Arabs instead. On 6 November 1973, the European Economic Community (EEC) called upon Israel to accept UN Resolution 242, by which the Arabs would recognize Israel's right to exist in exchange for Israeli withdrawal from territories seized during the 1967 war. This move had the desired effect, as the Arabs subsequently exempted community nations (except the Netherlands) from future production cuts. But Western Europe's united front was short lived. After a December summit meeting in Copenhagen failed to yield a common voice regarding the oil crisis, Britain, France, and other EEC nations began bilateral negotiations with various producing countries designed to swap industrial goods and technological aid for oil. In a clear violation of both the letter and the spirit of community regulations, they also refused to ship oil to the embargoed Dutch, beginning such shipments only after the Dutch threatened to withhold natural gas from Belgium, France, and West Germany if they did not receive oil assistance from their allies.[30] By early 1974, the Arab oil producers had shrewdly divided the Atlantic Alliance, pitting the Western Europeans against both the Americans and each other.

The French and the British were the most vehement about distancing themselves from the Americans and pursuing independent approaches to the Arabs. Partly this was a practical matter: As French President Georges Pompidou noted, while the United States received only 10 percent of its oil from Arab countries and could afford to alienate them by supporting Israel, France was "'entirely dependent'" on Arab oil and hardly in a position to do the same. It is also probable that the French and British opposed American policy as a way of avenging what they saw as earlier American betrayals elsewhere. The French, for example, had never quite forgiven officials in Washington for scotching their plans to employ NATO forces in the war against Algerian rebels. And the British, as Daniel Yergin has pointed out, saw opposition to the United States as a payback for what they considered the U.S. betrayal at Suez. Just as the Americans had abandoned them in favor of the Egyptians in 1956, so now did they abandon the Americans. Events had apparently come full circle, and although British Prime Minister Edward Heath denied personally that he "'want[ed] to raise the issue of Suez,'" he admitted that it was "'there for many people.'"[31]

Europe's oil-driven mentality displeased U.S. officials, who viewed the events of 1973 within a Cold War context. For them, the Yom Kippur War and the oil embargo were more than manifestations of the Arab-Israeli conflict; they were also components of the ongoing struggle between communism and capitalism. The Arab states, especially Egypt and Syria, received extensive arms support from the Soviet Union, and their victory in the Yom Kippur War would allow the Soviets to dominate the entire Middle East. To prevent such an eventuality, the West, led by the United States, had to assist Israel, even if doing so angered the Arabs and contributed to the oil embargo. But it also had to prevent the kind of humiliating Arab defeat that might invite Soviet intervention and thereby transform the Yom Kippur War into World War III. To this end, Secretary of State Henry Kissinger undertook a frenzied campaign of shuttle diplomacy that finally resulted in a cease-fire on 25 October.[32]

No thanks to the European NATO nations, though, which did not share Washington's geopolitical view of the 1973 crises and which wanted nothing to do with a possible superpower engagement in the Middle East. To avoid becoming embroiled in a Soviet-American confrontation, the Western European NATO partners generally refused to support U.S. efforts to resupply Israel during the October war. Aside from the Netherlands, only Portugal granted landing rights to U.S. planes carrying supplies to Israel, an act that earned it Arab enmity and got it added to the list of countries completely cut off from Arab oil. France continued throughout the conflict to ship tanks to Libya and Saudi Arabia; Turkey even allowed Soviet planes carrying supplies to Egypt and Syria to violate its airspace without protest.[33] The Western Europeans also made it clear that they would block any U.S. attempt to use NATO facilities against the Soviets in the Middle East. Their proximity to Soviet missiles in Eastern Europe and their fears of a Soviet attack overrode their sense of alliance solidarity, prompting Kissinger to lament that they were acting "as if the [Atlantic] alliance did not exist."[34]

American-European differences were also evident in the handling of the embargo. To Washington's way of thinking, the Arabs had made the oil weapon work by subordinating their individual differences to a common goal. Successfully resisting the embargo required consumer nations to do the same rather than adopting a *sauve qui peut* ("every man for himself") approach and cutting their own deals with the Arabs at the expense of their allies. Such action only played into the Arabs' hands, allowed them to raise oil prices dramatically, and weakened NATO's position in the Middle East and throughout the world. It also threatened to ally Western Europe more closely with the Arab cause, a development that would seriously complicate U.S. efforts to achieve a permanent Arab-Israeli settlement.[35] Given the intra-NATO differences over the Yom Kippur War and the oil embargo, 1973 hardly turned out to be the "Year of Europe" that Nixon and Kissinger had envisioned.

The disjointed Western response to the oil embargo was finally resolved in February 1974, when the NATO nations and Japan convened, under U.S. auspices, for the Washington Energy Conference. Coming as it did on the heels of the scramble for Arab oil, the conference was, in Kissinger's words, more like "a clash of adversaries" than "a meeting of allies."[36] Tensions were indeed high as the attending nations advanced different solutions to the oil problem. Britain and France, for example, called for a distinctly European approach to energy problems, while West Germany backed an American plan for consumer unity.[37] The deadlock was only broken when President Richard M. Nixon hinted that U.S. military commitments to NATO depended on alliance cooperation in the field of energy. Specifically, he issued a veiled threat to pull U.S. troops out of Europe unless the NATO allies abandoned their intransigence on oil.[38] Because the Western Europeans were ultimately unwilling to compromise their overall security by breaking with the Americans on energy, they agreed to join the U.S.-sponsored International Energy Agency, a supranational organization designed to provide the kind of concerted alliance energy policy that had been sorely lacking during the 1973-74 Arab embargo. In keeping with its past efforts at greater independence from the United States and the NATO alliance, France declined to join.[39]

The 1973 embargo had far-reaching ramifications for the international community. It marked the first successful Arab use of the oil weapon and indicated that in the future, producer countries would not hesitate to use their new economic power to achieve their political goals. The embargo also effected a significant redistribution of wealth from the developed West to the developing Middle East and allowed the Arab oil exporters to emerge (at least for a time) as philanthropists to the least developed nations of the world.[40] For the NATO countries, the embargo revealed the fragile sense of community that bound them together and the ease with which autarkic self-interest could tear them apart. It also marked the apogee of Soviet influence in the Arab world and ushered in a period of improving relations between the United States and key Arab states like Egypt and Saudi Arabia.

AMERICAN UNILATERALISM IN THE MIDDLE EAST

The period after 1974 witnessed a significant increase in the American presence in the Middle East, as Washington assumed primary responsibility for protecting Western interests in the region. Although U.S. policymakers continued to worry about the possible expansion of Soviet influence in the region, they also became more concerned than previously about the potentially destabilizing effects of indigenous Middle Eastern nationalism and intra-regional disputes. Both of these threats could plunge the Middle East into armed conflict and imperil vital Western petroleum and security interests in the region. To protect those interests, the United States augmented its regional presence and demonstrated its resolve to use force in defense of its Middle Eastern position, even if doing so meant acting without its NATO allies.

Immediately following the Yom Kippur War, the United States emerged as the driving force behind an Arab-Israeli settlement. Years of painstaking step-by-step diplomacy finally yielded the historic 1978 Camp David Accords and the 1979 Egyptian-Israeli peace treaty, which greatly reduced the chances of another Arab-Israeli war and went a long way toward stabilizing the entire Middle East.[41] Acclaim for the Egyptian-Israeli treaty was not universal. The other Arab states denounced Egypt for selling out to Israel, but because Egypt was the key to any viable Arab bloc, their opposition was in the end ineffectual. The Western Europeans were also critical, largely because the treaty made no provision for settling the Palestinian question; in June 1980 they issued their own, more pro-Palestinian policy statement, the Venice Declaration.[42] But if European opposition prevented a united Western front regarding the Arab-Israeli dispute and served as a harbinger of future obstacles to a permanent peace, it did not derail progress toward a settlement. By the late 1970s, the United States had clearly emerged as the dominant Western power in brokering an end to the long-simmering Arab-Israeli dispute. When Jimmy Carter left the White House in 1981, that conflict appeared to be receding as a major source of Middle Eastern instability.

This did not mean that all was well in the region, however. On the contrary, just as Arab-Israeli tensions were ebbing, the Iranian Revolution and the Soviet invasion of Afghanistan destabilized the Middle East and seriously threatened the Atlantic Alliance's position there. The 1978 Islamic Revolution in Iran, which transformed what had been the West's staunchest Middle Eastern ally into a hostile, anti-Western state, was seen as a gain for Moscow because it was a loss for Washington.[43] The almost concurrent invasion of Afghanistan, which bordered Iran, was even more threatening. It conjured up U.S. fears of a Soviet master plan to gain access to a warm-water port and oil reserves in the Persian Gulf, possibly by capitalizing on the turmoil surrounding the Iranian Revolution. It also altered the East-West balance in the region by placing Soviet troops within striking distance of vital Middle Eastern oilfields and important NATO military bases.[44]

Both of these developments refocused the alliance's attention on the importance of developments in the Middle East,[45] though neither yielded a truly unified response. Officials in Washington saw the Iranian and Afghani incidents from a global perspective and called for a common Western front. After Iranian militants seized the U.S. embassy in Tehran in November 1979, Washington pressed its European allies to apply economic sanctions against Tehran and to reduce the size of their embassy staffs there. Similar calls for united action, ranging from boycotting the 1980 Olympic Games to military support for anti-Soviet rebels, followed the invasion of Afghanistan. But these pleas went unheeded, as the European NATO allies continued to emphasize local concerns over global ones and to believe that the U.S. government overexaggerated the threats inherent in the Iranian and Afghani crises. For the Europeans, the overriding goals in the Middle East remained preventing another oil shortage and avoiding conflict with Moscow, and those goals could best be attained by a neutral response to the problems in Iran and Afghanistan.[46]

In a fashion that was becoming increasingly common, after 1980 the United States acted unilaterally to meet what it saw as new challenges in the Persian Gulf. In the Carter Doctrine, issued in January 1980, Washington indicated its intention to defend its Persian Gulf interests from outside threats—that is, Soviet aggression—by any means necessary, even a resort to force. To back up this new policy, the Carter administration began and the Reagan administration completed plans to upgrade U.S. capabilities for dealing with threats in what Washington now called Southwest Asia. In 1983, these plans resulted in the U.S. Central Command (CENTCOM), a rapid-response force that could quickly address regional tensions.[47] To be sure, CENTCOM did enhance the Western presence in the Persian Gulf and probably contributed to greater stability in the area. But as Thomas H. Etzold noted in 1985, because it amounted to yet another drain on dwindling U.S. resources and thus limited Washington's commitment to NATO's European theater, it forced the other allies to pick up the slack and thereby reap the whirlwind of their failure to join the United States directly in defending alliance interests in the Middle East.[48]

Other episodes throughout the 1980s reflected Washington's tendency to act unilaterally in the Middle East. For example, the United States took the lead in trying to stabilize Lebanon, where rival Christian, Muslim, and Palestinian elements had been locked in civil war since 1975. Over time, both Syria and Israel had sent troops to Lebanon—Syria because it wanted to prevent a victory by radical Muslims and Palestinians, Israel because it wanted to stop Palestinian guerrilla attacks coming from southern Lebanon. Ostensibly to stabilize the situation and allow the Lebanese government to reestablish order but ultimately for their own individual reasons, the United States, France, and Italy joined in a multinational force in Lebanon. Although the initial task was completed rather easily, permanent peace was more difficult to arrange, and the United States seemed on the brink of being dragged into a Vietnam-style quagmire. The October 1983 suicide bombing of U.S. Marine headquarters in Beirut that killed almost 250 Americans eliminated the threat of a protracted American presence in Lebanon and convinced the Reagan administration to reverse course. In early 1984, Washington announced that the marines were being moved to a more defensible position. Lebanon had not been stabilized, and the intervention ultimately proved fruitless.[49]

The United States also arrogated to itself responsibility for neutralizing Libya's Muammar Qaddafi, who had become its latest Middle Eastern bête noire. After assuming power in 1969, Qaddafi had nationalized Western oil interests in Libya and launched a concerted attack against Western interests in general, to the point of condoning and allegedly supporting international terrorists. In April 1986, in retaliation for what was thought to have been the Libyan-backed bombing of a nightclub in West Berlin that killed two U.S. soldiers and injured scores of others, U.S. bombers struck Libyan targets at will, killing many but failing either to dislodge Qaddafi from power or to deter him from supporting anti-American terrorism. Moreover, American heavy-handedness in dealing with Qaddafi elicited strong opposition from the European NATO partners, who advocated a political rather than a military settlement of U.S.-Libyan differences. France and Spain were especially outspoken against U.S. intervention, refusing overflight rights to U.S. bombers headed for Libya.[50] All things considered, the unilateral American interventions in Lebanon and Libya failed to accomplish their main goals. But they did indicate how determined the United States had become to protect its Middle Eastern interests from perceived threats, even if it had to act without its NATO allies to do so.

Concurrent with these instances of intra-NATO squabbling regarding the Middle East was the Iran-Iraq War that raged from 1980-1988 and evinced NATO-nation cooperation but not explicit NATO action. The war stemmed from a long-standing border dispute between Iran and Iraq rather than from outside (that is, Soviet) pressures and evolved for the most part without much third-party intervention. To be sure, U.S. policymakers, and their counterparts in Western Europe, feared that an Iranian victory would mean the spread of Islamic fundamentalism throughout the Gulf region and threaten Western interests in Saudi Arabia and elsewhere. But aside from France, which openly aided Iraq in the conflict, NATO nations refrained from supporting either side and sought instead to stay out of what became an increasingly bloody stalemate.[51] They did, though, take an active interest in keeping the conflict from spreading and in protecting the continued flow of oil through the Persian Gulf. To this end, early on in the war, the United States, along with Britain and France, had individually sent warships to the Gulf region not only in a show of force but also to escort foreign-owned oil tankers through the Persian Gulf. The allies expanded their efforts after the Iranians began attacking Kuwaiti oil tankers in the Persian Gulf in the summer of 1986. These attacks could seriously affect the United States and Western Europe, which received 15 and 46 percent of their oil, respectively, from the Persian Gulf. They could also provide an opportunity for an expansion of Soviet influence in the region if Moscow decided to assist Kuwait in protecting its Gulf tankers. To thus avert what officials in Washington saw as a double-sided danger, the United States agreed to reflag Kuwaiti tankers under the Stars and Stripes and to provide those tankers with naval escorts through the Gulf. The major NATO partners, including France, Great Britain, Italy, Belgium, and the Netherlands, added their own naval vessels to the transport effort and thereby helped to effect an independent but coordinated alliance response to what all could agree was a serious threat to their common interests in the Middle East.[52]

The driving force behind the concerted Western response to the Iran-Iraq War was clearly the United States. Washington's de facto involvement in that conflict served to confirm its determination to protect Persian Gulf stability from all perceived challenges, be they external or internal. The Soviet Union of the Gorbachev era was becoming less and less of a threat to Western interests in the Middle East, a belief given impetus by the dramatic events in Eastern Europe in 1989-90. American policymakers now came to appreciate the real danger posed by indigenous regional tensions and began formulating a strategy for dealing with them. They increased the U.S. military presence in the Gulf; they strengthened their ties to moderate Middle Eastern states like Kuwait and Saudi Arabia; and they even sought to improve their relations with Iraq, which they saw as less of a threat to Western interests in the Middle East than Iran.[53] As later developments made clear, however, that assumption could hardly have been more inaccurate.

Iraq's August 1990 assault against Kuwait elicited the same determination to protect U.S. interests in the Persian Gulf as previous regional crises. It also provided still another opportunity for alliance cooperation. The international community, including the United States, its NATO allies, and the Soviet Union, was quick to condemn the Iraqi invasion. Over thirty nations also eventually joined the U.S.-led coalition that pulled off Operation Desert Shield/Storm and forced Iraq out of Kuwait. The long-term consequences of the Gulf War are not yet clear. But it is probably safe to say that the conflict solidified the position of the United States as the primary Western power working for stability in the Persian Gulf and protecting smaller, oil-rich Gulf states like Kuwait and Saudi Arabia from outside attack, even now that the end of the Cold War had removed the specter of Soviet expansion from the horizon. Indeed, the American, and by extension, Western, interest in preventing the destabilization of the Gulf region remains constant. All that has changed, as the Gulf War revealed, is the potential catalyst of destabilization.[54]

TOWARD FUTURE ALLIANCE COOPERATION IN THE MIDDLE EAST

Although the end of the Cold War has eliminated the threat of Soviet expansion in the Middle East, other obstacles remain to the NATO goal of regional stability, one of which is the continuing Arab-Israeli conflict. The 1979 Egyptian-Israeli peace agreement did not lead directly to a permanent peace accord; in fact, the 1980s witnessed an escalation of Arab-Israeli tensions rather than their diminishment. Israel sought to solidify its control over the occupied territories, even in the face of American opposition. In December 1987 the *intifada* erupted and plunged those territories into almost daily violence. The post–Gulf War Madrid conference in the autumn of 1991 was hardly the vehicle for a permanent peace that its organizers had hoped for. Still, the historic handshake between Yitzhak Rabin and Yasir Arafat in Washington in the fall of 1993 opened the door to a permanent peace, and progress toward that end is finally under way. It can be expected that the NATO nations, especially the United States, will continue to work for a permanent Arab-Israeli settlement. But it is doubtful that resolving the conflict is as important as it was during the Cold War, when the Soviet Union served as the primary arms supplier for Syria and could have intervened on behalf of its client if the Arab-Israeli conflict had heated up significantly. Now the Arab-Israeli conflict is seen more or less on its own terms, as a potentially destabilizing force in the Middle East but not as something that challenges the East-West balance of power or might plunge the Middle East into superpower confrontation.[55]

Potential instability in Turkey, the only NATO member actually located in the Middle East, also threatens the alliance's position in the region. Since joining NATO in 1952, Turkey has had a tempestuous relationship with its alliance partners, especially the United States. U.S. use of Turkish air bases without permission during the 1958 Lebanon crisis, the U.S. decision to place Jupiter missiles in Turkey, the subsequent decision to withdraw those missiles without consultation, and the lack of U.S. support for Turkey's position during the 1964 Cyprus crisis poisoned Turkish relations with the United States. Ankara and Washington also split over such other issues as the Yom Kippur War, the recognition of the Palestine Liberation Organization, and how to respond to the Iranian hostage crisis and the Soviet invasion of Afghanistan. At that same time, economic and geostrategic realities were pushing Turkey closer to the Soviet Union. As a result, during the 1970s Turkey seemed to straddle the fence between East and West, retaining its NATO ties but accepting Soviet development assistance. By the late 1980s and early 1990s, though, its orientation had changed. In 1987 it applied, albeit unsuccessfully, for membership in the European Community; five years later it became an associate member of the new Western European Union with hopes of full membership in the future. Although Turkey's Western orientation can be expected to continue, economic and political turmoil and continued conflict with NATO ally Greece could destabilize the country and thus imperil larger alliance interests in the region.[56]

These are but two sources of instability in the post–Cold War Middle East. Both are indigenous to the region; neither will be solved by NATO action alone. With the end of the Cold War, regional problems that had been subordinated to the threat of Soviet expansion in the Middle East have risen to the forefront. But whereas the United States was relatively successful in keeping the Soviets out of the region, it will probably be less able to control the course of essentially regional problems. The bipolar worldview that guided so much of Washington's postwar foreign policy no longer applies to the post–Cold War world. It must now be replaced with one that gives pride of place to regional actors and takes greater account of their traditional animosities. The Soviet challenge to the Middle East is gone. But threats to Western interests in the region remain, as does the need for Atlantic Alliance cooperation.

NOTES

1. For general accounts of the Iranian nationalization crisis see Fakhreddin Azimi, *Iran: The Crisis of Democracy, 1941-1953* (London: I. B. Tauris, 1989), 257-338; and Homa Katouzian, *Musaddiq and the Struggle for Power in Iran* (London: I. B. Tauris, 1990), 113-55.

2. For the British side of the nationalization crisis see Wm. Roger Louis, *The British Empire in the Middle East, 1945-1951: Arab Nationalism, the United States, and Postwar Imperialism* (Oxford: Oxford University Press, 1984), 632-89.

3. Sir Oliver Franks (British ambassador, Washington) tel. 427 to Foreign Office, 11 February 1952, Foreign Office Correspondence, Record Class FO 371, 98685/EP15314/31, Public Record Office, Kew, England (hereafter FO 371, with filing information); Franks tel. 439 to Foreign Office, 12 February 1952, FO 371, 98685/EP15314/32.

4. NSC-117, "The Anglo-Iranian Problem," 10 October 1951, U.S. Department of State, *Foreign Relations of the United States, 1952-1954* (Washington, 1989), 10:220-22 (hereafter *FRUS*, with year and volume number).

5. Paper prepared in the Department of State, "The Present Crisis in Iran," undated, *FRUS, 1950* (Washington, 1978), 5:509-19.

6. For initial American thinking see, for example, William Rountree (director, GTI) memorandum of conversation, 18 April 1951, General Records of the Department of State, Record Group 59, 641.88/4-1851, National Archives, Washington, DC (hereafter RG 59, with filing information).

7. See Loy W. Henderson (American ambassador, Tehran) tel. to State Department, 25 August 1952, *FRUS, 1952-1954* 10:458-60; and Bruce tel. 481 to American embassy, Tehran, 25 August 1952, RG 59, 888.2553/8-2552.
8. Burton Y. Berry (U.S. ambassador, Baghdad) tel. to State Department, 17 August 1953, *FRUS, 1952-1954* 10:746-48.
9. For detailed examinations of the coup see Mark Gasiorowski, "The 1953 *Coup d'Etat* in Iran," *International Journal of Middle East Studies* 19 (August 1987): 261-86; and Kermit Roosevelt, *Countercoup: The Struggle for the Control of Iran* (New York: McGraw Hill, 1979), 169-99.
10. For an account that links earlier developments in Egypt with the Iranian oil crisis see H. W. Brands, "The Cairo-Tehran Connection in Anglo-American Rivalry in the Middle East, 1951-1953," *The International History Review* 11 (August 1989): 434-56.
11. For a general account of the Suez crisis see, for example, Peter L. Hahn, *The United States, Great Britain, and Egypt, 1945-1956: Strategy and Diplomacy in the Early Cold War* (Chapel Hill: University of North Carolina Press, 1991), 211-39. For an emphasis on oil diplomacy and alliance politics see Ethan B. Kapstein, *The Insecure Alliance: Energy Crises and Western Politics since 1944* (New York: Oxford University Press, 1990), 96-124.
12. For accounts of the crisis by British participants see, for example, Anthony Eden, *Full Circle: The Memoirs of Sir Anthony Eden* (London: Cassell, 1960); and Harold Macmillan, *Riding the Storm, 1956-1959* (London: Harper & Row, 1971).
13. Daniel Yergin, *The Prize: The Epic Struggle for Oil, Money, and Power* (New York: Simon & Schuster, 1991), 482.
14. For Anglo-French-Israeli collusion see, for example, Hahn, *Strategy and Diplomacy*, 224-27; and Yergin, *The Prize*, 485-88.
15. Eisenhower quoted in Hahn, *Strategy and Diplomacy*, 232, 215, 218.
16. Macmillan quoted in Yergin, *The Prize*, 492. For the importance of American sanctions see Diane B. Kunz, *The Economic Diplomacy of the Suez Crisis* (Chapel Hill: University of North Carolina Press, 1991).
17. For world systems theory see, for example, Thomas J. McCormick, "World Systems," in *Explaining the History of American Foreign Relations*, ed. Michael J. Hogan and Thomas G. Paterson (New York: Cambridge University Press, 1991), 89-98.
18. Eden quoted in Kapstein, *Insecure Alliance*, 112.
19. Macmillan quoted in Brian Lapping, *End of Empire* (New York: St. Martin's Press, 1985), 266.
20. See William Stivers, "Eisenhower and the Middle East," in *Reevaluating Eisenhower: American Foreign Policy in the 1950s*, ed. Richard A. Melanson and David Mayers (Urbana: University of Illinois Press, 1987), 192-219.
21. See Hahn, *Strategy and Diplomacy*, 238.
22. See William B. Quandt, "U.S.-Soviet Rivalry in the Middle East," in *East-West Tensions in the Third World*, ed. Marshall D. Shulman and William H. Sullivan (New York: W. W. Norton, 1986), 32.

23. The connection between Suez and Dien Bien Phu is made in Scott L. Bills, "The United States, NATO, and the Third World: Dominoes, Imbroglios, and Agonizing Reappraisals," in *NATO after Forty Years*, ed. Lawrence S. Kaplan et al. (Wilmington: Scholarly Resources Inc., 1990), 160.
24. See, for example, William B. Quandt, *Decade of Decisions: American Policy toward the Arab-Israeli Conflict, 1967-1976* (Berkeley: University of California Press, 1977), 65-68, 105-27; and Steven L. Spiegel, *The Other Arab-Israeli Conflict: Making America's Middle East Policy, from Truman to Reagan* (Chicago: University of Chicago Press, 1985), 158-65.
25. For an Arab perspective on this period see Mohamed Heikal, *The Road to Ramadan* (New York: Quadrangle, 1975).
26. For Arab thinking regarding the embargo see George Lenczowski, "The Oil-Producing Countries," in *The Oil Crisis*, ed. Raymond Vernon (New York: W. W. Norton, 1976), 59-72.
27. Figures from Yergin, *The Prize*, 625.
28. Royal Dutch/Shell executive Geoffrey Chandler quoted in Robert J. Lieber, *Oil and the Middle East War: Europe in the Energy Crisis* (Cambridge: Center for International Affairs, Harvard University, 1976), 16. For more on company efforts to handle the oil crisis see Yergin, *The Prize*, 619-22; and Robert B. Stobaugh, "The Oil Companies in the Crisis," in Vernon, ed., *The Oil Crisis*, 179-202.
29. See Yergin, *The Prize*, 623-24; and Frank R. Wyant, *The United States, OPEC, and Multinational Oil* (Lexington: D. C. Heath, 1977), 131-32.
30. For the European response to the Arab oil embargo see, for example, Kapstein, *Insecure Alliance*, 166-68; Yergin, *The Prize*, 626-29; and Wolfgang Hager, "Western Europe: The Politics of Muddling Through," and Hans Maull, "The Strategy of Avoidance: Europe's Middle East Policies after the October War," in *Oil, the Arab-Israel Dispute, and the Industrial World: Horizons of Crisis*, ed. J. C. Hurewitz (Boulder: Westview Press, 1976), 34-51, 110-37.
31. Pompidou and Heath quoted in Yergin, *The Prize*, 627-28.
32. On U.S. diplomatic efforts to end the Yom Kippur War see Alan Dowty, *Middle East Crisis: U.S. Decision-Making in 1958, 1970, and 1973* (Berkeley: University of California Press, 1984), 199-277.
33. See Kapstein, *Insecure Alliance*, 165; and Lieber, *Oil and the Middle East War*, 12.
34. Walter Laqueur, *Confrontation: The Middle East and World Politics* (New York: Quadrangle, 1974), 207.
35. See Yergin, *The Prize*, 629; and Lieber, *Oil and the Middle East War*, 20.
36. Henry Kissinger, *Years of Upheaval* (Boston: Little, Brown, 1982), 905.
37. See Kapstein, *Insecure Alliance*, 171-75; and Yergin, *The Prize*, 629-30.
38. See Kissinger, *Years of Upheaval*, 916.
39. For the International Energy Agency see Kapstein, *Insecure Alliance*, chap. 8; and Wilfrid L. Kohl, "The International Energy Agency: The Political Context," in Hurewitz, ed., *Oil, the Arab-Israeli Dispute, and the Industrial World*, 246-57.
40. For this development see Zuhayr Mikdashi, "The OPEC Process," in Vernon, ed., *The Oil Crisis*, 211.

41. See Spiegel, *Other Arab-Israeli Conflict*, chaps. 7 and 8.
42. For the Palestinian question see Janice Gross Stein, "Alice in Wonderland: The North Atlantic Alliance and the Arab-Israeli Dispute," in *The Middle East and the Western Alliance*, ed. Steven L. Spiegel (London: George Allen & Unwin, 1982), 60-72; for the European position see Raymond Cohen, "Twice Bitten? The European Community's 1987 Middle East Initiative," *Middle East Review* 20 (Spring 1988): 33-40.
43. For Iran see, for example, James A. Bill, *The Eagle and the Lion: The Tragedy of American-Iranian Relations* (New Haven: Yale University Press, 1988), 216-60.
44. For concerns about Afghanistan see Gianni Bonvicini, "Out-of-Area Issues: A New Challenge to the Atlantic Alliance," in *The Atlantic Alliance and the Middle East*, ed. Joseph I. Coffey and Gianni Bonvicini (Pittsburgh: University of Pittsburgh Press, 1989), 2; and Dominique Moisi, "Europe and the Middle East," in Spiegel, ed., *The Middle East and the Western Alliance*, 31.
45. See, for example, The Atlantic Council of the United States, Working Group on Security Affairs, *After Afghanistan—The Long Haul: Safeguarding Security and Independence in the Third World* (Boulder: Westview Press, 1980); and Lawrence S. Kaplan, "The United States, NATO, and the Third World: Security Issues in Historical Perspective," in *East-West Rivalry in the Third World: Security Issues and Regional Perspectives*, ed. Robert W. Clawson (Wilmington: Scholarly Resources Inc., 1986), 3.
46. See Lincoln P. Bloomfield, "Crisis Management outside the NATO Area: Allies or Competitors?" and S. I. P. van Campen, "NATO Political Consultation and European Political Cooperation," in *Allies in a Turbulent World: Challenges to U.S. and Western European Cooperation*, ed. Frans A.M. Alting von Geusau (Lexington: D. C. Heath, 1982), 53, 70-71.
47. See Jed C. Snyder, *Defending the Fringe: NATO, the Mediterranean, and the Persian Gulf* (Boulder: Westview Press, 1987), 116-19.
48. See Thomas H. Etzold, "The Soviet Union in the Mediterranean," in *NATO and the Mediterranean*, ed. Lawrence S. Kaplan, Robert W. Clawson, and Raimondo Luraghi (Wilmington: Scholarly Resources Inc., 1985), 44-45.
49. See Maya Chedda, *Paradox of Power: The United States in Southwest Asia, 1973-1984* (Santa Barbara: ABC-Clio, 1986), 153-73.
50. See Maurizio Cremasco, "Do-it-Yourself: National Approaches to the Out-of-Area Question," in Coffey and Bonvicini, eds., *The Atlantic Alliance and the Middle East*, 180-85; and Snyder, *Defending the Fringe*, 113-16.
51. For French policy see Cremasco, "Do-it-Yourself," 159.
52. See Michael A. Palmer, *Guardians of the Gulf: A History of America's Expanding Role in the Persian Gulf, 1833-1992* (New York: Free Press, 1992), 108-9, 118-27.
53. See ibid., 150-62; and H. W. Brands, *Into the Labyrinth: The United States and the Middle East, 1945-1993* (New York: McGraw-Hill, 1994), 192-96.
54. See Phebe Marr, "The Persian Gulf after the Storm," in *Riding the Tiger: The Middle East Challenge after the Cold War*, ed. Phebe Marr and William Lewis (Boulder: Westview Press, 1993), 109-35.

55. See William Quandt, "The Arab-Israeli Conflict in the 1990s: Prospects for a Settlement," in ibid., 91-107.

56. See Cremasco, "Do-it-Yourself," 166-69; and Graham E. Fuller, *Turkey Faces East: New Orientations toward the Middle East and the Old Soviet Union* (Santa Monica: RAND, 1992). For an earlier view of Turkey's importance see Bruce R. Kuniholm, "Turkey and NATO," in Kaplan, Clawson, and Luraghi, eds., *NATO and the Mediterranean*, 215-37.

13

NATO
and Scandinavia

Eric S. Einhorn

The evolving relationship between the North Atlantic Treaty Organization (NATO) and its three Scandinavian member-states and two nonmember Nordic countries, Sweden and Finland, has amply demonstrated the quip by Danish sage Robert Storm Petersen that "nothing is harder to predict than the future." While the European and North American security policy galaxy gives birth to new or reinvigorates older entities—the Conference on Security and Cooperation in Europe (CSCE), the North Atlantic Cooperation Council (NACC), the Partnership for Peace (PFP), the Western European Union (WEU), and the European Union (EU)—it is not readily clear what membership in such organizations means. As recently as 1988, NATO remained a contentious issue in Denmark and Iceland, and more discreetly so in Norway. Swedish and Finnish membership in the alliance would have been unthinkable. The pattern of Scandinavian security policies seemed set, and the debates remained surprisingly spirited despite their numbing repetitiousness. New issues had certainly arisen during the 1980s: NATO Intermediate Nuclear Forces, pre-positioning of military stocks in Denmark and Norway, and the restrictions on nuclear weapons on NATO ships. And there were numerous encores of earlier themes: the role of the Keflavik air base, the ability of Sweden to provide for its own security, and Finland's mystical obligations to the Soviet Union under the latest versions of the Treaty on Friendship, Cooperation, and Mutual Assistance (FCMA).

Most of these issues are now history, and useful Scandinavian diplomatic studies are clarifying the subtleties of these earlier debates.[1] Hence this investigation will draw only selectively from the past, focusing on those issues that continue to strongly influence security policy and NATO in northern Europe. Our concern here is with continuity and change. What remains of the classical Scandinavian security *problematique*? What are the options facing the Nordic countries? What tendencies are reflected in the security policy decisions of the past couple of years?

It is useful to recall the distinction between Scandinavia—more strictly, Denmark, Norway, and Sweden—and the Nordic region, which includes the three kingdoms plus Iceland and Finland. The term *Scandinavia* will be used informally. A viable but overlapping "Baltic region" encompassing the restored states of Estonia, Latvia, and Lithuania along with Russia, Poland, and reunified Germany has reemerged. There are also ambiguities over the security policy role of the European Union, to which Finland, Sweden, and Norway are pending members, and the Western European Union, to which several Scandinavian states send observers. Such geopolitical confusion is regrettable but rather normal in the historical context of northern Europe's international relations.

At no time have the five Nordic states embraced a common foreign policy. Since World War I they have communicated closely on foreign policy matters, and more recently the Nordic Council has added foreign and security policy issues to its agenda.[2] An important principle in the Nordic region has been that each country's foreign and security policy has an impact on the others. As Arne O. Brundtland has concluded, the Nordic view "asserts that it is an advantage for each Nordic country that each Nordic country be successful in its foreign policy."[3]

Historically, the Nordic countries have shared some common geopolitical perspectives. Three regions have been the focus of their foreign and security policies: the Nordic/Baltic region, Western Europe, and Eastern Europe, primarily Russia. The two world wars added an Atlantic dimension as a fourth region, when the United States supplemented Britain as the restorer of the European balance so critical for the survival of small states. Finally, the postwar period, especially the decolonization of Asia and Africa, reinforced a nascent global perspective that first appeared in modern form with the participation of the Nordic countries in the League of Nations and later in the United Nations.

Since the attempt to create a nonaligned Scandinavian Defense Union failed in 1948-49, attempts at common Nordic security policies have resulted in an amalgam of diplomatic consultation, political rhetoric, and occasional outside interference. The 1948-49 negotiations were the most ambitious effort to create a common Scandinavian (Finland and Iceland did not participate) foreign and security policy. They failed, however, basically because Norway sought closer ties with an emerging Western defense alliance. The perceived military weakness of the three Scandinavian countries after World War II lay behind Oslo's shift. One diplomat characterized Scandinavia's collective defense potential with a devastating mathematical formula: "0+0+0=0." A firm and credible guarantee of assistance from outside was critical for Norway and, more ambiguously, also for Denmark. Sweden wanted Scandinavian security policy to aim at repeating its World War II feat: to remain outside of another European war.

Without any concrete commitments, the ideal of Nordic balance emerged in the 1960s as the desired pattern of Cold War security policy.[4] This theory focused on Denmark, Norway, and Sweden and implied that these countries would maintain a status quo in their security policy so long as no outside power sought to introduce radical changes in the region. This stance coincided with their common strategic assumption that the Nordic region would not be a main theater of East-West confrontation and that the major powers would calculate that upsetting the "Nordic balance" would be contrary to their interests as well. The rarely uttered position presumed that the Soviet Union would neither make unreasonable demands on Finland nor seek additional concessions from the other Nordic countries. Denmark and Norway, for their part, would maintain conditions on their NATO membership, such as permanent foreign bases or nuclear weapons on their territories during peacetime. The Soviet Union, in turn, would not be inclined to reconsider the region's security policy.[5]

The end of the Cold War changed many of the fundamentals of Nordic security policy without changing long-term perspectives. In brief, ever since the end of Sweden's Great Power ambitions in the early eighteenth century, the Baltic/Nordic region has been a secondary region for European security concerns. Larger European conflicts, such as the Napoleonic Wars and World War II, have often spilled into the North, but during World War I the region managed to maintain neutrality as the operational priorities of the belligerents spared the Baltic and Scandinavian areas (except for defensive demands such as the mining of the Danish Straits by Denmark at Germany's behest but without British objection). The most recent period of "tension" in the region occurred during the 1980s, when NATO and especially the United States sought to confront the Soviet Union in the North (U.S. Forward

Maritime Strategy implied preemptive naval and air operations against the Kola Peninsula) and the Soviet naval buildup threatened to alter the strategic importance of the region.[6]

The events of 1989-1991 that "ended" the Cold War have had commonly shared as well as specific consequences for the Nordic countries. First, the withdrawal of all Soviet/Russian forces from the southern shore of the Baltic (East Germany and Poland) and nearly all from the Baltic states has removed the threat of sudden military attack. Russian forces remain in the Kaliningrad region and St. Petersburg, but the general Russian withdrawal is still the most significant change in the military balance since 1945.

Second, the reunification of Germany, but with a reduced German military establishment, reinforces the largest economic power in Europe without augmenting significantly its military potential. Indeed, the economic and political distractions of reunification, the reduction of German military forces (as a result of the "two-plus-four" agreements of 1990), and the general reluctance of Germans to ease their constitutional and political restraints on external military action have eased the traditional military security concerns of Central Europe to their lowest level since the mid-1920s. Additionally, reunified Germany is leading efforts to reinforce European security.[7]

A third change is the acceleration of European integration under the Maastricht Treaty. The addition of foreign and security policy issues into the European formula has already produced new challenges to Scandinavia with the revitalized WEU, the imminent expansion of the EU by up to four new members (including Norway, Sweden, and Finland), and the extension of NATO's political role, first through the NACC and then with the PFP program. At the very least, these changes will force a reevaluation of foreign and security policies in both the NATO and non-NATO Nordic countries.

Fourth, the Nordic region must accommodate structural changes occurring within NATO (for example, the closing of Allied Forces North headquarters, AFNORTH, near Oslo), the reconfiguration of military structures within major and minor NATO states, and the challenges of demanding participation in distant peacekeeping operations under the United Nations.

The remainder of this study will summarize the responses of the individual Nordic countries to the post–Cold War security situation in Europe by focusing on the role of NATO in their security planning. Although the concern here is with what their relations with NATO and other European security organizations will be now, current patterns continue to reflect earlier perspectives.

DENMARK

Denmark chose NATO as a "second best" solution to its security needs in 1949, and this ambivalence has remained. Although public supporters of NATO membership have always outnumbered the opponents, Denmark's commitments to NATO have been a frequent topic for vigorous domestic debate. No one familiar with this reluctant ally can be surprised that as recently as May 1988 the Social Democrats, then the main opposition party, instigated a challenge to the Danish NATO policies of a Conservative-led coalition, thereby providing the main theme of a sudden parliamentary election. Although Denmark had joined NATO under a Social Democratic government in 1949, the Social Democrats on twenty-three occasions during the 1980s attached conditions to Denmark's NATO commitments in the form of "footnotes" to NATO declarations. When a frustrated U.S. ambassador inquired of the government why it did not make such parliamentary opposition a question of confidence, he was astounded to learn that the government did not consider NATO and national security policy that important. In April 1988 the center-right government did draw the line and made gains in the ensuing election.[8]

As in most countries, Denmark's national security policy discussions occur on two planes. At the technical/administrative level, Denmark makes the best of its limited resources. Until the end of the Cold War, Danish defense units were rated thin in quantity but high in quality. With its position commanding the straits connecting the Baltic and North seas, Denmark's main value to NATO was geographic. For centuries, Denmark's location provided it with military and economic advantages, but during this century it made the Danes vulnerable to the security needs of Germany, Russia, and the Atlantic powers. Moreover, Greenland, now a self-governing autonomous country for which Denmark makes defense and foreign policy (and to which Danes provide enormous economic subsidies), has since 1940 been of vital strategic interest to North America. Greenland, the Faeroe Islands, and even Denmark proper also offered important warning and intelligence posts. Danes performed these security functions competently, as did the Americans in Greenland. Danish officers contributed their usual professional competence to the Baltic approaches command in Kiel, Germany, at AFNORTH headquarters in Oslo, and, less visibly, at NATO headquarters in Belgium.

Politically, Denmark could not reconcile the post-1945 consensus that neutrality, backed by minimal military forces, had been politically and morally unacceptable with the historical consensus (at least since 1864) that

Denmark could not realistically be defended against a determined invader. Added to this situation was the historical tradition, also dating back to the nineteenth century, of using defense and security issues for narrow partisan advantage. Denmark followed Norway in refusing to allow permanent NATO and foreign forces to use bases on Danish soil. The Danes also rejected the placing of nuclear weapons in Denmark except in wartime or when foreign attack appeared imminent.[9] This latter principle, which the opposition wanted to apply to NATO naval craft operating in Danish waters, precipitated the "NATO election" of May 1988.

The end of the Cold War in 1989-90 came at a most convenient time for all sides. The Social Democrats had painted themselves into a corner by a series of political miscalculations, including an overplaying of the "footnote" policy. The government sought to raise Denmark's profile in the emerging European security regime based on the CSCE, the North Atlantic Cooperation Council (NACC), and an expanding European Community (EC). By late 1990 Denmark's new NATO activism based itself on a policy that NATO should be the principal source of European defense, especially against peripheral conflicts (for example, in the Balkans) that could threaten European peace and democracy.[10]

Added to these shifts, the government assigned a Danish frigate to the international coalition responding to the Iraqi invasion of Kuwait in 1990. Although Danish armed forces had participated in nearly all major UN peacekeeping missions since 1949, the dispatching of a warship to a distant conflict was unprecedented. Additionally, more than 1,000 Danish land forces backed by heavy armor joined other international units in the former Yugoslavia in 1992. Denmark also announced the same year that it would form by the end of 1995 a 4,550-strong rapid reaction brigade for NATO's Rapid Reaction Corps.[11]

The periodic multiparty defense agreements that determine the organizational and financial commitment to defense for a number of years provide a clear indicator of Danish security policy. The current accord, reached in April 1991, just as the post–Cold War era was taking shape, received the support of all of the main political parties except the Socialist People's party on the left and the Progress party on the right. It called for significant reductions in personnel, heavy equipment, and funding. Although the size of the Danish armed forces had remained steady for nearly a decade, plans called for reductions starting in 1992 and reaching more than four thousand by 1997 (that is, from twenty-nine to twenty-five thousand). The government also suspended the acquisition of additional heavy tanks and naval patrol craft. Despite the emphasis on budgetary considerations, some Danish military and civilian defense observers asked during the fall 1991 NATO Action Express exercise: "Whom were they to be defending against?"[12]

The Western European Union's revival in the 1990s again placed Denmark at odds with other European states. Never a party to the WEU, Denmark held "observer" status at an organization that did nothing. For more than forty years the issue had not come up. In 1988 Spain and Portugal joined the WEU, and Iceland and Norway followed by seeking to upgrade their WEU status from observer to "associate." Denmark remained skeptical because it did not want to integrate its defense into an untried organization. Nor did the Danes want to weaken the commitment of the United States to the maintenance of Western European security. Although current and future threats remained unclear, for the moment, the United States remained a superpower and unburdened by tragedies of European history, unlike Denmark's large neighbor to the south.

Denmark signed the Maastricht Treaty forming the European Union in December 1991, but the agreement proved enormously controversial, in part because of the vague references to a common EU foreign and security policy. After voters rejected the treaty in a required referendum in June 1992, Denmark secured significant concessions at the European Community's Edinburgh summit in December. A second referendum in May 1993 approved the revised union treaty following a "national compromise" by the parties the preceding fall. But with Maastricht largely approved, the domestic consensus began to unravel. Former foreign minister and Liberal party leader Uffe Ellemann-Jensen, possibly the most enthusiastic "European" in Danish politics, called for a reappraisal of the Edinburgh reservations and for aloofness toward WEU. He noted that events had transpired to weaken Denmark's concerns that WEU would become an alternative to NATO. The United States was increasingly accepting WEU as the European "pillar" in NATO. Much of the opposition, for its part, sought to "contain" Denmark's European integration and even found NATO the least undesirable option.[13]

Now it is Europe that has become the symbolic topic of Danish foreign and security debates. European Parliament elections in June 1994 confirmed Denmark's minimalist views on European integration. The principal "Euro-enthusiast" in Danish politics is Uffe Ellemann-Jensen, who advocates another referendum on Denmark's commitment to the European Union, in this case emphasizing the WEU issue. His party gained only marginally in the June elections, but he will have another chance in the September 1994 national elections. In line with the other mainstream parties, that campaign has moved away from European issues.

Basically, Denmark is trying in traditional small-state fashion to keep as many security policy options open as possible. NATO is tried and trusted; indeed, public support for NATO has never been higher.[14] The renewal of the U.S. commitment to NATO pleased Denmark, even as America accommodated the WEU and proceeded with its own force reductions. Danish commitments in the former Yugoslavia's conflict, technically a UN operation but with NATO infrastructure and support playing a growing role, augur strongly against an isolationist policy. Remarkably, the former leader of the pacifist Socialist People's party, Gert Petersen, who has opposed NATO during more than three decades of parliamentary service, proclaimed at the party's annual convention in May 1994 that there would be chaos in Europe if NATO disappeared without a credible replacement.[15]

NORWAY

Norway has historically been the most committed Scandinavian member of NATO. The trauma of World War II brought about fundamental and enduring changes in the national defense consensus. It was Norway's insistence on formal ties to a Western/Atlantic defense arrangement that scuttled Scandinavian Defense Union talks in 1949.[16] Nevertheless, from the outset Norway conducted its NATO affairs so as to avoid unnecessary provocation of the Soviet Union. In 1949, Norway declared that it would not allow permanent foreign bases on its territory except in time of war or if threatened by imminent attack. Although Norway did integrate much of its warning and operational capabilities into the NATO system in the 1950s and 1960s, it kept permanent operational NATO facilities off its territory.[17]

Norway is notable among the Nordic countries in that it alone maintained and increased its defense expenditures during the post-détente era of 1977-1990. Norwegian national security concerns resulted from the perception that, although the political rhetoric of the Soviet Union was more restrained after 1970, Moscow still pursued a steady and significant military buildup in areas of greatest sensitivity to Norway: the Kola peninsula and the Arctic regions and seas. Many of these concerns linger now, despite the radical changes in Russia's political and foreign policy character.

Norway's relationship to NATO is increasingly complicated by the country's evolving relationship with the European Union. Skeptical about the advantages of full membership in the European Union, Norwegians have often stressed the primacy of NATO as the focus of the country's foreign and security policy in Europe.[18] Foreign and security issues had not played a significant role in the debate preceding the referendum defeat of Norway's first application for European Community membership in 1972.[19] But in the renewed discussion it is evident that the European Union's foreign and security policy ambitions, as articulated in the 1991 Maastricht Treaty on European Union, have not been a popular selling point in Norway.

Additionally, Norway's strategic situation is one of the least changed of the European NATO states. While the populous south has clearly benefited from changes in the Baltic, the north still shares a border with the most militarized region of Russia. Norway clearly faces a different situation with Russia than it had with the Soviet Union. The Kola and Barents Sea region is now home to larger, if considerably weakened, Russian forces that have been withdrawn from Central Europe and other former Soviet bases. Even the naval forces have been augmented by elements of the Black Sea fleet, including a large aircraft carrier. The military effectiveness of these units is generally admitted to be a shadow of the old Soviet establishment, but it is still substantial, especially since Norway deliberately avoids significant military installations in its northernmost regions (Nordland, Troms, and Finnmark counties). The growing military and civilian environmental risks, stemming from neglected mineral refining installations, wrecked nuclear-powered submarines, and carelessly dumped nuclear wastes, have exacerbated regional uncertainties. Social consequences of the collapsing Russian economy on the substantial civilian population of the Kola region are also a Norwegian security concern. All of these issues share one common problem: they are unprecedented in the NATO debate and radically different from the threats against which NATO planned during the Cold War.

Norway's security debate has thus entered uncharted waters and is muddled by the EU debate. Will European security move increasingly onto the European Union agenda? Will the U.S. commitment stabilize at a level that has meaning for peripheral regions such as Norway? How will peacekeeping actions in areas like the Balkans affect Norway's relationship with NATO?

The minority Labor government of Gro Harlem Brundtland presented its plans prior to the 1993 elections in a traditional four-year defense planning document or Report to Parliament in January 1993.[20] The Conservatives, the main opposition party, attacked the proposed cuts as a return to pre-1940 Labor party pacifism, known disparagingly as "the policy of the broken rifles." Conservative defense policy spokesman Ingvald Godal called it the "kiss of death for Norwegian defense," in part because it called for a reduction of defense personnel by thirty-two hundred over five years and about the same number for the following five years. Equipment budgets were also to be severely cut. The implementation of these plans has started trimming Norwegian forces. In 1993, active armed forces fell just under thirty thousand personnel, a decline of more than seven thousand (more than 20 percent) from the 1985 level.[21]

Then Defense Minister Johann Joergen Holst defended the proposals as less drastic than those of Norway's neighbors: Sweden, Finland, and even Russia. Former Conservative Prime Minister Kaare Willoch, who has headed the multiparty parliamentary defense commissions, warned that political pressures to preserve jobs would squeeze matériel modernization.[22] Later, the chair of the parliament's Foreign Affairs Committee, Laborite Haakon Blankenborg, noted that the United States was reducing its commitments to Europe and implied that the European Union was emerging as the focus of security as well as economic policy concerns. Defense Minister Joergen Kosmo confirmed that in his opinion NATO's role as a consultative and planning organization seemed to be weakening and that NATO was increasingly ratifying decisions made elsewhere. His Conservative counterpart noted that one such alternative forum was the Western European Union (WEU), which was open only to countries belonging to both NATO and the EU.[23]

By 1994, Norwegian security and NATO policies became enmeshed in the larger debate about membership in the European Union. Non-Socialist opponents of the EU, primarily in the Center party, emphasized the formal distinction between NATO and the EU. Norway, they noted, remained a solid NATO member; membership in the CSCE further reinforced its influence in European security issues. EU opponents on the left-wing of Norwegian politics could rarely bring themselves to use NATO as an excuse for rejecting EU membership. They often recycled arguments that had been employed against NATO for more than forty years. Now it was the EU that would deprive Norway of its political and economic sovereignty and bind it to a German-dominated exclusively Western European bloc. Lost would be historic ties to the other Nordic countries, solidarity with emerging countries in Eastern Europe (for whom ties with the EU cannot come fast enough), and that classic invisible constituency for a radically different Norwegian foreign policy, the less developed countries.[24]

The pro-EU camp sees future security policy as less compartmentalized. The new, less explicitly military, components of national security in the 1990s (for example, environmental and social) are not part of the NATO bailiwick. While the United States is likely to remain a guarantor of NATO's military security, as a non-European state it is not likely to become deeply engaged in confronting these low-level threats. It is natural, the pro-EU camp argues, that Norwegians become part of an emerging European political community based not on the traditional relations between sovereign states but on over-lapping integrative elements. Full membership in the European Union is therefore essential for access to these discussions and decisions.[25]

SWEDEN

Sweden has long followed a policy of pragmatic and opportunistic neutral-ity. Whereas the Swiss maintain a discreet neutrality, the Swedes have proudly flown their nonaligned banner as they pursue an active and often quite demonstrative foreign policy. No one can name a significant Swiss diplomat, while Folke Bernadotte, Dag Hammarskjöld, and Olof Palme were well-known world statesmen in their day.

How then can one include nonaligned Sweden in a discussion of NATO's future? Sweden chose to continue its historic policy of nonalignment in peace as a precondition to neutrality in war following the collapse of the Scandinavian Defense Union negotiations in 1949.[26] Periodically for the next forty years Swedish politicians and diplomats would interpret nonalign-ment as more flexible than neutrality during war. While at times the discus-sions approached an almost theological level, the principles were less abstract. Swedish nonalignment (*alliansfrihet*, literally translated as "alliance-freedom") was an independent policy chosen and adjusted by Swedish gov-ernments as the best means of protecting the country's security and interests. This approach made Sweden's position fully compatible with active mem-bership in the United Nations, membership in other intergovernmental international organizations (for example, the Organization for Economic Cooperation and Development and the European Free Trade Association in the 1960s), and, at times, a demonstrative foreign policy (for example, against U.S. policy in Vietnam after 1965 and Central America after 1981).[27]

Stockholm demonstrated sensitivity but prudence concerning the "Nordic balance." As Finland's special relationship with the Soviet Union developed positively after 1955, when Soviet forces were withdrawn from the Porkkala base near Helsinki, Sweden's active discussion of such a regional balance became less overt. Relations with the developing NATO military structure were generally treated with discretion.[28] Recently declassified doc-uments indicate that after 1951 in case of a European war, Swedish defenses would allow NATO aircraft to operate over Swedish airspace and that help was expected from the West.[29] Indeed, as the current Conservative Swedish Foreign Minister Margaretha af Ugglas recently wrote, Swedish nonalignment depended on a cohesive and strong NATO.[30] Ironically, U.S. documents from the same period show relatively little interest in NATO for active assistance to Sweden. It is, of course, difficult to know what an isolated attack on Sweden would have meant in a European context. No one could have considered that a likely contingency.[31]

Sweden's foreign policy profile sharpened notably under the influence of Olof Palme's power (starting from 1969 to 1976 and again from 1982 until his assassination in 1986). Palme rejected Western European integration and advocated a so-called Social Democratic Third Way. Critics claim that during its heyday, Palme's policy, although perhaps not by design, was nonetheless congruent with many Soviet aims for Europe with its backing of nuclear-free zones, no U.S. nuclear missiles in Europe, and "no first use" policy for nuclear weapons.[32]

Palme's successor, Ingvar Carlsson, focused again on Swedish domestic politics, but until early 1990 he maintained the Swedish position, first proclaimed by Tage Erlander in 1961, that membership in the European Community would not be compatible with nonalignment. In short order, however, Carlsson guided a dramatic shift by proposing Swedish membership in the EC (neutral Austria had already applied and Finland was about to make a similar decision). The application stated Sweden's insistence that its traditional nonalignment continue to be respected. At the time the EC was only vaguely committed to European Political Cooperation, which oversaw regular discussions of foreign policy matters affecting the EC. This arrangement, it was conjectured, would not place much stress on Sweden's pragmatic nonalignment.

After the September 1991 elections, a non-Socialist coalition came to power, led by Conservative Carl Bildt, already well known for his outspoken positions directed against the fading "Palme line." The new government continued Sweden's approaches to the EC and sought to accommodate the Social Democrats, who had, after all, actually made the great reversal. Following the signing of the Maastricht Treaty, Bildt found no problems with the strengthening of a common European foreign and security policy. The treaty does not contain specific defense commitments and thus does not force Sweden (or the other nonaligned Western European countries) to abandon their strictly defined security policies. Nevertheless, the Swedish parliament's latest statement on neutrality qualifies the conditions of neutrality by stressing that nonalignment could keep Sweden out of a European war. Neutrality would not be automatic; the current government has even talked openly of commitments to the Baltic states in the wake of Russia's emerging neonationalism in 1994.[33]

More challenging will be Sweden's relationship with the Western European Union as that arrangement develops into the core of the European Union's collective defense system and continues its close ties to the NATO system. Bildt believes that the entry of Finland, Norway, and Sweden into the EU will give its Common Foreign and Security Policy a better northern European perspective. Security in the Baltic area will receive a higher priority. Rigid blocs and alliances are no longer on the agenda, but rather Sweden will participate in several organizational arenas: the EU, the CSCE, the Conventional Forces in Europe mechanism, and the United Nations.[34] Over time, the current center-right government wants Sweden to participate actively in shaping the EU's next stage of security policy cooperation, scheduled to begin in 1996.[35]

Although joining the European Union will now require support from the Swedish electorate in a referendum scheduled for late 1994 (a similar process will be followed in Norway and Finland), the political leadership in both the government parties and the Social Democratic opposition is supportive. Pierre Schori, the main opposition spokesman on foreign policy, emphasizes the scope of the common challenges facing Europe and notes that the final EU negotiations for the four applicants specifically recognized their different security policies and his belief that the military dimension will be less important in the EU's Common Foreign and Security Policy.[36]

If they return to power following the September 1994 parliamentary elections, the Social Democrats will be more restrained in pursing security policy in a European context. Membership in the EU will be decided in a referendum a month later. Sweden has declared its intention to become an associate member of the Western European Union as part of EU entry. Swedish forces are deployed in the Balkans as part of a sizeable European contingent that, although nominally under UN auspices, depends on NATO support. Currently, Swedish and Danish military units are conducting joint training exercises in preparation for service in Bosnia.[37]

Sweden is unlikely to join NATO, but it has been increasingly interested in the PFP proposals, which would include the non-NATO, Western European democracies (Austria, Finland, and Sweden) as well as the new democracies of Eastern Europe. Sweden has accepted the invitation to join the PFP, which will probably be a more active commitment to collective security than the CSCE but will not be a formal obligation according to the terms of the North Atlantic Treaty. Indeed, the Western states (NATO and non-NATO) see the PFP mainly as a diplomatic and confidence-building measure, while the Eastern European states worry whether it is a significant guarantee of their security.[38]

FINLAND

Finland's relations with the Soviet Union during the Cold War were a weather vane for northern Europe. The concept of "Nordic balance" was rooted in concern for Finland's situation. For more than forty years the decisive factor in Finnish security policy was the Treaty of Friendship, Cooperation and Mutual Assistance (FCMA), first signed with the Soviet Union in February 1948 and periodically renewed. Building on the restrictions demanded of Finland in the Paris Peace Treaty of 1947, FCMA gave the Soviet Union nebulous but nonetheless real influence over Finnish foreign and security policy (the so-called *droit de regard*). At times this leverage stretched into domestic politics as well. Although the Western powers feared the worst when Stalin demanded the treaty, Finns often expressed surprise that the West did not trust Helsinki's ability to manage its own affairs. Finland moved steadily out of the shade of its Soviet neighbor, starting with the Soviet evacuation of the Porkkala base in 1955-56. Ironically, by the 1980s some Western hard-liners saw Finnish neutrality as too close to the Soviet line. Four criticisms leveled against Finland included (1) an anti-Western bias in foreign policy statements, (2) self-censorship of any criticism of Soviet foreign policy (for example, Afghanistan), (3) use of the special relationship with Soviet leaders to strengthen the domestic political influence of the president (especially in the case of long-serving Urho Kekkonen), and (4) economic dependence on the Soviet Union for more than 20 percent of its exports—a very profitable relationship for Finland until the collapse of the Soviet economy.[39]

The survival of an independent, democratic, and eventually very prosperous Finland bordering on the Soviet Union is a remarkable foreign and security policy achievement. Mikhail Gorbachev's perestroika, followed by the dissolution of the Soviet Union, released Finland from the terms of the FCMA treaty, but geography and history still counsel caution toward its big Russian neighbor. Finland's security problems are more akin to those of the former Soviet bloc states in Eastern Europe than those of the other Nordic states. Although Finland has long been closely tied to the Western economic system, Soviet and Eastern European trade was significant. Following the collapse of the Eastern economies, Finland experienced a severe three-year economic recession; hence, its interest in closer economic ties with the European Union reflects a desire to recover lost ground.

Second, Finland is acutely sensitive not only to political developments in Russia but also in the Baltic states and to eastern Baltic diplomatic relations in general. Nothing could contribute more to long-term Finnish security and economic prosperity than the survival of political democracy and an economic recovery in the region. These are areas in which the European Union can assist. NATO is seen as part of an evolving security system for Europe that includes the CSCE, which emerged out of the Helsinki Accords of 1975.

Despite its past orientations, Finland is an applicant to the European Union and accepts the general foreign and security policy principles in the Maastricht Treaty. In Finland, too, a national referendum in September 1994 will decide EU membership. Finnish public opinion has appeared to be the most positively disposed of the three Nordic applicants. Political concerns surpassed economic factors following the political unrest in Russia in late 1993. Doubtlessly extremist Vladimir Zhirinovski's references to Finland as part of a future Russian empire have caught the attention of the Finns.

The new pattern of Finnish foreign and security policy has become clearer since 1992. Overtures by Swedish neutralists for a new neutral Nordic bloc were dismissed. U.S. Defense Secretary Richard Cheney visited Finland in June 1992 following Finland's choice of the American F/A-18 fighter over the developing Swedish JAS aircraft. Disappointed Swedes claimed the decision was part of a Finnish approach to NATO, while the Finns and many more objective observers stated that they had simply chosen the better plane.[40]

Finland joined the North Atlantic Cooperation Council (NACC) in June 1992, before any of the other European neutrals, and has kept an open attitude toward the Maastricht's foreign and security policy requirements. Erkki Tuomioja, a leading Finnish Social Democratic (opposition) parliamentarian, commented that this aspect of the EU would first be negotiated after 1996 and that longtime member-states, such as Britain and France, would have interests to protect. Moreover, the Finns felt that keeping U.S. and Canadian ties to European security would be desirable. Tuomioja saw Finland's security situation as rather different than that of the former Warsaw Pact states, which are seeking to pull NATO's shield eastward. Finland, he implied, had not needed NATO in the past and would not require protection in the foreseeable future. Finland would promote disarmament and low tensions in the Baltic region.[41]

Nevertheless, pending EU membership and concerns about political stability in Russia following the unsettling events of late 1993 influenced Helsinki's official position on the Partnership for Peace program. In December 1993, Finnish Foreign Minister Heikki Haavisto explained that Finland would find a closer association with NATO consistent with maintaining its nonalignment. The Foreign Policy Committee of Parliament approved the PFP in April 1994.[42]

Helsinki is hedging its bets. For Finland, the EU is attractive on immediate economic terms, but its security and foreign policy development is less clear. Finland is not a candidate for membership in NATO or the WEU, but it does have a stake in the development of a European security system that incorporates Russia on acceptable terms. Finland will maintain its credible but limited defense potential while continuing to rely upon diplomacy, often in conjunction with the other Nordic states, to promote political stability and economic recovery in the eastern Baltic. Russia poses a problem for Finnish security somewhat differently than the former Soviet Union did. But habits linger. Just prior to Finland's first post–Cold War presidential election in early 1994, the Russian Embassy in Helsinki presented a note protesting two radical right Finnish groups, the IKL and Greater Finland, that echoed extremist groups of the 1930s. Russian Ambassador Yuri Deriabin, an experienced specialist on Finnish affairs, referred to the 1947 Peace Treaty prohibiting fascist and ultranationalist movements;[43] this protest that came less than a month after Zhirinovski's electoral breakthrough in Russia. Finns were reminded once again that while politics changes, geography is permanent.

ICELAND

Iceland is often excluded from analyses of Nordic security policy and the region's relationship with NATO. Its strategic geographic position in the North Atlantic removes it by a thousand kilometers from the other Nordic countries (excepting Greenland and the Faeroes) but also accounts for its enduring importance in NATO's operational planning for more than forty years. Iceland has no regular armed forces, and the Icelandic Defense Force consists almost entirely of U.S. military personnel. Icelandic membership in NATO was a controversial domestic issue from the start, but for the United States and the alliance, the small installations on Icelandic territory were crucial for air transport (until long-range transport became common), North American air defense, and North Atlantic air and sea defense operations.[44]

Iceland's security policy is, therefore, based on NATO membership and the 1951 U.S.-Iceland defense agreement, which, in turn, evolved out of a bilateral relationship stretching back to 1941.[45]

By the late 1980s, the periodic and often fierce political debates in Iceland about NATO bases had subsided. Although the leftist People's Alliance party and the pacifist Women's List still called for closing the bases, Icelandic opinion had become bored with the issue. The rise of Soviet power in the Atlantic, popularized by Tom Clancy's novel *Red Star Rising*, which gives a plausible if sensational account of an effective Soviet surprise attack on Iceland, and a new political maturity defused the issue. Some three thousand U.S. (mainly naval) personnel were based at Keflavik. Small contingents from other NATO members (for example, the Netherlands and occasionally Canada and Norway) gave legitimacy to the American and official Icelandic claim that the base was for NATO and not exclusively for the United States. Additional radar installations on the island completed the picture. The permanent U.S. air defense unit at Keflavik totaled eighteen F-15 aircraft by the mid-1980s, supplemented by nine P-3 antisubmarine patrol craft, and two E-3 air warning and control aircraft. The dramatic decline in Soviet military aircraft entering the Icelandic air region and Soviet submarines passing the Greenland, Iceland, United Kingdom (GIUK) sea defense line presaged Gorbachev's "New Thinking" on international relations, as did the U.S.-Soviet summit held in Reykjavik in November 1986.[46]

The end of the Cold War and the cessation of Soviet and then Russian military operations in the North Atlantic altered Iceland's position. First, the revival of the Western European Union, of which Iceland became an associate member in 1993, places Iceland in something of a political and security no-man's-land. Beyond this status, the application by all of the Nordic European Free Trade Association (EFTA) members other than Iceland for membership in the European Union threatens economic isolation. Additionally, the United States began to plan significant force and operational reductions in the Keflavik base, initially without Icelandic input. In short, just as a broad foreign and security policy consensus emerged in Iceland, the country's principal partners turned their attention elsewhere. Those Icelanders who had for two generations agitated to be left alone might now have their wish fulfilled, to the chagrin of most of the political leadership.[47]

One might question why Icelanders, reluctant allies during the depths of the Cold War, might become so security-conscious at a time when the fiercest forces plying the North Atlantic were environmental activists such as Sea Shepherd. NATO membership had given Iceland a seat in the most important political entity in the Atlantic community for four decades. There were implicit economic advantages, including EFTA and the considerable economic activity connected with the Keflavik base. NATO installations provided an infrastructure for civilian aviation, air traffic control, and emergency air rescue services. In time and with some expense, a number of these services have been turned over to civilians, but the cuts came at a time of severe economic difficulty for the Icelandic economy.[48]

In 1992, Iceland secured an American promise that it could participate in the planning for the future role of the Keflavik base. An Icelandic defense planning committee undertook contacts with American defense officials while Iceland moved closer to the WEU. The government also declared that the bilateral relationship with the United States would remain the foundation of Iceland security policy.[49]

In April 1993, Foreign Minister Jon Baldvin Hannibalsson reported that Iceland would continue to follow an active foreign policy in NATO and the WEU: with the Nordic countries in accommodating Baltic security interests and with the United States on the Keflavik issue. Remarkably, Olafur Ragnar Grimsson, the leader of the People's Alliance party, the historic opponent of NATO and the Keflavik base, said in parliament that his group could support the government's security policy. NATO, he noted, was evolving into a "peace league" that would enforce UN decisions. In this regard, the Keflavik base would be part of a larger international peacemaking effort. His party colleagues were less enthusiastic, and they reiterated the party's position that the base should be closed and Iceland withdrawn from NATO. The government's proposal that Iceland become an associate member of the WEU narrowly passed 29-26 on 23 April.[50]

Conversations in August 1993 between Icelandic Prime Minister David Oddsson and Vice President Al Gore in Washington moved the negotiations forward. The relationship with the United States was renewed on 4 January 1994, when Foreign Minister Hannibalsson signed a new U.S.-Icelandic agreement with Secretary of Defense William Perry. The United States pledged not to make significant changes in the base and its forces without consulting Iceland. In practice, the parties agreed to reduce the Icelandic Defense Force fighter group from twelve to four aircraft with future reductions possible. About 380 of the base's 3,000 personnel would be removed. Naval patrol, rescue helicopters, and radar stations would continue to operate as Icelanders prepare to assume the latter two functions.[51]

The current foreign policy challenge for Iceland will be to adjust its relations with Western Europe if the three Nordic applicants join the

European Union. Iceland has not considered the EU, in large part because of its fisheries interests, but it does want to maintain the European Economic Area agreements, which extend the European single market for most trade items to EFTA countries. Economic isolation is so ominous that some Icelandic politicians are beginning to rethink the standing rejection of the European Union. The Social Democratic party, part of the governing coalition, has promised to reassess the EU at its forthcoming party congress, and polls in mid-1994 showed a large upsurge in public support for an Icelandic application to the European Union if the three Nordic applicants join (70 percent, including a majority in all parties). Indeed, some Icelandic leaders were even willing to consider association with the North American Free Trade Association as an alternative to mid-Atlantic isolation.[52]

Security policy is not currently a major factor, and it appears again that Icelandic participation in security organizations (NATO and WEU) has the advantage of guaranteeing this small democracy a place at the table with larger partners. Economic isolation is the current threat, made more credible by six years of economic stagnation. For fifty years, Iceland was more important to the Atlantic powers than the reverse; at present, that historic relationship has given Iceland a critical chance to remain in the changing Atlantic community.

CONCLUSION

This chapter has sketched the evolving but complex relationship between Scandinavia and NATO. Forty-five years have left their mark on several emerging perspectives. First, the end of the Cold War has had an enormous impact on foreign and security policy conditions for the Nordic countries. Their policies traditionally aimed at strengthening deterrence, diplomacy, détente, and reform in northern Europe. All had based their policies on the likelihood that an East-West military conflict would be unacceptable and unnecessary, and hence could be avoided. They understood that military preparedness, unilateral or collective defense, was part of the equation for peace in Europe. None felt that security policy was primarily military defense.

Post–Cold War northern Europe vaguely resembles the situation prevailing in the 1920s. The two potential threats to Scandinavia at that time, Germany and Russia, had become focused inward and no longer seemed to pose an immediate military or political danger. New international organizations pledged accommodation for historic disputes in Europe and promised protection for small states, new and old. Neutrality had succeeded in 1914-1918, but just barely. Collective security under the League of Nations was an alternative to neutrality, but there was no clear sense of whether the new commitments would be costly. All of the Scandinavian states became solid league citizens, but when the atmosphere darkened in the 1930s, each sought unilaterally to protect itself, and not all avoided disaster during World War II.

The emerging European security system faces more immediate challenges than did the restrained system of the 1920s. The Persian Gulf War of 1990-91 demonstrated that collective security could be enforced with sufficient political will and the accumulated strength of NATO. Currently, the Bosnian crisis has shown that raw military power is still dependent upon political will and opportunity.

The Nordic countries have two options at present. They can work within the emerging European Union and the Western European Union for a close linkage among political, economic, and security interests. The EU and WEU are unlikely to be monolithic or truly federal institutions in the foreseeable future. The Nordic members will certainly want a pragmatic confederal model to function before taking bold new steps. Alternatively, they can face semi-isolation. Those that do not join the EU/WEU framework will have other options, including bilateral relations with the EU (a continuation of the European Economic Area agreements) and secondary organizations (for example, the CSCE). The Nordic Council will also remain a secondary organization for the Scandinavian countries on most policy issues, including security concerns. A Baltic framework is under construction but unlikely to amount to much for probably another decade, and then only if Russia can be accommodated.

NATO remains an essential Atlantic and Western connection for Iceland, Norway, and Denmark. Through the Partnership for Peace that link may extend to Sweden and Finland without creating new divisions. The United States cannot be a substitute for those nations' European neighbors, but the Atlantic connection is well ensconced and functioning satisfactorily. It will also be a pillar of the next European security regime, if one is established, and provide ties with Eastern Europe, Russia, and the other former Soviet republics. As stated earlier, politics changes, but geography endures. And history connects. That is the substance behind Scandinavia's evolving relationship with NATO.

NOTES

1. See, for example, the comprehensive study by Rolf Tamnes, *The United States and the Cold War in the High North* (Aldershot, England: Dartmouth, 1991).

2. The Nordic Council is an intergovernmental organization founded in 1952 (Finland joined in 1955) consisting of the five Nordic countries and the three autonomous territories of Greenland, the Faeroe Islands, and the Aaland Islands. For an early account of the council see Stanley V. Anderson, *The Nordic Council* (Seattle: University of Washington Press, 1967).

3. Arne O. Brundtland, ed., "Svensk og Finsk Sikkerhetspolitiske Revolusjon og Litt om Norske Interesser," in *Norsk Utenrikspolitisk Aarbok 1992* (Oslo: Norsk Utenrikspolitisk Institutt, 1993), 20.

4. These events are summarized well by Nils Andren and Gylfi Gislason, "The Nordic Countries between East and West," in *Nordic Democracy,* ed. Folmer Wisti (Copenhagen: Det Danske Selskab, 1981), 677-90. See also Nils Andren, "Changing Strategic Perspectives in Northern Europe," in *Foreign Policies of Northern Europe,* ed. Bengt Sundelius (Boulder: Westview Press, 1982), 73-106.

5. For additional details see Johann Joergen Holst, "Five Roads to Nordic Security," *Cooperation and Conflict* vol. 7, no. 2/3 (1972): 133-37.

6. The Scandinavian debates surrounding the Forward Maritime Strategy are discussed by Rodney Kennedy-Minott, "The Forward Maritime Strategy and Nordic Security," in *Nordic Security at the Turn of the Twenty-first Century,* ed. Ciro E. Zoppo (Westport: Greenwood Press, 1992), 201-17.

7. There are, of course, significant nonmilitary security concerns in Germany and Central Europe more generally, including the enormous social, economic, and political problems of the changes since 1989. The problem of immigrants and refugees and the related rise of political extremism is certainly unsettling (and duplicated on a lower level in Scandinavia). Finally there are the modern problems of environmental degradation. None of these issues is part of the "traditional" security agenda, but all are clearly entering the debates.

8. *New York Times,* 26 April 1988. The ambassador's remarks were made to the author several years earlier.

9. See the discussion of Danish and Norwegian restrictions on NATO in Ingemar Doerfer, "Scandinavia and NATO: à la carte," *Washington Quarterly* 9 (Winter 1986): 15-30.

10. Christian Thune, "Danish Defense Policy," in *European Security after the Revolutions of 1989,* ed. Jeffrey Simon (Washington: National Defense University Press, 1991), 420.

11. International Institute for Strategic Studies (IISS), *The Military Balance, 1993-1994* (London: Brassey's, 1993), 32, 40-41.

12. See *Nordisk Kontakt,* 1991: no. 10, 31-33; and Nikolai Petersen, "Danish Security Policy after the Cold War: Adaption and Innovation (Aarhus: Department of Political Science reproduction, 1994), 15-16.

13. *Nordisk Kontakt,* 1993: no. 12, 40-41.

14. European Community (Union), Statistical Service, *Eurobarometer*, nos. 35, 38, 39.
15. *Politiken*, 24 May 1994, reported by Leif Andersen, "Danske Nyheder pr. 94.05.24," Internet. A younger SPP politician, Hens Toft, reacted angrily to Petersen's faint praise for NATO. He claimed that NATO was fighting a war in the former Yugoslavia. The meeting closed with its traditional call for the immediate abolition of NATO. Although the party, with its typically 10-15 percent of the vote could be a significant parliamentary partner in a center-left coalition, its rigid foreign and security policy position has stood in the way. It will probably continue to do so.
16. Magne Skodvin, *Norden eller NATO? Utenriksdepartementet og alliansespoergsmaalet 1947-1949* (Oslo: Universitetsforleget, 1971), 170-75.
17. Exceptions were made for the AFNORTH headquarters at Kolsaas just outside Oslo, warning and electronic navigational equipment, training exercises and occasional intelligence operations (for example, the U.S. U-2 aircraft used Norwegian bases in the 1950s). In the 1980s there was controversy over "prepositioning" of NATO matériel in Norway. Compare with Knut E. Eriksen, "Norge i det vestlige samarbeid" in *Vekst og Velstand; Norsk politisk historie 1945-1965*, ed. Trond Bergh and Helge Pharo (Oslo: Universitetsforlaget, 1977), 239-45.
18. This is especially true of the non-Socialist (especially Center) opponents of European Union membership. Leftist opponents have usually been opponents of Norwegian membership in NATO (or at least Norwegian defense efforts based on NATO). EU opponents in the divided Labor party come from that party's NATO skeptics and minimalists.
19. Compare with Nils Oervik, ed., *Fears and Expectations; Norwegian Attitudes toward European Integration* (Oslo: Universtitetsforlag, 1972), esp. 310-28.
20. *Stortingsmeldingen: Hovedretningslinjer for Forsvarets Virksomhet og Utvikling i tiden 1994-98.* Such reports to Parliament are not the same as multiparty parliamentary commission reports or "crown commissions." They are the government's policy intentions subject to parliamentary debate and action and the basis for electoral debates.
21. IISS, *Military Balance, 1993-1994*, 55, 225.
22. *Nordisk Kontakt*, 1993: no. 1, 76-77.
23. Ibid., 1993: no. 11, 74-77.
24. For a sketch of the ideal Nordic alternative see, for example, Sverre Lodgaard, "Redefining Norden," in *Nordic Security in the 1990s*, ed. Jan Oeberg (London: Pinter, 1992), 281-300. The entire volume makes a case for the Nordic option from a leftist perspective.
25. Haakon Blankenborg, "Sikkerhet i Norden: fra balanse til fellesskap," *NK tema: Saekerhet*, 1994:1 (special supplement to *Nordisk Kontakt*, 1994: no. 3): 57. See also Arne Olav Brundtland, "Litt om Nordisk Utenriks- og Sikkerhetspolitisk Samarbeid," in ibid., 32.
26. For a concise but clear discussion of the 1948-49 Scandinavian defense talks see Barbara Haskel, *The Scandinavian Option: Opportunities and Opportunity Costs in Postwar Scandinavian Foreign Policies* (Oslo: Universitetsforlaget, 1976).

27. For a detailed analysis of Swedish foreign policy through 1965 (that is, before the demonstrative policies of Olof Palme and others) see Nils Andren and Ake Landqvist, *Svensk Utrikespolitik efter 1945* (Stockholm: Almqvist & Wiksell, 1965), esp. 84-88, 101-36. As "nonalignment" came to mean the nationalist foreign policies of many newly independent states after 1960, translation of the Swedish expression *alliansfrihet* became problematic. In a later study Andren proposed "not-alignment" as a better term, but only he seems to use it. See Nils Andren, "Changing Strategic Perspectives in Northern Europe," in *Foreign Policies of Northern Europe,* ed. Bengt Sundelius (Boulder: Westview Press, 1982), 103.

28. See John Logue, "Sweden," in *Europe's Neutral and Nonaligned States,* ed. S. Victor Papacosma and Mark Rubin (Wilmington: Scholarly Resources Inc., 1989), esp. 88-97.

29. Reported in *Nordisk Kontakt,* 1994: no. 2, 81-83. There were also joint naval exercises, and Sweden had nearly full access to Western military technology. For the latter see Ingemar Doerfer, *System 37 Viggen: Arms, Technology, and the Domestication of Glory* (Oslo: Universitetsforlaget, 1973).

30. Margaretha af Ugglas, "Sweden's Security Policy in Post–Cold War Europe," *NATO Review* 42, no. 2 (April 1994): 12.

31. See Paul M. Cole, "Competing Interests in the Nordic Region," *Scandinavian Studies* 64, no. 4 (Fall 1992): 616-19.

32. For this perspective see Ingemar Doerfer, "Sixty Years of Solitude: Sweden Returns to Europe," *Scandinavian Studies* 64, no. 4 (Fall 1992): 602-4. See also Ann-Sofie Nilsson, "Swedish Foreign Policy in the Post–Palme Era," *World Affairs* 151, no. 1 (Summer 1988): 25-33.

33. The strong showing of the Zhirinovski nationalists in the Russian parliamentary election in December 1993 has given Scandinavia food for thought. *Nordisk Kontakt,* 1994: no. 2, 84.

34. Sweden, Foreign Ministry, "Swedish Security Policy in a Changing Europe," speech by Prime Minister Carl Bildt at the Royal Academy of Military Science, Stockholm, 7 December 1993 (unofficial translation).

35. Af Ugglas, "Sweden's Security Policy," 15.

36. Pierre Schori, "Sverige mellan Maastricht och Sarajevo," *NK Tema: Saekerhet,* 1994, no. 1 (special supplement to *Nordisk Kontakt*): 65-67.

37. Af Ugglas, "Sweden's Security Policy," 12.

38. Ibid., 13.

39. Ward Thompson, "Postscript: Reflections of an American Diplomat," in *Finland and the United States; Diplomatic Relations through Seventy Years,* ed. Robert Rinehart (Washington: Institute for the Study of Diplomacy, Georgetown University, 1993): 111-15.

40. The Saab JAS aircraft has been plagued with developmental problems while the U.S. F/A-18 is operational. It was the first major U.S. military aircraft acquired by the Finns. *Nordisk Kontakt,* 1992: no. 5, 1-9, 14-15.

41. Erkki Tuomioja, "Finlands Saekerhet och foeraendringarna i Europa," *NK Tema,* 68-73.

42. *Nordisk Kontakt*, 1993: no. 12, 53.

43. Ibid., 1994: no. 1, 37.

44. A comprehensive summary of Iceland's role in NATO defense operations is Albert Jonsson, *Iceland, NATO and the Keflavik Base* (Reykjavik: Icelandic Commission on Security and International Affairs, 1989).

45. In 1941, U.S. forces relieved British forces that had peacefully occupied Iceland (then still part of the Danish realm) following the German occupation of Denmark in 1940. The origins of Iceland's security policy are best sketched in Donald E. Nuechterlein, *Iceland, Reluctant Ally* (Ithaca: Cornell University Press, 1961), esp. chaps. 2 and 5.

46. Air intercepts in the Icelandic zone fell from 170 in 1985 to 60 in 1989. Ibid., 30, 53-57. By 1992 the number was down to zero.

47. See Bjoern Bjarnasson, "Islands Vei i Sikkerhetspolitikken," *NK Tema*, 1993, no. 1, 58-60.

48. Excessive fishing of the North Atlantic has significantly reduced Icelandic catches. Maritime products constituted 79 percent of Icelandic merchandise exports in 1990-1993. Since 1988, the Icelandic economy has been in recession with a cumulative 7 percent decline since the peak of 1987. Iceland, Central Bank, *Economic Statistics Quarterly* 15, no. 1 (February 1994): 23, 25.

49. *Nordisk Kontakt*, 1992: no. 3, 58-61.

50. Ibid., 1993: no. 5, 57-59.

51. Ibid., 1993: no. 7-8, 56-58, and no. 12, 56-59.

52. *News from Iceland* no. 219 (May 1994): 1, 4, 15.

Official Perspectives

14

NATO after the January 1994 Summit:
The View from Brussels

Erika v.C. Bruce

For more than forty years, the Atlantic Alliance found itself locked in a critical confrontation with the Soviet Union. The alliance won the Cold War, and the Soviet bloc remained saddled with a crippled and uncompetitive economic and social system, a discredited political structure, a bankrupt ideology, and unresolved internal conflicts that had been suppressed for decades. During the Cold War years, Western Europe, under the defense umbrella of the alliance and with the earlier massive support of the Marshall Plan, not only recovered but became through the European Community and its economic partner, the European Free Trade Association, one of the strongest economic regions in the world. Even Western European countries that were not members of the alliance and, indeed, many Third World states were beneficiaries of the security and stability that the North Atlantic Treaty Organization (NATO) provided.

Since 1989 the world has witnessed a succession of dramatic developments: the demolition of the Berlin Wall; the unification of Germany within the Atlantic Alliance; the disintegration of the Soviet empire and then of the USSR itself; the liquidation of the Warsaw Treaty Organization; the transformation of countries in Central and Eastern Europe (CEE) and the Baltic into free and independent states; the creation of embryonic democratic institutions in these nations and the former republics of the USSR; the beginnings of free-market economies in Eastern Europe; the expansion of the

European Union (EU); and the development of a European commitment to create a new security and defense architecture for the Continent.

For a short interlude, most of us lived in a dream world, believing that the need for large military establishments had finally disappeared. That dream soon blurred or, perhaps, dissipated entirely amid the harsh realities of Europe's resurrected heritage of ethnic, national, religious, and territorial discord. With the benefit of historical hindsight, it was probably predictable. In any case, a number of critical trends and issues influenced governments, political and intellectual elites, and pressure groups in the formulation of policy as the alliance moved toward the January 1994 summit.

First, since 1990, wars, coups d'état, and violence have shaken the confidence of the West in a "Europe whole and free" and a security zone extending "from Vancouver to Vladivostok." Shortly after the Cold War's end, hostilities flared up in the former Yugoslavia. Europe blindly refused to recognize the inflammatory ingredients and the inevitable chain reaction of that conflict, and in the absence of decisive action to snuff it out at birth the conflict was allowed to blaze into civil war and genocide. In comparison, the velvet divorce of the Czech and Slovak republics represented a rare example of civilized human behavior.

Second, in a related pattern, we have seen and continue to witness conflicts that have erupted in and among the republics of the former Soviet Union (FSU) with the prospect of still others in the future. Third, NATO is continually reminded, mainly by the United States, of the large stockpiles of weapons of mass destruction that remain intact in the hands of states that may be neither stable nor reliable.

Fourth, those of us in the alliance are conscious of the profound economic, social, and political challenges plaguing Russia and the other republics of the FSU. The Soviet system had imposed a peace on conflicting forces and communities that are now again resurfacing. We are sensitive to the facts that Russia's armed forces remain the largest in Europe, that their morale is dangerously low, and that they probably possess the only nationally organized structure in the country. The military had been accustomed to playing a major role in the political life of the USSR and may only be a short move from assuming a center-stage position in the near future. As events in Bosnia have clearly shown, we can no more ignore Russia today—no matter how crippled it may seem to be—than we could in decades past.

Last, United Nations (UN) failures in Somalia and Haiti have reminded governments and their general publics, now well informed by instantaneous media coverage, of the limitations of intervening in civil conflicts that are of little direct, national interest and where warring parties are unwilling to negotiate even a viable cease-fire. The Gulf War is now regarded as a unique operation unlikely to be repeated anywhere else in the near future.

In this new political climate and in the midst of a long economic recession, there have been two competing, if not incompatible, forces shaping the foreign, defense, and domestic policies of Western governments. On the one hand, taxpayers have insisted on reducing their countries' military forces, expenditures, and commitments. On the other, alliance governments have urged NATO to redefine its role, expand its strategic scope, develop relationships of trust and cooperation with Eastern Europe (including Russia and the republics of the FSU), and enlarge its membership. Clearly, NATO is expected to serve as a guarantor of peace and security throughout Europe.

Soon after the Cold War ended, the Atlantic Alliance did, in fact, move decisively to redesign its strategy, restructure its forces, and, in tandem with Russia and the other nuclear-weapons republics of the FSU, reduce its conventional military and nuclear forces. Furthermore, it proposed concrete ways for NATO, the countries of Central and Eastern Europe, and the FSU to collaborate in building a new Europe. Among the more important initiatives, in December 1991 it established the North Atlantic Cooperation Council (NACC), bringing all of these governments into a permanent association with NATO, in the hope that the NACC would serve to project stability beyond the frontiers of NATO's membership and throughout Europe. These innovations proved insufficient, however, to provide the sense of security that Russia's neighbors sought. They understandably wanted to crowd in under NATO's security umbrella, and it was largely due to their collective pressures that the question of NATO's enlargement was added to the summit's agenda.

At this point, it is also appropriate to mention some of the more important European perceptions of America's role in the alliance. Simply stated, the United States has always been regarded as the one essential and predominant nation in NATO. Public support in Europe for the United States's continued military presence has ebbed and flowed, usually rising when any serious threat appeared on the horizon. There remains the solid conviction, however, that American forces are the guarantor of security.

Fascinated by American society, Europeans watched with keen interest the 1992 presidential campaign, the election of Bill Clinton, and his subsequent first year of governance. Clinton's policy statements, by placing top priority on American domestic issues, generated considerable uneasiness among Europeans. They worried that this tilt might signal a substantial decline in Washington's commitment to what Europeans perceived as the responsibilities of the United States in the international community and, more particularly, in Europe. Did it mean, in blunt terms, that a new isolationism was emerging?

In this context, President Clinton also indicated that America, as the only remaining superpower with global interests, would not attempt to assume a lonely leadership role in the international community as the world's police force. There would have to be shared responsibilities. Again Europeans asked if this was another theme in the prelude to a decline in America's willingness to play the principal role in world affairs. Then, later in 1993, statements from Washington implied that Asia had moved to the top of the list of America's international priorities. Where did this place Europe? Many Europeans waited impatiently for the answer.

These and other related developments, such as the massive cuts that all Western countries were making in their armed forces, intensified feelings among Europeans that they could no longer depend so heavily on the American security structure. Such sentiments took on added meaning in the new debate over the continued justification for NATO. The media and the general public on both continents demanded peace dividends and asked with increasing insistence why scarce resources should be poured into an alliance whose main enemy had disappeared. Some of this initial criticism did diminish somewhat toward the close of 1993, as risks to Europe's stability attracted more attention. Against this background of uncertainty, President Clinton called for a NATO summit in which he would declare unequivocally that the United States accepted its responsibilities in Europe and that there would be no return to an isolationist policy.

Several points are worth mentioning about the 1994 summit. First, it provided the right forum, on the right continent, and at the right time for President Clinton to define his administration's foreign and defense policy objectives and, in that setting, to renew its commitment to NATO and to a changed and changing Europe. Second, Clinton clearly wanted to provide fresh impetus and strength to the reorientation and direction of the alliance's role in the new Europe and, in particular, to open the way for more intensive and productive relations with CEE, Russia, and other republics of the FSU. Third, in this scenario, President Clinton, with his NATO allies, wanted to strengthen NATO's and Europe's capacities to project security and stability. The ratification of the Maastricht Treaty had completed the foundation for the EU to develop, through the WEU, its own defense structure and consequently to carry a greater share of the responsibilities for leadership and the burden of defense. Last, the summit provided a timely international forum for the European leaders of the alliance to define, in their turn, the importance they were giving to the development of a credible European Security and Defense Identity (ESDI) and their expectations for constructive support from a United States that had not always been "enthusiastic" about the development of a separate European defense force. In more general terms, they wanted to strengthen the common efforts that America and Western Europe wished to pursue in their relations with CEE and the FSU. In a sense, a pan-European NATO could serve to accompany the EU and other European states into that part of the Continent that had been isolated for so long.

It is relevant here to refer to an episode that can be regarded as Clinton's first important presidential step in Europe on the road to the summit and that helped to shape the favorable impression he wanted to—and did—create on his first official visit to Europe. In Brussels's City Hall on the evening before the summit's opening session, the president addressed 250 young men and women drawn from thirty countries, "the future leaders of Europe," as he described them. His statement provided a solid and comprehensive review of American domestic and foreign policies and served, in the pre-summit hours, as an excellent introduction to his reaffirmation that Europe remains central to the interests of America. "The bonds," he declared, "that tie the U.S. and Europe together are unique. You remain our most valued partner." To emphasize this commitment, he confirmed that America would maintain one hundred thousand troops in Europe.

Decisions at the summit did give concrete shape to expectations mentioned earlier. First and foremost, the alliance heads of state and government reaffirmed the fundamental importance of the transatlantic relationship and the indispensable commitment of the United States to Europe. At the same time, they restated their strong support for the development of the European Security and Defense Identity. Both commitments are intended to provide a sound and enduring basis for constructive cooperation in the years to come. The strong support for the development of the ESDI was not only of special importance to Europe. It was also seen as a major reorientation in America's attitude, as noted earlier, toward an independent European defense organization outside NATO but operating in close cooperation with it. In this context, it is of interest to note that the Summit Declaration mentions strengthening the ESDI seven times, the European pillar of the alliance five times, and the WEU an even more remarkable eight times.

France's leading newspaper, *Le Monde,* acutely observed on 11 January 1994: "The United States, since the beginning of the Clinton Administration, has come a long way toward European positions, and notably those of France." It added, "The Declaration should respond to a number of French demands . . . the development of a European identity in the field of security and defense, and in the reinforcement of the European pillar of the alliance through the move toward the WEU." The *Observer* of London on 16 January posed the question of whether the declaration "represents a success in the French campaign to diminish American influence in Europe."

In deciding to strengthen the ESDI and the WEU, summit leaders clearly recognized that a stronger, economically powerful Europe was now able (and some will add that it has been for some time) to participate more equitably in the Continent's responsibilities for maintaining stability and sharing the costs of defense.

The second important initiative, again under American leadership, was the concept of Combined Joint Task Forces (CJTF), an idea familiar to the U.S. Armed Forces. The alliance's military forces and structures would be changed to make them more flexible and to allow NATO assets to be used in crisis management and peacekeeping operations. With this policy it would be possible, for example, for European members of the alliance to use NATO troops and resources, under European command, perhaps from the WEU, for missions in which the United States and Canada did not wish to get involved. Moreover, it would also allow for joint peacekeeping operations with partner countries.

The summit's third major decision was the Partnership for Peace (PFP). The creation of the NACC in 1992 had been among the first major initiatives reaching out to the states of CEE and the FSU. But historical reflection, two coups d'état in Russia, and President Boris Yeltsin's threatening objections to a closer association of CEE with NATO have demonstrated that NACC was only a first step toward more substantive measures. Within NATO the question of expansion was placed in the larger context of how best to project stability throughout the East. Granting membership presented only one of several options, and it raised a number of difficult questions: Which countries? Were any able to contribute effectively to the common defense? What would happen to those left out? Would expansion lead to a new division of Europe? What was Russia's role to be? Were the parliaments of all sixteen allies prepared to defend new members against attack?

The response to these considerations was the PFP, which stated that NATO "expected and would welcome" eventual expansion. This new, imaginative program is based on an American initiative, first suggested years ago, according to former Defense Secretary Les Aspin, by General George C.

Marshall, and now wisely resurrected by President Clinton. It is no exaggeration to declare that if it is carried forward as planned, it will truly transform the relationship between NATO and the participating states in CEE. It is designed to open the way for any NACC member to develop, bilaterally, "customized" cooperative political and military relations with NATO for the purpose of joint planning, training, and exercises that will strengthen their ability to undertake, among other activities, joint peacekeeping missions. It will also facilitate transparency in national defense planning and the democratic control of defense forces. No other NACC member can veto the program developed by a partner with NATO. A most important aspect is the privilege of a partner to consult with the alliance whenever it feels its independence is threatened. In the short term, the Partnership for Peace program will open the way for partners to develop their credentials for full NATO membership.

As much praise as this initiative attracted, it also found criticism in the Eastern and Western press. There was the perception that Russia's objections to NATO's move into CEE—following Poland's decision to apply for membership in NATO—had been the godmother of the PFP program. Alliance members were quite aware, of course, that powerful forces in the FSU still regarded NATO as an aggressive, imperialist organization and that this new initiative, the PFP, might be seen as an attempt by NATO to extend its sphere of influence up to and indeed into territories long considered Russia's domain. This perception is, of course, incorrect. PFP was created to facilitate the process of transformation that the CEE states must go through on the road to eventual membership in NATO and the development of a continental security structure. Moreover, any continental security system must be designed to embrace all European countries, including Russia.

After the summit, President Yeltsin renewed his objections to NATO's expansion through the PFP program. He stated: "This [expansion] is the path towards new threats for Europe and the world. Russia is not a guest in Europe." The world must acknowledge Russia, he declared, as the guarantor of stability in the entire territory of the former Soviet Union.

In another important summit decision, the alliance, again led by the United States, also reaffirmed its commitment to reducing, if not eliminating, all weapons of mass destruction. Europe followed with great interest President Clinton's visits to Ukraine, Belarus, and Russia in his efforts to persuade their governments to move ahead with the program for downsizing their nuclear arsenals.

Finally, the summit reiterated the allies' conviction that the war in the former Yugoslavia must be settled "at the negotiating table, and not on the battlefield" and that only the parties to the conflict could conclude a peace agreement. Summit leaders, following President Clinton's lead, reaffirmed their support for the UN and WEU efforts to secure a settlement and for America's willingness to contribute to its implementation. They stated that NATO would continue to carry out the tasks requested of it by the UN, including monitoring the no-fly zone, and that it was prepared to carry out air strikes in order to prevent the strangulation of Sarajevo, "of the 'safe areas' and other threatened areas."

This coverage would not be complete, however, without a few words about the decision on Sarajevo taken by the NACC, under Franco-American leadership, one month later, on 9 February: to carry out NATO air strikes at the end of a ten-day deadline against "heavy weapons, along with any of their essential military support facilities . . . within the Sarajevo exclusion zone, unless controlled by UNPROFOR [UN Protection Force]." The NACC also agreed, "at the request of the UN Secretary General," to authorize air strikes against ground forces "in and around Sarajevo . . . responsible for attacks against civilians in that city."

Some reflections on how the public image of NATO has changed since the summit and the February initiative are appropriate. First, the alliance decision, taken on 9 February, has brought NATO back to "center stage," as Dr. Manfred Wörner, then NATO's secretary- general, put it. It constituted a persuasive reminder that the alliance is the only defense organization capable of mounting a credible and forceful operation in attempting to bring an end to the violence. More precisely, it showed persuasively that, with the authority of the UN, NATO was ready to use its military forces in the interests of peace and humanitarian assistance. The first shots in combat ever fired by NATO, when American aircraft downed four planes in the no-fly zone, modestly confirmed that the alliance has met the test of its willingness to take forceful military action. It must be noted that it had previously been impossible, for a number of reasons, to enlist the unanimous support of all alliance governments for military intervention. Only *after* the United States had reaffirmed its commitment to Europe and had become decisively engaged in Bosnian peace efforts did all members became persuaded to support the use of intervention by force.

Second, the threat of active intervention in Bosnia served as a further illustration of the alliance's new role in crisis management. One might well ask what the image of the alliance would have been if, after the 9 February bombing of civilians in Sarajevo, NATO had done nothing. One public opinion seminar indicated that NATO would have seriously diminished, if not demolished, its credibility. Third, NATO's decision served to emphasize, at a time when there had been some doubt on both continents about the role of the United States in Europe, the importance of American leadership and military forces in carrying forward NATO's responsibilities. Finally, the alliance's intervention resulted unexpectedly in the welcome return of Russia to European security consultations on what intervention would be feasible and effective in the Bosnian conflict and, by implication, in the shaping of the new strategic structure of Europe.

An accurate picture of the thinking in Brussels would be incomplete without more coverage of the developing relationship between NATO and Russia. Russia expressed its intention to join the PFP program. Russian Foreign Minister Andrei Kozyrev, in the *New York Times* of 19 March, expressed his government's views on the role that Russia, in cooperation with the United States, might play in building a more peaceful Europe. Russia, he affirmed, remains a superpower, and there must be realistic collaboration based on the principles of strategic partnership agreed by Presidents Clinton and Yeltsin in Vancouver and Moscow. At the same time, he acknowledged the need for American leadership in the world, because of its strength and special position in NATO and the Group of 7. But this did not imply, he added, that the United States should attempt to establish a "global hegemony," since America could not cope with every world problem alone.

As a related aspect of Russia's role in the new Europe, Yeltsin and Kozyrev, writing in the 11 January 1994 *Izvestia*, clearly stated Russia's interests in its neighbors, the "near-abroad." NATO can recognize these interests but without accepting any claim for Russia's interference or intervention in those countries against their will and in violation of the terms of the Conference on Security and Cooperation in Europe. In this connection, Secretary of State Warren G. Christopher remarked to a congressional committee in 1993 that the United States had no objection to Russia serving as a guarantor of "regional stability."

It is generally acknowledged that it would be a serious mistake to take advantage, or be seen as trying to take advantage, of Russia's current weaknesses and difficulties. As a nation, it can never be isolated diplomatically, whatever its domestic situation. The West must help the reforms to succeed. With words of caution in his 19 March 1994 article in the *New York Times*, Kozyrev expressed his fear that "in Moscow when democracy needs all the help it can get, we hear Western threats to reduce economic cooperation with Russia." Against this background, it is fair to say that there was an almost audible sigh of relief and satisfaction in Brussels when the Russian government declared its intention to join the PFP.

It is appropriate to conclude by recalling an old Roman epigram that states: "If you want peace, prepare for war." Pursuing this policy is much less costly in human lives and resources than fighting a war. NATO's first forty-five years confirm the wisdom of this principle, a principle that was twice disregarded on both continents in the first half of this century, but that when implemented carried us so successfully through the Cold War. It must remain our guiding principle for the next forty-five years and beyond.

NATO has led the way, since the end of the Cold War, in responding to the realities and challenges of a changing political and strategic environment in Europe. Most recently the January 1994 summit has put in place the framework for the new European/North Atlantic security structure. A Europe at peace remains a dream, but it is surely a dream all must pursue.

This positive evaluation of the summit has been, and is, optimistic, although only the future will determine the real, concrete results in the years ahead. One might well ask a number of questions:

- Will the transatlantic partnership and will America's leadership remain strong and firm?
- Will the European Union develop the defense credibility to which it has committed itself?
- Will the alliance and Russia, through the PFP, succeed in laying the foundations for a genuine pan-European defense entente stretching from Vancouver and San Francisco, through Europe, to Vladivostok?
- Will the reduction of weapons of mass destruction ever reach the point where the world is spared the threat of madmen?

These are among the formidable and inescapable challenges of our common agenda for the years ahead. We are convinced that the 1994 summit has pointed us in the right direction.

15

Partnership for Peace and the Transformation of North Atlantic Security

*Joseph Kruzel**

Although there is considerable sentimental reflection on the first forty-five years of the North Atlantic Treaty Organization (NATO) and gloomy commiseration about its present plight, I personally believe NATO is an organization that may well play a more important role in the next half-century than it served during the Cold War phase of its existence. The transformation of NATO has already begun with the Partnership for Peace (PFP).

Reflecting on the historical record of European security teaches Americans that they cannot ignore conflicts in Europe. The fiftieth anniversary commemoration of D-Day reminded us that "transatlantic security" is not a slogan but a fact written on the pages of history with the blood of thousands of American troops. Our security is inextricably bound to the security of Europe.

When NATO was founded forty-five years ago, Europe was physically devastated but full of hope. World War II was over. Freedom-loving nations were victorious. There were dangers ahead, but there was an opportunity to build a secure, unified Europe. That was the vision presented by George C. Marshall when he stepped up to the microphone to give his now-famous commencement speech at Harvard in June 1947. His vision was inclusive, offered to all

---

* Joseph Kruzel was one of three Americans killed in a road accident in Bosnia on 19 August 1995 while on a U.S.-sponsored peace mission to end the Balkan conflict.

of Europe, from the Atlantic to the Urals, including the Soviet Union and the countries of Eastern Europe. His dream, a continent of prosperous democracies cooperating in international relations to the mutual security of all, excluded no country. But events intervened: Stalin declined the offer, the Iron Curtain descended, and only half of Marshall's vision was realized.

Now, more than forty-five years and a Cold War later, we have an opportunity to pick up where the Cold War left off, to rededicate ourselves to Marshall's vision of a Europe whole, secure, and free. That vision is now within our grasp. But to seize it, we must do three things.

First, we must reaffirm that the Euro-Atlantic region is one, indivisible geopolitical region, and that as a consequence the United States is in Europe to stay—no *ifs*, *ands*, *buts*, or *untils*. For as far into the future as it is possible to see, so long as the Europeans want the United States to be part of their security domain, we will be there, not just in spirit, but with a substantial military presence as well.

Second, we must support the success of democratic and economic reforms in Central and Eastern Europe, and that includes Russia, Ukraine, and the other former Soviet republics. We should pay special attention to the courageous efforts of reformers in these nations. Freedom and prosperity are the best guarantees of security and stability in all of Europe. And third, we must develop a new security system based on the realities of today's Europe, one that transcends the artificial lines that divided Europe during the Cold War. This is the purpose of the Partnership for Peace.

As we envision it, the partnership will provide a framework for detailed, operational military cooperation for multinational security efforts that would have NATO at its core. The nations of the partnership will participate with NATO in a range of military activities, including joint military planning, training, and exercises as well as search and rescue missions, disaster relief, peacekeeping, and crisis management. PFP is a process to take us from where we are today to this new stage of security cooperation.

Individual nations interested in PFP have been invited to sign a framework document. By signing this document, partners commit themselves to certain principles of international conduct. They accept the protection and promotion of fundamental freedoms, human rights, justice, and peace through democracy. Partners also pledge themselves to the preservation of democratic societies. Partners affirm their commitment to refrain from the threat or use of force against the territorial integrity or political independence of any state, to respect existing borders, and to settle disputes by peaceful means. They also agree to transparency in national defense planning and budgeting and democratic control of defense forces as goals of their defense posture.

In return, NATO promises to develop a planning and review process for evaluation of forces and capabilities that might be made available by partners for multinational training, exercises, and operations in conjunction with alliance forces. NATO invites partners to send representatives to NATO headquarters and to a partnership coordination cell located right next door to SHAPE, the Supreme Headquarters of Allied Powers in Europe. For its part, NATO pledges to consult with any participant if that partner perceives a direct threat to its territorial integrity, political independence, or security.

Once the framework document is signed, each new partner submits a presentation document identifying the facilities, resources, and forces it is willing to make available to the partnership and the extent of its intention to participate in joint training, planning, and operations. A partner will also identify what it intends to do to achieve civilian control of the military and make defense budgets and policies transparent, that is, taking them out of the half-light of national defense ministries and making them visible to the citizenry.

It is important to note that there are two things PFP will *not* provide: the NATO security guarantee and automatic membership at some future time. First, regarding the security guarantee, Article 5 of the North Atlantic Treaty requires each member to regard an attack on one as an attack on all. This article's guarantee will not be extended to partners.

The next big question—whether joining the partnership is a ticket into NATO—is answered negatively. Partners will not automatically become eligible for membership into NATO. They do not even have to want to join NATO.

What partners *will* get is an opportunity to work with NATO to develop the principles, purposes, and capabilities of NATO members. While partnership is no guarantee of membership, active participation will likely be an essential condition of future NATO membership.

There are some big advantages in this approach to current NATO members as well as for partners. First, it does not redivide Europe. We spent two generations trying to lift the Iron Curtain, and we do not want to replace it by drawing another line. PFP gives all nations the same chance to take part, but makes the results dependent on the effort of each partner. Second, PFP sets up the right incentives. In the old, Cold War world, NATO was an alliance created in response to an external threat. In the new, post–Cold War world, NATO can be an alliance based on shared values of democracy and the free market. PFP rewards those who move in that direction. Third, PFP requires that partners make a real contribution. It does not just ask what

NATO can do for its new partners. It asks what the new partners can do for NATO. Security consultations, for instance, will be available to active partners, to those who make a contribution and involve themselves in the multinational activities that are the heart of NATO. Fourth, it keeps NATO at the center of European security concerns and thereby keeps American involvement at the center of Europe. Finally, it puts the question of NATO membership for the partners where it belongs—at the end of the process rather than at the beginning. After we have some experience with the partnership process, it will be much clearer who among the eligible nations genuinely wants to buy into the NATO ideas of shared democratic values and cooperative security.

There have been complaints that the partnership treats all former Communist states alike, regardless of their intentions. In fact, it gives every state an equal chance to make its intentions clear before it is taken into the new security system. The partnership process offers equality of opportunity but judges results entirely on the behavior of individual states.

The partnership process imposes no timetables or hard-and-fast rules governing how much the partners must do, or how soon. They can work at their own pace. At first, some states may be content with merely signing the framework document, while others may limit themselves to token participation. However, active and committed partners—those that jump right into planning, exercises, and training with allied forces and participate in regular political consultations—will have an edge. They will pick up NATO's standard operating procedures, habits of cooperation, and routines of consultation more quickly.

That is how PFP will work. In turn, what will it mean? This question involves the old debate about NATO, one that has been around almost as long as the alliance itself: Is NATO an institution of collective defense or collective security? Does the alliance defend its members against external aggression, in which case it would be a collective defense mechanism, or does it defend against internal threats? In the latter case, it would be a collective security organization. The conventional wisdom is that NATO has always been a collective defense system, the means by which the Soviets and their Warsaw Pact allies were kept out of Western Europe. NATO was the embodiment of Western collective defense. As such, it protected the allies from the Soviet Union and in the end won the Cold War.

If the truth be known, conventional wisdom may give NATO too much credit. Factors other than the prowess and firmness of the Atlantic Alliance contributed to the demise of the Soviet Union. But if NATO is perhaps given too much credit for bringing down the Iron Curtain, it is certainly not given enough credit for the other signal achievement of its forty-five-year history, and that is the multinationalization of the defense policies of its member-states.

Reflecting on the last half-century of world history, most would agree that the most dramatic event was the fall of communism. That story had all the ingredients of great drama—good guys and villains, the tension of impending catastrophe, and, eventually, a happy ending. It was a made-for-TV movie.

The other dramatic story of the last fifty years does not enjoy such glittering visuals, because it is basically a nonstory of the dog that did not bark. It is the tale of nonviolence among states that, before the creation of NATO, were not famous for that virtue. In the seventy-five years before NATO, France and Germany fought three bitter wars that expanded into two world wars. The history of NATO, therefore, is not only the story of a successful defense of the free world against communism but also of peace within the alliance. It has been a collective security organization as well as one concerned with collective defense.

Political scientists often speak of dyad-years of conflict as a measure of violence in the international system. One war between two countries for one year equals one dyad-year of war. Looked at in this way, one could say that the history of NATO is over ten thousand dyad-years of peace. This is NATO's second great accomplishment, and one much less heralded than its stand against communism.

Many scholars maintain that this nonviolence is a consequence of democracy. States that are democratic do not go to war against each other. With some exceptions, this proposition has held since World War II. One exception was the "Cod War" between Iceland and the United Kingdom, an exception so trivial that it proves the point.

I would like to offer a different theory. It is not simply democracy that inclines states away from fighting; rather, it is multinational defense planning. It is building a security relationship in which defense professionals, military and civilian, get to work together, train together, and develop habits of cooperation, coordination, and integration that become second nature.

One of the most instructive experiences I have had in this job was the task of leading a U.S. delegation to NATO headquarters to present the U.S. defense plan for 1994 to the Defense Planning Committee (DPC). In a large conference room I laid out American defense policy for the next year as it pertained to NATO: so many ships in the Mediterranean, so many fighter wings, so many divisions in Europe, and so on. I was interrogated by representatives of other NATO countries, who complained that the United States was making dangerous cuts in its defense capabilities.

My first reaction was to rise up and say, "Who are you to criticize the United States? Especially when your own defense budget isn't in such great shape itself." But I caught myself when it suddenly dawned on me that this is what it means to make defense policy in a multilateral context. This is how NATO keeps the peace among its member-states. It is a means of mutual reassurance that countries are not planning against each other. How can they do otherwise, when they plan together and work together in the DPC?

This process is at the heart of what we are offering in the Partnership for Peace. We are not giving our new peace partners shiny new military equipment, and we are certainly not offering them a security guarantee. But we are proposing that they move their defense planning process out of the half-light of national defense ministries in Central and Eastern Europe and into the cold light of NATO conference rooms in Brussels. Let them defend their defense policies before DPC representatives. Let them suffer the interrogation. Let them sit through interminable committee meetings at NATO Headquarters. The result, if history is any guide, will be another ten thousand dyad-years of peace.

One of the most ingenious aspects of PFP is that it hedges the cosmic bet about the future of Russia. Russia will be a part of the European security system by dint of its geography and power. It will not go away. It is in the interest of us all, especially Russia, that Russia's role be a constructive and cooperative one. The path of partnership cooperation has the potential to be a powerful tool to help integrate Russia into Europe.

As policymakers, we are realistic that Russia's foreign policy, under any government, will be shaped by Russian interests. As a Great Power, Russia will, like all nations, have some interests different from ours and from its neighbors'. A partnership between nations does not mean a perfect coincidence of views, but a broad recognition that common interests in a strong and multifaceted relationship provide a basis for working out concrete problems in ways that respect the interests of others.

Our hope is for a future European security sphere in which no nation threatens its neighbors. There should be no common enemies in the future Europe. We seek a European security system embracing the United States and Canada, as well as all of Europe. It must be rooted in common commitments to democracy and free economies. It must be rooted in mutual respect for human rights. And it must be rooted in the independence of states and the security of borders.

As President Clinton has said, ours is a vision of a Europe that, for the first time ever, would not be divided by present conflict or lingering animosities. Russia must therefore take its place in the new European security architecture. The PFP provides a unique path to such a security system. It is based on this proposition: While the United States with its allies will do what is necessary to preserve our collective security if the worst happens, we will do all we realistically can to prevent the worst from occurring. The dual nature of that policy underlies the concept of the PFP. It moves us forward, while maintaining a hedge if we should be unsuccessful.

The PFP is built around an optimistic scenario, and its goal is an optimistic outcome. It avoids drawing new security lines in Europe. Our objective, as Strobe Talbott has put it, is a Russia "integrated into the West rather than contained by the West."

But there is also a hedge against pessimistic outcomes. If Russia hews to a course of internal reform, respect for its neighbors' independence, and cooperation within the West, NATO will continue to evolve in the direction of maximum inclusiveness. If, however, reform in Russia falters, NATO will be there to provide the allies with collective defense and will already have been working through the partnership with the active participants to promote regional security. In short, Russia has a choice. And the choice Russia makes will significantly shape the future of NATO and the Partnership for Peace.

I have been frank in describing our concerns, as well as our hopes about Russia, but let me be clear. It would be deeply premature and profoundly wrong to let such concerns make us abandon our attempts to achieve the fundamentally new Europe we seek in the PFP. We believe the PFP will help to bring about what we all want—Marshall's vision of a peaceful, stable, secure, and unified Europe.

Every so often, in my travels around the United States and in Western Europe, I encounter people who ask me why NATO doesn't declare victory, shut its doors, and go out of business. After all, isn't the Cold War over? Isn't NATO's assignment completed? It is a fair question, and I have given you my answer here.

But let me close with a striking fact: In all of my travels around Central and Eastern Europe, in my conversations with hundreds of government officials in countries from Estonia to Albania, no one has ever questioned the relevance of NATO. Their question is, "How do we get in?" They see the relevance of this middle-aged institution, its value. They understand its contribution to collective defense and collective security. Their enthusiasm will give NATO new vigor. Their participation will give the alliance new breadth and relevance. The result will be a NATO transformed to fit the geostrategic realities of a new Europe, providing security and stability in the next forty-five years just as it did for the last forty-five.

CONTRIBUTORS

BOLESLAW A. BOCZEK, professor emeritus of political science at Kent State University, holds a doctorate in international law from Jagiellonian University and a Ph.D. in political science from Harvard University. Author of *Flags of Convenience* (1962), *Taxation in Switzerland* (1976), and *Historical Dictionary of International Tribunals* (1994), he also has written numerous articles, monographs, and reviews dealing with NATO, the Warsaw Pact, international law and organizations, and international security in Europe.

ERIKA V.C. BRUCE served from 1990 to 1994 as director of information and press of NATO in Brussels. Born in Vienna, she obtained her baccalaureate in Vienna and then earned her diploma and doctorate in political economy and business administration from the Universität für Wirtschaftswissenschaften, Vienna. She also obtained a master's degree in archaeology from Sir Wilfred Laurier University in Canada. Prior to joining NATO, she held a number of posts, including director general of the Program and Policy Branch of the Social Sciences and Humanities Research Council of Canada, clerk of the Committees Branch of the Senate of Canada, and coordinator of official languages for the same body.

CLAUDE CARLIER earned his doctorate from the University of Montpellier and is a professor at the Sorbonne, vice president of the Institute for Defense History, and director of the Center for Aeronautical and Space History in Paris. Included among his publications are *L'Aéronautique française 1945-1975* (1983), *Marcel Dassault, La légende d'un siècle* (1992), and *Chronologie aérospatiale 1940-1990* (1993).

ERIC S. EINHORN is professor of political science and chair of the department at the University of Massachusetts at Amherst. He received his B.A. from the University of Pennsylvania and his M.A. and Ph.D. from Harvard University. He has written extensively on Scandinavian issues and has published, among other titles, *National Security and Post-War Politics in Denmark: Some Principal Issues, 1945-1961* (1975) and *Modern Welfare States: Politics and Policy in Social Democratic Scandinavia* (coauthored; 1989).

MARY ANN HEISS is assistant professor of history at Kent State University, where she teaches courses on U.S. foreign relations. She studied for her B.A. and M.A. at Miami University (Ohio) and received her Ph.D. from Ohio State University with a dissertation entitled "The United States, Great Britain, and Iranian Oil, 1950-1954." She has served as associate editor of *Diplomatic History* since 1991.

ALAN K. HENRIKSON is associate professor of diplomatic history at The Fletcher School of Law and Diplomacy, Tufts University, where he directs The Fletcher Roundtable on a New World Order. He received A.B., A.M., and Ph.D. degrees from Harvard University and also holds B.A. and M.A. (Oxon.) degrees from Oxford University, which he attended as a Rhodes scholar. Among his publications are *Defining a New World Order: Toward a Practical Vision of Collective Action for International Peace and Security* (1991) and *Negotiating World Order: The Artisanship and Architecture of Global Diplomacy* (edited; 1986).

WALTER L. HIXSON, associate professor of history at the University of Akron, was educated at the University of Kentucky (B.A.), Western Kentucky University (M.A.), and the University of Colorado (Ph.D.). His research focuses on U.S. policy during the Cold War, and he has published *George F. Kennan: Cold War Iconoclast* (1989). He has also written *Witness to Disintegration: Provincial Life in the Last Year of the USSR* (1993), a memoir and analysis based on his ten-month residence as visiting Fulbright lecturer at Kazan State University in Russia.

ROBERT S. JORDAN, who holds doctorates from Princeton and Harvard universities, is research professor of international institutions, professor of political science, and senior research associate in the Eisenhower Center at the University of New Orleans. From 1992 to 1994 he served as visiting professor in the Department of National Security Studies of the U.S. Air War College, and earlier he taught at the U.S. Naval War College, the University of South Carolina, Columbia University, SUNY Binghamton, George Washington University, and the University of Pittsburgh. His more recent publications include *Generals in International Politics: NATO's Supreme Allied Commander, Europe* (1987), *Maritime Strategy and the Balance of Power: Britain and America in the Twentieth Century* (coedited; 1989), *Alliance Strategy and Navies: The Evolution and Scope of NATO's Maritime Dimension* (1990), *Europe and the Superpowers: Essays on European International Politics* (edited; 1991), and *International Organizations: A Comparative Approach* (coauthored, third ed.; 1994).

LAWRENCE S. KAPLAN is university professor emeritus of history and director emeritus of the Lemnitzer Center for NATO and European Community Studies at Kent State University. He received his B.A. from Colby College and his Ph.D. from Yale University. Before arriving at Kent in 1954, he served three years as a historian with the Historical Office of the U.S. Secretary of Defense. A preeminent scholar of NATO's history, his long list of publications includes *A Community of Interests: NATO and the Military Assistance Program, 1948-1951* (1980), *The United States and NATO: The Formative Years* (1984), and *NATO and the United States: An Enduring Alliance* (1988). He has also coedited six volumes based on the proceedings of Lemnitzer Center conferences or projects. Now based in the Washington area, he is a contract historian at the Department of Defense, adjunct professor at Georgetown University, and visiting lecturer at the University of Maryland.

SEAN KAY is a lecturer and senior doctoral student in political science/international relations at the University of Massachusetts. He received his B.A. and M.A. in political science from Kent State University and his M.A. in international politics from the Free University of Brussels. During his stay in Brussels he was also a research fellow at the North Atlantic Assembly of NATO and a corecipient of a NATO fellowship. He has published several articles, including "NATO and the CSCE: A Partnership for the Future," *Paradigms* (Winter 1993).

JOSEPH KRUZEL was one of three Americans killed in a road accident in Bosnia on 19 August 1995 while on a U.S.-sponsored peace mission to end the Balkan conflict. He was U.S. deputy assistant secretary of defense for European and NATO policy, having taken a leave of absence from his position as associate professor of political science and director of the Program on International Security and Military Affairs at Ohio State University. He published extensively on European security issues and served as editor-in-chief of *American Defense Annual*.

S. VICTOR PAPACOSMA, professor of history and director of the Lyman L. Lemnitzer Center for NATO and European Community Studies at Kent State University, received his A.B. from Bowdoin College and his M.A. and Ph.D. from Indiana University. He has written extensively on Balkan issues and particularly on twentieth-century Greek politics. Among his publications are *The Military in Greek Politics: The 1909 Coup d'État* (1977), *Politics and Culture in Greece* (1988), and coedited volumes of Lemnitzer Center conference proceedings, *Europe's Neutral and Nonaligned States* (1988) and *NATO after Forty Years* (1990).

STEVEN L. REARDEN, an independent consultant in Washington, DC, who specializes in contemporary foreign affairs and national security issues, earned a B.A. from the University of Nebraska and a Ph.D. from Harvard University. He has been an adviser to the Departments of State and Defense and to the U.S. General Accounting Office and has held several academic research appointments. Rearden's publications include *The Evolution of American Strategic Doctrine: Paul H. Nitze and the Soviet Challenge* (1984), *History of the Office of the Secretary of Defense: The Formative Years, 1947-1950* (1984), and *The Origins of the U.S. Nuclear Strategy, 1945-1953* (1993), which he coauthored with Samuel R. Williamson, Jr.

GARY SCHAUB, JR., is a doctoral candidate in the Graduate School of Public and International Affairs at the University of Pittsburgh. He has an M.A. in political science from the University of Illinois at Urbana-Champaign. His current research concerns the use of threats of military force in international relations and European security.

STANLEY R. SLOAN is the senior specialist in international security policy in the Congressional Research Service (CRS) of the Library of Congress. He was educated at the University of Maine (B.A.), Columbia University's School of International Affairs (M.I.A.), and the School of International Service at American University. Prior to assuming his position at the CRS, he was employed at the Central Intelligence Agency from 1969 to 1975. Among his extensive publications are *NATO's Future: Toward a New Transatlantic Bargain* (1986), *Conventional Arms Control and Europe's Future* (1989), and *NATO in the 1990s* (edited; 1989).

PHIL WILLIAMS is director of the Ridgway Center for International Security Studies and a professor in the Graduate School of Public and International Affairs, University of Pittsburgh. He has written and edited, among other books, *The Carter Years: The President and Policy Making* (1984), *The Senate and U.S. Troops in Europe* (1986), and *Superpower Detente: A Reappraisal* (1988), and published articles in such journals as *Survival, International Affairs,* and *The Washington Quarterly.*

INDEX